CULTURE AND COSMOLOGY:

Essays on the Birth of World View

Harry Coffin Stafford
The Florida State University

University Press of America™

Library of Congress Catalog Card Number: 80-5642

To my parents George Timothy
and Evelyn Coffin, Stafford

TABLE OF CONTENTS

v

ACKNOWLEDGEMENTS

The author has received encouragement and valuable assistance from many in the research, writing and preparation of this manuscript for publication. The scholarly advice of Professors Richard Rubenstein, John Priest, Raymond Sheline, and John Carey proved invaluable in the initial preparation of this manuscript from 1974-76.

Preparing the manuscript for publication would have proved impossible without the professional expertise and generous efforts of Richard and Margaret Van Sciver. Finally, I want to thank Brenda S. Freeman for her patience, encouragement, and considerable time in the final stages of manuscript preparation.

The author is also very grateful for the following permissions to quote previously copyrighted material: To Harper and Row, Publishers, Inc., for permission to quote Werner Heisenberg's *Physics and Philosophy*, ©1958; to the Bobbs-Merrill Company, Inc., for permission to quote G. M. A. Grube's translation of Marcus Aurelius, *The Meditations*, ©1963; to the Houghton Mifflin Company, Inc. for permission to quote John Mansley Robinson's translations of the Presocratics in his *An Introduction to Early Greek Philosophy*, ©1968; to the M.I.T. Press, Inc., for permission to quote from Benjamin Lee Whorf's "Science and Linguistics" from his book *Language, Thought and Reality*, ©1956.

CULTURE AND COSMOLOGY:

ESSAYS ON THE BIRTH OF WORLD VIEW

INTRODUCTION

OUR FIVE senses mediate that which we call "reality." Thus we begin our discussion of world view by exploring the role that they play. The five senses are only sensitive to a small set of stimuli in the larger cosmic spectra (the seemingly infinite and multi-faceted bursts of energy constituting the known universe). Thus what we call reality is only *a special case*—a symbolic and necessary creation and abstraction—a narrow and selective response to cosmic signals.

Our neurological sensors serve as *channels* through which spectral signals travel. Our sensors thus also serve as living spatio-temporal casts which mold reality into shapes and relations which we identify *as* reality. In this (very real) sense our neurological equipment—in its channeling and shaping functions—serves as a selective monitoring system by which the world is made known to us, and through which in part we create that world which we deem "objective reality."

This reification of the world as a world of external objects and relations is partial truth, and only partial error, yet a critical limitation for our self-understanding. It is only partial error because this *special case* which we identify *as* objective reality is in fact a legitimate *facet* of reality.

The error lies in the exclusiveness and finality that we attribute to this special case, not recognizing the subjective conditioning and inherent bias of our neurological equipment. To recognize the *creative* apprehension and casting of our world is to acknowledge: 1) the relativity and contextuality of what we deem "reality"; 2) the structural limitations of our world views; 3) the richness of structural models available to us for shaping our "world picture"; 4) our freedom (within the relative sophistication and flexibility of our sensory equipment) to *reshape* our world in images evocative of greater utility and harmony. Indeed, where do shapes, colors, solids, textures, etc. come from? These arise not from the elusive structure of radiant energy in atomic patterns of the "object" *alone,* but likewise from the elusive structure of radiant energy making up the "subject." Continuously the *mind* contributes to the organic world of interaction its symbolic modes which we perceive as size, shape, color, solidity, etc. These are not properties of the physical world *sui generis,* but are complex symbols of subjective-objective interaction, participant properties of *both* subject and object. This perspective is not an assertion of solipsism or pure anthropomorphism. Symbology is an organic process involving continuous interactions between the nervous system, the

1

mind, cultural categories, and the spectra of reality impinging upon us which we normally label "the material world."

Thus we would affirm neither an extreme Kantian position, whereby the phenomenal world is in contraposition to unknowable "things in themselves," nor the alternative of naive realism where perceptual experience is conceived as direct information about *"the* real world." We would propose that the situation is more mediate: we relate to *a* real world (in that we are organically connected to, and perceptually cognizant of, a reality outside of ourselves); we are participant creators of that world through the peculiarities of our perceptual equipment, our space-time location, and the rational propensities of our minds. As opposed to Kant, we would affirm that our knowledge of the world is not merely an apprehension of appearances, but of *real* occurrences or shapes of reality. Moreover, the categories of our minds, such as space and time, appear to be largely cultural variables. (Though as Noam Chomsky asserts, we may possess, *a priori,* a set of very basic structural predispositions, i.e., an "innate grammar." But Chomsky's mental structures are more flexible and less philosophically predetermined than Kant's categories.) Although as "common sense" would have it, we do actually traffic with a real world, it is only a *portion* of the real world which impinges upon our peculiar physiological apparatus and space-time frame. Einstein has demonstrated that, though there seem to be universal laws, they must be *translated* into the context of our finite setting of space-time.

Our contemporary apprehension of the physical world suggests that *all* reality—if we may extrapolate from the known to the unknown—is a dynamic and continuous *process.* As such, it seems unlikely that any static absolutes exist. Such a position does not negate the regularity, continuity and lawfulness of nature, but does exclude abstract absolutes, as anthropomorphically construed. The recurrent dichotomy of "things as they truly are" as opposed to "things as they appear to be" betrays a substantialist bias. Such a bias attributes some absolute status to an abstract reality, which may only be known "intuitively," "rationally," or "spiritually," but in any case *not* in physical experience. A more organic apprehension of reality, as suggested by the physical and psychological sciences, accepts no division between "the really real" and "appearances." It rather affirms a continuity (which we grasp with only tentative consistency and incomplete conceptualization) of our experience with reality as a whole. Thus, though our world is *only* a "special case" of reality—a fact of vital significance—it is also a "special case" of *reality,* a fact of equally vital significance. Our cultural models of reality are not thereby erroneous *unless* they are reified as absolutes or granted a status of ultimacy (or unless they falsify the experience of the empirical world). As long as they remain faithful to experience—flexible and subject to modification, correction or expansion—cultural models of the world are not only necessary, but highly useful. We will explore such models as we proceed. The physiological delimitations of world view remind us of our obviously inherent anthropocentrism; of our interdependence with, and creative appropriation of, our natural environs; and, of the comparative richness of cultural dynamics.

STRUCTURES OF CONSCIOUSNESS: FIRST AND SECOND ORDER

Although this is not a treatise on physiological epistemology, it is quite necessary that we should attempt to delineate the parameters of world view. By the term "structures of consciousness" we designate certain patterns of perception which arise *either* by nature of the processes of the human organism, *or* by nature of the processes of history and society, *or* by the interplay of both factors. Those structures which are primarily organic are the proper domain of physiology and psychology, and will herein be approached indirectly in terms of the process of socialization. This task will occupy the first two chapters. Organic structures might be termed "first-order structures." We would affirm that the human body preestablishes a certain "psychological space-time" orientation, deriving from the first-order structures, i.e., our visual, tactile, aural, gustatory and olfactory equipment (and perhaps certain mental predispositions such as Chomsky's hypothesized "innate grammar").

For the balance of our investigation we will be concerned with "second-order structures." These might also be termed "the psycho-social structures of consciousness," because of their derivation from 1) first-order structures and 2) cultural processes, myths and models (all of which derive in part from organic roots). These psycho-social structures define and refine the cosmos, and thus impose more narrow limits or "tunnel focus" upon reality.* These second-order structures will be analyzed historically and typologically, with special emphasis upon both roots and expressions of contemporary world pictures. The term "typological" refers to the generality of such an analysis. At this point it is germane to summarize the purpose and accompanying methodology of this study.

Beginning with an awareness of our physiological limitations, the purpose is to describe further refinements of world view which occur through socialization, and which have occurred historically in classical patterns of Western thought. The study culminates with an investigation of issues raised

---

*An example of the distinction between "first-order" and "second-order" structures of consciousness is the relative meaning of "black" and "white." Physiologically, "black" and "white" are simply symbols identifying the variable sensitivity of the eye to light rays. "Black" is caused by complete absorption of light rays, and "white" by the reflection of all the rays that produce color. This is on the level of first-order structures. However, culturally "black" and "white" have sometimes accrued further connotations of value. Perhaps deriving from the primitive fear of the night and darkness and the unknown, "black" has been taken for "menacing" or "evil," and "white" for "purity" or "goodness." Such a value judgment is on the level of second-order structures of consciousness.

by contemporary world views. The methodology of the historical sections employs typological analysis to identify recurrent common denominators. Our intention is thus representative and exploratory, not exhaustive.

The following outline is a sample typology of second-order, psycho-social structures of consciousness.

A Sample Outline of Psycho-Social Structures

Simple Structures

Space	: Hierarchy (Vertical)	
	authority (sacred and profane)	church or religion
	cosmic picture	various institutions
	family structure	bureaucracy
	state	
	Symmetry-Geometry (Horizontal, Radial)	
	"place"/"space" of propriety	language
	man–woman–child	aesthetic norms
	kinship	mechanical structures
	architecture and artifact	institutional
	cosmic picture	structures
Time	: Linear-Sequential	
	beginnings and ends	ethical or status
	childhood to old age	models (arrival,
	cosmogony to apocalypse	perfection, etc.)
	institutional orders	history, by some views
	(schooling, etc.)	everyday "schedules"
	: Cyclical-Seasonal	
	seasons	history, by other views
	clock time	mythical recurrence
	night/day sequences	and archetypes

Composite Structures

Absolute Space-Time or Eternity:
(which may incorporate any of the above patterns)
      eternal patterns or archetypes
      being versus becoming
      realms of revelation, inspiration (by some models)
      mystical experience (by some models)
      aesthetics (by some models)

Relative Space-Time or Becoming:
(which may also incorporate the above patterns)

becoming versus being	mystical metamorphoses
growth, progress	organic processes
creative inspiration and novelty	and unity

Models of Consciousness

The foregoing chart is a simple outline of spatial and temporal psycho-social structures. One of the most difficult tasks in the analysis of culture is a choice of models which, though comprehensive enough to prove worthy of wide utility, are nevertheless flexible enough to prove applicable without undue distortion to the actual historical data. It is with this goal in mind that the following three-fold scheme of consciousness is introduced, to which we will return sporadically.

Cultural structures of consciousness seem adaptable to a taxonomic scheme drawn from the vocabulary of organisms and ecology. The relevant terms are *sessile, motile* and *holistic*. As applied to cultural consciousness, the terms are used as symbols for recurrent patterns in Western world views.

Zoologically, *sessile* refers to organisms which are not self-propelled. These organisms, moved by environmental forces such as air or water currents, remain within a somewhat fixed environment and do not move about seeking food. Examples of sessile organisms include barnacles, polyps and starfish. In a different sense, a tree or flower is sessile by virtue of its stationary attachment to the earth and its dependence upon its environs for growth and nourishment. Sessile animals, such as the starfish, often exhibit a design of *radial symmetry*, with no distinct head and a circumferential exposure to the environment. The term *sessile*, applied to psycho-social structures, is used metaphorically. As such the term suggests modes of consciousness which are 1) primarily *spatially* oriented, exhibiting little penchant for vital self-propelled changes; 2) generally rigid, geometrically "shaped," and hierarchically stratified. Sessile consciousness would seem to be the dominant mode of consciousness in Western mythical and scientific cosmologies prior to the twentieth century. Sessile consciousness would correspond roughly to various labels (sometimes used indiscriminately), such as Apollinian, Olympian, orthodox and mechanical. Sessile consciousness would define life's ultimates more in terms of "being" rather than "becoming," and generally would envision the cosmos as a singular predetermined order.

Zoologically, *motile* organisms are those capable of self-generated, active movement. Motile organisms are not carried along by winds or tides for food, protection and procreation, etc., but are equipped with structures of locomotion, from simple cilia or flagella or pseudopodia to sophisticated muscular systems. Motile organisms are found on all levels from a simple unicellular animal to human beings. As opposed to the radial symmetry of sessile organisms, motile organisms generally exhibit bilateral symmetry and an elongation in the direction of motion. Most motile organisms have a clearly defined head. In applying the term *motile* to psycho-social structures of consciousness, we must realize that in the strictest sense all human beings are motile organisms. However, by motile *consciousness* we mean attitudes or beliefs which demonstrate flexibility, movement and dynamism; or historically, a sense of novelty, development, or becoming. Actually, it is difficult to isolate any predominantly motile world views widespread prior to the nineteenth century. Yet to varying degrees, motile tendencies seem evident in, for example, Dionysian and chthonic elements of Western culture, the nomadic and prophetic consciousness of Israel (and her sense of history), the Hellenistic milieu, primitive Christianity, and certain facets of the Renaissance. Of course we might identify many individuals who seemed propelled by a motile sense, such as Abraham or Alexander the Great (who legendarily wept when he had "no more worlds to conquer"). However, in most cases where motile tendencies seem certain, an equal case could be marshalled for sessile motivations. In any case, by *motility* a strong *temporal* orientation is indicated. Moreover, just as an extreme sessile consciousness would entail spatial rigidity, cultural fixation and ultimately death, so an extreme motile consciousness would suggest rootlessness, anomie and ultimately chaos.

The third term, *holistic,* is of a different genre than sessile and motile. Holism refers to a balanced ecosystem, where both sessile and motile constituents harmoniously interact. In terms of consciousness, *holism* would imply not only homeostatic balance between sessile and motile elements, but also the balanced interrelationship of human culture and consciousness with the whole natural order. Holism suggests a consciousness which, as strongly cognizant of the interdependence of all things, is attuned to both the orders and processes of nature. Holism seeks the implementation of a healthy, orderly transformation of culture and consciousness in dialogue with the cosmos in all of its dimensions. As an analogue to Einsteinian physics, holism is a *space-time* orientation which presupposes the significance of historical and organic context and processes. Mythically speaking, if sessile organisms seem to "trust" their environment to supply their needs, and motile organisms manifest restless energy in actively *seeking* their needs, holism would suggest a modulated passive/active, yin/yang, Eastern/Western, grace/works, "right lobe"/"left lobe" rhythm of life processes. Further ramifications of holism will be explored in later discussion.

An Overview

The ensuing discussions proceed as a three-pronged investigation, with each avenue constituting a major section of the work.

The first section, "Socialization and World View," raises critical questions regarding the emergence of world view through the processes of socialization and language acquisition. This section underscores the critical role of these contiguous processes as *constants* in the relationship between culture and cosmology. These discussions are designed to be heuristic, not exhaustive. (The multi-variegated phenomena of socialization merit far more extensive investigations than the limited scope of this writing.)

The second section, "An Historical Typology of Culture and Cosmology in the West," selectively identifies structures of consciousness of pervasive typological influence in the evolution of Western culture from the Presocratic philosophers through Newton. Chapter three compares mythopoeic thought with the revolutionary ideas of the Greek Presocratics. Chapter four approaches the Judeo-Christian and classical world views by means of a similar comparison. Chapter five is transitional, selecting "structures of consciousness" which seem particularly formative from the Hellenistic Era to the Renaissance. The final chapter of the second section sketches the contours of the mechanical model of the cosmos. This world view arose in the early modern period and has continued as a dominant (but not exclusive) world picture, affecting not only modern science, but many other facets of modern culture.

The final section, "Cosmology and Modern Consciousness," explores key structures of world views reaching into the present. Chapter seven describes certain structures of political consciousness which have in part shaped the modern world. Chapter eight is a more creative excursion into two pervasive institutional structures: bureaucracy and technology. Chapter nine isolates five general models of man which, though by no means a comprehensive sampling, represent popular perspectives among intelligent contemporary Westerners. It should be noted that the recent influence of Eastern models of man is beyond the scope of this present work. Chapter ten broadly outlines the revolution in scientific cosmology in this century, especially Einsteinian relativity and quantum mechanics. Chapter eleven addresses the eschatological ramifications of technology and cosmology in our age. It suggests a perspective for a more integral relationship between science and other facets of culture in the future.

With the advent of new cosmological theory, and with the continuing expansion of investigation into all realms of knowledge, older cosmological frames (and their derivative cultural consciousnesses) seem increasingly inadequate for a viable account of many life processes. The final chapter, "Towards a New Holism," describes emerging perspectives which challenge old models and suggest the need for new ones. Three appendices have been added to propose some directions for further exploration.

The express purpose of this book is to provide a tentative and heuristic typology for identifying the roots and implications of prominent world views in the West, both as they are culturally communicated and historically propagated. This study, which is an exercise in the quest for *perspective,* is offered as a hopeful contribution to that end.

SECTION I

SOCIALIZATION AND WORLD VIEW

CHAPTER I

SOCIALIZATION, TEMPORALIZATION AND WORLD VIEW

DEFINITION OF SOCIALIZATION

USUALLY ABOUT the second year[1] the major socialization of the child in our culture begins. Socialization entails the progressive acquisition of characteristics, behavior-patterns, values, motives and beliefs, considered appropriate by a given culture. Berger and Luckmann identify three moments within the dialectical process of society: externalization, objectification and internalization.[2] The social order, continuously created by man, is the result of mutual externalizations. Society is a human product. Yet the social order seems to exist objectively apart from any one person or group of persons. Institutions seem to be "givens." Objectification describes the process whereby externalizations take on the character of objects or givens. If objectification is not considered as rooted in externalization, or if institutions, values or ideologies are conceived as existing ontically, in their own right, and apart from man, they assume the character of "things." This process is called reification (from the Latin *res*, "thing"). The final "moment" in the dialectic of society is internalization. Internalization implies the inner appropriation by the individual of the external social order. Social reality and value become internal reality and value. Internalization includes perhaps as its major mechanism socialization. Socialization is said to occur in two phases: primary socialization, the first inductions of the child into society; and secondary socialization, subsequent expansions of the social world. The fundamental act of socialization—and of the acquisition of a cognitive world view—is the acquisition of language. Understanding the functions of language is a vital key in the unlocking of the ethos and world view of a socially-constructed reality. We shall turn to the question of language after first examining how world view emerges through socialization.

SOCIALIZATION: HOW IT OCCURS[3]

The Nature-Nurture Conflict

A debate still raging among psychologists, biologists and others is the question of just how the structures of consciousness arise. The two fundamental positions include the environmentalists, who assert that the mind of the neonate is like Locke's *tabula rasa* or blank slate, and the nativists

11

who posit inherited traits or tendencies which to a greater or lesser extent preshape the individual and define the parameters of his development.

Behaviorism

The chief environmentalist position is behaviorism. The early behaviorists, such as Pavlov and Watson, illustrate the influence of the mechanistic world picture upon psychology. Pavlov, of course, is noted for his famed experiments in "conditioned response." Here the organism responds to mechanical cues with learned ritual behavior. John B. Watson, who developed his theory of rewards and punishment, believed that the so-called phenomenon classically known as "mind" could not be studied directly at all.

The most famous contemporary behaviorist is B. F. Skinner, who asserts that behavioral controls can reshape human society. In *Beyond Freedom and Dignity* Skinner argues for the obsolescence of such concepts as freedom and dignity which, he asserts, only befuddle man's efforts to solve his real problems. In *Walden Two,* Skinner paints a picture of a modern utopia based on behavioral technology. In this novel, human autonomy is depicted as a myth, and the new society can be created by strict models of behavior reinforced by a sophisticated system of rewards and punishment. Skinner's utopia includes communal ownership of land and buildings, egalitarian relationships between men and women, devotion to art, music and literature, liberal rewards for constructive behavior, and freedom from jealousy and gossip and *from* the ideal of freedom.[4]

Although behaviorism does explain a significant portion of human action and reaction, the main objection is the charge of reductionism. Not only does man's inner self become a myth, but more significantly, behaviorism does not account for all of the empirical data regarding human behavior. Telling criticisms of behaviorism have been usefully summarized by Munsinger.[5]

Ethology, a newly budding science of the study of the natural behavior of animals, has renewed and expanded the role of instinct. Instinct it appears means not simply an inherited tendency, but a pervasive mode of action in animals.

> The instincts can be extremely specific and well developed as in the case of the newly hatched cuttlefish, which very expertly catches the first passing shrimp it sees. Or it can be less specific and imperfectly developed. A newly hatched gosling follows the first moving thing it spots—whether mother goose, rolling basketball, or passing ethologist—and after this initial "imprinting" the gosling can never be dissuaded from its chosen mother figure.[6]

Ethologists have also discovered complex structures of social behavior, in some cases paralleling human culture. Munsinger notes that some anthropologists (Lionel Tiger and Robin Fox)

> have been laying stress upon the large number of traits that most human

cultures have in common. These include such practices as incest taboos, religious propensities, marriage, and the clubby fellowship of men in groups. The suspicion is gathering strength—though also amidst controversy—that far more human individual and cultural behavior than had ever been realized has its roots in genes, not in chance or choice and certainly not in stimulus-response conditioning.[7]

A word of caution should be raised here. Structuralism and systems philosophy expose the structural similarities of the entire organic order. (We shall explore this position further in a later chapter.) From this perspective there seem to be pervasive structural types, but such affinities do not account for the eccentricities which also pervade human social life.

Further objections to behaviorism include observations from linguistic science (Chomsky's assertion that every child is born with certain structural capacities for language), and computer theory (which, drawing an analogy between the brain and the computer, asserts that the brain is far more structurally complex than the computer). Behaviorists have responded to these criticisms with a certain revisionism which allows some significance for genetic endowment.[8]

Jean Piaget

The most influential alternative to a behaviorist model of human learning presently is to be found in the work of the child psychologist (and self-styled "genetic epistemologist") Jean Piaget. Piaget's theories, at first resisted because of a paucity of experimental data, have received growing confirmation and widespread recognition in recent years. Although Piaget views the process of learning primarily as an adaptation to the environment, he sees man as structurally equipped from birth to become a social being and an order-seeker. Cognitive acts, genetically rooted in certain structures of consciousness, are the child's way of organizing his environment in meaningful categories. Logical behavior emerges in the creation of taxonomic (classificatory) and relational systems.

> Even the simple statement, "This is green," implies the acquisition of such skills and hence cannot be regarded as a reference to a simple perceptual datum. When we talk intelligently of green, this presupposes that we have learned to classify objects according to their color and to differentiate one color from another.[9]

Piaget has developed four basic categories to describe the process of human learning.

The first of Piaget's categories is the *schema* (plural *schemata*). Schemata are structures of the mind (comparable to bodily structures, organs, etc.). These cognitive structures are inferred to exist. Wadsworth has compared the construct nature of schemata to Freud's Id and Ego, and points out that their function is much like an index file.[10] New cards (schemata) are added to encode new experiences. For example, upon first seeing a cow, a child, having no appropriate schema, may call it a "big dog." At birth the child exhibits certain "global schemata," such as sucking, which are reflexive and undifferentiated.[11] These are essentially instinctual. Only later do the schemata assume a distinct intellectual character. The psycho-social structures of consciousness which we have heretofore outlined would seem to parallel Piaget's schemata to a certain extent. However, Piaget's schemata are more particular. Ideally there is a schema or set of schemata which encompasses every bit of positivistic data. Our space-time categories would group such schemata in larger patterns or general cognitive structures of Western civilization.

Piaget's second and third categories refer to the ways in which schemata are ordered and expanded in the learning process. *Assimilation* is "the cognitive process whereby a person integrates new perceptual matter or stimulus events into existing schemata or patterns of behavior."[12] When the child identifies a cow as a big dog he *assimilates* the stimuli into existing cognitive structures. On the other hand, when a stimulus is found to be incongruous with existing schemata (as the foregoing example would prove to be), a child must either create or accept a new schema or modify an existing one. These options are both forms of *accommodation*. It should be noted here that assimilation and accommodation are processes which can be largely socially predetermined—that is as part of the larger process of internalizing social norms and values.

In considering the socialization process and the emergence of world view, Piaget's categories are instructive. Processes parallel to assimilation and accommodation continue throughout life. With assimilation the stimuli are "forced" to fit within given structures. With accommodation the opposite is true: one is forced to change his schemata to fit the new stimuli. For example, if one is imbued with a given ideological frame (Christianity or Marxism, for example), new data, which do not fall within the purview of that frame create an effective crisis. One may distort the data in order to assimilate it (such as cramming a square peg into a round hole), thereby falsifying the data or disfiguring the schematic integrity (either the peg or the hole must give). One may also properly modify one's system to *accommodate* such data (thereby altering the frame itself). If one's model will not accommodate the new data, one must either ignore the data or find a more adequate model. An example or two will illustrate. In the realm of value judgments we constantly operate with sweeping generalities such as "all Arabs are bad." Upon meeting a good Arab one must either ignore the Arab, deny his worth, or alter one's categorical niches to allow room for good Arabs. Another example would be the flat earth cosmology which is assumed in many places in the Christian scriptures. Here actual positions held are illustrative. The fabled "Flat Earth Society" in London simply denies the veracity of all evidence to the contrary, since God has clearly stated the facts. More flexible traditionalists may quite easily accept the world picture of modern cosmology, yet find various means of adaptation or rationalization to protect the trustworthiness of the scriptures, such as "the scriptures are completely inspired as concerns matters of faith and doctrine; but God accommodated himself to the cosmological frame of the day." Still others may suspect that since the scientific and historical data of the scriptures do not conform to modern standards of accuracy, that matters of faith and doctrine may stand in need of revision as well. Some may feel that the entire cognitive frame of the scriptures is inadequate for modern man, and that a new world view must be discovered. The relevance of assimilation and accommodation should by now be obvious, and we could enumerate examples of similar cognitive crises from the realms of the social and physical sciences, aesthetics, etc.

The final category of Piaget is *equilibrium,* a kind of psychic homeostasis which depends upon a balance between assimilation and accommodation. If assimilation predominated in the acquisition of world view, one would end up with a very few large categories which would be unable to allow for adequate discrimination or refinement. If assimilation never occurred, and the person always accommodated, a seemingly infinite assortment of unrelated and chaotic schemata would befuddle the mind. Equilibrium on a social level is the human quest for *cosmos* (world order) as opposed to chaos. Returning to our initial models of structures of consciousness, we may perhaps see some parallels here. Consciousness which leans strongly towards the sessile pole will favor assimilation over accommodation in the quest to secure the stability of its spatially-oriented structures. Motile consciousness may tend towards indiscriminate accommodation and disorder, in the quest for novelty. Holistic consciousness will seek a dynamic equilibrium between well-attested schemata, whose accuracy proves sufficient through ample experience, and the acquisition of new schemata on a continuing basis as is necessary for an open stance.

SOCIALIZATION AND WORLD VIEW: THE EMOTIONAL COMPONENT

In our discussion thus far we have excluded a critical factor in the process of socialization and the emergence of world view: the emotional component. Structures of personality are the domain of the psychologist and the social psychologist, and are generally tangential to the scope of this book. However, one example of the relationship between emotional and structural components is the dated but classical study of swaddling techniques by Ruth Benedict entitled "Child Rearing in Certain European Countries."[13] Alan Dundes comments in his introduction to this article:

> Whether or not the swaddling hypothesis or modifications thereof are ever satisfactorily validated, there can be no question of the importance of the

initial parental response to neonates in the development of the world view and personality of those infants when they become adults.[14]

Benedict and a task force of interviewers investigated patterns of infant swaddling practices and later adult expectations among children of Central and Eastern Europe. The most severe techniques are found in Russia. The baby is completely submerged by mummy-like wrappings and placed in a blanket, which is taped with criss-cross lashings. Sometimes the wrappings threaten the infant's capacity to breathe and must be loosened. In addition, the baby is not rocked, "but is moved horizontally from right to left and left to right."[15] The ostensible purpose behind this custom is the belief that the infant is inherently violent and must be prevented from hurting itself. Since the tightly-bound toddler's one mode of contact with the outside world is its eyes, Benedict postulates that this ancient custom may explain the significant role of the eyes in Russian literature as "the mirrors of the soul." Benedict further conjectures that the relative acceptance of violence in Russian society, from Czarist days to twentieth century revolutionary forms, has some roots in the attitudes held towards the infant as illustrated by the swaddling technique. In a similar vein, Eric Ericson, in a discussion of Maxim Gorky's youth, proposes that the alternating rigid binding and release of Russian infants exemplifies a recurrent cultural pattern in Russia—a rhythmic dialectic oscillating between firm, static restraint and explosive catharsis.[16] Because of the dates of Benedict's (1949) and Ericson's (1950) studies, only further investigation would establish whether or not these swaddling customs (and Benedict's further examples), are still prevalent. Furthermore, it might be relevant to observe that the dates of both Benedict's and Ericson's studies are squarely in the midst of an era of significant anti-Russian propaganda, when various attempts to "explain" Russian "violence" were widespread. However, even if these studies bear evidence of this trend, they are not without some empirical substantiation and illustrative merit.

The other two examples developed by Benedict concern the Polish baby and the Jewish baby, whether in Poland or the Ukraine. In Poland the infant is not regarded as violent, but rather as extremely fragile. Here the binding supports the child, not from violent outbursts, but from "breaking in two." Swaddling is conceived as the first step in the process of "hardening." One is particularly hardened by suffering, so suffering, too, is accorded great value in Poland. According to Benedict, Poles prove their worth by recounting their sufferings. Polish patriots refer to Poland as "the crucified Christ of the Nations."[17] Thus if the crying baby receives no attention, it will strengthen its lungs. Beating helps harden the child. In Russia weaning is a gradual process; in Poland the act is designed to be quite sudden. In later life there is no greater concern to the Pole than defending his honor.

By contrast, the Jewish baby in Poland is swaddled with great comfort. A soft pillow, loose bindings and the lullabies of the mother accompany the process. Benedict sees the high respect of the home in the Jewish family as being rooted in the warmth shown the child in the early years, especially before facing the rigors and severe discipline of the *cheder*, the elementary school entered at three or four years of age. The author also surmises that the warmth of swaddling lays part of the groundwork for the "complementary system" of Jewish social relations. By complementary she means "paired actions as dominance-submission, nurturance-dependence, and command-obedience . . ."[18] Here the pattern is called "nurturance-deference." The obligation of the subservient party is not through reciprocal action, but rather through assuming responsibility in a cyclical pattern. Thus the baby becomes an adult and in turn shows the same care for a new generation.

In evaluating the significance of Benedict's study we must bear in mind, as we have mentioned, its particular limitations because of age. To what extent these customs have been corroded by more modern practices is unknown to this writer, since Poland has been a Soviet satellite since 1947. Nevertheless, it is likely that further empirical studies would substantiate the correlation between attitudes and expectations of adults towards children, embodied in methods of care, and later attitudes and psycho-social structures of consciousness manifest by the mature individual. The emerging world view and the attendant self-image of the growing person will tend to reduplicate cultural structures of hierarchy, authority, geometrical kinship or social roles and the like. The externalizations and objectifications, emotively charged through accumulated experience and even unconscious memory, become internalized (usually) to a substantial degree in the process of socialization.

THE SHAPE OF A CHILD'S FIRST WORLD AND THE EMERGENCE OF SESSILE CONSCIOUSNESS

The earliest environment of the human organism is the mother's womb. It is perhaps here that the sense of *timelessness* of the neonate and early infant is rooted. Freud refers to this undifferentiated state as "oceanic consciousness."[19] The earliest structure of consciousness of the child seems to be an indiscriminate spatial awareness. Time, at the beginning, is an insignificant factor.

Spatial Components

Philosophically, we might assert that for the infant, *being* incorporates becoming. The *being* of the child is a spatial awareness, although certainly not a sense of static location, but in fact just the opposite: an undifferentiated environmental flux. Piaget calls this early stage of human life the *Sensori-Motor Stage* (from approximately birth to two years). The baby only gradually distinguishes itself from its environment. Behavior during these early months is primarily motor. From a Freudian perspective the dominant principle of this early stage is the Pleasure Principle. The child's earliest temporal awareness pivots around the centers of basic biological orientation: ingestion, elimination, sleep, fondling and attention, and elementary exploration. According to Piaget the most important acquisition of the Sensori-Motor Stage is the *schema of the permanent object*. The permanence of an object is not *a priori* an automatic response. Piaget notes that an infant of five or six months will not perceive an object in front of him if it is screened from his vision.[20] On the contrary:

> The outer world is only a series of moving pictures which appear and disappear, the most interesting of which can reappear when one knows very well how to manage it (for example crying long enough if it is a question of someone whose return is desired).[21]

Furthermore, the external world consists of "only moving pictures without substantiality or permanence and, above all, without localization."[22] Only around nine or ten months does the child finally learn to discover that the shielded object is still there, and only at eighteen months does he discover a notion of *generalized space* which includes the *permanence* of the object and a discrimination of his body and other spaces. The schema of the permanent object is therefore a structure of consciousness arising from the coordination of rudimentary neurological equipment—the five senses—in the forming of an elementary picture of the world. This schema marks the acquisition of a temporal dimension—continuity—which enables the emergence of generalized space and sessile consciousness. Apart from this acquisition the foundations of such concepts as space, time and causality could not be laid.

One word of caution: in terms of modern quantum theory the schema of the permanent object involves an element of deception as well as a necessary truth. We have noted that the physiological process entails the *channeling* and *casting* of the 'signals' of reality into the world that we know. Piaget himself acknowledges that "nothing is innate in structures and that everything must be gradually and laboriously constructed."[23] In a (perhaps esoteric, but important) sense, the "oceanic" undifferentiation *preceding* the permanent object is *as accurate*—if not more accurate—as a picture of reality as the schema of the permanent object. Simply speaking, we know that no object is permanent. We know also that we *do not perceive* the full radiant spectrum of any object, or facet of the larger whole of reality. We necessarily and creatively *monitor* reality into the world which we *call* "reality." Thus our emerging knowledge of the world is *never* a copy of some "objective world," for the objective world itself is a psycho-social, and not an ultimately-real, construct.

A second structure of consciousness of the early child is what we might call "simple hierarchy." At the beginning the fetus is enclosed within an hierarchical and all-encompassing structure. At birth, and for many months until the infant acquires some measure of social perception and independence, he/she is almost completely manipulated and maneuvered by the mother, nurse, or family member in whose care the infant is placed. The child is aware of its dependence and vulnerability, but of course is unable to attach any value or social significance to the situation at this point. The simple hierarchy structure of consciousness slowly evolves with the differentiation and identification of family members and perhaps a few relatives or other persons close to the family. Slowly, too, it is learned that some of these figures possess greater authority than others (e.g., mother and father, as opposed to Aunt Sue).

A third structure of consciousness emerging in late infancy, following the schema of the permanent object, is what we might term "radial symmetry," a "centering" and differentiation between self and environment. Radial symmetry assumes the identification of a generalized space. Piaget has noted that for the neonate

> there is no space that contains objects, since there are no objects . . . There is a series of spaces differing one from another and all centered on the body proper.[24]

These "egocentric spaces" emanate from certain centers of the body: the buccal space of the mouth as the first center, then visual, tactile and auditive space. But these spaces are not coordinated until generalized space and the permanent object are deciphered. For Piaget, when the infant learns to isolate its body as a functioning whole and passes from an "oceanic" consciousness, a veritable Copernican Revolution has occurred.[25] Yet with the loss of the world as extension-of-self, and thus as an all-encompassing (if asymmetric) egocentrism, there emerges a radial egocentrism. Now all objects and persons are identified according to their "space" or "place" with regard to the budding ego. Only by the loss of the world can the ego be born. Only with the emergence of time does individual history begin.

Temporal Components

According to the radial centrality of the young child it is not surprising that its essential timelessness is modified little at first. The Eternal Now, the immediacy of the present, the satisfaction of the biological demands of the moment dominate. As the child begins to develop some sense of time, it is not surprising either that time for the child is quite literally different from adult time. Time passes more quickly the more we are socialized, because we move from spontaneous, short-term activities (such as contemplating a caterpillar), to planned, sequential, long-term goals: earning a degree, buying a house, etc. In childhood one more or less lives in a psycho-temporal environment of *kairoi*.[26] As one grows, artificial schemata or *chronoi* are imposed upon consciousness.

Significantly enough, there is now physiological evidence which suggests that the "slower" time of the child is not just a difference in symbolic ap-

prehension. Seymour Kety has noted that the consumption of oxygen by the brain falls rapidly from childhood to adolescence, and continues to decline gradually into old age.[27] Kety concludes that this effect makes time pass faster with advancing age. It has also been demonstrated that our metabolic rate influences perception of time, and Lecomte du Nouy's experiments have shown that time for a twenty- and fifty-year-old man is roughly four and six times faster than for the five-year-old child.[28] In addition, the child is not aware of mechanical causation, "natural law," or the rotation of the earth around the sun. The seemingly (obvious) transparent realities—cause and effect, Aristotelian logic, and empirical fact—are *not* innate to the province of the child. In the Sensori-Motor Stage the child has not yet even discriminated broad categories and generalities: the world is full of concrete particulars and infinite novelties. Each experience is unique and intimate.

Piaget terms the period following the emergence of what we have called "radial symmetry" the Preoperational Period, from about two to seven years. At the outset of this period the child develops another significant structure of consciousness, the "symbolical function"—"the capacity to represent something with something else."[29] Speech is, of course, the most crucial symbolizing activity. Other forms of symbolical function include discriminatory (as opposed to purely motor) play, the use of gestures and the formation of mental pictures. The symbolical function is generically necessary to the assumption of chronological time (the representation of recurring sequences by signs or symbols: day, night, the seasons, the delineation of clock time and its terms).

Sessile Consciousness

According to our classifications of consciousness we can initially label early childhood consciousness as *sessile* (although *pre*-sessile might be more appropriate). It is spatially oriented and given to structurally rigid conceptions. This latter statement will be qualified, but its meaning lies in the budding nomistic tendency of children after infancy. In fact, Papalia and Olds write of childhood:

> With all their lively impudence, children are the great traditionalists. In line with Piaget's statements about the rigidity of children's conceptions of rules and morality, children pass on what they have heard as The Revealed Truth. They will not tolerate theories that contradict what they "know."[30]

The nomism of children reflects a possible morphic tendency[31] (a tendency towards increasing orders and hierarchies, as opposed to entropy) in the organic world. The young human seems anxious to fit everything in its "place"—to locate spatially both itself and "world" in a meaningful order. In Piaget's *Preoperational Period* changes occur so quickly that this nomistic tendency proves necessary for homeostasis. The development of language, rapid conceptual transformation, burgeoning hierarchies of social structure, intrusive "attacks" upon the egocentric cosmos (and the necessity of recognizing the worlds of others), and the frustrations of cognitive equipment and coordination underdeveloped for the demands of the social task, all contribute to the frustrations of the growing child. As a child moves from home to nursery school, and from nursery school to grammar school, the protective shield of infancy is slowly corroded; demands to acquire adult skills increase, and fear of failure becomes a more haunting demon. Essentially, then, the sessile tendencies and rigidity in the child are crowded and challenged at every turn.

SOCIALIZATION AND TEMPORALIZATION

The process of socialization dissevers the child from the quasi-eternal security of infancy. Beginning with the acquisition of the schema of the permanent object, the child is increasingly bombarded with the demands of new stimuli and suddenly mushrooming assortments of new assimilations and accommodations, accompanied by the necessity for continued equilibrium. From infancy through early school years the child commonly makes a series of structural "errors" (according to the socially-defined "real" world). Common structural errors for this phase of development are: 1) *syncretism*, an overgeneralized nomistic tendency of the child; the lack of discrimination in ordering the details of the world; making disjointed connections and analogies between words, events and objects; 2) *juxtaposition*, a comparable tendency, where the child fails to connect the details of the world in a logically coherent order (e.g., in drawings where parts and pieces do not "fit"); 3) *confusion of appearances and reality;* the child awaking in the dark night may confuse the clothes draped over a chair for a wolf; 4) *centering*, a technical term which indicates the inability to process information from two different sources, resulting in an unrefined geometric perspective (e.g., it has been demonstrated that children frequently fail to recognize equal amounts of liquid volume if they are poured into asymmetrical containers—an error still made by some adults); 5) *cause and effect and syllogistic logic* as tools of thought are undeveloped; 6) *nonreversibility*, by which Piaget indicates the child's inability to retrace his thought processes, or return from effect to cause. Piaget asks why the processes of logical thought and perception do not appear as soon as speech and the symbolical function enter as working tools.[32] His answer is that in actuality a *relearning* process on the level of thought must accompany what has already been mastered on the level of action. New cognitive structures require time for absorption. The spatial security and atemporal tendencies of sessile consciousness cannot dwell long secure in the child. Socialization demands not only certain patterns of action, but a modicum of sophistication on the level of communication. Communication in its normal verbal form entails an acutely temporal linear structure. Thus with socialization comes temporalization and the pressures to polish the cognitive processes in order to avoid the foregoing list of "errors."

Socialization thus means temporalization. Leaving the *kairoi* of filled moments, the child must learn the *chronoi* of defined minutes, hours, days, months, years; he must learn the world of alarm clocks and school bells, of planning, logical thought and action. Life becomes serialized, the individual acquires a history, and time becomes linear. We might assume that sessile consciousness passes into motile consciousness, but such is not entirely the case. We have noted already the stabilizing function of sessile elements.

From ages seven to twelve a child is acquiring more complex spatial perceptions as she/he learns the skills of the *Concrete Operational Period*, including distinguishing appearances from reality; learning fundamental logical, mathematical and geometric operations; and increasing verbal efficiency. The simple hierarchy of infancy has proliferated many times over into relatives, teachers, and other adults, religious organizations, schools, and a budding awareness of mysterious bureaucracies constituting civil authority and government. Television and mass communication have speeded the evolution of this hierarchical structure of consciousness. Simultaneously, the hierarchies entail a complex geometrization. The child's egocentric world becomes a polycentric world of competing egos and purposes. The social world appears interrelated in complex and meaningful (if as yet esoteric) patterns. The *being* of early infancy is now subsumed under the temporalized *becoming* of a social self.

THE EMERGENCE OF ADULT MODES OF CONSCIOUSNESS

During Piaget's Concrete Operational Period, and Period of Formal Operations (from age twelve on), we have a growing tension (between two modes of consciousness, sessile and motile) which demands resolution. As we develop, we evolve from an egocentric to a polycentric world; yet, in a real sense, we are always egocentric insofar as there is no other center of external perception. We may be challenged by competing perceptions, external to ourselves, which no longer allow us the simple comforts of radial symmetry. Our world may gradually undergo complex geometrization. The ever-present demands and challenges of becoming may increasingly crowd upon us from late infancy on. Yet at each stage most of us envision a return to some idealized state of being (sessile consciousness): "when I grow up," "when I finish school," "when I find my job," "when I am married," etc. We are haunted by yearnings: if not for the innocency of childhood, at least for its spontaneity, and security of "place" and "space." The resolutions of such tensions vary according to a complex of psychological and social factors.

Physiologically, man is a motile creature. As Ruth Benedict has pointed out, human cultures certainly appear, when contrasted with other social structures in the animal kingdom (such as ant societies whose structures have remained stable for sixty-five million years), to be dynamic and flexible.[33] However, in more short-range terms (e.g., decades or centuries), adult modes of sessile consciousness seem abundant. This is certainly the case historically, as we shall see. Yet owing to the complexity of social variables such as sexual, racial, ethnic and economic strata, a social taxonomy based upon the sessile-motile scheme is not easy to construct. For example in the U.S., W.A.S.P. middle-class conformity, with its array of professional, domestic, economic and religious status symbols, is not necessarily a strictly "sessile" condition; it may appear as restless dissatisfaction and continuous striving for a more satisfying lifestyle. Moreover, whether because of external prejudice, internal lack of motivation, subcultural world views, or a complex of factors, many "ghetto" peoples seem typical of sessile staticism. Although the "civil rights movement" in the United States has undoubtedly propelled many minority persons into a more motile frame, others seem still bound to various ghettos and sessile modes of life and consciousness. Examples of both motile dissatisfaction and sessile rigidity seem interspersed among Native Americans, Appalachian whites, Mexican-Americans, blacks and various other minority groups. Certain religio-ethnic groups, such as the Amish in Pennsylvania, appear to have maintained a little-altered sessile consciousness for many decades. In other instances, sessile patterns seem tied to a vicious cycle of poor education or illiteracy, prejudice, poverty, cultural isolation, malnutrition, disease, etc. Thus "sessile consciousness" in adulthood can mean many things: a sense of "having arrived," a conviction of the superiority of a revered tradition, or a hopeless capitulation to apparently predetermined conditions. Sessile consciousness entails a *spatial* orientation, and self-conceptions based upon occupying a given "place" or "space" vary widely in their perceived symbolic value according to class, sex, race, ethnic identity or economic status.

As an adult option motile consciousness is more difficult to define than the sessile mode; the latter is relatively easier to quantify in terms of visible and measurable cultural variables. Furthermore, *as* a mode of consciousness, motility cannot be equated simply with revolutionaries, social reformers or mobile home owners. In addition, it may be quite difficult to determine whether certain minority persons, whose striving would seem to indicate a high motile index, are in fact seeking a sessile status with its attendant signs and artifacts. Finally, it is critical whether we define our terms psychologically or culturally, since social location is not easily equated with psychological values and goals by simple formulae. If motility indicates consciousness concerned with growth and development, then what are its appropriate *material* signs and artifacts? Motile consciousness is hardly quantifiable (except perhaps to a certain extent by psychological testing), since its primary constituents are qualitative "intangibles" such as psychic, spiritual or relational values. Although we might argue that the same is true for *sessile* consciousness, the fact remains that the sessile mode is more preoccupied with quantifiable values such as "space" or "place" or material status.

Because of its fundamental psychological dimensions, *holistic conscious-ness,* perhaps even more than motility, is difficult to locate empirically. Holism, as we have suggested, means psycho-social homeostasis and dynamic equilibrium. It connotes the healthy balance between assimilations and accommodations, between sessile solidity and motile openness and flexibility. Ideally such a consciousness transcends the redundance of egocentrism by placing the "I" within an organic and social continuum. Here the joys of a substratum of identity, of an emergent integrity (wholeness), of trustworthy "givens" of personality (responsibility, honesty, openness, etc.) constitute a continuing sessile structure of reference. At the same time holistic consciousness promotes a healthy self-critical capacity and an openness to new experience, further growth, knowledge and expansion of consciousness: all motile elements. But the "whole is greater than the sum of its parts." Holism avoids reduction of the personality. Both the "orders" and "novelties" of the world impinge upon us in unknown ways, and the expansion of consciousness is a process not explicable in rational terms alone. The point is, we should not attempt to establish a uniform social or behavioral profile for holistic consciousness. We must leave room for the strangeness and beauty, the sudden clarity or unexpected mystery, of that nature of which we are a part. The ramifications of holistic consciousness will be further explored in the concluding chapter of this study.

TEMPORALIZATION AND HAPPINESS

A Study in Time

The significance of time for world view is highlighted by a unique experiment designed by Bernard S. Aaronson. Aaronson reports his investigation in an article entitled "Behavior and the Place Names of Time."[34] The study included two subjects, one who was hypnotized and another who served as a control. Both subjects were given relevant psychological tests before, during and after the experiment and were under the observation of several independent clinical diagnosticians. The two subjects were engaged in two sets of test conditions: *ablation* conditions, where various categories of time were obliterated by hypnosis (or for the control, by mild self-hypnosis and role-playing); and *expansion* conditions, where the subjects were induced to envision a designated time category as greatly protracted or extended. The results of these experiments are summarized as follows:

In the ablation set, the first condition imposed was *no past*. The hypnotized subject "became confused, irritable, and given to mild acting-out."[35] Memory was greatly impaired, and the subject tended to waive propriety and express his real feelings (in some socially unacceptable ways). The no-past condition also precipitated a loss of inhibition, and the MMPI (Minnesota Multiphasic Personality Inventory) profile resembled the patterns of "people with bizarre acting-out syndromes."[36] The simulator reported considering two responses: an eradication of memory evoking present confusion, or a liberation from the past. The latter course was chosen, and a sense of rebirth and freedom to act and interact ensued. His MMPI "showed a marked decline in obsessive rumination."[37]

The second set of conditions, *no present,* induced a state of immobility and rigidity in the hypnotized subject. He responded neither to his name nor any stimulation, such as pain. The experimenters compared the state to catatonia. Because of the severity of the reaction this condition was terminated immediately and appropriate suggestions were given. "When awakened, he responded with great fear and relief."[38] The subject recalled an emotionless experience, the memory of which filled him with horror. He "described his condition as a state of unbeing, like death."[39] The simulator's response to *no present* was also quite interesting, beginning with

> a burst of good-natured but very marked aggressiveness. He attributed his mood to reading Allen Ginsberg's *Howl.* He felt that . . . the masks and falseness which clutter behavior and obscure true being . . . could be stripped away and that then people could live . . . [40]

The subject displayed hyperactivity, and MMPI results again showed a decline in obsessive rumination, but with an increase in rebelliousness and active inclinations. Of course *no present* in a *literal* sense was impossible for the simulator, though his behavior may indicate how a person *feels* when the present is devalued.

The *no future* conditions produced in the hypnotic subject "a euphoric, semi-mystical state"—a sense of a boundless present in which the subject's interest in detail and interaction was greatly increased. The simulator found *no future* suggestions initially depressing, but developed a sense of stoical acceptance, devoid of both anxiety and anticipation.

The ablation conditions were continued in a series of combination sets: no past and future, no present and future, and no past and present. Because of the severe reaction of the hypnotic subject to the *no present* condition, both sets involving present were deleted from the hypnotic study. The simulator responded to *no past and present* with restless anticipation. His MMPI showed "some increase in atypical thinking."[41] In the *no present and future* condition the control subject dwelt in past experience and displayed neurotic and irritable behavior. His MMPI displayed a pattern of excessive worry and guilt over impulses, and an attendant cycle of loss of control.

The *no future and past* unexpectedly created in the hypnotized subject a response almost identical to the *no present* suggestion: rigidity, inflexibility and a catatonic-like state. Again the experimenters terminated quickly this phase. For the simulator, the same suggestion made him unaccountably sleepy. Though the subject recalled ample sleep the previous night, he napped for a while, and afterwards displayed lethargic disinterest in the laboratory environment. His MMPI indicated increased dependency, passivity and depression. After the completion of the *ablation* conditions, *control* conditions of no suggestions were observed in both subjects. No significant deviation from their normal behavior or MMPI profiles was noted.

The *expansion of the past* evoked in the hypnotized subject a sense of happiness and preoccupation, with a marked reduction in concern for present happenings around him. His MMPI showed little change. The role-playing subject negotiated the *expanded past* with similar patterns: decline in compulsiveness was suggested by his MMPI. The *expanded present* produced in the hypnotic subject a certain sense of happiness and immanence, but no key personality alterations were noted. The simulator became immersed in the moment, happy and active; but the intensity of his activity left him exhausted at day's end. The MMPI reflected a notable decline in obsessiveness. The *expanded future* produced a marked happiness and mystical elation in the hypnotized subject, a condition also reflected in his MMPI. In particular, fear of death declined. Deadlines seemed unimportant. For the simulator the *expanded future* increased self-confidence, and again his MMPI profile testified to considerable reduction in obsessiveness.

In the combined expansion series, *expansion of past and present* made the hypnotic subject happy. He exhibited a pervasive concern for the origin of things, and seemed to envision the components of his environment in terms of their historical context and progressive unfolding from past to present. On the other hand, the simulator became very depressed, hypochondriachal and withdrawn, interpreting the suggestion as deterministic, i.e., that the present was completely preestablished by the past. The MMPI reflected these attitudes.

Expanded past and future caused the hypnotized subject to trace the course of his life and reflect upon the future. The sense of the present declined and his MMPI reflected "an increase in obsessive, ruminative thinking."[42] Afterwards, the subject remembered that he was "as close to being a philosopher as he could possibly be."[43] The simulator responded in a similar fashion, becoming pensive and somewhat withdrawn.[44]

In the *expansion of the present and future* the hypnotic subject felt happy and believed "he had triumphed over death." His euphoria was followed by restlessness and bizarre behavior in which he:

began to pin obscene slogans to the backsides of people in the laboratory. After he had gone off to relieve himself, he returned from the lavatory trailing ribbons of toilet paper, with which he proceeded to festoon the doors of the rooms in the laboratory . . . While in the lavatory, he had drawn a cartoon of a face on the mirror over the washbowl.[45]

The simulating subject likewise displayed a marked optimism and greater aggressiveness and energy. His MMPI again reflected a decline in obsessive tendencies. Following the expansion series a second set of *control* conditions as before evidenced no significant changes in personality profile of the two subjects.

The results of the foregoing study are analyzed by Aaronson. The correlation between models for time and behavior is obvious. The serial understanding of time as past, present and future seems to require each term as necessary to the other. Each term contributes to psycho-social consciousness. Aaronson concludes that "the past provides us with meanings and inhibition of response."[46] Such an "inhibition of response" and selectiveness of stimuli is basic to the establishment of meaning. *No past* conditions resulted in socially obnoxious abandonment of inhibitions on the one hand, or interpreted in another light, a sense of rebirth.

In the *expanded past* conditions, both subjects responded in terms of a narrowed frame of interest, in the same way that old people do.[47]

Expanded past and present seemed to induce an historical sense, or else a sense of fatalism or determinism. Since past differentiations monitor present stimuli, selecting input which becomes part of our identity, it is not surprising that the expanded past conditions should evoke reflection on origins. Aaronson believes that these conditions support the "disengagement theory" of ageing:

disengagement is an outcome of the socialization process, which selectively reinforces a narrowing range of reinforcements until the individual is socialized out of life.[48]

(It seems to me that the latter years of certain great men might not support this thesis. For example, Alfred North Whitehead did some of his most innovative and seminal thinking in his late sixties and early seventies.)

The present is the actual locus of all behavior. *No present,* as well as *no future and no past,* produced in the hypnotic subject a state which seemed like "unbeing." The *expanded present* produced no crucial changes in the subjects, except a tendency towards a flooding of stimuli. A relative devaluation of the present, as in the *expanded past and future,* elicited a philosophical reflectiveness in the subjects. Aaronson notes that

Nelson (1965) has pointed out that the message of the great religious leaders, such as Christ and Buddha, is a message of an extended present in which the individual can control his destiny because he has stepped out of the flow of time, and causation moves through rather than around him.[49]

The future is the repository of goals and deadlines, of hope and anxiety. The final terminal point of death lies in the future. *No future* and *expanded future* both produced euphoric and mystical responses in the hypnotized subject. The simulator found the former depressing, but responded to the latter with a sense of hope. *Expanded present and future* precipitated a kind of manic elation in both subjects.

Aaronson's study, like all manageable experiments, has necessary limitations. Both subjects were twenty-two year old male college graduates. Would variables in age, sex or culture significantly alter the responses? Since we assume that our sense of time and its psychological coefficients are largely socially derived, how would a yogi, or one imbued with time frames other than linear, react to a similar experiment?

The Meaning of Time: Social and Historical Variables

Haeckel's theorem that "ontogeny recapitulates phylogeny" suggests that the processes of socialization and history should bear some resemblance. Without too much superimposition, we find such a parallel between mythopoeism and Piaget's Preoperational Period. (The term mythopoeism derives from the Greek words *muthos*, "myth," and *poieein*, "to make," and refers to the "mythmaking" cognitive structures of ancient man.) Mythopoeism will be discussed further in a later chapter, but the parallels with the Pre-operational Period are as follows: 1) *a qualitative apprehension of space*, such as the mythical "maps" of childhood and primitive culture which differentiate home from foreign ground, places we belong and places we do not, sacred and profane locales, friendly and hostile territory; 2) *a qualitative apprehension of time*, the importance of *kairoi*, children looking forward to birthdays and *holidays*, the seasonal festivals and holy days of archaic man, a synchronicity (an acausal, but meaningful simultaneity of events, such as astrology assumes) of cosmic and social or personal events; 3) *an ego-, family-, or tribe-centered world* with attendant appropriate legitimating myths, explaining how "we" are related to "them" out there; 4) *the unity of subject and object,* with the infant body and world undifferentiated, with personifications of toys, trees, animals; in ancient man the animistic assumptions regarding the natural world; 5) *cause and effect envisioned personally,* as "the rock (personified) tripped me up" or "a cloud chased me and rained on me," etc.; 6) *the coalescence of the symbol and the thing signified,* where possessions are ontological extensions of the self (borrowing mommy's or daddy's things); or, words have power (curses, voodoo, witchcraft, magic, etc.).

In the light of Aaronson's study, we will focus here solely on comparative temporal structures. The infant seems to be an *atemporal* being, with neither past nor future, and no means of defining its present *as* present. In early childhood, the "past" of infancy quickly becomes a shadowy memory ("a long time ago, when I was little . . . "). We must remember that for the child time indeed *is* longer. The "past" is chronologically brief, but disproportionately critical psychologically, harboring the roots of self-concept. In Aaronson's *no past* conditions, the hypnotic subject responded with a loss of social inhibitions, and confusion and irritation. Socialization, rooted in the past, was removed. The simulator chose instead a sense of rebirth and liberation—a way of escaping from the sometimes shackling bonds of socialization.

In the mythopoeic mind the present identity of the social group is rooted in archetypal events. Though the past is not conceived historically (in the modern sense), *loss* of such a mythic framework would be disastrous to social identity. (Such losses have occurred many times over historically.) Aaronson was unable to test the hypnotic subject in the *no past and present,* but the simulator exhibited atypical thinking and restless anticipation. Comparable social examples fit the structure we have labeled *motilism.* For a people who feel socially enslaved or trapped, the future *alone* looms before them, a harbinger of both dread and hope. As the Jerome Kern song goes: "I gets weary, and sick of tryin', I'm tired of livin' and feared of dyin' . . ." Socially oppressed minorities may also envision the future as mythic liberation ("We shall overcome"); religious apocalypticism and millenialism, or the classless society of Marxism, are similar perspectives.

Expansion of the past produced in both subjects an historical sense, with diminished concern for the present. Here we might place a conservative middle-class consciousness, happy in its traditions and memories (*as long as* not disturbed by the present or future). *Expansion of the past* would be a *sessile* time frame. *Expansion of the past and present* was taken by the hypnotic subject again as a cue to historical awareness. Comparatively, mythopoeism roots all significant events in past archetypes. In the case of the simulator, who responded with a sense of fatalism, we might recall the philosophical determinism of Stoicism. *Expansion of past and future* created excessive concern with cause-and-effect and accompanying ruminations in both subjects. Here we might compare a people—Post-Exilic Israel, for example—who live in a limbo between past memories and future hopes.

The ablation suggestion of *no present* induced an intolerable condition for the hypnotic subject, a sense of non-being or death. The *no future and past* produced an almost identical reaction, for the present (in the linear scheme) has *being* only in relationship to a past and future. *No present* for the simulator elicited a state of rebelliousness which might be interpreted as a desire to move into the future, posthaste; we are reminded again of the perspective of oppressed peoples. *No present and future*—omitted for the hypnotic subject—was taken by the simulator as a signal of loss of control (present), and a sense of guilt and anxiety (schizophrenic retreat into the past). Perhaps another alternative consciousness of psychically oppressed persons is represented here.

Just as the childhood comprehension of the past is disproportionate to its actual chronological span, so the future seems to the child vast and illimitable (or certainly indefinite beyond immediate expectations). The indefinite future for psycho-socially secure children is a vague, but happy anticipation. On the other hand, for repressed minorities the future may seem bleak; there may seem to be "no future." Similar behavioral phenomena may be observed in the elderly. Even a belief in an afterlife must remain largely an unknown, and the tendency in most elderly persons is to retreat to past memories. *No future* for the hypnotic subject inspired a mystical sense—a boundless present open and unhurried. The role-player appropriated the condition with a more psycho-social awareness—at first depression, then stoical acceptance. If mythical arrivals are taken from us we are condemned to live in the present, a prospect with both positive (responsibility) and negative (loss of anticipation) implications. Thus the future can mean limitless possibilities or increased burdens and responsibilities, an extension of a hopeless present, an opportunity for liberation, or combinations and nuances of all these expectations. Or as Alfred North Whitehead proposes, the future is a promise of the continuous flux into the present of novelty—a therapeutic counterbalance to sterility and boredom.

As we consider the processes of socialization and temporalization we must recognize the psycho-social complexity of any time category and its relative meanings: security or guilt, opportunity or limitation, expansion or contraction, freedom or boredom, etc. The time frames (especially non-linear) of other cultures doubtlessly would yield a diverse array of values in tests such as Aaronson's. In general we may conclude that the individual or culture best equipped to define the strange phenomenon of time demonstrates, with balanced reciprocity, both sessile joys and motile challenges.

FOOTNOTES

[1]Paul Henry Mussen, John Janeway Conger, and Jerome Kagan, *Child Development and Personality* (New York: Harper and Row, 1969), pp. 258-59.

[2]Peter L. Berger and Thomas Luckmann, *The Social Construction of Reality* (New York: Anchor Books, 1967), pp. 52-61; 129-163.

[3]Harry Munsinger, *Fundamentals of Child Development* (New York: Holt, Rinehart and Winston, 1975), p. 160 ff. Munsinger's discussion of cognitive development constitutes an excellent general survey.

[4]Ibid., p. 169.

[5]Ibid., pp. 172-73. Munsinger makes the following points: 1) Skinnerian determinism denigrates human free will according to theologians (like Reinhold Niebuhr), humanists (like Carl Rogers), conventional psychologists and Freudians; 2) Arthur Koestler charges that behaviorism ignores consciousness, mind, imagination and purpose; 3) "Peter Gay speaks of 'the innate naivete, intellectual bankruptcy and half-deliberate cruelty of behaviorism'," 4) others cite authoritarian/ totalitarian implications of behaviorism, and the ethical ambiguity of manipulating others; Richard Rubenstein portrays the danger of some future controller stamping out all dissent; and, Rollo May argues that "the capacity to rebel is of the essence in a constructive society;" 5) Munsinger asks, who

is to determine the social norms of good and evil, or who is to define pleasure and pain, reward and punishment?

[6]Ibid., p. 231.

[7]Ibid.

[8]Ibid., p. 230.

[9]The Encyclopedia of Philosophy, s.v., "Piaget, Jean," by Wolfe Mays.

[10]Barry J. Wadsworth, *Piaget's Theory of Cognitive Development* (New York: David McKay Co., 1971), p. 11.

[11]Jean Piaget, *The Origins of Intelligence in Children* (New York: Norton and Co., 1963), p. 35.

[12]Wadsworth, p. 14.

[13]Ruth Benedict, "Child Rearing in Certain European Countries," in *Every Man His Way,* ed. Alan Dundes (Englewood Cliffs: Prentice-Hall, 1968), pp. 292-301.

[14]Ibid., p. 293.

[15]Ibid., p. 296.

[16]Erik H. Erikson, *Childhood and Society* (New York: Norton and Co., 1963), pp. 388-392.

[17]Benedict, p. 298.

[18]Ibid., p. 300.

[19]Sigmund Freud, *Civilization and Its Discontents* (New York: Norton and Co., 1962), pp. 11-12; 14; 15; 19.

[20]Jean Piaget, *The Child and Reality* (New York: Viking Compass, 1974), pp. 13-14.

[21]Ibid, p. 14.

[22]Ibid.

[23]Ibid., p. 15.

[24]Ibid.

[25]Ibid., p. 16.

[26]The distinction between *kairos* and *chronos,* Greek words for time, is a theological distinction ostensibly found in the New Testament. Although it has been pointed out that these words are often used synonymously, the distinction proves useful for describing two different "kinds" of time. *Kairos* refers to special moments or events, "filled time," which alter the course of history. *Chronos* refers to measured time flowing in a linear direction. *Kairos* fits the consciousness of childhood because it is event-oriented, qualitative time.

[27]James L. Christian, *Philosophy* (San Francisco: Rinehart Press, 1973), p. 102.

[28]Ibid.

[29]Diane E. Papalia and Sally Wendkos Olds, *A Child's World* (New York: McGraw-Hill Book Company, 1975), p. 489.

[30]Ibid.

[31]The morphic tendency in the organic world is discussed cogently by Lancelot Law Whyte, *The Universe of Experience* (New York: Harper Torchbooks, 1974).

[32]Piaget, *The Child and Reality,* p. 17.

[33]Ruth Benedict, "The Science of Custom," in *Every Man His Way,* ed. Alan Dundes (Englewood Cliffs, N.J.: Prentice-Hall, 1968), p. 183.

[34]Henry S. Aaronson, "Behavior and the Place Names of Time," in *The Future of Time,* eds. Henri Yaker, Humphry Osmond, and Frances Cheek (Garden City, N.Y.: Anchor Books, 1972), pp. 405-436.

[35]Ibid., p. 412.

[36]Ibid., p. 413.

[37]Ibid., p. 414.

[38]Ibid., p. 415.

[39]Ibid.

[40]Ibid.

[41] Ibid., p. 417.
[42] Ibid., p. 422.
[43] Ibid.
[44] Ibid., p. 424.
[45] Ibid.
[46] Ibid., p. 428.
[47] Ibid.
[48] Ibid., p. 429.
[49] Ibid., p. 430.

CHAPTER II

LANGUAGE AND WORLD VIEW

Language Acquisition and its Biological Bases

SINCE THE acquisition of language and the acquisition of world view are integrally related processes, it is important to ask *how* language is learned, and to describe the role of biological referents.

Theories of Language Acquisition

Papalia and Olds[1] outline four competing theories of language. 1) *Behaviorism:* As in other matters, stimulus-response conditioning is considered *the* significant factor in the learning of language. The mind of the infant is a *tabula rasa.* As the young child utters a cacophony of sounds, only those which resemble patterns of established vocalization are reinforced. In behaviorism the role of innate biological structures has been traditionally ignored. 2) *Cultural Relativism and Cultural Determinism:* The authors assert that these theories

> minimize the importance of individual differences and heredity in the acquisition of language. Their adherents believe that children have innate predispositions for learning language but that it is learned because it is a social necessity.[2]

Furthermore, both Sapir and Whorf, proponents of these positions, stress the world-shaping functions of various languages as critical modes for understanding cultural differences. We shall return to this thesis. 3) *Interactionism:* Jean Piaget, the foremost theorist of this position, asserts that language is learned by children naturally—that they are biologically predisposed for its acquisition. But the innate capacity a d structural bias of the child for language are developed only through interaction with the environment. Facility of expression evolves concomitantly with the internalization of the rational processes. 4) *Preformationism and Predeterminism:* These theories, popular among contemporary linguists, stress the natural, innate capacity for language. "Language occurs naturally, without training, just as walking does."[3] Linguists who espouse such a view, point to certain cultural "universals" to substantiate their claims.

> All normal children learn their native language . . . In all cultures, children display remarkable similarities in learning language. They follow the same stages for both prelinguistic and linguistic speech. They use the same kinds of one- and two-word sentences, in the same kind of "telegraphic" speech, innocent of articles, prepositions, and word endings. Since there are

universal aspects of acquisition and of linguistic structure common to *all* languages, there must be inborn mental structures that enable children to build grammars, or systems of rules.[4]

Not surprisingly, the preformationist-predeterminists challenge behavioral presuppositions;

they claim that knowledge of language is infinite, in the sense that we can always create new and longer sentences; it would be impossible to have learned all the language we are capable of expressing by simple operant conditioning. Also, small children do not imitate adult speech. When they try to, they typically repeat only some of the words and omit parts of speech.[5]

According to this stance, much of the language of children reflects not the speech of others, but a kind of internal grammar. This position underscores the profound role of innate neurological mechanisms.

Biological Bases of Language

All animals communicate in some fashion. Animal communications initially revolve around basic survival "givens": food, mating, hunting, warning signals, etc. Ants and bees have complex systems of communication. Man, who monitors reality through his basic biological sensors, constructs his world selectively and transmits signals, both verbal and non-verbal, of comparable discrimination and complexity. Man's speech, like all animal communication, seems to be originally a biological survival tool; its basis seems to lie in innate structures within the brain. In recent years the analogous structures of the computer and the brain have spawned various comparisons. The brain far excels the most sophisticated computer in function and (we must assume) in structural capacity.

In 1968 a "language lump" was found in the brain by Normal Geschwind and Walter Levitsky of Boston University.[6] This lump exists normally in the left lobe of the brain, and seems to be related to the primary role of that lobe in speech process. Damage to various parts of the brain will, of course, affect speech:

The critical acoustic area for the recognition process for words lies in the left temporal lobe; people injured there may not be able to distinguish "b" from "p," or "d" from "t," and may be prevented from writing because they cannot think of the components of the words.[7]

The investigator, Nigel Calder, cites a poignant variable which illustrates the difference between cultures in their apprehension of the world:

Strikingly enough, Chinese children, whose words are pictorial rather than phonetic, are not affected in this way, and Chinese injured in the acoustic area do not lose their ability to write.[8]

A further example of physical *structure* and its vital role in speech is the parietal region of the brain where the ability to shape letters "resides." Injuries here may produce "mirror-writing" (where handwriting runs from right to left). Such mechanical and structural examples do not exhaust contemporary claims for the rooting of language in the brain.

Perhaps the most convincing case for mental "innateness" among contemporary theorists is presented by Noam Chomsky of M.I.T. Chomsky asserts that the mind contains a "deep structure" of great complexity and sophistication which is comparable to an innate grammar. The child, through utilizing transformational rules which follow biological patterns, is able to construct an infinite number of sentences. (Chomsky asks how are children able to construct sentences which they have never heard if such structures do not exist?) As might be expected, Chomsky's theory has stirred both enthusiasm and skepticism. Such a position does explain a wide variety of observations and experiments. Its usefulness as a model is well established, but its coincidence with the actual structure of the brain and the exact mechanics of language acquisition has yet to be confirmed. It seems fairly likely that Chomsky's theory is at worst an over-simplification, and at best only an approximation. Yet its contours challenge effectively many of the bland assumptions of behaviorism (or purely sociological explanations as well). Although Chomsky maintains that language is a uniquely human phenomenon, chimpanzees have developed hand-gesture vocabularies of up to thirty-four signs, and utilizing colored plastic shapes to represent words, a vocabulary of 130 words.[9] Although the significance of these feats is contested, they do seem to suggest that a structural basis for using sophisticated sign language must be granted the chimps. Of course, the monkeys were trained in a "social setting" by humans using behavioral reinforcements.

Thus studies in language acquisition indicate a significant role of innate biological structures, which seem to be passed on in the genes through generations. Furthermore, as Piaget has clearly demonstrated, intelligent behavior precedes the acquisition of language. However, language is equally a social construction insofar as, apart from some mythical and primal beginnings, it has been part and parcel of the process of socialization historically. Moreover, it is through socialization that language acquires its distinctive world-shaping role in the lives of cultures and individuals.

FUNCTIONS OF LANGUAGE AND LEVELS OF ABSTRACTION

The Symbolic Character of All Language and the Ontological Error
Language is symbolism. S. I. Hayakawa writes that

> human beings have agreed, in the course of centuries of mutual dependency, to let the various noises that they can produce with their lungs, throats, tongues, teeth, and lips systematically stand for specified happenings in their nervous systems.[10]

That system of agreements—of mutually accepted symbols—is language. Hayakawa goes on to assert that there is "no necessary connection between the symbol and that which is symbolized."[11] These assertions may strike us as peculiarly self-evident; however, the symbolic character of all language has *not* been a self-evident fact to the large bulk of humanity historically, nor to many people today.

Words derive their meaning from their cultural usage. The English expression "I am hungry" translates into the French *J'ai faim* or the German *Es hungert mich.* The mere vocal sounds of these three expressions are meaningless apart from semantic agreement; there is no *a priori* reason for assuming one to be a more suitable vehicle of meaning than another. The problem becomes more complicated as we move to more abstract symbolisms. Christian missionaries have encountered perplexing situations when critical images or concepts have proved untranslatable into a native dialect. This writer remembers a report of an attempted translation of "Behold the lamb of God" from John's Gospel into a dialect with no word for lamb. Shall the translator choose another animal? Can another animal bear the same semantic value as the lamb in Jewish sacrificial imagery? What if this people has no language of sacrifice? These questions reflect the obvious dilemmas of translation, not only of *words,* but also of *concepts.* Not only do we face difficulties in moving from one culture to another, but also in moving from one historical period to another (as Chaucerian English illustrates). To what extent *can* we understand different peoples in different places at different times? Certainly the historian knows that he must try to move behind the words or through the words to a vicarious participation in the world of experience. Language, then, mediates reality. Words may signal unique experiences, but no language has remained sacred. Words appear and disappear with the passage of history. Experiences, concepts, or realities that persist may carry with themselves persisting symbols, but in any case will continue to be couched adequately even if their original semantic symbols disappear. As Mauthner says:

> Language is merely an apparent value, like a rule of the game, which becomes more binding as more players submit to it, but which neither alters nor comes into contact with the world of reality.[12]

Thus as symbols, words have no *ontic* reality. Yet as we examine history we find such a reality attributed to words over and over again. In mythopoeic thought there is indeed an ontic coalescence of the symbol and the thing symbolized. Especially *names* partake of the essence of their referents. Cassirer cites this example:

> Knowledge of the name gives him who knows it mastery even over the being and will of the god. Thus a familiar Egyptian legend tells how Isis, the great sorceress, craftily persuaded the sun-god Ra to disclose his name to her, and how through possession of the name she gained power over him and over all the other gods . . . Egyptian religious life in all its phases

evinces over and over again this belief in the supremacy of the name and the magic power that dwells in it.[13]

This phenomenon is carried over into Jewish and Christian traditions as well. The name of Yahweh has become unutterable in Jewish liturgy after the Exile. In the New Testament, the name of Christ possesses special efficacy (Philippians 2:10). The name phenomenon is widespread in other ancient cultures. How did words become "taboo?"

Since language has been the most effective social tool among human beings it is not difficult to see how this logical error (which may be called the "ontological error" owing to the status of "being" assigned to the word itself) arose. Language from the beginning has been a chief tool for regulating behavior, from primitive communications regarding food, sex, and shelter to the language of kinship, tribal authority, and religion. Thus it is understandable that the mediating symbol which bore the message of expected behavior and attitudes should itself become invested with ontic status—that it should literally "carry" the reality with it. The problem arises when the ontic status of words continues to provide a mystification of structures of behavior, authority, or concepts, when these patterns themselves have ceased to be meaningful.

We might underscore the point by making this value judgment: any sort of language that causes us to focus on the symbols themselves rather than the experience symbolized serves to break down the process of communication. Once a concept is outworn or an experience has evolved beyond its former historical referents, dead symbols cannot forever linger as disembodied ghosts. Twentieth century man, faced with a pandemonium of authoritative-sounding voices and competing myths, must as never before penetrate into the authenticity of experience and life, behind verbal masks, if he is to begin again the process of world-building.

The Functions of Language

As we have already noted, language is a critical expression of man's nature as a social being. Through the verbal facility man exists "in relationship" to other persons, and not in isolation. Substitute symbologies, both gesticulative and written, have been developed to incorporate language as part of the socialization of even the mute and the blind. What then are the primary social functions of language?

1) *Language as a tool of survival* is a function we have suggested previously: primitive man it seems evolved language in part as a means of enhancing social solidarity in procuring and producing food; in the spheres of sexual relations and shelter; and in structures of kinship, authority and religion; 2) *langauge as a tool of ordering and meaning-formation (nomic tool)* makes life meaning-*full* by ordering the disparate experiences of the senses into structured categories and generalizations; language creates models and thus serves as a

"handle" on reality; 3) *language as a mythical tool* is similar to the second function; myths (in a broad sense) are stories and archetypes which legitimate social patterns and explain the world; 4) *language as a magical tool* in a broad sense helps man to manipulate the world; language invested with ontic status is believed to effect immediate results: e.g., incantations for the sick, prayer and liturgy to the gods, songs of love and poetry, and (often in the modern world) the symbolism of mathematics and the jargon of medicine; 5) *language as a mode of power or manipulation* is closely allied to the magical function; others may be controlled through language, especially when it is invested with the potency of "decree"—political, religious, etc.—or, propaganda (imposing ideas, actions, ideologies or world views upon others through the power of words); 6) *language as an aesthetic tool* mediates man's sense of beauty through creativity, e.g., musical and poetic expression; 7) *language as a mode of psychic elimination* can serve to rid the mind of stress, frustration, fear and anger by objectifying, creativity or interjection (e.g., cursing, emotional exchanges, analysis of thought and feeling, singing or writing poetry, etc.), just as the body has mechanisms for eliminating waste and noxious chemicals; 8) *language as alienation:* because language *mediates* reality it can also *alienate from* that reality, i.e., words create barriers to understanding feelings or experience; Burrow writes

> In short, as a result of his early training, the child is enveloped not so much within a spontaneous field of total, bionomic reactions as within a field of vicarious symbols that more and more replaces his total world of objective actuality.[14]

Thus language can alienate one from the immediate world of nature or experience, from other persons, or finally from one's self through rationalization, self-deception or verbalization to avoid action or integrity; 9) *language as a mode of reconciliation, relationship and love* explains feelings, overcomes barriers of hostility and experience, provides vicarious experience and sympathetic identification and participation, establishes and maintains relationships, reminds man of evocative truths, celebrates significant feelings and overcomes the isolation of the egocentric self. These functions of language are not discrete and most often occur in conglomerate form. As we examine the wide variety of psychic and rational uses of language, its significance in shaping man's world and its dangers in creating simplistic formulas or categories should become clear. In addition, our use of language cannot be adequately understood until we examine the various levels of abstraction of words and word constructions.

Levels of Abstraction

It is not our purpose to set forth a scientific scheme which captures the complex hierarchy of abstractions in language. However, several observations should underscore the importance of considering levels of abstraction in evaluating what we say. All language, as we have argued, *mediates* reality. At best we are *twice* removed from reality as soon as we speak. We are *once* removed when we channel the world through our five senses—and already we have shaped the world in our own image. Verbalizing the impressions of our perceptions is a further act of abstraction. In many instances, we might argue that the abstraction goes no further than this. For example, I describe a simple armchair which sits in my living room, and it seems to me that the description should be apparent to any independent observer. But this is not necessarily the case. First of all, I am an English-speaking person, so I use the word "chair" which would be meaningless to many persons on this earth. Secondly, I describe the chair—its apparent height, width, dimensions, etc.—from my own perspective and valuation. Although we can be reasonably sure that most adults would describe the chair in similar terms, differences would undoubtedly exist. Am I looking at the chair from the front, back, or side? Standing or sitting? What if I am color-blind? What if I look at the chair in the aura of a rose-colored glow created by the diffusion of sunlight through pink curtains? Am I examining the chair in sunlight, in late afternoon shadows, or in artificial evening light? What if I am a child, to whom the chair takes on gigantic proportions? It becomes obvious now that the simple act of abstraction is already a reasonably complex, though certainly useful, generalization. We are all familiar with the further example of the frenzied witnesses to a crime who are unable to agree upon what they have seen. Studies have shown that these witnesses are easily swayed by any suggestion (for example, by an investigating officer). Yet returning to the more mundane, each of us takes for granted that his/her descriptions of physical objects and events, as well as personal experiences, are more or less objectively accurate. In fact, *no verbalization* is equivalent to objective reality: abstraction, and abstraction upon abstraction, not to mention simple errors of perception, color the entire process of verbal communication. Obviously we *do* communicate effectively—and yet how often we do not!

The problem, of course, becomes far more complex as we pass from physical descriptions and events to (what *we* call abstract) ideas, models, and value judgments. Embler cites the common error of taking diagrammatic models as accurate charts of the way reality objectively *is*—for example Dante's depiction of Hell, Purgatory, and Paradise, or a contemporary example, Freud's chart of the Id, Ego and Superego.[15] Or consider the lofty abstractions: God, Nirvana, Sin, Salvation, Freedom, Equality, Space, Time, Good, Evil, etc. We would not argue that these concepts are devoid of meaning, but rather suggest how absolutely critical it is that we recognize their medial position with regard to reality and their distinct relativity with regard to experience. A single example should help illumine the highly abstract nature of assumed "factual statements." We assert that "X is a bad man." "X is a bad man" is a statement of an entirely different order from "this is a pencil." We must define "bad man" by some reference to the appropriate qualities or actions characteristic of such an opprobrium. Such an assertion may have widely divergent points of reference both personally and socially. He is a "bad man" because:

he smokes cigarettes
he stole a car
he killed a man
he will not play baseball with his son
he likes dirty magazines
he is a Democrat
he does not attend church, etc., etc.

Obviously to substantiate a judgment certain actions may be referred to a "higher court of opinion," such as civil law or religious tenets. But the simple statement "he is a bad man" is an abstraction of a high order which varies widely from person to person, or from culture to culture. Such a statement may simply be a mode of "psychic elimination"—a means of expressing something like "I don't like him" or "I am mad at him" or "I fear him" (because he is different), etc. Particularly in the realm of ideas and value judgments we should constantly remind ourselves of the *process* of abstraction in which we are engaged.

THE COEFFICIENTS OF LANGUAGE AND ITS RELATIVITY

Cognition and the Necessity of Language

Imagine yourself at this moment flung unexpectedly from this world. Your present knowing self awakes and finds itself in the body of an octopus-like creature, which can move not in horizontal-linear space, but only in a series of vertical magnetic ridges which require complex manipulations of your many tentacles. To your astonishment you discover that there is no phonic communication in this world at all. Soon you comprehend that communication takes place through emitting an innumerable array of subtle hues of color in varying combinations via a small spout-like aperture on your head. Your vision is four-dimensional. As the extraordinary requirements of new learning assail your new senses, you discover the world you have left behind rapidly fading from memory. This fanciful excursion is a fable on cognition and language—which we usually assume to be necessary to intelligent life. We might just say that the process of socialization in human society, which normally entails learning language, does not *prove* anything about the intelligence of an infant, or even such esoteric matters as the possible preexistence of the soul. Forsaking the world of myth, we discover that even in our social world, language—especially in its spoken form—is not essential to cognition (though we might argue that it is essential to culture as we know it).

There are several sets of data which suggest that cognition and the acquisition of language are not always integrally related processes. A report on deaf children provides relevant data:

> Furth (1970) has studied deaf children in the U.S. and says that they don't learn reading, writing, and speaking until fairly late. In fact, most U.S. deaf children are *not* different from children who hear. Both develop similar cognitive sequences at similar rates. Furth concludes that language has only an indirect effect on cognitive development. He believes language accelerates cognitive development, but that it is not necessary for thought.[16]

A familiar case-in-point is Helen Keller who, though blind and deaf in infancy, became a well-known writer and lecturer.

Non-verbal communication, the subject of extensive study in recent years, illustrates further modes of intelligent communication. Eye movements, posture, facial expressions, gestures and positioning of the body constitute a complex and effective means of meaningful interchange. Although we find that nonverbal communication is primarily affective in content, relating to such matters as dominance, territory, sexuality, anger and fear, it nevertheless constitutes clear evidence of a wider range of intelligent symbology.

One further example of communication apart from verbal channels is telepathy. Abundant evidence—more in fact than for some physical laws which we take for granted—points to the existence of nonverbal channels of intelligent communication between persons, normally referred to an "extra-sensory perception" (which may prove to be not *extra*-sensory, but simply following sensory channels not yet discovered). For one unfamiliar with the experiments and implications of research in this area Arthur Koestler's *The Roots of Coincidence*[17] is an excellent introduction.

Emotional and Behavioral Indices of Language

The relativity of language is further indicated by the indices of connotation and action. Most of us are familiar with the common example illustrating the difference between denotation and connotation. The word home *denotes* a dwelling or domicile, but *connotes* warmth, intimacy and comfort—or does it? That simply depends upon whose home we are talking about! To a ghetto child (who may be in a *poor* ghetto or a *rich* ghetto) "home" may connote absent parents, hostile conditions and a stifling atmosphere. An evocative example which further illustrates the varying connotations of language is reported by Daryl J. Bem.[18] In a study done by Rokeach (1968) a cross-section of individuals was asked to rank twelve terms of value, including "wisdom," "a comfortable life," "a world at peace," "salvation," "maturity," etc. The researcher was especially interested in the ranking of two democratic values, "freedom" and "equality." Included in the study were three groups who manifest divergent attitudes concerning civil rights demonstrations: participants, those who did not participate but were sympathetic, and those who were unsympathetic. *Freedom* ranked high for all three groups, averaging first place for participants and those sympathetic, and second place for those unsympathetic. *Equality,* however, averaged as follows: third place for participants, sixth place for those sympathetic, and eleventh place for those unsympathetic. Bem observes:

> This last pattern is almost identical to that obtained from fifty policemen in a midwestern city who ranked *freedom* first but *equality* last. Similarly, unemployed whites ranked *freedom* third and *equality* ninth. One begins to appreciate the depth of the racial split in our society when one compares these groups with a group of unemployed Negroes: they ranked *freedom* tenth and *equality* first.[19]

These studies again underscore the significance of levels of *abstraction* in language, as well as varying connotations. Midwestern policemen may consider themselves to be protectors of *freedom,* civil rights demonstrators may consider themselves to be advocates of *freedom,* and unemployed blacks may feel that the white man's *freedom* is a sham since it connotes oppression and unequality, thus *equality* seems to be a more significant value. In each case *freedom* is conceived differently: freedom *from* crime and drugs, freedom *for* minorities to enjoy opportunities and equal rights, or the freedom of *one class* to oppress or withhold economic benefits from another! Part and parcel of these judgments are the concomitant behavioral indices accompanying such words.

What kind of *action* does the word *freedom* evoke? Anti-communist propaganda? Harsh penal codes and strict law enforcement? Lobbying in behalf of powerless minorities? Revolution? New sexual mores? Obviously *freedom* elicits not only widely divergent emotional response, but likewise a staggering and often contradictory variety of actions. Another example of the behavioral index of connotations is the usages and contexts of the word *love.* "Love" may be invoked in behalf of romantic infatuation, selfish manipulation, philanthropic gestures, authentic confrontation between persons, or in more bizarre (though not too rare) instances—murder and warfare! Simply speaking, to understand the real intent—as well as the overt content—of language, we must measure its emotive significance and the patterns of action and value which accompany its use. The author of John's *Gospel* in the New Testament understood that deed verifies (or falsifies) word when he affirmed that "the Word became flesh and dwelled among us . . ."[20]

Environmental Coefficients

The influence of environment upon culture (and therefore language) further underscores the relativity of language. Even as language to some extent shapes our view of the world, so nature may directly influence language and world view. Our first example is drawn from B. L. Whorf's anthropological studies:

> We (English-speaking persons) have the same word for falling snow, snow
> on the ground, snow packed hard like ice, slushy snow, wind-driven flying
> snow—whatever the situation may be. To an Eskimo, this all-inclusive
> word would be almost unthinkable; he would say that falling show, slushy
> snow, and so on, are sensuously and operationally different, different things
> to contend with; he uses different words for them and for other kinds of
> snow. The Aztecs go even farther than we in the opposite direction, with
> "cold," "ice," and "snow" all represented by the same basic word with
> different terminations; "ice" is the noun form; "cold," the adjectival form;
> and for "snow," 'ice mist.'[21]

Skiers have different terms for snow as well. It is obvious that in the case of
the Eskimo, the Aztec and the skier, the environmental coefficient of their
respective worlds creates markedly divergent significances for snow and ice.
Although we would assume that peoples living close to nature would develop
systems of classification for their environments, because of our bias regarding
the superiority of modern science to "primitive" world views we might
suspect such taxonomic systems to be crude and contradictory; but such is not
the case. Levi-Strauss shatters this myth in his thoroughly documented study
The Savage Mind.[22] One of many examples given by Levi-Strauss is the account
of the anthropologist E. Smith Bowen, who describes her astonishment at the
sophistication of a certain African tribe in their knowledge of the plant
world:

> I also found myself in a place where every plant, wild or cultivated, had a
> name and a use, and where every man, woman and child knew literally
> hundreds of plants . . . (my instructor) simply could not realize that it was
> not the words but the plants which baffled me.[23]

Levi-Strauss concludes that

> Native classifications are not only methodical and based on carefully built
> up theoretical knowledge. They are at times comparable from a formal
> point of view, to those still in use in zoology and botany . . . It was a
> professional biologist who pointed out how many errors and misunder-
> standings, some of which have only recently been rectified, could have been
> avoided, had the older travellers been content to rely on native taxonomies
> instead of improvising entirely new ones.[24]

Levi-Strauss cites other such cases, but our primary point is the influence of
environment on the world which we name and classify. A secondary point is
man's propensity for taxonomic systems—his predisposition for ordering his
environment.

Cultural Location and Language

A final and substantive set of factors which expose the relativity of
language we may call "cultural location."

"Cultural location" is also "historical location"—a consideration
absolutely fundamental to the understanding of language. For language, like
culture, evolves. Through the ages words spring to life or die, and changes
occur in phonetics and phonemics, denotation and connotation, and the norms

of syntax. We call "durst," "haply," and "twain" archaisms and now say "dared," "by chance," and "two." For establishing definitions etymologies are usually misleading because they do not take into account the evolution of a word through history and its widely divergent uses. A good example is the word "myth." The original meaning of the Greek *muthos* is debated; one suggestion is that it first meant "thought."[25] In Plato *muthos* "is exalted to the position of being the adequate expression of a revelation,"[26] as for example in Plato's myth of the cave. At the other extreme is the warning against "myths" as erroneous fables opposed to Christian revelation, as found in the New Testament letters *Timothy* and *Titus*.[27] In the broader spectrum of ancient literature *muthos* assumes a vast array of nuances, including "proverb," "statement," "answer," "command," "commission," "proposal," "promise," "account," and "story."[28] Later *muthos* is considered antithetical to *logos,* as "fairy tale" to "credible account," "the mythical form of an idea as distinct from its dialectical presentation" or "popular myth" as contrasted with its "deeper, extracted meaning."[29] Today myth is used in an equally varied fashion, in some cases with historical precedence and in others with modern nuances. Myth today can refer to "an erroneous fable" (orthodox religious usage), "a thematic expression of pervasive imagery" (in literary circles), "an explanation of natural phenomena" (an anthropological view), "a sacred archetype" (a psychological and anthropological use), "an allegory of truth" (a philosophical and theological perspective), and a "total world view" (a sociological and historical usage). In common parlance the expression "oh that's just a myth" bears the same off-the-cuff dismissal as the label "old wives' tale." The main point is that the history of the term "myth"—though evocative and fascinating—can hardly provide us with any proof of what its meaning today *must be.* That history does provide us with a wealth of insight into shifting world views in Western civilization, and an array of significant perspectives for understanding myth. In any case, the history of a word such as myth further establishes the relativity of language *vis-a-vis* culture and world view.

A crucial determinant in the acquisition of language—and in its relative significance and development—is the role of "significant others."[30] Normally these are parents. Through them the child not only learns to speak, but generally learns to speak in a manner befitting the social class, vocabulary and accents peculiar to the parents. This process involves both the mastering of speech and the construction of a social world:

> . . . all identifications take place within horizons that imply a specific social world. The child learns that he *is* what he is called. Every name implies a nomenclature, which in turn implies a designated social location. To be given an identity involves being assigned a specific place in the world. As this identity is subjectively appropriated by the child ("I *am* John Smith"), so is the world to which this identity points . . .[31]

In this initial intimate setting the child learns his name and learns the names of other persons and things—what they are, how they are to be regarded, and how they function. From this core experience the child extrapolates to the world at large and assumes a stance towards "generalized others." Thus the world acquires an objectivity, and language mediates between the growing person and the emergent world (for the world emerges out of every individual, just as every individual emerges out of the world).

Moreover, in the process of socialization human beings are not only introduced to verbal communication in a particular language (and in some case, languages), but also *within* this process they follow highly individual paths according to a cluster of social factors. First, as we noted, there is (normally) the family. Secondly, we have socioeconomic "class" (which may shift at times for some families) and the added eccentricities of regionalism (and further variations *within* a region). A third set of influences converges in a child's formal educational environment where academic training is combined with the influence of teachers and peers. A final set of factors resides within the individual: hereditary factors, learning facility, and perhaps peculiar eccentricities or vocabulary stock which may be assumed to enhance uniqueness.

Each of the above variables should refine and correct generalizations we make regarding the *structure* of language and world view. Social and personal eccentricities create peculiar divergences from the norm and, cumulatively, create the norm itself.

The Structures of Language and World View

Physical Location and World View

In our introduction we suggested the necessary relationship between our physical sensors and the reality "out there." We noted that the five senses serve as channels which "pick up" only a limited portion of signals which are constantly flashing forth throughout the universe. Thus what we call reality—as we suggested—is from the beginning a "special case." Before approaching the role of language in structuring our world, we must recall this predetermination.

There is another side to predetermination where language is involved. Not only do the senses preestablish "the real world," but also culture through language—its chief effecting instrument—tells us from infancy what we may sense. Here we are faced with the fabled dilemma of the chicken and the egg. And the solution may well be the same: whichever first appeared we have *both* chickens *and* eggs in our world of experience. Yet if we move imaginatively across the panorama of our everyday visible world, it is not difficult to see how certain primitive structural elements—in our language and our thought—arose. The world of physical geography has always presented to man (apart from perceptive seafarers, dreamy-eyed stargazers and entranced mathematicians) a flat earth. The flat earth cosmology is native to a simple common sense purview. Even though we now witness the magnificent "earthrise" from the moon, beamed via satellite to our TV sets, the fundamental planes of man's practical existence are up and down—horizontal and vertical.

The horizontal plane we have long associated with time, action, and the delimiting of the ephemeral; the vertical with space, hierarchies of status and authority, eternal values and ideals. Likewise, language reflects the two planes of man's existence. The horizontal plane is especially evident in verb forms, which in Indo-European languages normally denote time, time sequence and action. The horizontal plane also includes spatial functions—terms of breadth, length and width. The vertical plane is apparent more in the verb to be, and nouns of identity and location. In the written form of most languages the horizontal plane demarcates the movement of the text. In terms of *value*, most people—if asked to establish a ranking of common usage—would produce similar hierarchies of a random sample set of nouns such as cow, chair, man, governor, ocean, tree, napkin and angel; or door knob, automobile, arm, citizen, nature, book and king. Although variations would occur, we might expect:

angel	nature
governor	king
man	citizen
cow	arm
ocean	automobile
tree	book
chair	door knob

Some might substitute book for automobile, or place nature on a lower level, etc.; but the idea of a hierarchy of value or significance is common to our cultural orientation. Of course, grammatical and logical structures are far more complex than the simple two-plane depiction, yet the acquisition of complex geometrical schemes and relations follows the two basic axes of our visible horizon. Our language contains a bias inherited from our basic physical orientation.

A simple comparison might make the point clearer. Picture a man, an ant and a fly in a small box-shaped room. The man's perception of the room follows two planes (and three dimensions): the horizontal and the vertical.

The ant, unhindered by our more acute gravitational limitations, can move with equal facility on any of the six surfaces inscribing the cubic room, including the ceiling. The ant—if capable of language—might develop a far more complex geometrical grammar, including perspectives like perpendicular movement and "upside down" as normal parlance. The fly, even more flexible than the nimble ant, might not only relate to the ant's multi-dimensional geometrical scheme, but add its own asymmetrical flight patterns, enriching the affective tone of things quite remarkably. Our point is a simple one: as we examine the role of language in shaping our world view we should not be surprised to see the two-plane bias recurring here and there in various ways, and we should bear in mind the structural elements implicit within our physical location. And, as we shall see, historical, cultural and environmental factors further alter such structural components.

Selectivity and Language

When we consider the inherent *selectivity* of language, its role in shaping world view is especially evident. Not only does what we name establish world bounds, but also *how* we name what we name.

The selectivity of language is intimately connected to its integrative function, since any *ordering* of experience requires focus, disposition of components, generalization, abstraction, arrangement and hierarchy. Our creations of categories of experience or perception involve the processes spoken of by Piaget as assimilation and accommodation. For example, we have *social delineations* (such as kinship terms, institutional titles like "chairman," etc.), *biological constants* (names of the parts, functions and movements of the body, terms relating to sex, food, sleep, etc.), *terms of social interactions* (involving work, play, learning, territory, defense, relationships, love, etc.), *environmental terms and interaction* (names of trees, rocks, elements, etc. and terms for exploitation, chemical and ecological processes, etc.), and *aesthetic and spiritual expressions* (such as religious language, poetry, aesthetic terms, etc.). Within these overlapping (but by no means exhaustive) categories, we name—and selectively order—environment and perception.

Berger and Luckmann describe the "zones of meaning" created by the process of selectivity as "semantic fields."[32] "Vocabulary, grammar, and syntax are geared to the organization of these semantic fields."[33] Gender, number, verbs of action or being, and terms of relative social intimacy (such as *du* and *Sie* in German), for example, are variable elements which may in part order semantic fields. These fields enable "biographical and historical experience to be objectified, retained and accumulated" and constitute both individual and social memory or oblivion.[34]

> By virtue of this accumulation a social stock of knowledge is constituted, which is transmitted from generation to generation and which is available to the individual in everyday life . . . Participation in the social stock of

knowledge thus permits the "location" of individuals in society and the "handling" of them in the appropriate manner.[35]

The most common semantic field is the knowledge of everyday life, which is mainly "recipe knowledge," "knowledge limited to pragmatic competence in routine performances."[36] This everyday-life reality "appears as a zone of lucidity behind which there is a background of darkness."[37] This "background of darkness" includes not only specialized knowledge esoteric to the average individual, but also basic structures of perception and belief upon which "everyday reality" naively rests.

Selectivity necessitates integration of experience and the creation of semantic fields. A further degree of this discriminating and ordering process is the creation of pictures of reality which we call "world views." A world view may remain semi-conscious or seemingly unconscious throughout a person's life. It may be more or less coherent—more or less understood. Or, it may be intellectually grasped, theoretically analyzed and deliberately structured, again to a greater or lesser degree. A world view may be assimilated from institutional semantic fields (e.g., religion, political party, bureaucracy, technology, academic discipline). The official or tacit world views of institutions and ideologies may be mingled with structures acquired through primary socialization processes. Frequently the individual is eclectic, acquiring—usually haphazardly—fragmentary belief structures from diverse sources. The world views of most persons appear to contain many disparate elements locked in a quasi-integrated conglomerate. What role does language play in the acquisition of a world view? Allen Dundes asserts that

> the structure of a given language influences the categories of perception and thought of speakers of that language . . ., but the extent of the influence continues to be debated.[38]

Two men especially have emphasized (and perhaps overstated) the importance of language in the construction of world view. The first of these is Benjamin Lee Whorf (a celebrated pupil of the equally celebrated linguist Edward Sapir. Whorf's theory (the Whorfian, or Sapir-Whorf, Hypothesis), proposes that the acquisition of language requires the assimilation of culture and a basic structuring of world view. A second savant, Alfred Korzybski, the father of "General Semantics," believes that the acquisition of the structures of language entails the assimilation of underlying metaphysical categories which shape the way in which reality is understood and described. Korzybski's most noted interpreter is S. I. Hayakawa.

Benjamin Lee Whorf

Whorf depicts the silent, tacit workings of language in the structuring of world view like a law before it has been discovered:

> . . . if a rule has absolutely no exceptions, it is not regarded as a rule or as anything else; it is then part of the background of which we tend to remain

unconscious. Never having experienced anything in contrast to it, we cannot isolate it and formulate it as a rule until we so enlarge our experience and expand our base of reference that we encounter an interruption of its regularity. The situation is somewhat analogous to that of not missing the water till the well runs dry . . .[39]

The Law of Gravitation, Whorf asserts, could not have been formulated *as* a law until it could be placed in the perspective or context of a larger cosmos. Thus he continues

. . . our psychic makeup is somehow adjusted to disregard whole realms of phenomena that are so all-pervasive as to be irrelevant to our daily lives and needs.[40]

Perhaps an example of Whorf's observation might be weeds. Normally as we pass a vacant lot or walk along a country road, we are oblivious to the vast and variegated world of weeds. However, when they begin to invade our garden it is another matter. Whorf, of course, is not talking about either weeds or natural laws, but language. The grammatical structure of our language is something we rarely, if ever, question. Whorf asserts that "we dissect nature along lines laid down by our native languages." Language provides us with certain fundamental contours of a model of reality. At the outset our perspective is biased.

An excellent illustration of Whorf's point is Werner Heisenberg's discussion of the difficulty created by the incursion of new, alien theories in twentieth century physics which could not be contorted to fit the vocabulary of classical physics.

To the underlying fundamental ideas of this language (of classical physics) belonged the assumptions that the order of events in time is entirely independent of their order in space, that Euclidean geometry is valid in real space, and that the events "happen" in space and time independently of whether they are observed or not . . . Into this rather peaceful state of physics broke the quantum theory and the theory of special relativity . . . no language existed in which one could speak consistently about the new situation.[41]

Heisenberg points out that the problem was especially acute with the theory of general relativity, based on non-Euclidean geometry, where the description necessarily "now follows the scientific language of the mathematicians."[42] Heisenberg continues:

The most difficult problem, however, concerning the use of the language arises in quantum theory. Here we have at first no simple guide for correlating the mathematical symbols with concepts of ordinary language . . . our common concepts cannot be applied to the structure of the atoms.[43]

It has become necessary, in order to speak of the quantum theory "to use an ambiguous rather than an unambiguous language, to use the classical concepts in a somewhat vague manner . . ."[44] Thus Niels Bohr introduced the principle of complementarity which asserts that two (essentially contradictory) descriptions must be given the atom, which follows both "particle" and "wave" behavior. Heisenberg concludes that these pictures "have only a vague connection with reality, that they represent only a tendency toward reality."[45] It is precisely situations like Heisenberg describes that Whorf wishes us to recognize. Heisenberg's discussion also underscores a point to which we shall return: the structures of our language and the structures of new cosmological theories are not always harmonious bedfellows.

Whorf himself believes that fundamental cosmological concepts are rooted in our grammar, but are not to be found in the grammars of other languages. That we are bound by predetermined modes of interpretation regarding nature Whorf believes is apparent if we compare Indo-European languages with certain Native American languages.

The concepts or categories of *substance* and *event* illustrate such interpretive differences. In the Indo-European tradition we divide reality into "lumps, chunks, blocks, pieces . . . a 'stuff,' 'substance,' or 'matter' that answers to the water, coffee, or flour in the container formulas."[46] Likewise, our languages are *binomial*, divided into two classes—nouns and verbs— which have "different grammatical and logical properties."[47] Yet nature is not polarized. Whorf continues:

> Why are "lightning, spark, wave, eddy, pulsation, flame, storm, phase, cycle, spasm, noise, emotion" nouns? They are temporary events. If "man" and "house" are nouns because they are long-lasting and stable events . . . what then are "keep, adhere, extend, project, continue, persist, grow, dwell," and so on doing among the verbs? If it be objected that "possess, adhere" are verbs because they are stable relationships rather than stable percepts, why then should "equilibrium, pressure, current, peace, group, nation, society, tribe, sister," or any kinship term be among the nouns?[48]

As we compare the Hopi language, we discover that although there is a class of nouns, there is no subclass of mass nouns. Nouns in Hopi have an individual sense, and even mass nouns are not exact, but "vaguely bounded events."[49] For example, "water" never means what we assume is the *substance* of water, but refers to *a particular mass* or *quantity* of water. Thus in Hopi one speaks not of "a glass of (the substance) water," but *ke-yi,* meaning "a water" and implying a given quantity. Moreover, in Hopi

> "lightning, wave, flame, meteor, puff of smoke, pulsation" are verbs— events of necessarily brief duration cannot be anything but verbs. "Cloud" and "storm" are at about the lower limit of duration for nouns. Hopi, you see, actually has a classification of events (or linguistic isolates) by *duration-type* . . .[50]

Furthermore, Whorf notes that in Nootka, a language of Vancouver Island, all words would seem to be verbs. For Nootka has only one class of words for all kinds of events. Thus

> "A house occurs" or "it houses" is the way of saying "house," exactly like a "flame occurs" or "it burns." These terms seem to us like verbs because they are inflected for durational and temporal nuances, so that the suffixes of the word for house event make it mean long-lasting house, temporary house, future house, house that used to be, what started to be a house, and so on . . .[51]

A similar disparity between Indo-European and Hopi is to be found in the ways in which the two language-types represent time. Hopi, according to Whorf, is a timeless language. "It recognizes psychological time, which is much like Bergson's 'duration,' but this 'time' is quite unlike the mathematical time, T, used by our physicists."[52] Just as Hopi does not objectify certain events as nouns, so too, plurality and cardinal numbers are treated differently. We speak of an abstraction "ten days," yet we *experience* only one day at a time. In Hopi, days are not abstract quantities which may be objectified, but rather experiences lived. Therefore, "ten days is greater than nine days" in Hopi would be "the tenth day is later than the ninth," for days are not quantities to be compared, but expressions of continuing experience. Likewise, one does not speak of "this (seasonally recurrent) entity summer," but of "summer now" or "summer recently."[54] So Hopi verbs have no *tenses*, but verb "aspects" which express "intensity, tendency, and duration of causes or forces producing manifestations."[55]

As concerns *space,* Hopi again refuses to abstract. Here the similarity to mythopoeism (see chapter three) is clear:

> The Hopi thought-world has no imaginary space. The corollary to this is that it may not locate thought dealing with real space anywhere but in real space, nor insulate real space from the effects of thought. A Hopi would naturally suppose that his thought (or he himself) traffics with the actual rosebush—or more likely, corn plant—that he is thinking about . . .[56]

Whorf does seem to feel that Hopi "space" is more similar to our own—that there are at least spatial constants rooted in our psyches (as we suggested earlier).[57] "We see things with our eyes in the same space forms as the Hopi."[58]

The ramifications of Whorf's contentions are manifold, especially in terms of "time." "Indo-European" appears to follow what we have called "sessile consciousness" in its perceptions: time is envisioned more spatially. The *historical sense* is dependent upon *objectifying* time as a sequence of events (which at the extreme are reduced to atomistic isolates). Comparatively, Hopi is "subtle, complex and ever-enveloping, supplying no ready-made answer to the question of when 'one' event ends and 'another' begins."[59] We might wonder how a Hopi might respond to Aaronson's time-ablation and time-expansion experiment, since past, present and future are *not* objectifiable "quantities" in the Hopi mind. Even more evocative is Whorf's suggestion that a Hopi physics would be quite possible, yet markedly different from our own.[60] Time and velocity would have to be replaced by intensity. Acceleration would perhaps be replaced by variation. Whorf notes that scientists from such differing cultures might have a difficult time communicating. At a cursory glance, it seems as though a language like Hopi—apparently more motile or perhaps holistic in consciousness-frame— might be better suited for expressing some of the subtleties of contemporary physics. How would a Hopi scientist formulate verbally the data behind Bohr's complementarity principle?

Alfred Korzybski

Alfred Korzybski's theories closely parallel or intersect Whorf's at many points. Korzybski's main premise runs:

> A language, any language, has at its bottom certain metaphysics, which ascribe, consciously or unconsciously, some sort of structure to the world . . . Now these structural assumptions are inside our skin when we accept a language—*any* language . . . We do not realize what tremendous power the structure of an habitual language has. It is not an exaggeration to say that it enslaves us through the mechanism of semantic reactions and that the structure which a language exhibits, and impresses on us unconsciously, is *automatically projected* upon the world around us . . .[61]

S. I. Hayakawa, a leading exponent of Korzybski's views, points out that Korzybski "has concluded that prescientific structural assumptions, primitive metaphysics, etc., underlie the language (and accompanying semantic reactions)"[62] of much futile behavior in the modern world. Korzybski's assumption has not gone unchallenged. Max Black[63] provides an extensive critique of Korzybski's views. (I do not feel that Black adequately grasps Korzybski's fundamental points.)

The main weakness which Korzybski cites in modern Indo-European languages is what he calls their "Aristotelian" structure. As we have moved in modern times from Euclidean to non-Euclidean geometry and from Newtonian to Einsteinian physics, so Korzybski proposes that we must move from Aristotelian to non-Aristotelian language structures. Just what does he mean by Aristotelian language structure? Hayakawa identifies four elements which constitute the Aristotelian structure of Indo-European languages. The first of these: the "is" of identity which tends to obscure the difference between words and things. The word takes on "thinghood"; it becomes reified or assumes ontic status. We have already referred to this tendency as the "ontological error." Whereas Piaget underscores the critical importance of the child acquiring the "schema of the permanent object," Hayakawa quotes Trigant Burrow[64] to the effect that with the identification of permanent objects the child loses the spontaneous field of experience. We may guess that Hayakawa finds the Hopi scheme less rigid. We wonder how Piaget would respond to the more monistic Hopi grammar. The legacy of regarding the knowledge of words as the knowledge of things is especially important as we examine rigid ideological stances, e.g., any system such as religious orthodoxy which asserts some "absolute truth." Words—by the very nature of their mediatory and abstracting function—cannot express "absolutes." F. H. Heinemann suggests that the philosopher Heidegger's lapidified jargon exemplifies what he calls "the monomorphic fallacy":

> Words are here taken for "essences." On the basis of the monomorphic fallacy it is falsely assumed that because there is the *one* word "truth," there ought to be *one* essence corresponding to it, called the essence of truth. Since the days of Plato this mistake has been repeated over and over again, but it remains a mistake even in the writings of the most sublime minds.[65]

A second facet of Aristotelian structure is *elementalism*. By this, Korzybski means that traditional Indo-European languages divide the indivisible world into atomistic, self-contained entities, e.g., substance, form, body, mind, cause, effect.[66] The elementalist error, like the "is" of identity, results in the obscuring of the interrelationships and processes of the world. (Recall Whorf's discussion of *substance* and *event.*) The most notable philosophical instance of elementalism is perhaps the mind/body duality. According to Korzybski, this problem is fundamentally semantic in nature. For mind and body are not discrete *things* to which we can attach permanent independent status. Neither the "mind" nor the "body" is static: in fact they constitute one functioning whole. "Mind" and "body" simply describe modes of experience of the self in the world.* It is asserted, for example, that the physical mind/body complex completely replaces itself every seven years on a molecular level.

Just as Whorf has identified the bipolarity of noun and verb in Indo-European, so Korzybski notes how our languages are laced with polarities of value: true/false, black/white, right/wrong, up/down, etc. "He who is not for us is against us."[67] Particularly here we should recognize that such ideological and cultural polarities, when taken as ontological absolutes, have wreaked havoc throughout history. How easily we have lumped persons into categories of good/evil, Christian/non-Christian, moral/immoral, etc. These objectivated categories create artificial dichotomies which often completely obscure 1) the complex nuances of action and reaction and 2) the widely variant relevance of context, both of which must be considered in making value judgments.

The final Aristotelian fallacy identified by Korzybski is the lack in discriminating levels of abstraction. We have alluded to this in our previous discussion.

Language and World View: An Appraisal
Although it may be argued that the claims of Whorf and Korzybski are exaggerated, both men present clear evidence for the point which we wish to establish—that language is *a* critical determinant of world view. Yet certain questions remain unanswered.

For example, Chomsky claims that the structures of grammar are innate. Yet Korzybski and especially Whorf (in his study of Native American languages) suggest that language structures are cultural and historical phenomena reflecting the world view of their native speakers. Can we argue that what is *innate* is not grammar, but perhaps the *morphic* tendency of man to order his environment? Physiology and culture seem to interact at times, as in the case where a Chinese person may continue to write his pictograms after

---

*The unity of the physical mind/body experience does not answer the thorny question of a "transcendent" continuity of experience such as the "soul."

damage to the acoustic region of the brain, whereas an English-speaking person suffering the same damage may not be able to write. Environmental factors may also affect world view (or components of it) in ways reflected by linguistic differences—as for example the role of "snow" in Eskimo and Aztec cultures.

Support for the supposition of the preconditioning of world view by language might seem to be forthcoming through the observation of bilinguals. It seems to be true that a bilingual may follow one behavior pattern when speaking one language, and another when speaking another. However, this split behavior may simply reflect *associations* and *expectations* identified with the cultural location of the language, and not necessarily prove that differences are rooted in the structure of the languages themselves.

Furthermore, if it can be proven that world view is *to a degree* preconditioned by language structure, we must still ask how the structure itself may have emerged—or changed. We must inquire how *actual behavior* of a native tribe, for example, is modified by Westernization. Does the native language serve as a buffer against new world views? As a mere cultural symbol? Or is it possible to adopt behavior radically different from what *seems* to be demanded by grammatical structures, and yet at the same time retain those structures as functioning modes? What about contemporary physics and the apparent inadequacy of key classical terms for new concepts?

We must conclude with several observations. The structure of language does seem to affect our apprehension of the world—including vital co-efficients of life such as space, time, action and identity. Whether we might argue, as Korzybski does, that we have Aristotelian metaphysical presuppositions (resembling what we have called a sessile frame-of-consciousness) rooted in Indo-European grammar, or argue instead that the presuppositions spring from European ideologies and institutions, seems to be of relative, and not ultimate significance. For in either case the classical world views of the West do reflect a sessile frame, and secondly, that frame *is* reflected in the grammar (even if because of the historical evolution of ideology and institutions).

It would seem that the relationship between language and world view is both dialectical and dialogical. It is dialogical through the "conversation" of culture and language; it is dialectical through the evolutionary interplay of both, illustrating that language appears to be culturally-predetermined—and culture, too, seems notably linguistically-predetermined. For the purposes of understanding *how* we shape reality, therefore, we would do well to be aware of the structuring of the world implicit in language as well as the cultural history to which language is linked.

55

FOOTNOTES

[1] Dianne E. Papalia and Sally Wendkos Olds, *A Child's World* (New York: McGraw-Hill Book Company, 1975), pp. 194-96.

[2] Ibid., p. 195.

[3] Ibid.

[4] Ibid.

[5] Ibid., p. 196.

[6] Nigel Calder, *The Mind of Man* (New York: The Viking Press, 1973), p. 194.

[7] Ibid., p. 196.

[8] Ibid.

[9] Ibid., pp. 202-208.

[10] S. I. Hayakawa, *Language in Thought and Action* (New York: Harcourt, Brace and World, 1964), pp. 26-27.

[11] Ibid., p. 27.

[12] *The Encyclopedia of Philosophy*, s.v., "Semantics, History of," by Norman Kretzmann.

[13] Ernst Cassirer, *Language and Myth* (New York: Dover Publications, 1953), pp. 48-49.

[14] S. I. Hayakawa, "What is Meant by Aristotelian Structure of Language?" in *Language, Meaning and Maturity*, ed. S. I. Hayakawa (New York: Harper and Row, 1954), p. 221.

[15] Weller Embler, "Metaphor and Social Belief," in *Language, Meaning and Maturity*, ed. S. I. Hayakawa (New York: Harper and Row, 1954), p. 135.

[16] Harry Munsinger, *Fundamentals of Child Development* (New York: Holt, Rinehart and Winston, 1975), p. 221.

[17] Arthur Koestler, *The Roots of Coincidence* (New York: Vintage Books, 1973); also, a recent work by Alister Hardy, Robert Harvie and Arthur Koestler, *The Challenge of Chance: A Mass Experiment in Telepathy and Its Unexpected Outcome* (New York: Vintage Books, 1975), is quite useful.

[18] Daryl J. Bem, *Beliefs, Attitudes, and Human Affairs* (Belmont, California: Brooks/Cole, 1970), pp. 17, 18.

[19] Ibid.

[20] John 1:14 (RSV).

[21] Benjamin Lee Whorf, "Science and Linguistics," in *Every Man His Way*, ed. Alan Dundes (Englewood Cliffs, New Jersey: Prentice-Hall, 1968), p. 327.

[22] Claude Levi-Strauss, *The Savage Mind* (Chicago: The University of Chicago Press, 1966).

[23] Ibid., p. 6.

[24] Ibid., pp. 43-44.

[25] G. Stahlin, *"muthos,"* in *The Theological Dictionary of the New Testament*, 9 vols., ed. Gerhard Kittel and trans. G. W. Bromiley (Grand Rapids, Michigan: Eerdmans, 1964-75), 4:765.

[26] Ibid., p. 764.

[27] Ibid., p. 765.

[28] Ibid., pp. 766-67.

[29] Ibid., pp. 770-71.

[30] Peter L. Berger and Thomas Luckmann, *The Social Construction of Reality* (New York: Anchor Books, 1967), p. 131.

[31] Ibid., p. 132.

[32] Ibid., p. 41.

[33] Ibid.

[34] Ibid.

[35] Ibid., pp. 41-42.

56

[36] Ibid.

[37] Ibid., p. 44.

[38] Alan Dundes, ed., *Every Man His Way*, p. 319.

[39] Whorf, "Science and Linguistics," pp. 321-22.

[40] Ibid., p. 322.

[41] Werner Heisenberg, *Physics and Philosophy* (New York: Harper Torchbooks, 1962), pp. 173-4.

[42] Ibid., p. 177.

[43] Ibid.

[44] Ibid., p. 179.

[45] Ibid., p. 181.

[46] Benjamin Lee Whorf, "The Relation of Habitual Thought and Behavior to Language," in *Language, Meaning and Maturity*, ed. S. I. Hayakawa (New York: Harper and Row, 1954), p. 232.

[47] Whorf, "Science and Linguistics," p. 326.

[48] Ibid.

[49] Whorf, "The Relation of Habitual Thought and Behavior to Language," p. 232.

[50] Whorf, "Science and Linguistics," p. 327.

[51] Ibid.

[52] Ibid.

[53] Whorf, "The Relation of Habitual Thought . . ," pp. 230-31.

[54] Ibid., p. 234.

[55] Ibid., p. 237.

[56] Ibid., p. 241.

[57] Ibid., p. 250.

[58] Ibid.

[59] Ibid., p. 244.

[60] Whorf, "Science and Linguistics," p. 328.

[61] Hayakawa, "What is Meant by Aristotelian Structure of Language?," p. 218.

[62] Ibid., p. 219.

[63] Max Black, *Language and Philosophy* (Ithaca, N. Y.: Cornell University Press, 1949), pp. 223-57.

[64] Hayakawa, "What is Meant by Aristotelian Structure of Language?," p. 221.

[65] F. H. Heinemann, *Existentialism and the Modern Predicament* (New York: Harper Torchbooks, 1963), p. 105.

[66] Hayakawa, "What is Meant by Aristotelian Structure of Language?," p. 222.

[67] Ibid.

SECTION II

AN HISTORICAL TYPOLOGY OF

CULTURE AND COSMOLOGY IN THE WEST

CHAPTER III

MUTHOS AND LOGOS: A COMPARISON OF MYTHOPOEISM AND THE PRESOCRATICS

WE HAVE briefly defined mythopoeism (deriving from the Greek words *muthos,* "myth," and *poieein,* "to make") as a term applied to the cognitive disposition of ancient man. The most important statement of mythopoeic structures is H. and H. A. Frankforts' essay "Myth and Reality,"[1] to which we are chiefly indebted. The relationship between mythopoeic thought and the emergent "rational" thought of the West after the Presocratics has been widely debated. Lucien Levy-Bruhl,[2] Claude Levi-Strauss[3] and their anthropological heirs have challenged the smug assumption of the superiority of "scientific" to "primitive" thought. W. F. Albright[4] has argued that ancient man must not be saddled with the pejorative term "illogical," but in fact should be given credit for a highly creative "empirico-logical" capacity which, within the framework of a prescientific culture, exhibits its own sophisticated rationality and consistency. In the present chapter we will discuss similarities and differences between mythopoeism and the Greek Presocratics as a first step in outlining typological structures which have become constitutional elements of world views in the West.

MYTHOPOEISM AND THE PRESOCRATICS: CONTRAST

The first point of contrast between mythopoeism and the Presocratics concerns the distinctive purposes of their speculations. Cosmology for ancient man is his legitimating framework, not only for his culture but for himself. The sacred order of the cosmos establishes the sacred order of society, home and relationship. Archaic cosmologies are *religious,* since "religion is the human enterprise by which a sacred cosmos is established."[5] In fact we might argue that every *effective* or *evocative* cosmology has a religious flavor—as an expression of man's own sense of the sacredness of life and as a projection of that sacredness upon the world order. Thales of Miletus, the first of the Presocratics (whose writings we possess in fragmentary form), seems to have shared the mythopoeic sacralization of the cosmos when he reportedly said, "all things are full of gods." The Presocratics who followed Thales (with the notable exception of the Pythagoreans) "demythologized" (or "remythologized") the cosmos in naturalistic terms. Hippolytus, an early Christian bishop, reported of Democritus: "This man ridiculed everything— as if all human concerns were absurd!"[6] Hippolytus' own claim about the famed Atomist seems absurd to the unbiased investigator. However, the opinion expressed by the good bishop must have been shared by many of Democritus' fifth century B.C.E. contemporaries, for it is representative of that sense of horror which the scientific spirit often evokes in those to whom a sacred cosmos is the legitimating framework of their identity.

If we pursue the question of cosmic origin we find a comparable situation. In mythopoeism *cosmogony* is usually an archetype of the social order—and thus a pattern for the *nomoi* of the social world. For the Presocratics the quest for the *arche* ("beginning") seems to be motivated largely by "intellectual curiosity" (which cannot be divorced from man's quest for identity). Thales, who reportedly visited Egypt in his quest for wisdom, seems to have been influenced by the Egyptian world picture: the earth is envisaged as floating in the waters, the heavens supported by pillars. The Egyptian depiction of the cosmos illustrates the cultural archetypes often projected into a world picture.[7] The earth is conceived as a flat platter with a corrugated rim. The flat segment of the platter represented Egypt proper, the corrugated borders the foreign lands. The platter floated in water (which constituted both the underworld and the encircling river—the Greek *Okeanos.)* Above and below the earth were located symmetrical "pans" of heaven, thus constituting a three-tiered world. Four pillars supported the weight of heaven (or, alternatively, Shu, their air god did the honors.) The stars were variously depicted as hanging from the pan of heaven or spangling the belly of a cosmic cow. The sun was reborn in the East every morning and died in the West every evening, moving across the heavens in a boat, or rolling, like the pellet pushed by the common dung beetle. The shape and arrangement of the cosmos is mirrored by the shape and arrangement of society and the known world of experience: cow's bellies and dung beetles. Wilson suggests[8] that the elements of the universe were *consubstantial*—that is, there is a primal unity in the cosmos as a whole which means that the realm of human experience and behavior is a reliable frame of reference for non-human phenomena, such as the gods, cosmogony, etc. Thus the Egyptian cosmos is a *projection* of Egyptian social and cultural experience.[9] The world picture, for example, in some ways resembles an Egyptian temple. The "principle of free substitution, interchange, or representation"[10] between the visible and the invisible, the known and the unknown, means that food provided in the tomb of the dead is effective for nourishment in the life beyond; or pictures depicted on the tomb wall provide actual experience for the departed. The dwelling of the gods and their authority and activities resemble the dwelling of man and structures of authority and experience in Egyptian civilization. For example, the king of Egypt was one of the gods and the representative of the gods. His activities were considered divine in the appropriate setting. One text reports:

> Year 30, third month of the first season, day 9: the god entered his horizon.
> The King of Upper and Lower Egypt, Sehetepibre, went up to heaven and

was united with the Sun disc, so that the divine body was merged with him who made him.[11]

The gist of this mythopoeic scheme is an integral cosmos into which every facet of Egyptian life, belief and ritual would fit. On the other hand, for Thales, this world picture does not function as a *social* legitimation. Thales, perhaps dissatisfied with the cosmological myths familiar to us in Hesiod and Homer, went to Egypt—noted for its wisdom in antiquity—in quest for truth. What he brought back was distinctly Egyptian: both the world picture and his explanation that all things originated from *water* (for Egyptians the Nile was the source of all life, and the divine source of their livelihood and culture). Whether Thales was motivated by "pure" intellectual curiosity or not, there seems to be no suggestion that he was seeking out social legitimations.

In any case, Thales' pupil Anaximander went a step beyond his mentor. Thales' act of "demythologization" cast the Egyptian cosmology adrift from its social moorings. But Anaximander asks, how can all things derive from one element, water? Anaximander's desire to abstract the matter further from accepted opinion demanded a more universal explanation—and this he finds in the *apeiron,* the "Boundless" or "Infinite."[12] The Boundless is the source or reservoir of all living things: that out of which they arise and to which they return. The elements were not arranged by the gods, but rather separated out by a kind of vortex rotary motion.

> Earth, which is heaviest, is situated in the middle; water, which is next heaviest, encircles it as Ocean; beyond lies air; outermost of all is the fiery circuit of heavens.[13]

Anaximander has provided a rational, speculative explanation of the way things are. With Anaximander the world picture is abstracted and quantified one step further (although its speculative quality remains). We will not describe other explanations of the *arche* by the Presocratics, since their significance lies not in a departure from the naturalistic *intent* of Anaximander, but in the theoretical *content*. Mythopoeic models of cosmic order appear to be motivated by designs similar to institutional ideologies— both religious and social—throughout history. The Presocratics are forerunners of more scientific and philosophical explanations.

A second point of contrast between the cosmologies of mythopoeism and the Presocratics can be subsumed under the rubric *concreteness* vs. *abstraction.* *Space* for mythopoeism is defined qualitatively and according to the norms of social significance: sacred and profane places and grounds, home territory versus dangerous or alien lands "out there," etc. The "map" of mythopoeism is psycho-social, drawn not with the tools of the draftsman but with the contours of emotions and values—with the *ethos* of the social unit. For Anaximander however, who is credited with the first map,[14] a map is supposed to depict, objectively and quantitatively, how and where things are.

In a similar vein, for Anaximander's contemporary Anaximenes, the earth does not rest in water, but is flat, riding upon the air. The sun, moon and heavenly bodies—of fiery composition—ride in the air around the earth.[15] A further example of the abstraction and quantification of space is Zeno's paradoxes. Here the question of space has assumed an even more purely speculative function.

A similar differentiation may be established with regard to time, which is also qualitative in mythopoeic thought. There is no conception of an abstracted time—a series of passing moments unrelated to particular personal, social and cosmic experience. Significant moments in the passage of the year are archetypal cosmological expressions:

> Both in Egypt and in Babylonia the New Year, for instance, was an occasion of elaborate celebrations in which the battles of the gods were mimed or in which mock battles were fought.[16]

Frankfort continues:

> The deliberate coordination of cosmic and social events shows most clearly that time to early man did not mean a neutral and abstract frame of reference, but rather a succession of recurring phases, each charged with a peculiar value and significance.[17]

For most of the Presocratics, time *per se* is not discussed. The questions of nature involve time indirectly, i.e., in the "coming-to-be," and "process" and "decay" of things. But here time is conceived as the inevitable passage of events. In any case its psycho-social qualitative significance is missing. Heraclitus is credited with this typically enigmatic statement:

> Time is a child moving counters in a game; the royal power is the child's.[18]

Here it appears that Heraclitus speaks of the inevitable flux of events and change—the world as in a constant state of becoming. Time is conceived as defining the course of nature. Antiphon the Sophist remarked:

> Time is both a conception (*noema*) and a measure (*metron*), not a substance (*hypostasis*).[19]

In this terse statement Antiphon offers a sophisticated and quantified view of time. Time itself does not exist, but is a term which we use to measure certain relationships. Time has no substantial being. Isaac Newton would have done well to heed this saying of Antiphon. In his attempt to establish the priority of static Being in contradistinction to Heraclitus, Parmenides denied the existence of time.

For the Presocratics, time—when it does appear—is a function or measure of nature—an abstraction which is not conceived in terms of its psychological or social significance. The peculiar "scientific" *historical* sense of time is missing from both mythopoeism and Presocratic thought.

A third area of contrasts emerges as we consider the logical relationship between self and world, as depicted variously by mythopoeism and Presocratic thought. The differentiation between subject and object is a cherished cornerstone of scientific and "logical" thought. Piaget asserts that the acquisition of the schema of the permanent object (and even earlier, the child's learning to distinguish between body and world) is considered essential to the normally functioning intelligence in the process of socialization. Yet for early man, the isolation of the thinking mind from the context in which, out of which, and towards which it operates, is not a tacit assumption. On the contrary, mythopoeism (we assume) was far more naive, far more realistic, and far less arrogant about man's capacity to extricate himself from his world and treat it as "object."

> The fundamental difference between the attitudes of modern and ancient man as regards the surrounding world is this: for modern, scientific man the phenomenal world is primarily an 'It'; for ancient—and also for primitive—man it is a 'Thou.'[20]

The organic identity of self and cosmos generates a vital and integral world view for ancient man:

> The world appears to primitive man neither inanimate nor empty but redundant with life; and life has individuality, in man and beast and plant, and in every phenomenon which confronts man—the thunderclap, the sudden shadow, the eerie and unknown clearing in the wood, the stone which suddenly hurts him when he stumbles while on a hunting trip.[21]

In mythopoeic thought the great cosmic acts are personalized (as the myths of a primal male or female divinity, or the origin of the world through sexual generation). With the emergence of Presocratic thought the scientific element eclipses this personalizing tendency. While the Egyptians could personify "almost anything," including "the head, the belly, the tongue, perception, taste, truth, a tree, a mountain, the sea, a city, darkness, and death,"[22] and treat the world as "Thou," Aristotle reports that

> Anaximenes says that the earth, through being soaked and dried out, cracks and is shaken by the impact of falling peaks that have broken loose. This is why earthquakes occur during droughts and heavy rains; for during a drought the earth is dry and (as just explained) cracks. Then, when rains make it excessively wet, it falls apart.[23]

Thus for Anaximenes the disposition of earthquakes is not due to a wrathful god or to a personified earth element angered at man's impiety, but simply to objectivated natural causes. The Atomists were able to objectify their own perceptions, as this saying remarkably demonstrates:

> Sweet exists by convention, bitter by convention, color by convention; but in reality atoms and the void alone exist.[24]

The same kind of opposing tendencies of mythopoeism and Presocratic thought appear in the relationship between cause and effect. Mythopoeism evinces no interest in an impersonal principle or law which will explain natural phenomena. Just as the world appears as vitally living Subject, so the cause of events is not abstracted but personalized. We have noted that the great cosmic acts are given personal divine causation. So too, when a river refuses to rise it is the recalcitrant *will* of the river that is to blame.[25] Furthermore, a man does not just *happen* to die—he or some other person or god *wills* his death. Again, the personal cause and effect sequence explains the legitimation of social customs by cosmology: we perform this ritual *because* it reduplicates the act of the gods at the creation.

On the other hand, several of the Presocratics made astute observations regarding the causes of natural phenomena. Xenophanes of Colophon (sixth century B.C.E.) observed that

> The sea is the source of water and the source of wind. For there would be no winds to burst forth from the clouds were it not for the great sea, nor rivers nor showers of rain from heaven, but the great Pontus is the father of clouds, winds and rivers.[26]

Perhaps even more remarkable are Xenophanes' observations regarding fossils (as reported by Hippolytus):

> Xenophanes believes that a mixing of the earth with the sea is taking place, and that in time it will be dissolved by the moisture. He says that he has proof of this, namely, that shells are found inland and in the mountains. And he says that in Syracuse the impression of a laurel leaf has been found deep in the rock, and in Malta flattened forms of all sorts of marine animals. He says that these were formed long ago when everything was covered with mud, and that these impressions were dried in the mud.[27]

Other writers offer comparable explanations of natural causation. Theophrastus, an Atomist, theorized regarding dizziness:

> The head is by nature moist. When air gets into it and penetrates the moisture, forcing its way toward the blood vessels, it thrusts the moisture around in a circle . . . The motion being like that of a vortex, the moisture does not hold together uniformly but one part lags behind while the other goes ahead. That part which is forming a sediment settles, because it offers resistance, while that which is settling is dragged along by that in which it is sinking, because it is not in equilibrium with it. The result is dizziness and frequent falling down.[28]

For the Atomists, the causation of all natural events is traceable to the given collocation of atoms relevant to the particular effect—a remarkably modern judgment.

For mythopoeism, the personal and organic view of causation bears a close resemblance to C. G. Jung's theory of synchronicity, which proposes an acausal, but meaningful coincidence of events. The best illustration of Jung's principle is astrology, which posits a connection between the movements of the stars and planets and the occurrence of events on earth (including their quality and meaning). Contrary to popular misconception, the stars do not *cause* a war in the sense of some physical or even esoteric force acting upon the world. Rather, the configuration of stars and planets in the heavens (which themselves bear personal "character traits") matches, in a world organically coordinated, some situation in the social or personal sphere. There is a simultaneity of meaning, of action and reaction running through the entire cosmos, and testifying to its inherent unity and organic interdependence. But for the Presocratics, such an explanation would be generally untenable.

The end result of rational analysis carried to the extreme, surfaces in the world view of the Sophists. Robinson comments:

> It is the assumption that: Nature is devoid of mind and purpose, and that the world order is the product not of design, but of chance, i.e., of atoms in motion . . . so men are driven by the laws of nature, subject only to those appetites which drive other animals, restrained only by those fears which restrain them . . .[29]

If mythopoeism juggles key conceptual givens of the "logical" mind such as the subject/object schema and causality, it is not surprising that our neatly defined distinction between reality and appearance does not hold. Dreams and hallucinations, which we tend to jettison as meaningful but disorderly musings of the unconscious, are regarded by mythopoeism as integral elements in the total experience of reality. Mythical beasts take their place alongside natural species in primitive accounts. Moreover, the realm of the living and the realm of the dead—though separated—are equally real. For the dead appear in dreams and visions; thus they are part of human *experience* (as Albright's term for ancient conceptualization, "empiricological," suggests).

As we turn to the Presocratics, we find that their entire philosophical enterprise seems to be motivated by a desire to extricate "appearance" *from* "reality"; yet the experience of all men at the outset appears to be bounded by the same physiological determinants. The Ionic quest for the *arche* constitutes a Promethean attempt to locate the cosmos according to rational and natural explanation, and to liberate it from the entangling web of myth. The role of *observation* and *reflection* is established, yet the role of *experiment* is largely untapped. Speculation searches for a rationally-consistent theorem. For Heraclitus, the *logos* is an orderly animating principle pervading all reality. By becoming aware of the *logos,* men should be freed from their "sleep":

> Though the *logos* is as I have said, men always fail to comprehend it . . . For though all things come into being according to *logos,* they seem like men *without experience,* though in fact they do have experience . . . But other men are as unaware of what they do when awake as they are when they are asleep.[30]
>
> Eyes and ears are bad witnesses to men if they have souls that do not understand their language.[31]

Yet the illusions of the senses could lead the Presocratics to opposite conclusions regarding what is reality and what is appearance. For Heraclitus, the whole cosmos is in constant flux. The *appearance* of identity is misleading:

> Upon those who step into the same rivers flow other and yet other waters.[32]

Parmenides, distrusting the senses altogether, denied the ultimate existence of change (which thus becomes mere appearance). Parmenides asserts:

> But motionless in the limits of mighty bonds, it [the world order] is without beginning or end, since coming into being and passing away have been

> driven far off, cast out by true belief. Remaining the same, and in the same place, it lies in itself, and so abides firmly where it is . . .[33]

Though driven to opposite conclusions, both Heraclitus and Parmenides sought to distinguish clearly between reality and appearance.

A final point of comparison is the function of symbology in mythopoeic thought and the Presocratics. In mythopoeism a symbol coalesces with the thing signified. Before battle ancient kings might inscribe the names of rival powers on a clay pot which would be ritually smashed. The destruction of the symbol implied some real destruction of the enemy, and thus (hopefully) would secure the victory. The same conceptual understanding is at work in voodoo. In voodoo a name or a lock of hair, used in invoking a curse, is representative of the person (and in fact is as effective as the actual presence of the person, embodying part of his/her *essence*). A voodoo doll functions in a similar way, in that the doll actually partakes of the identity of the intended victim. The identification of the symbol with that which is symbolized reflects the same sense of organic interdependence and simultaneity as the synchronistic interpretation of causality. Therein the cosmos constitutes a *living* whole; there is no split between the "organic" and the "inorganic."

As we examine the fragments of the Presocratics, significantly the contrast in symbology with mythopoeism is not always as acute. Xenophanes perhaps provides us with the most remarkable prefiguration of modernity in these observations:

> Mortals believe that the gods are begotten, and that they wear clothing like our own, and have a voice and a body.
>
> The Ethiopians make their gods snub-nosed and black; the Thracians make theirs gray-eyed and red-haired.
>
> And if oxen and horses and lions had hands, and could draw with their hands and do what men can do, horses would draw the gods in the shape of horses, and oxen in the shape of oxen, each giving the gods bodies similar to their own.[34]

Xenophanes is identifying the cultural location and projection of the gods (and the relativity of symbology). Beyond these many cultural gods Xenophanes believes there is one god which is not like man in body or mind. But Xenophanes proceeds a step beyond the other Presocratics, recognizing the relativity of *all* human knowledge and thus the mediating role of *all* symbology and language (including his own!):

> No man knows the truth, nor will there be a man who has knowledge about the gods and what I say about everything. For even if he were to hit by chance upon the whole truth, he himself would not be aware of having done so, but each forms his own opinion.
>
> Let these things, then, be taken as *like* the truth . . .[35]

We remarked that the contrast in symbology with mythopoeism is not always as acute, but Xenophanes is the notable exception. The other Presocratics tend to identify their theoretical symbology *with* reality. Perhaps we should challenge Korzybski's labeling the "ontological error" *Aristotelian,* and likewise Heinemann's statement "from the days of *Plato* on." For Anaximander's source of all things, the *Infinite*, and Heraclitus' animating principle, the *logos*, both seem to be treated as substantial realities. In addition, *Parmenides* could be given the title, "the father of the ontological error," since it is he who identifies *thought* and *being*:

> For thought and being are the same. Thinking and the thought that is are the same; for you will not find thought apart from what is, in relation to which it is uttered.[36]

Robinson argues that Parmenides intends to say that thought and being are inseparable, not identical.[37] Nevertheless, in the long history of rationalism in the West *logos* has all too often been granted real ontological status. Yet since man *does* construct his world from his beliefs, *thought* and *being* do converge (not in an absolute sense, but in relative worlds which different peoples and different eras label "reality," and which by behavioral indices quite effectively constitute what is real). Xenophanes seems to have come close to espousing this perspective.

We initially distinguished the mythopoeic and Presocratic mentalities with the labels of *muthos* and *logos*—myth and reason. Before exploring points of commonality between mythopoeism and the Presocratics we need to reiterate how myth and reason relate to each other.

MYTH AND REASON

For Heraclitus *logos* (not quite "reason," since it is not only a "faculty" but also an ontological principle) is a means of abstracting from the concrete and explaining the disparity of our senses (thus we cannot step into the same river twice). This is what reason *does*, but what is reason? Reason is an ordering faculty, a mental propensity for correlating the phenomena of existence in a meaningful pattern. How then does reason differ from myth?

Reason depersonalizes, and is redundant and circular. Myth personifies and creates. Reason is redundant because it refers to *what is* in terms of pre-established categories which cannot be comprehended apart from *what is*. Myth, in its own way, is redundant. Myth creates divinities and stories out of the collective experience of mankind and the particular perception and imagination of individuals.

The patterns of myths are often similar, and to this extent there may be a structural similarity between myth and rational formulations. Myth is not *anti*-rational, but employs the rational faculties imaginatively and creatively, intuitively and organically. As it reaches more complex degrees of abstraction, as in the case of science, reason strives to make experience consistent and replicable, atttributes which myth does not always exhibit. Myths may be replicated in certain structures, perhaps even in psychic and emotive patterns of human *being* (as for example, Jung's theories of archetypes and the collective unconscious). However, with respect to particulars, there is no predictable pattern to which the details, or twists and turns, of myth must conform. Disparities such as number, sequence and order (which seem irrelevant to the larger purpose), occur in variations of the same myth. Myths are only in part quantifiable.

Reason, in its more abstract and scientific forms, is consistently quantifiable. For example, if independent investigators are working with the same data, their observations and conclusions are likely to manifest strong similarity or identity (as simultaneous "discoveries" by independent researchers illustrate).

Reason and myth also differ in focus and content; myth is usually associated with emotional, aesthetic, social, or spiritual concerns. However, both processes are contingent upon the thinking self in its individual and social biography and context. Creations of reified patterns—whether rational, pragmatic, mythical, or hybrid—suggest that man, consciously or unconsciously, with varying emotional content and intent, constructs his own world of meaning in all times and in all places. Behind such patterns we may discover certain habits of thought and life which provide us with clues to the meaning of existence and the bounds of reality in a particular era or culture.

POINTS OF CONVERGENCE BETWEEN MYTHOPOEISM AND PRESOCRATIC THOUGHT

As poignant as divergent world apprehensions between mythopoeism and the Presocratics, are convergent perspectives. In approaching the differences we could cite fairly specific categories such as reason/myth, subject/object, cause/effect, reality/appearance, etc. In the quest for order reality is filtered through such relational polarities. But as we examine the cognitive task of each mode of thought, distinct similarities emerge. The act of conceptualization itself—drawn into the service of constructing meaningful models of reality—bears a certain uniform character regardless of the mode of thought employed.

The most obvious and most basic similarity is the task of "world building." Both mythopoeism and the Presocratics enlist *nomic* processes in cognitive construction. Berger asserts that "every human society is an enterprise of world-building."[38] In this light both "reason" and "myth" function in similar ways. Both seek to bring order out of chaos and to discover satisfactory niches for the disparate data of our experience. The rational explanation of an earthquake may be that the earth is either too soggy or too dry, and falls apart (Anaximenes); a seismologist may cite faults in the earth's crust subject to subterranean tremors. But the mythical explanation still incorporates a kind of cause/effect rationality within its own framework. The earth god, angry because proper sacrifices have not been offered, erupts in a display of vengeful behavior. In each case a significant datum of experience—an earthquake—is fit into an orderly niche within a larger framework of meaning. The framework itself is predetermined by history, tradition, cultural location, and individual eccentricities.

Moreover, man is a world-builder because of an inherent *creative* faculty. For mythopoeism, *survival* was by no means the sole motive of myth-making. Myths serve not only as cohesive social bonds or cohesive frames of reference, by which self, social relationships, institutions, and world are integrally ordered; they also tease the imagination and the aesthetic faculties. Storytelling is not merely a mechanical routine for recounting important truisms, but a highly developed art form designed to excite the imagination, please the senses, and cultivate a sense of balance or beauty. Thus the discovery of oral traditions behind Homer and many of the biblical narratives, has shown us mnemonic devices and structural patterns of great complexity and genius. As we have seen, Levi-Strauss demonstrates that the taxonomic systems of many primitive peoples, which rival modern science in their sophistication and orderliness, must be attributed to intellectual curiosity and a scientific spirit. We should also note that the Presocratics are not without aesthetic sensitivity in *their* creative endeavors. The Presocratic writings are usually cited for their rational content and scientific predilections. But the Presocratics were artists at times as well. Consider these sayings of Heraclitus:

> The god is day, night, winter, summer, war, peace, satiety, hunger, and undergoes change as fire, when it is mingled with spices, is named according to the aroma of each.[39]
>
> Nature loves to hide.
>
> The lord whose oracle is at Delphi neither speaks out nor conceals, but gives a sign.
>
> The Sibyl with raving mouth, uttering things mirthless, unadorned, and unperfumed, reaches down a thousand years with her voice because of the god.[40]

Or Empedocles:

> At one time all the limbs that are the body's lot come together into one through Love, in the prime of flourishing life; at another, sundered by cruel strifes, each wanders apart by the breakers of life's sea. So it is with plants and water-dwelling fish, the beasts that lie up in the hills and winged sea birds.
>
> I will return to the path of song which I followed before, driving my chariot from one argument to another. When Strife had reached the lowest depth of the vortex, and Love was in the midst of the eddy, then all things came together in it to be one—not all at once, but they came willingly from this side and that. And as they came together Strife began to move out to the furthest limit.[41]

So the Presocratics can speak poetically—exhibiting a fascinating breadth of creativity and curiosity, covering the gamut in their speculations—sometimes brilliant, sometimes bizarre—speaking at once of the sublime and the mundane.

In addition, mythopoeism and the Presocratics cross paths in another way, venturing beyond the limits so often set for them. Mythopoeism is not void of science, nor the Presocratics of culture. Levi-Strauss speaks of what he terms the "Neolithic Paradox":

> It was in neolithic times that man's mastery of the great arts of civilization—of pottery, weaving, agriculture, and the domestication of animals—became firmly established. No one would any longer think of attributing these enormous advances to the fortuitous accumulation of a series of chance discoveries or believe them to have been revealed by the passive perception of certain natural phenomena. Each of these techniques assumes centuries of active and methodical observations, of bold hypotheses tested by means of endlessly repeated experiments . . . there is no doubt that all of these achievements required a genuinely scientific attitude, sustained and watchful interest and a desire for knowledge for its own sake . . .[42]

Just as great scientific advance accompanied an era when mythopoeism dominated, so too we cannot accept the writings of the Presocratics at all times as "pure" speculation (since all speculation uses cultural tools). A helpful example of the cultural predisposition of the Presocratics is Anaximander's "Law of Compensation."

For Anaximander the world exhibits an array of opposites which are constituents of reality: hot and cold, moist and dry, night and day, life and death, etc. The balance of the cosmos depends upon the harmonious proportion of these constituent facets. The one sentence remaining from a book of Anaximander's asserts that the opposites must "make reparation to one another for their injustice according to the ordinance of time."[43] The idea of balance or harmony of the world order seems to be deeply rooted in the Greek mind. In the body, "health lies in the maintenance of a balance of opposites."[44] When moist/dry or hot/cold are out of proportion *dis*-ease sets in. Robinson includes a passage from Herodotus to illustrate the Law of Compensation in Greek culture. It is the story of Polycrates, tyrant of Samos. About 540 B.C. Polycrates seized the throne, and phenomenal military successes and abundant good fortune followed him at every turn. A friend of Polycrates, Amasis, king of Egypt, wrote to warn Polycrates because of the *imbalance* of his successes. Following the advice of Amasis—to give up his most precious possession—Polycrates embarked on a voyage and cast his priceless emerald ring into the sea. Later, a fisherman brought Polycrates the gift of a handsome fish, and of course, the ring was found inside the fish. Soon afterward, Polycrates was brutally murdered on a diplomatic mission. The story illustrates two assumptions of Greek culture: the Law of Compensation must be satisfied, and one cannot change his fate. The same laws are foundational to Greek tragedy; success and pride *(hubris)* lead to *hamartia* ("overstepping the bounds"), and the balance must be restored by the tragic blow. Sophocles remarks in *Antigone:*

> Above all, happiness depends on wisdom. It is never right to sin against the gods. Great blows repay great words of boasting men, and teach us wisdom in old age.[45]

Returning from culture to cosmology, Anaximander envisioned the cosmos itself as exhibiting the Law of Compensation in its periodical death and rebirth out of the Boundless.

A final instance of the wedding of culture and cosmology is Anaximenes' theory of the microcosm and the macrocosm. Anaximenes asserts that "the living creature is a world-order in miniature."[46] This statement is not too far removed from the mythopoeic understanding of symbology and the organic and personal interdependence of the world order. As we have noted, for mythopoeism the social order is a reduplication of the cosmic order, and events of the sacred calendar are reduplications of events enacted by the gods in the cosmogony. In Anaximenes, we have a first step in the process of demythologization. Yet the microcosm/macrocosm perspective is foundational to the very Greek society in which the *polis* is to reduplicate the divine order of things. Thus in Anaximander and Anaximenes we have not only elementary physics, but the expression of vital cultural principles. Mythopoeic and Presocratic thought, both anthropomorphic endeavors, have much in common. And indeed, is not the *Principia* of Sir Isaac Newton replete with absolutes and divine legitimation? Perhaps seldom (if ever, since the tools of science are also cultural tools) have scientists really disengaged themselves from culture.[47]

A final example of the merging of mythopoeic and rational thought is the Pythagoreans. Although from the sources it is difficult to tell what should be attributed to Pythagoras, and what to his disciples, it is clear that the Pythagoreans taught that the world order consists of numbers. Here we encounter a strange hybrid of *logos* and *muthos*. On the one hand the mathematical work done by the Pythagoreans represents a notable quantitative advance for early science. Yet on the other, the Pythagoreans assigned ontological status *to* numbers and incorporated them into the dogma of a mystical religious brotherhood. Pythagoras, it is claimed, first described the world order as *cosmos,*[48] expressing a conception that was "part of the Ionian tradition from the first."[49] As part of Greek culture in general, *cosmos* unites world order, aesthetic beauty, ethical balance, and harmony. Thus for Pythagoras, *cosmology* was at once a science, a religion, and a political and ethical philosophy. Perhaps this unity accounts for the profound and lasting imprint of Pythagoreanism upon Western civilization. Pythagoras' assertion that the heavenly bodies revolve in exact mathematical ratios equivalent to musical consonances left its mark on Western cosmology for well over two thousand years. Before Plato, Pythagoras introduced a fatal ontological dualism which has colored the entire course of Western thought. Robinson cites the following statement of Philolaus (which he asserts is authentic and "no doubt" a reflection of Pythagoras' own sentiment):

> For the sake of punishment the soul is yoked to the body and buried in it as in a tomb.[50]

Robinson feels that this dualism derives from the Ionian physics of Anaximenes, based upon the compression and dilation of air. The heavenly bodies are more rarefied, light and fiery. The compressed states of air produce successively water, earth, and stone. With the Pythagoreans this physics bears a value judgment: the heavenly bodies are "pure" and "immortal." The earthly atmosphere is "impure" and subject to time and decay. Robinson concludes:

> The difference between the two realms amounts to a radical breach in the natural order. For the history of Western thought it was fateful; for in the form which it was to receive at the hands of Aristotle it prevented the development of a rational system of celestial mechanics down to the time of Galileo . . .[51]

Robinson fails to note how (perhaps even more) fateful this dualism has been in the history of Western ethics and religion—especially in neo-Platonic and Christian theologies. In its more extreme forms (e.g., the Orphic *soma=sema*, "body"="tomb") this dualism is tantamount to a curse upon the body, all physical pleasures, and the earth itself.

With the Pythagoreans we see that clear-cut distinctions between mythopoeism and the Presocratics are only broad generalizations or representative types. Though at times *logos* has seemed clearly dominant and at others *muthos* has held the field, as often as not from the days of the Presocratics the two have been strange and subtle bedfellows. Man cannot extricate himself from the cultural world which has been long established, and into which he is born. Language is a cultural vehicle and our chief conceptual tool employed both by reason and myth in anthropomorphic processes of world-building. Even mathematics (as the Pythagoreans illustrate in a somewhat extreme fashion) cannot be disengaged from culture.

FOOTNOTES

[1] H. and H. A. Frankfort, "Myth and Reality," in *Before Philosophy*. H. and H. A. Frankfort, John A. Wilson, and Thorkild Jacobsen (Baltimore: Penguin Books, 1972), pp. 11-36.

[2] Lucien Levy-Bruhl, *Primitive Mentality* (Boston: Beacon Press, 1966).

[3] Claude Levi-Strauss, *The Savage Mind* (Chicago: The University of Chicago Press, 1973).

[4] W. F. Albright, *From the Stone Age to Christianity* (Garden City, N. Y.: Doubleday Anchor Books, 1957).

[5] Peter L. Berger, *The Sacred Canopy* (Garden City, N. Y.: Doubleday Anchor Books, 1969), p. 25.

[6] John Mansley Robinson, *An Introduction to Early Greek Philosophy* (Boston: Houghton Mifflin Company, 1968), p. 214.

[7] John A. Wilson, "Egypt: The Nature of the Universe," in *Before Philosophy,* pp. 39-70.

[8] John A. Wilson, "The Function of the State," in *Before Philosophy*, p. 72. (Rudolf Anthes, in his article "Mythology in Ancient Egypt," in S. N. Kramer's *Mythologies of the Ancient World* (New York: Anchor Doubleday, 1961), pp. 15-90, underscores the unique and dynamic interchange (with particular intent of legitimating the divine kingship), between Egyptian mythology and political history (pp. 36 ff., 46 ff., 63 ff.). Anthes demonstrates the remarkable sophistication of the Egyptian intellect from the earliest times (p. 23 ff.), and records his skepticism regarding the term "mythopoeism" (p. 28), citing the Egyptians' diverse, flexible and ostensibly self-conscious use of symbols in their culture, as in the modern West. Although Anthes is quite right in noting that "This was not the period of primitive man," (p. 28), "common sense"—in itself a cultural variant—cannot be enlisted as witness to a uniform apprehension (between Egyptian and modern Western man) of the role and function of symbols. This is to suggest that the use of the term *mythopoeism*—though doubtlessly of as many variant forms as ancient cultures—by no means implies a pejorative value judgment.

[9] Wilson, "The Function of the State," p. 72.

[10] Ibid, p. 82.

[11] Ibid.

[12] Robinson, pp. 23-25.

[13] Ibid., p. 27.

[14] Ibid., p. 32.

[15] Ibid., p. 44.

[16] H. and H. A. Frankfort, "Myth and Reality," p. 34.

[17] Ibid., p. 35.

[18] Philip Wheelwright, ed., *The Presocratics* (New York: The Odyssey Press, 1966), p. 71.

[19] Ibid., p. 260.

[20] H. and H. A. Frankfort, "Myth and Reality," p. 12.

[21] Ibid., p. 14.

[22] Wilson, "Egypt: The Nature of the Universe," p. 49.

[23] Robinson, p. 46.

[24] Ibid., p. 202.

[25] H. and H. A. Frankfort, "Myth and Reality, p. 24.

[26] Robinson, p. 50.

[27] Ibid., p. 51.

[28] Ibid., p. 210.

[29] Ibid., p. 289.

[30] Ibid., p. 94.

[31] Ibid., p. 96.

[32] Ibid., p. 91.

[33] Ibid., p. 115.

74

[34] Ibid., p. 52.

[35] Ibid., p. 56.

[36] Ibid., p. 110.

[37] Ibid.

[38] Berger, *The Sacred Canopy*, p. 3.

[39] Robinson, p. 94.

[40] Ibid., p. 96.

[41] Ibid., p. 160.

[42] Levi-Strauss, *The Savage Mind*, pp. 13-14.

[43] Robinson, p. 34.

[44] Ibid., p. 35.

[45] Ibid., p. 38.

[46] Ibid., p. 48.

[47] David Bakan in *The Duality of Human Existence* (Boston: Beacon Press, 1966), pp. 23-29, sees Newton's scheme as "a fulfillment of Calvinistic theology," (p. 24), and the world machine as Newton's desacralized version of Calvin's perfectly predestined and lawful order. Newton's distant God seems to reflect the strong Calvinistic stance on divine sovereignty and transcendence.

[48] Robinson, p. 77.

[49] Ibid.

[50] Ibid., p. 58.

[51] Ibid., p. 59.

CHAPTER FOUR

THE ROOTS OF WESTERN CULTURE:
THE JUDEO-CHRISTIAN AND CLASSICAL WORLD VIEWS.

THE TWO mainstreams leading into the complex sea of Western Civilization are the Greco-Roman and Judeo-Christian traditions. Again through establishing a comparative typology, we shall explore similarities and differences in the conceptual legacies frtm Greece and Israel. We shall also approach the intermingling of these two traditions in the Christian synthesis.

POINTS OF CONTRAST

Reason and Revelation

By analogy, the two strands of Western Civilization might be described physiologically, the Greek rational strand comprising the left hemisphere of Western consciousness, and the Judeo-Christian revelational strand, the right hemisphere. However, the picture is far too complex for such an historical phrenology. For example, the Presocratics played a formative role in the speculative-rational disposition of the West; however, we must also remember the cognitive contributions of Babylonia, Egypt and Persia. It is reported that Thales journeyed to Egypt, and the intellectual traffic in the classical Mesopotamian/Mediterranean world is a fruitful topic which has yet to be fully exploited. Certainly the interfusion of cultures by the Hellenistic Era is well known. However, there are two vital shifts from mythopoeism, one each in the earlier traditions of the Greek and Hebrew worlds. In the Presocratics we see the cosmos stripped of sacred *muthos* and reclothed in the garb of naturalistic *muthos*. In the rise of the nation Israel, the world is stripped of a sacred *nature muthos* and clothed in the *muthos* of sacred *history*. So from the tenth century B.C.E., both Hebrew and Greek cultures drift slowly away from the sacred nature myth-complex of the Ancient Near East. By the Hellenistic Age the Greeks have erected an intellectual edifice of reason based on nature, and the sacred writings of Israel reflect a theological credo of revelation based on history. The diagram on page 76 illustrates some of the currents flowing through the two traditions. (Each current flows both ways, and each leads to and from society and man.) Using the diagram, we see that the *classical* Hebrew world view evinces a connection (C) not to be found in Greek conceptual contributions. Though the above scheme is subject to

75

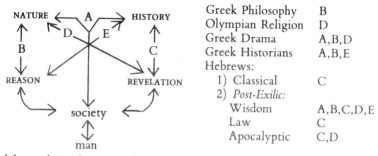

Greek Philosophy	B
Olympian Religion	D
Greek Drama	A,B,D
Greek Historians	A,B,E
Hebrews:	
1) Classical	C
2) *Post-Exilic:*	
Wisdom	A,B,C,D,E
Law	C
Apocalyptic	C,D

debate, the Hebrew Wisdom Movement may represent the most synthetic and holistic cognitive tradition.

Reason and revelation* appear to comprise two fundamentally different ways of knowing: but perhaps it is more accurate to say that they are two variant modes of engaging the world or constructing a world picture.[1] A case in point is the method of dialogue brought to fruition by Socrates and Plato. This method assumes that truth is innate within nature and within man—both of which are rational—and that open inquiry and conversation among men, and between man and nature, will bring truth to light. In this sense Socrates and Plato seem to have moved beyond the Presocratics, who were first theorists of nature, and too often concerned with belittling their opponents. Yet even in Plato's writings his antagonists often seem more like straw men than independent thinkers.

In the Hebrew tradition dialogue as an avenue to truth is missing (with possible exceptions being conversations between man and God, which tend to be mainly divine monologues). Yahweh, the God of the Hebrews, established his *covenant* modeled on the format of the old Hittite treaty form between overlord and vassal, stipulating obligations and privileges devised by Yahweh. The covenant singled out Israel as Yahweh's chosen people and defined the pattern of life they were to lead "among the nations." The covenant is not intended to create dialogue among men of differing world views, or to challenge nature to share her secrets with Israel. It is rather a channel for one voice alone to speak, the voice of Yahweh, which thunders from Sinai, inspires charismatic leaders, and grasps the prophets with the urgency of the divine word. The laws of the covenant clearly define the style of life and *ethos* incumbent upon the chosen people. Ideally at least, the way of the covenant is envisaged as one way, the voice of the covenant God as one voice, and Israelites reject this route only at great cost. Social ostracism is tantamount to divine ostracism, because the social unit is also the religious

---

*"Reason versus revelation" is a *conceptual* contrast relevant to Western world views. The Greeks were certainly fully religious persons; even while rationalism and skepticism began to obscure Olympian piety, the cult of Dionysus flourished.

community, and its laws are the laws of God. Of course historically, deviant belief and practice constantly threaten the ideal norm.

In Platonism *truth* is interwoven in the very structure of the cosmos; and, though not obvious to the casual glance or the uninformed senses, it is available to the disciplined and committed inquirer through rational contemplation. And even if the phenomenal world is only a shadow copy of the bright and eternal world of the forms (and the highest form, the Good) through philosophical awakening one can transcend the illusory world of the senses and in some sense *know* the eternal ideas. In classical Israel the mode of *knowing* is not abstract and intellectual, but personal and communal—available through the *cultus* and way of life revealed by Yahweh in the Law. If for the Greeks the *polis* represents a rational cosmic pattern derived from nature, for the Hebrews the covenant community embodies the revealed historical pattern typified in the commandments:

> Behold, I set before you this day a blessing and a curse: the blessing, if you obey the commandments of the Lord your God . . . and the curse, if you do not obey the commandments . . . (Deuteronomy 11:26-28)

Confronted by a mélange of competing traditions in the Hellenistic milieu, early Christianity generally adheres to the Hebrew preeminence of revelation:

> Where is the wise man? Where is the scribe? Where is the debater of this age? Has not God made foolish the wisdom of the world? . . . For Jews demand signs and Greeks seek wisdom, but we preach Christ crucified, a stumbling block to Jews and folly to Gentiles . . . (I Corinthians 1:20-22)

Here Paul challenges Jews and Greeks alike. The problem for the Jews is (from Paul's point of view) their blindness to the fulfillment of the historical purposes of Israel in the person and mission of Jesus, the Messiah ("Anointed One"). For both the classical Hebrew and early Christian traditions (apart from certain variations in the Wisdom Movement, Hellenistic Judaism, or the later Christian Synthesis), *revelation* is the one reliable mode of knowing the truth. For the Greeks truth is apprehensible with man's highest faculty, the faculty of reason.

Reason—for Plato and Aristotle—focuses on the abstract and the unchanging. Plato's forms are eternal. They are the archetypes and patterns out of which the phenomenal world of becoming, change and decay is constantly reborn. Aristotle's answer to the Presocratic quest for an *arche* is the Absolute or "Unmoved Mover"—a postulate for the cause or beginning of all change and material form. In each case the highest (in Plato's vertical scheme) or first (in Aristotle's horizontal scheme) source, norm or cause, is an eternal and unchanging abstraction. These abstractions seem remote from the existential dilemmas of human life. On the other hand, the Judeo-Christian God reveals himself in intimate connection with his people—and seems as concrete as his people among whom he dwells. In the Hebrew tradition he is successively God of the Patriarchs, God of Moses, God of David, and God of the prophets. In each case he is a God who discourses with man. Yahweh certainly does not regularly appear, as do the gods of Olympia who traffic with men as present *actors,* siring immortal heroes by mortal women, turning the course of battle in the guise of a famous warrior, etc. Yahweh is rather present with men—in the broad range of human events—by his spirit, infusing his people with preternatural courage and wisdom through precarious turns in their historical trek. Yahweh is both *deus absconditus,* hidden in the strange and fatal exigencies of life and history; and *deus revelatus,* addressing Moses on quaking Sinai, leading Gideon's small band against the Midianites, calling men to obedience with the irresistible force of his word. For early Christians he becomes the "God and father of our lord Jesus Christ," who has altered the course and meaning of history by "becoming flesh and dwelling among us." Beside the Judeo-Christian God, Plato's Eternal Form of the Good and Aristotle's Absolute stand immobile, but predictable, rational, nomistic to the utmost, imbuing the world with harmony and order. The Judeo-Christian God can act with caprice in the name of preserving his integrity and the integrity of his purposes. In the fervor of raising up and bringing down men and nations according to the iron dictates of his will, his actions surely appear to be beyond the grasp of reason. Yet as a merciful God, his "mind can be changed" by the righteousness of a few or the repentance of many (and his mercy may extend to an alien people such as Ninevah, as in the expedient Post-Exilic parable of Jonah).

Nature and History

The epistemological functions of reason and revelation for the Greeks and Hebrews are meaningless apart from their larger frames of reference: nature and history. In these two realms the *identity* of the Greek and Hebrew peoples is rooted respectively. For the Greek world, the reflection of the macrocosm ("large world" nature as a whole, the world order) in the microcosm ("small world," nature in miniature, the individual or the state) *roots* both individual and society in nature. Thus the same norms and harmony which keep the world order in balance keep the *polis* and the individual in balance (as the Law of Compensation illustrates). In Plato's *Republic* "justice," the chief virtue, is the balance which ensues when both social class and individual are assigned by nature vocations suited to the welfare of the whole. "Natural Law," a concept of Stoic philosophy reflected in Roman Law, was first a Greek ideal. Proper relationships derive from nature and are reflected in the *polis.*

The native population of Greece was from the first an *agricultural* people. The Dorian invasion of the twelfth century, culminating a millenium of migrations into the Greek peninsula, precipitated a final, gradual syncretization of Greek religion. As W. K. C. Guthrie has shown, the "gods of the

Greeks were complex characters, with both Northern and Mediterranean strains in their ancestry . . ."[2] Guthrie concludes that it was part of the Greek genius to preserve "the old alongside the new."[3] Thus in classical Greece, the dominant strains of religion include the more ancient cult of Demeter, the Mother of life, as well as the "official" Olympians. The Olympians' character stems from 1) the wedding of the gods of the invaders with those of the indigenous peoples; 2) from socioeconomic changes such as urbanization (politicizing the gods), the rise of small industry, and the expansion of trade and commerce. The cult of Dionysus, seemingly of Thracian (and perhaps Phrygian) origin, was initially unacceptable among the Greeks; but its affinity to the ancient fertility rites soon won it a distinctive—if at times "underground"—role in Greek life. In fact, Greek religion never eradicated its primitive *agrarian* bias. Even though Zeus—the patriarchal sky god of the nomadic invaders—became the dominant force, he shared his prestige with a large family and was sometimes identified with an already existing local deity. In many cases, Guthrie asserts, "the indigenous deity took the name of Zeus, but remained essentially what he had been before."[4]

The patriarchal forebears of the Hebrews were a *nomadic* people, tending their flocks and herds, moving with the seasons, following the watercourses (as their modern-day heirs, the Bedouins). The wandering Habiru (diverse nomads appearing in Ancient Near Eastern texts, at times as bandits and brigands), are the probable ancestors of the Hebrews. In the Exodus (ca. 1280 B.C.E.), a band of mixed peoples left Egypt, wandering in the deserts for some time before finally settling in Canaan; they gradually intermingled with distant kin, but used force to gain hegemony. During this time the Hebrews followed Yahweh, initially depicted as a fierce desert patriarch, stern and loyal to his people, but ruthless with all "who opposed his will." The constant mobility of the Hebrews and their progenitors, plus the decisive event of the Exodus (in Hebrew lore a magnificent victory of Yahweh over the Egyptians and the occasion of his calling a people), defined Yahweh's nature once and for all as a God of history. After the arrival in Canaan, a life-and-death struggle between Hedrew and native began—an inherent conflict between a pastoral and nomadic people and an agrarian people. If, to the Hebrews, the Canaanites and their favorite god Ba'al appeared to be degenerate un-believers with no ethics, certainly the Hebrews must have appeared to the Canaanites as intrusive, ruthless and uncultivated outsiders, with no respect for established culture or territories. Moreover, the conflict intensified as two sacred cosmoi and their attendant cultic practices were at stake: Yahweh and the Sinaitic revelation versus Ba'al and company and the rites of an agricultural (earth) religion. Needless to say, the Hebrews' assimilation of many of the elements of Canaanite life sapped away the prestige of Yahweh, as the history of continual apostasy in Israel so vividly testifies. Yahweh's theological nature altered to meet shifting cultural norms, agricultural economy, and the eventual inroads of urbanization, trade and commerce. However, Yahweh's victory over Ba'al is not to be disputed—as an *historical* God he provided the rallying norm of continuity for Israel through history long after Ba'al was buried with his culture. Thus in the Hebrew tradition (though under Solomon, Israel seemed very much like another Eastern monarchy), the nomadic roots persisted, and the children of Israel (and later their Chistian descendants) are "the pilgrim people." The imagery of "pilgrim" has left an irrevocable imprint on the Western mind (e.g., the early settlers in America in quest of a new Canaan; or in a contemporary popular vein, the adventures of the starship "Enterprise" of the TV series *Star Trek* depict pilgrims on a cosmic scale, still waging battles in the universal struggle of good and evil). Furthermore, the duality of nature and history in Western consciousness renders us exiles, at home neither in the one nor in the other. The dual auspices of nature and history also appear as dual causation as we survey the world.

Even though the Olympian religion evolved dramatically, nature remained the supreme hidden god. The Greeks recognized this, as *moira* ("fate") commanded greater power than Zeus (as Hera addresses Achilles):

> We shall keep you safe for this time, O hard Achilleus. And yet the day of your death is near, but it is not we who are to blame, but a great god and powerful Destiny *(moira).*[5]

Zeus, himself, was originally a god of nature:

> First and foremost he (Zeus) is the god of the sky and weather whom all Indo-European peoples acknowledged under names variously derived from the same root . . . His constant epithet in Homer is Cloud Gatherer. He sends the rain, the lightning, the thunderbolt and the thunder.[6]

Yet it is the Presocratics who saw behind the veneer of cult to nature itself, searching for natural causation, and disengaging the myth of nature from the gods. The heritage of Heraclitus, of *moira,* and of the macrocosm/microcosm scheme, passed into Stoicism where the cosmos becomes a rational, predetermined and integral system. The work of the Presocratics, especially filtered through Aristotle, becomes the cornerstone of modern science and the predilection for *natural* causation. So if stories like the River Xanthos rising to do battle with Achilles in the *Iliad* remind us of the strong mythopoeic inclination to personify nature, we must remember that to some, like the Presocratics, such personification was transparent. Yet, personified or demythologized, in the Greek world nature ultimately determines the events of history. Fate is preestablished for a man, a society, or even the world order which, like the seasons, dies and is reborn at proper intervals. Achilles addresses Lykaon, the suppliant he is about to slay:

> Do you not see what a man I am, how huge, how splendid and born of a great father, and the mother who bore me immortal? Yet even I have also my death and my strong destiny *(moira),* and there shall be a dawn or an afternoon or a noontime when some man in the fighting will take the life from me also . . .[7]

Nature sets the bounds of existence. In the gods of Olympus these bounds are personified and given concrete expression. To challenge the limits is man's fatal flaw, expressed as *hamartia* ("missing the mark"), *hubris* ("invading or trespassing the divine sphere"; "overarching pride"), *agnoia* ("ignorance"), or *ate* ("delusion"). In each case, through stupidity or blundering willfulness, man upsets the balance, transgresses the limits, and (according to Anaximander's Law of Compensation) must repay the world with tragedy. For the Greeks

> Human guilt is the confusion of the existing order, the disruption of an objectively given state (nature), which man must make good by his suffering and the misfortune which strikes him, and sometimes by his destruction.[8]

The gods, the guardians of nature, must act as agents of *nemesis* to redress the imbalance created by man's ignorance:

> Human guilt follows from the limitation of human knowledge, not as personal moral guilt, but as guilt given with existence itself. Since man "in his ignorance is set to act, and by his action to have a part spatially and temporally in the unlimited nexus of cause and effect, with unforseeable consequences for which he is thus not responsible, all action is guilt."[9]

Though the latter statement is somewhat strained, it nonetheless remains true that for the Greeks (as well as for the Hebrews), human existence entails guilt. But guilt here is not the personal moral guilt of history, but natural guilt of existence, owing to man's limitations and mortality, and above all to his ignorance of the laws of nature and destiny. (It is no wonder that the quest of the Presocratics was aimed at disclosing the causative forces and designs of nature.) Thus Agamemnon can blame his foolish behavior on Delusion *(ate)* the elder daughter of Zeus:

> Yet what could I do? It is the god who accomplishes all things. Delusion is the elder daughter of Zeus, the accursed who deludes all; her feet are delicate and they step not on the firm earth, but she walks the air above men's heads and leads them astray. She has entangled others before me. Yes, for once Zeus was deluded, though men say he is the highest one of gods and mortals.[10]

Zeus could be deluded, and *fate* looms behind the masks of the gods. Zeus himself makes this disclaimer in the *Odyssey:*

> Oh for shame, how the mortals put the blame upon us gods, for they say evils come from us, but it is they, rather, who by their own recklessness win sorrow beyond what is given, as now lately, beyond what was given, Aigisthos married the wife of Atreus' son, and murdered him on his homecoming, though he knew it was sheer destruction, for we ourselves had told him . . . And now he has paid for everything.[11]

Man, acting out of his nature—if in willful disregard for the laws *of* nature—brings upon himself the fate decreed by nature! Stoicism attempts to transcend the *tragic* element of this scheme; by contemplation and understanding of the world order one may live "in accordance with nature."

As we turn to the Judeo-Christian tradition we are struck by the contradistinction of perspectives. Whereas for the Greeks nature determines history, for the Hebrews the God of history rules and determines the course of nature. Unlike Plato's Demiurge (the Divine Craftsman who shapes the world out of the raw materials *of* nature), the God of the first chapter of Genesis establishes nature out of the void and out of chaos, as a meaningful order. The natural order arises after a period of creative days or epochs. In the creation story of chapter two, after a brief flirtation with nature's innocence, man and woman are thrust out of the garden in an historical trek marked by the intervening of God's calling and providence. Nature *serves the purposes* of history, as the Flood purges the earth for the righteous descendants of Noah, or as Joshua commands the sun to stand still so that he may finish the battle. In the Greek world man is the microcosm of the macrocosm, reflecting the natural order. For the Hebrews man becomes lord of the earth, commanded to tame, to rule and to subdue (and as a king bore the welfare of his people in his suzerainty, so too, man is responsible for the earth—an implication often ignored in Western tradition). Yet in Genesis two, the second creation account, man is set at enmity with nature. To Adam and his heirs in exile from the garden paradise, the earth rises up as a strange savage or wild beast to be tamed. If nature is not harnessed, it will destroy. Although for the Hebrews Yahweh is always God over nature, an ambivalence remains concerning the world order. Even its aesthetic colorations (as in the Psalms or the poems of Job) are the handiwork of the God of history. The end of nature is thus determined by history and *not* vice versa. In classical Israel there are no cycles of world order. Eschatology first appears as an historical hope for the fulfillment of Yahweh's purposes and the extension of his sovereignty throughout the earth. When the task of *history* is complete, then and only then could nature be redeemed (Isaiah 65:17 ff.). With the distrust of nature, perhaps rooted in the conflicts with Ba'al, it is not surprising that after the Exile the oppressed Jews should turn to Zoroastrian apocalyptic schemes.[12] Including warring forces of good and evil and the split within nature, this scheme offered both renewed *historical* hope in present time of crisis, and new legitimation for Jewish identity in the light of the flagging Davidic covenant.

Finally, the orientations of nature and history create variant understandings of social community. Ideally, the Greek *polis* is patterned after the cosmos, and its laws are rooted in nature. In Pythagoras the harmony and geometrical balance of the cosmos is meant to apply to the social order.[13] Plato illustrates a strong Pythagorean influence in the *Republic,* where the State—a macrocosm of the individual—is divided into classes corresponding to parts of the soul: rational (the philosopher-king and the ruling class), spirited (the warriors), and appetitive (the workers). Aristotle asserts:

> The proof that the state is a creation of nature and prior to the individual is that the individual, when isolated, is not self-sufficing; and therefore he is like a part in relation to the whole. But he who is unable to live in society . . . must be either a beast or a god . . . A social instinct is implanted in all men by nature . . .[14]

But the Greeks were never able to achieve unity among themselves. The particularism embodied in various city-states triumphed over any concept of world political order. Both Alexander (tutored by Aristotle) and Stoicism conceived of a world state based on the natural brotherhood of men. Alexander attempted to translate the ideals of Hellenism learned from Aristotle into a world *Realpolitik,* just as Rome enlisted Stoicism as its chief philosophical legitimation. In each case the ideal became distorted by reality; yet the legacy of "cosmic" politics remains fundamental to the West.

Israelite society was rooted in historical tradition. Communally, it recalled the heroically embellished (yet surprisingly realistic) events from the Exodus to Sinai, and the settlement in Canaan. Israel's this-worldly orientation was not a belief in harmony with nature, but a belief that God, the lord of nature, would tame its elements and force it to yield a bountiful life, if only the people would obey his ordinances. Thus Israel's culture was theocratic— dependent upon Yahweh for political stability and for material prosperity. The "this-worldly" character of Hebrew culture is reflected in her sense of values; following the Torah and participating in cultic life brought its own rewards: worldly success, a good reputation, a secure and large family, etc. *Mishpat,* a term usually translated "justice," indicates a society properly functioning in obedience to the revealed will of Yahweh. *Shalom* or "well being" refers to the material and spiritual welfare of the whole man, and of the community where *mishpat* rules. In these terms there is some similarity with the Greek *cosmos.* Nonetheless the chasm between history and nature remains in the two societies.

Man and Immortality

The final area of significant contrast is Greek and Hebrew anthropology. Man's nature is not conceived statically in either society, so our observations will concern dominant types emerging from the two traditions. In the Hesiodic/Homeric tradition man is created in the *imago dei* just as surely as the gods are projections of man. Homer particularly glorifies the Heroic code of *arete,* which is in essence courage in the face of mortality. Of course Homeric man is at the mercy of fate and the gods, and more fundamentally of nature itself. With the evolution of Greek society human nature acquires added dimensions. In classical Athens man is a political being as well as a rational being, as in the immortal words of Pericles:

> We differ from other states in regarding the man who holds aloof from public life not as 'quiet' but as useless; we decide or debate, carefully and in person, all matters of policy, holding, not that words and deeds go ill together, but that acts are foredoomed to failure when undertaken undiscussed.[15]

Aristotle writes that man is a political animal by nature—as Marx later says, "a species being." Man's political nature is rooted *in* nature (recall again the microcosm/macrocosm scheme). According to Sextus Empiricus, the followers of Pythagoras and Empedocles believed that

> there is a certain community uniting us not only with each other and with the gods but even with the brute creation. There is in fact one breath pervading the whole cosmos like soul, and uniting us with them.[16]

The scheme of microcosm/macrocosm is integral to Greek thought, beginning with Anaximenes, and in various ways enunciated by the Pythagoreans, Heraclitus, Empedocles, Stoicism and Neoplatonism. The idea also pervades the mystical doctrines of Orphism, Gnosticism and Hermeticism.[17] Plato assumes this belief in *Meno,* where, expounding the doctrine of recollection, Socrates says:

> The soul, then, as being immortal, and having been born again many times, and having seen all things that exist, whether in this world or in the world below, has knowledge of them all; and it is no wonder that she should be able to call to remembrance all that she ever knew . . . for as all nature is akin, and the soul has learned all things, there is no difficulty in her eliciting . . . out of a single recollection all the rest . . .[18]

And regarding the world soul out of which the soul is born, Plato asserts in *Timaeus:*

> Now when the Creator had framed the soul according to his will, he formed within her the corporeal universe, and brought the two together, and united them centre to centre . . .[19]

As significant as the divine, political, and natural facets of man's selfhood in Greek thought is the doctrine of the dualism between soul and body, and the psychical and material worlds. This dualism seems to have emerged from two separate, though related streams—Orphism and Pythagoreanism. From these two traditions arose the paronomastic equation of *soma* and *sema*—the "body" is equal to a "tomb." The body as the prisonhouse of the soul is an idea woven as a continuous thread in the fabric of Western tradition. Given classic expression by Plato, the duality of body and soul recurs in Platonism and Neoplatonism, Hellenistic Judaism, and Christian orthodoxy. This idea is certainly not original with the Greeks. In Egypt the concepts of *ka* and *ba*—the *ka* a surviving spiritual double of the earthly man and the *ba* a less physical and immortal soul—illustrate at least one very similar concept in the Ancient Near East prior to the Greeks.[20] Probably the idea was imported into Greece from the East.[21] But it was the Pythagoreans whose religious philosophy influenced Socrates and Plato. In Plato it is difficult at times to ascertain how negative a value judgment concerning the body and the material world is implied. It is clear that *psuche* (which often should be translated "mind") is the source of health for the whole man, yet Plato implies the inferiority of the body and its hindrances to development.[22] More closely linked to the Eternal Forms, it is the *psuche* through which contemplation and knowledge are possible. By contrast, Aristotle's *hylomorphism* affirms the material world and the body as real occasions of the forms, reflecting their essence. Aristotle's aesthetic doctrine of the imitation of nature clearly illustrates his greater respect for the material order and the body. Moreover, classical Greek sculpture plainly idealizes the body's naturalistic expression. Aristotle followed Plato in at least one respect, in exalting the *nous* and identifying *theoria* as the supreme activity of human being. For the legacy of the immortality of the soul we are indebted primarily to the Pythagoreans and to Plato.

As we move to the Hebrew world we again confront mental soil quite alien to Greek conceptions. Prior to the Hellenistic Era when Judaism (as the entire Near East) began its interchange and accommodations with Greek culture, classical Israel depicted man as a unity—soul and body—created in the *imago dei*. Man is not immortal, but has forfeited eternal life (in the Garden Myth) because of disobedience. The early Hebrew conception of an afterlife appears as insubstantial and relatively insignificant as that of Homer. This point has been recently debated by Ringgren,[23] but the consensus of opinion still seems to underscore the thoroughgoing this-worldly nature of the Hebrew understanding of man. Without examining all of the relevant Hebrew terminology, we might point out that the term *nephesh* means essentially "breath" and designates the animating source of human life (ultimately springing from the *ruach* or spirit of God). Jacob notes that

> *nephesh* is the usual term for man's total nature, for what he is and not just what he has. This gives the term priority in the anthropological vocabulary, for the same cannot be said of either spirit, heart or flesh . . . It *(nephesh)* has no existence apart from the body . . .[24]

Thus Hebrew anthropology is *monistic*. Man acts out his life upon the stage of concrete communal history focused in the *praxis* of covenant existence. The highest activity of man is not reason or contemplation, but that which is expressed in the *shema:*

> Hear, O Israel: The Lord our God is one Lord; and you shall love the Lord your God with all your heart, and with all your soul, and with all your might. (Deuteronomy 6:4,5)

Jesus later added "you shall love your neighbor as yourself" to this commandment; and indeed this expresses the Hebrew spirit: a present life of integrity in obedience to the Torah and in responsible action among fellow men. The Hebrew community, a theocracy in its ideal and ultimate form, nonetheless recognized that man's existence was social existence, and in this respect paralleled the Greek *polis*. But for the Hebrews such a concept was rooted in historical election, and not in nature. The changes that occurred in Hebrew anthropology after the Exile (587 B.C.E.) are worthy of note because of their influence on the eventual Christian synthesis of Greek and Hebrew ideas.

With the advent of Persian hegemony in the Near East (the latter sixth through the late fourth centuries B.C.E.), the Jewish communities, scattered in the so-called Diaspora or Dispersion throughout the old Babylonian Empire, began to adopt the apocalyptic motifs of the Persian religion, Zoroastrianism. Zoroastrianism divided the cosmos into warring powers of light and darkness, and anticipated a final cataclysmic encounter between Ahura Mazda, the god of light and ultimate sovereign, and Angra Mainyu (or Ahriman), the demonic power of darkness. Following the victory of Ahura Mazda would be the resurrection of the dead and a last judgment. During the ensuing centuries many Jews were also exposed to Hellenic thought, especially Platonism.[25] Foremost among Hellenistic Jews was Philo Judaeus (ca. 20 B.C.E.-C.E. 40), whose Platonic view of the soul is typical.[26] By the first century there were at least three different ways of looking at man among the Jews: the classical this-worldly orientation affirmed by the Sadducees, the Zoroastrian-influenced apocalypticism shared in general by Pharisees, Essenes and Zealots, and a cosmopolitan Platonic stance especially prominent among the educated Jews of Alexandria. "Orthodox" Christianity at first opted for the common Palestinian doctrines of the Pharisees, Essenes and Zealots. But from the late second to early fifth centuries, influenced by educated Romans, Christian theologians assimilated a strong Neoplatonic orientation which is expressed in the classical creeds, the thinking of St. Augustine, and finally in the general cosmic scheme of the middle ages. We have omitted one significant influence—probably incipient in some New Testament passages—gnosticism, a diverse syncretistic movement which arose in the Hellenistic world. Gnosticism in general propounded a strong dualistic doctrine where body and soul, matter and the spiritual world, and God and man are widely separated and antithetical both in essence and in ethical nature.

Considering the combined forces of apocalyptic teaching, Platonism and Neoplatonism, gnosticism (widespread by the second century), and even certain of the mystery cults, it is no wonder that the Christian orthodox synthesis finally succumbed to dualism. Furthermore, since early Christians after the Jerusalem Assembly (49 C.E.) considered their movement separate from Judaism, and since Judaism had absorbed these dualistic doctrines, it is not surprising that Christianity did not consider it a contradiction to its Hebrew heritage to adopt many of the Greek positions. This choice, made gradually and perhaps unwittingly over a period of three centuries, was to have a profound effect upon Western psychology down to the present day. Because of the far-reaching consequences of the *synthesis* of the Greek and Hebrew traditions, we will devote some further space to its discussion.

The old doctrine of Adam's Fall was initially a description of man's *historical* condition. As the Hebrews considered man's mortality, guilt and death, they must have asked questions (which seem implicit in Genesis two and three) such as 'why is man condemned to die,' 'why does he have to slave over the soil to subsist,' 'why does woman suffer pain in childbirth,' and the like. Surely the God of history had some design in the historical realities of man's fallenness. The myth of the Garden is evocative not only because it captures the heart of these questions, but because at the same time it explains why man was cut off from nature and condemned to history. For the Hebrews, the Fall and its implications are acutely historical in that they do indeed describe man's historical state. So guilt for the Hebrews is *historical guilt*. The importance of this point is that for classical Israel *historical guilt* could be *remedied within history*. Not only were there provisions made for sins both deliberate and accidental in the sacrificial code, Yahweh was a merciful God to the repentant, and obedience brought earthly rewards. The *way out* of historical guilt is through a this-worldly life of integrity based upon following the graciously revealed laws of God.

> And because you hearken to these ordinances, and keep and do them, the Lord your God will keep with you the covenant and the steadfast love which he swore to your fathers to keep; he will love you, bless you, and multiply you; he will also bless the fruit of your body and the fruit of the ground, your grain and your wine and your oil, the increase of your cattle, and the young of your flock, in the land which he swore to your fathers to give you. (Deuteronomy 7:12,13)

Similarly for the Greeks, various solutions arose to provide a "good life" in the face of their understanding of the human condition. But guilt for the Greeks, as we have seen, is *natural guilt* (or guilt rooted in the natural order). Various ways of expiating nature were provided in the Olympian and Dionysian religions. In general a life of integrity in the family, in the polis, with reverence for the gods, assured man of honor if he did not err by *hubris*, bringing upon himself the tragic consequences of the Law of Compensation. For Plato, Aristotle, and Stoicism, rational thought and contemplation were highly valued modes of transcendence; and the Stoic norm of "living according to nature" reflects the general classical spirit. Moreover, the freedom from the pangs of mortal existence became further assured with the gradual dissemination of the idea of immortality. Thus the inferiority of the *body* and material life in the scheme of things could be compensated for in various ways, especially by cultivating the soul.

With the Christian synthesis, a deadly amalgamation of the Hebrew and Greek traditions occurred. By combining Hebrew and Greek concepts, Christianity absorbed into its heart a contradiction which has haunted the Western psyche ever since. The *union of historical and natural guilt* was ultimately to leave Western man with "no exit." The diagnosis which follows is perhaps oversimplified, but should help illumine certain deeply ingrained fissures in the Western psyche. As we have said, *historical guilt* for the Hebrews could be alleviated *within history*. But when history is *removed* as an effective arena, trouble ensues. This occurs in a series of dramatic events including the conquest of Israel by Assyria, the fall of Judah and the destruction of the Temple, and the deportation of Jews from Palestine culminating in centuries of exile. The state of Judah and the Temple — two critical *historical* institutions of Jewish identity — were removed in one sweeping blow. Thus in the Post-Exilic Era, Jews sought out various solutions for this disruption of their faith (especially a challenge to the Davidic Covenant which had seemed to *guarantee* the permanence of the Temple and the State). Zoroastrian-influenced apocalypticism, strict piousness centered in the Torah, practical integrity espoused in the Wisdom Movement, and the synthesizing of Hebrew heritage with Greek philosophy all served as avenues of reconstruction for the shattered Jewish psyche. For Jews who followed Jesus of Nazareth, he was the historical Messiah who provided spiritual liberation and new meaning for history (though not political vindication). However, the absorption of Greek dualism by Christianity precipitated a crisis of consciousness. *Dualism* which declares the material world and the body to be inferior to the mind, is not fatal (though perhaps not desirable) as long as avenues of fulfillment or liberation are open for the mind. But the Christian *revelation,* when combined with such a dualism, did *not* provide for such fulfillment, but in fact specifically stated its futility:

> Where is the wise man? Where is the scribe? Has not God made foolish the wisdom of the world? For since, in the wisdom of God, the world did not know God through wisdom, it pleased God through the folly of what we preach to save those who believe.   (I Corinthians 1:20,21)

Thus the "word of the cross" is foolishness to the rational mind, and in Romans 1:21 Paul asserts that the Gentiles "became futile in their thinking and their senseless minds were darkened." For Christianity, the dilemma created by *natural guilt* and particularly by dualism could not be solved *through* nature, but only through revelation and a *super*natural transformation.

At the same time, *historical guilt,* as understood within classical Israel, no longer was subject to an *historical solution. Dualism* renders the material world and life in the body suspect and inferior. Prosperity is not a boon but a temptation of the devil; Jesus is purported to have suggested that it was hard for a rich man to enter the Kingdom of God. Furthermore, the ability to *choose* a life of integrity on one's own efforts is necessary to a viable *historical* existence. As Joshua says:

> Now therefore fear the Lord, and serve him in sincerity and in faithfulness; put away the gods which your fathers served beyond the River, and in Egypt and serve the Lord. And if you be unwilling to serve the Lord *choose* this day whom you will serve, whether the gods your fathers served in the region beyond the River, or the gods of the Amorites in whose land you dwell; but as for me and my house, we will serve the Lord. (Joshua 24:14,15)

Yet for Christianity the will is severely crippled (apart from God's *super*-natural intervention). Paul clearly illustrates this point:

> I do not understand my own actions. For I do not do what I want, but I do the very thing I hate . . . For I know that nothing good dwells within me, that is, in my flesh. I can will what is right, but I cannot do it. For I do not do the good I want, but the evil I do not want is what I do. (Romans 7:15,18,19)

Not only is the will crippled for Paul; the body (Romans 7:14,23,24) and the world (Romans 8:20) have been rendered helpless as well. No worldly solution is available. All that remains is a trans-worldly redemption.

The consequence of the Christian synthesis for the West is this: both classical Hebrew and classical Greek world views are emptied of their respective patterns of the good life. The *naturalistic* judgments of dualism cut off the avenue of history by rendering this world and the body inadequate vehicles for fulfillment. The *historical* judgments of revelation testify to the inferiority of nature and reason and turn these avenues into dead ends. The *only* way that remains is the way of revelation—which, though promising new life in the present and future—*can never restore historical integrity or the integrity of nature and reason* to the former status which they enjoyed in the respective Hebrew and Greek traditions. Why? Because the all-inclusive Christian synthesis judges as inferior *all* facets of life in this world, the restoration of which may occur only *under* the divine activity of *grace*. Historical existence, nature, and reason remain forever *subservient to* the divine revelation and enjoy no significant status of their own. Alan Watts calls such a situation a *double bind*. For the situation of the individual is this: his will is crippled, his body suspect, the material world is controlled by the devil—all historical avenues of self-realization are cut off. Nor is the scenario complete. Since the whole man is tainted by sin, his intellect is incompetent and the activity of *theoria* is a dead end. Original sin has blocked out the hope of illumination from the intellect (though Paul says there is enough light to judge a man, but not enough to save him). The classical Israelite could exercise initiative and achieve happiness through following the Torah and participating in cultic life. The Platonist could exercise initiative by cultivating his rational tools and developing his soul through the light of reason and nature. But for the classical Christian, the sole way of achieving happiness and salvation is not through his own efforts, but by the grace of God (mediated in various ways in Christian tradition, through the Church, through the Bible, through pious exercise, etc.). Self-worth is thus not the achievement of the individual, but a gift of God.

As long as one accepts the verdict and the solution of the Christian synthesis, the problem is not without alleviation. Even if this life is to be endured and not enjoyed, it is easier to endure if you believe that you are among the saved and will eventually enjoy eternal life. But the situation is not so simple. For *beliefs* shape consciousness, and the shape of Western consciousness has for many centuries been dependent upon the Christian synthesis. The structures of Christian consciousness remain within Western man, but the mythical framework has been largely abandoned in the process of secularization; thus *all* avenues of escape seem closed: the *historical* solution, the *natural* solution, *and* the *supernatural* solution. The only options for such a crisis in consciousness are despair or the quest for a new world view.

Of course the picture we have painted is somewhat extreme, and yet not without justification if we examine the situation of twentieth century secular (?) or Christian (?) man. Obviously Western civilization may cite its accomplishments. Historically, various compromises have occurred to dull the brunt of the orthodox dilemma. Moreover, Greek naturalism and Hebrew historicism are not the *only* strands of Western world view, nor is the Christian synthesis the only synthetic approach to emerge in Western history. However, the Hebrew and Greek orientations are the *chief* components from antiquity, even though Roman utilitarianism, statecraft and law or medieval Islamic scholarship, etc., are certainly significant. In fact the Roman *practical* spirit has doubtlessly turned the attention of many away from such ruminations. Indigenous religions and traditions have played significant roles both in Europe and in the Americas. Such factors have tempered the inherent tension between the Greek and Hebrew elements in the Christian synthesis, and of course there has been a variety of forms of Christianity other than the dominant orthodoxy. So the picture is far from a simple one. However, the nature-history dilemma is real and does merit consideration in the attempt to understand Western psyche.

POINTS OF IDENTITY[27]

Sense Experience and the Phenomenal World
Although Heraclitus and Empedocles defended the reliability of the senses, the balance of the Presocratics (especially Parmenides, Zeno, Melissus and Democritus) found the senses to be inadequate or misleading. Plato upheld the negative judgment of Parmenides, and although granting perception a place in the soul, considered it inferior to rational knowledge. Platonic dualism confines the body (through which perception must operate) to a realm of flickering shadows—mere reflections of the real world of Eternal ideas. The mental faculties of the soul alone, less condemned to immediacy, are true participants in the Eternal.

In a similar vein we should not be surprised that a tradition which asserts that true knowledge is revealed by God's spirit, should limit the perspicacity of the senses. With regard to the senses, proximate perspectives inform the Judeo-Christian and Greek rationalistic traditions. (We must remember here the fertile interchange of the Hellenistic Era.) Considering the contexts, we discover that the distrust of the senses reflects essentially different motives: in Greek rationalism a celebration of man's rational faculty; in the Judeo-Christian milieu, an emphasis upon the necessity of divine revelation. The agreement thus bears further comment. If the Greek rationalistic and Judeo-Christian traditions have denigrated the senses, then what are the roots of Western science?

Respect for nature and the senses is widespread in antiquity. In the wordly orientation of classical Israel, we find a marked respect for man's sensory and observational powers. For example, Psalm eight acclaims

When I *look* at the heavens, the work of thy fingers,
    the moon and the stars which thou hast established;
what is man that thou are mindful of him,
    and the son of man that thou dost care for him?
Yet thou hast made him little less than God,
    and dost crown him with glory and honor.
Thou hast given him dominion over the works of thy hands;
    thou hast put all things under his feet . . .   (Psalm 8:3-6)

The Psalmist applauds the majesty of the cosmos as perceived by his senses. Similar sentiments are poeticized in the cosmic songs at the end of Job and in the Post-Exilic work Ecclesiastes. Yet apart from the eclectic dimensions of Ecclesiastes, the fact remains that all such observation and reflection in the Hebrew scriptures is *already* informed by revelation, ". . . the work of thy fingers." Observation of nature and its marvelous order appears to be more prominent in Hebrew literature than in the New Testament, but the scientific spirit seems little indebted to biblical origins.

The roots of science are complex. The astronomical/astrological observations of the Babylonians and Persians, the expert mathematical and geometrical sophistication exhibited in the pyramids, the analytical and mathematical tools developed by the Presocratics, and most significantly, the work of Aristotle, all must be considered formative expressions of early science. Furthermore, if we take seriously Levi-Strauss' "Neolithic Paradox" (plus his observations on taxonomy in primitive cultures), we must antedate the scientific spirit by some thousands of years. Considering the development of language and other elementary cultural artifacts, perhaps the scientific spirit is in fact integral to human nature.

In the classical period of Western culture, Aristotle stands above all others as a man of science. It is true that the mathematical and geometrical theories of Pythagoras profoundly influenced Plato, who for example in *Timaeus* depicts the universe as a perfect sphere. But Plato seems influenced largely by aesthetic and philosophical preconceptions rather than scientific concerns. Aristotle breaches Plato's chasm between the phenomenal and essential worlds, since matter is the vehicle whereby form is actualized and essence is realized. Being, for Aristotle, is manifest *in* becoming, and the universal *in* the particular. In addition to this solution to the Platonic dilemma, Aristotle contributed another critical insight—the world is *process.* Essence is not to be found in some static frozen realm of eternal forms, but is manifest in the ongoingness of things. Science then derives two fundamental assumptions from Aristotle: first, the phenomenal world *is* an expression of the "true forms"; second, the *process* or unfolding of the phenomenal world is not an aberration, but a legitimate expression of Being. Windelband asserts that "being is that which comes to existence in the processes of Nature. This self-realization of the essence in the phenomena, Aristotle calls *entelechy.*"[28] In addition, Aristotle contributed significant theories of logic and causation, and developed taxonomic systems for the interrelationships of natural phenomena—all of which express Being. Upon the foundation of observing characteristics and interrelationships of phenomena, generalization and classification can be built. Aristotle developed his elementary scheme of cause and effect (from first to final cause) with an eye for the significance of process. Because of all these contributions, Aristotle deserves chief credit for laying the philosophical groundwork of modern science, and for *providing a perspective* out of which science is possible. After the full flowering of the Christian Synthesis, it was the resurrection of Aristotle which trumpeted the dawn of modernity. It was not first by Christian thinkers, but by the great Muslim philosophers Alkindi, Alfarabi, Avicenna and Averroes (Ibn Rushd) that Aristotle was restored.

The critical factors, then, making "world" an object of scientific inquiry in the West include: 1) The Greek concept of *cosmos* whereby the universe *is* a world order; 2) the Presocratics' naturalistic speculations for an intelligible cosmogony; 3) the systematic investigations of Aristotle; 4) the historical sense of the Hebrews and the Greek historians; 5) pre-classical influences such as Babylonian astrology/astronomy; 6) post-classical thinkers of the Hellenistic Age such as Aristarchus, Archimedes, Eudoxus, Theophrastus, Euclid and Ptolemy.

Science eventually did mature in the Christian West. The distrust of matter characteristic of the Platonic-Christian synthesis, though generally hostile to science, may be cited for one "contribution": the *objectification* of the world as "other" or "alien." When the Presocratics loosed nature from mythopoeic personalism, they paved the way for dualism, whereby the world as "other" may be treated dispassionately, analytically, as an "it" for our inquiry and explanation.[29] Hebrew historicism and apocalypticism, combined with dualism in the Christian Synthesis, forbade the West any *worship* of nature which now would become the object of scientific inquiry. It is also just this combination of *historicism* and *dualism* which threatens—as ecology has diagnosed—the health and safety of the natural order.

Cosmos or Chaos, Nomism or Anomie

Both the Greek and Judeo-Christian traditions, (and perhaps culture and nature as well), strive to create world order. The whole of classical Greek society is built upon the premise of an aesthetic harmony and order manifest ideally in the political sphere, in art, in religion, and in particular lives. The microcosm—whether the social order or the individual—should reflect the macrocosm. In classical Israel the nomistic elements derive from the sense of historical continuity, the Torah, the cult, the prophetic faith, and the concepts of *mishpat* and *shalom* (where Hebrew thought approaches Greek concepts of *cosmos*). *Mishpat* is used to describe God's miracles against Egypt (Exodus 7:4), but refers more frequently to "judgments" or "ordinances" of Yahweh—the various facets of his revealed law (e.g., in Deuteronomy, the Psalms and Ezekiel). But the larger theological implications of the word entail the idea of world order. In Jeremiah 8:7 we read that

> Even the stork in the heavens knows her times
> and the turtledove, swallow and crane
> keep the time of their coming;
> but my people know not
> the ordinance of the Lord.

In Genesis one, *Mishpat* is implied in the mythic order of the days of creation, and the taxonomy of nature declared "good" by Yahweh. This affirmation somewhat counterbalances later denigrations of the material order. In Psalm 89:8-14 the natural order is attributed to Yahweh whose throne is founded upon *mishpat* (vs. 14). Of great importance to the origins of social conscience in the West, are passages where *mishpat* includes the welfare of the poor and the oppressed (e.g., Psalms 72:2, 103:6, 146:7, Isaiah 1:17 ff., Amos 5, 7, etc.) Micah affirms

> He has showed you, O man, what is good;
> and what does the Lord require of you
> but to do justice *(mishpat)*, and to love kindness,
> and to walk humbly with your God?
> (Micah 6:8)

In a similar fashion, *shalom* ("well-being" or "peace")—a condition of wholeness informing cultic duties and righteous acts of justice among men—affects the natural order. In Job the righteous man helps the afflicted, the fatherless and the poor; and as a result:

> At destruction and famine you shall laugh,
> and shall not fear the beasts of the earth.
> For you shall be in league with the stones of the field,
> and the beasts of the field shall be at peace with you.
> (Job 5:22,23)

Of course, the experience of Job challenges this simplistic equation of righteousness with automatic peace and safety. As righteous Job faced calamity, so also Post-Exilic Jews, righteous as well as unrighteous, were uprooted from their *cosmos*. Nevertheless, the above statement is typical of classical Hebrew belief. In Zechariah (8:11 ff.) the eschatological restoration of *shalom* brings to the earth peace, renewed fertility, and productiveness. Jeremiah's vision of the destruction of Jerusalem includes the concomitant desolation of nature:

> I looked on the earth, and lo, it was waste and void:
> and to the heavens, and they had no light.
> I looked on the mountains, and lo, they were quaking,
> and all the hills moved to and fro.
> I looked, and lo, there was no man,
> and all the birds of the air had fled.

> I looked, and lo, the fruitful land was a desert,
> and all its cities were laid in ruins before the Lord,
> before his fierce anger.   (Jeremiah 4:23-26)

This cosmic upheaval and chaos is attendant upon the ignoring of social justice and *mishpat,* as is clearly shown in chapter five, where there is no one "who does justice," and the cause of the fatherless and the needy is ignored (vs. 28). In Zechariah 8:12-16 *shalom* again includes both society and nature. Following the loss of the State (after 587 B.C.E.), Hebrew cosmology and eschatology were ripe for the influence of Persian apocalypticism. For as the social order broke apart and anomie ensued, it was easy to believe that the natural order was not only disrupted, but also the scene of cosmic warfare between light and darkness. With but one more step Greek dualism could be incorporated, combining Zoroastrian demonism with the denigration of the material world. During the Maccabean Era some Jews adopted just such a view, which then became a dubious heritage of the Christian Synthesis.

In early Christianity the full-blown synthetic dualism of Hebrew, Zoroastrian, and Greek roots was not yet complete, and some tension remained between various possibilities. The position of Jesus is uncertain, but he does not seem to have affirmed an ontological dualism. The Zoroastrian scheme, primarily an ethical dualism, was nonetheless couched in cosmic terms. Like the Hebrew prophets, Zoroastrianism assumed a coalescence between ethics and cosmic harmony. But ethical dualism, and even cosmic conflict, do not imply that the material order in itself is inferior. Paul moves closer to ontological dualism, in Romans 8:19-21:

> For the creation waits with eager longing for the revealing of the sons of God; for the creation was subjected to futility, not of its own will but by the will of him who subjected it in hope; because the creation itself will be set free from its bondage to decay and obtain the glorious liberty of the children of God.

It may seem a subtle point to critics, but Paul does *not* say here, or anywhere else, that the material world is evil. Paul is expressing a position not far removed from the Hebrew prophets: namely that the historical presence of sin in the world has brought death and decay, and that eschatological redemption will transform the natural, as well as the moral, order. A pertinent question is whether certain passages in Colossians and Ephesians—historically attributed to Paul—in fact reflect another tradition within the early Church. (Of course as Paul matured he may have changed his mind on certain matters.) In Colossians 1:15-28 and 3:11, as well as Ephesians 1:9, 10, 20-23 and 2:11-3:11, the most far-reaching and radical statements in the New Testament regarding the effects of Christ's redemption are recorded. Here Christ has become the Cosmic Lord in whom creation itself subsists, and through whom all of creation is reconciled to God. Not only has the barrier between Greek and Jew been removed, but all men partake of the unity of Christ's cosmic body: "Here there cannot be Greek and Jew, circumcised and uncircumcised, barbarian, Scythian, slave, free man, but Christ is all, and in all." (Colossians 3:11) These significant passages lay the foundation for a universal monism—a route seldom traveled in Christian thought. In the West too often it is not the vision of *cosmos* that has triumphed, but the dire picture of dualistic strife and chaos, leading irrevocably to some mythical apocalyptic upheaval. Yet the vision of Ephesians and Colossians will continue to haunt the prophets of doom until they alter their world view or disappear in a real apocalypse which they have helped precipitate.

Why has the fear of chaos haunted the West, and what are its roots? We can only conjecture here. Both classical Hebrew and classical Greek societies faced threats from primitive "earth" religions. For the Hebrews, the threat was the native religion of Canaan—the cult of Ba'al and his cohorts (established in Palestine to its advantage before the Hebrews arrived). For the Greeks, the challenge to the classical Olympian religion (and also to philosophical rationalism) issued forth from the older native fertility cults, and later the rites of Dionysus.[30]

Although many contrasts exist between the religion of Yahweh and the Olympian religion (e.g., divergent orientation to history and to nature, differing uses of anthropomorphism, etc.), there are also similarities.[31] For example, Mt. Sinai was sacred to Yahweh. The old Canaanite deity, *El* (linguistically related to the Hebrew "god"), was "the one of the mountains." The *location* of God is two-fold. In the horizontal dimension the Covenant links him to the history of his people; in the vertical he is god of heaven, inhabiting the hierarchical domain of a three-storied universe. The Greek pantheon dwells in the sky on Mt. Olympus, yet manifests certain horizontal dimensions—particularly in protecting the various *poloi*. In both cases Law (whether the Torah, or the laws of the *polis),* is given hierarchical legitimation—a kind of *spatial* permanency implicit in the vertical mythical frame. In other words, the vertical location of deity provides a sessile stability for society. Wheelwright underscores the spatial quality in Greek culture:

> While it would be unwise to oversimplify so complicated a phenomenon as Greek religion, it can be suggested very tentatively that the Olympian mode of thought in religion had counterparts in the emphasis which the Greeks gave to such spatial ways of thinking as geometry, land-surveying, architecture, and the first steps of physical science. The Olympian influence shows itself, too, in Greek ethics—in the dominant emphasis that is put on moderation and the golden mean, which appears to have conceptual affinities with the primitive mythic command against overstepping territorial boundaries.[32]

Though the Hebrew historical orientation certainly implies a motile and temporal disposition, there is also a strong sessile element in the belief that the Covenant and the Law are eternal: "For ever, O Lord, thy word is firmly fixed in the heavens." (Psalm 119:89) A comparative chart follows to illustrate common elements in Olympian (or ouranian, from *ouranos*, "heaven") and Hebrew religion as opposed to the threat of Dionysus or Ba'al:

Olympian, Ouranian or Law-Oriented Religion	Dionysian, or Chthonic (from *chthon*, "earth")
spatially fixed norms	temporally oriented rituals
being or eternity	becoming or time
conservative	ecstatic
hierarchical, authoritarian	horizontal, participatory
cosmos, stability, static	*chaos,* change, dynamic

In opposition to classical Hebrew religion and Olympian religion are the chthonic religions of Ba'al and Dionysus. The chthonic cults are intimately allied with *eros* and *thanatos*—the forces of life and death manifest in the cycles of nature. Both Hebrew and Greek "orthodoxies" exhibit certain chthonic elements, such as animal sacrifice. Prophets of Yahweh or Apollo, for example, could enter states of ecstasy (from *ek-stasis,* "to stand outside one's self") or enthusiasm (from *en-theos,* being "in God"). Charismatic leadership, especially in Israel, arose spontaneously to meet temporal crises. But both religions were marked by dominant conservative trends (literally, conserving continuity), distrusting *eros* and fearing *thanatos* (the final dissolution of continuity). Wheelwright remarks:

> A distinctive kind of ethics grows out of this way of regarding the world (the chthonic rhythms), an ethics drawn from the character of the rhythmic life-death sequence itself. What, from the standpoint of organic nature and without reference to any alien standard of judgment, is the criterion of good and ill? From the standpoint of naturalistic biology it is not true to say that death represents the evil side of things, because death, no less than life, is an inseparable part of the ongoing life-death rhythm.[33]

Both Wheelwright and E. R. Dodds[34] assert that the strength of the chthonic element in Greek society has been vastly underrated; and it is well known to biblical scholars how pervasive the cult of Ba'al remained in Israel for many centuries. It would seem that the chthonic element has played the role in classical culture of a strong "underground" to the dominant conservative religions.* Christianity itself did battle with an array of chthonic cults, from the early mystery sects to the indigenous European religions. Since the Middle Ages the "occult" (meaning "hidden") has periodically reared its head. (It is significant that witchcraft and similar practices have remained popular on an underground level, especially in rural areas of Europe.)

In general, the chthonic opponents of classical Greek and Hebrew religions offered adherents a primordial means of transcendence and emotional catharsis not available within the later orthodoxies. Moreover,

---

*However, it is important to remember that the chthonic religions *preceded* the later orthodoxies, and were *driven* underground.

chthonic rituals directly confront the two most feared elements of human life, sex and death. For both are placed in their natural context: intercourse and procreation are understood in the context of the fertility and seasonal rebirth of the earth; death and sacrifice recall the yearly approach of winter and the return of all elements to the earth. Of course, the *eros/thanatos* rituals cut right across the accepted *nomoi* of the *polis,* or the Hebrew Covenant. In this sense the chthonic elements were feared primarily as threatening anomie or chaos. The threat became more intense the more the social order seemed to be tottering. It was in periods of great insecurity and danger that the prophets reminded Israel how she had strayed from the Covenant and joined in the practices of "other gods" (primarily Ba'al and other nature deities). When the axe finally fell, and Jerusalem was razed by Babylon, the abomination of alien earth cults must have seemed very real indeed. For both Post-Exilic Jews and early Christians (derived mostly from oppressed Jews or lower class Gentiles), the appeal of a lofty revealed law of God—which guaranteed *cosmos* both personally and communally (if not on a socio-political level where hope was mostly abandoned)—must have been very strong. At the same time, the appeal of "earth" or "mystery" religions which could offer immediate ecstasy and transcendence, must have created formidable and highly-feared opposition.* For the idea of *cosmic law* is much easier to digest when one's immediate personal and social situation *evidences* the presence of nomism: prosperity, family-security, recognition in the community, etc. And here is perhaps a key: poverty, famine, warfare, oppression, disease, have all struck with unremitting regularity in the course of human history. During these traumatic times when cosmic *nomoi* are most threatened, the appeal of both *eros* and *thanatos* for immediate release is strongest, and arouses vigorous attempts at repression. Freud underscores this point in *Civilization and Its Discontents* where he asserts that civilization itself is built upon repression. The question remains as to whether the chthonic drive of eros/thanatos is given greater strength by greater repression, or whether, if allotted some officially-sanctioned (or unofficially-accepted) outlet, it adds stability to the mainstream *cosmos.* The continuous recurrence of violence in history seems to suggest the inadequacy of most cosmic ordering structures in providing consistent, constructive, and viable release for man's aggressive instincts. Although we may only speculate, it would seem that some officially-sanctioned (or unofficially-accepted) outlet for ecstatic behavior—such as prophecy in classical Israel, Dionysian cultus in classical Greece, or the mysteries in Rome—probably contributes to the general stability of society. In each case we assume that the larger nomistic structure of central institutions is not threatened, but actually affirmed in some manner. Of course

---

* The promise of ecstasy, and emotional release from a sense of powerlessness, help account for the widespread popularity of highly dramatic, fanciful apocalyptic literature.

98

it could be argued that social stability has nothing to do with chthonic outlets, but is simply a function of political and economic security. However, modern probings into the meaning of personhood and community do seem to suggest that psychological and social health must include some acceptable means for self-transcendence or ecstasy, e.g., dance, athletics (an integral facet of classical Greek *cosmos*), aesthetics, religion, or similar healthy emotional and erotic outlets.[35] We might speculate that the dilemma created by the orthodox Christian Synthesis, shutting off natural channels of both history and nature, has contributed—albeit subtly and indirectly—to frustration and violence in the West. Survival in our era requires that now, as never before, we must explore healthy avenues of integrating the psyche's chthonic dimensions—an integral part of nature—into a holistic social order.

Summary

Because of the length of our discussion, it will be helpful to summarize briefly the main conclusions of this chapter: 1) the Greek component of Western consciousness tends more toward the vertical, the abstract, the rational—the Hebrew more toward the linear, the horizontal, the historical, the existential; 2) the Greek *cosmos* is an integral world order (microcosm /macrocosm) based upon the rational unity of nature—the Hebrew world view emphasizes historical continuity and obedience to the revealed law of God, with harmony, both social and cosmic, being fundamentally dependent upon ethics; 3) the Greek view of history is oriented to nature, its cycles and recurrences, and tends towards universalism—the Hebrew view of history acknowledges human temporality and envisions a linear eschatological goal; Hebrew consciousness was more often particularistic than universal; 4) the Platonic element of Greek heritage and late Jewish and Christian thought tends to degrade the senses and the material order—classical Hebrew, classical Greek, and Aristotelian perspectives generally affirm the material order and the body as viable means to knowledge and fulfillment; 5) Greek, Hebrew and Christian thought value "world order" of a fundamentally *sessile* nature, and exhibit extreme distaste for, and repression of, radical motile orientations such as the chthonic religions of antiquity.

FOOTNOTES

[1]Thus reason and revelation as variations on a single theme—world building—have much in common. Peter L. Berger discusses *pre-theoretical* and *theoretical* knowledge, each of which is employed in legitimating the social order. See *The Sacred Canopy* (Garden City, N.Y.: Doubleday, 1967; Anchor, 1969), pp. 30-32. However, research into man's two-hemisphere brain suggests that there may be some *generic* difference between "reason" and "revelation." See chapter eight of this book.

[2]W. K. C. Guthrie, *The Greeks and Their Gods* (Boston: Beacon Press, 1955), p. 27.

[3]Ibid., p. 28. See also p. 146 ff.

[4]Ibid., p. 51.

[5]Homer, *Iliad* (trans. Richmond Lattimore) 19.408-410.

[6]Guthrie, pp. 37-38.

[7]Homer, *Iliad,* 21.108-112.

[8]Gustav Stahlin and Walter Grundmann, *"hamartano"* in Gerhard Kittel, ed., *The Theological Dictionary of the New Testament,* Vol. I (Grand Rapids, Michigan: Eerdmans, 1964), p. 298.

[9]Ibid.

[10]Homer, *Iliad,* 19.90-96.

[11]Homer, *Odyssey* (trans. Richmond Lattimore) 1.32-43.

[12]John Priest notes that although the themes present in developed Jewish apocalyptism are heavily indebted in *literary form* and *imagery* to Zoroastrian materials, Zoroastrian motifs were incorporated only when indigenous needs within Judaism suggested their relevance. Such motifs were quickly adopted for specifically Jewish purposes. Recent research has indicated that apocalyptic themes in Israel seem to predate Zoroastrian influence. See Paul D. Hanson, *The Dawn of Apocalyptic* (Philadelphia: Fortress Press, 1975), and Klaus Koch, *The Rediscovery of Apocalyptic* (Naperville: Alec R. Allenson, Inc., n.d., German edition, 1970); translated by Margaret Kohl. As Richard Rubenstein observes, since God was Lord over nature, the apocalyptic resolution of history *beyond* this current world was in some sense incipient within Israel's cosmology from the beginning.

[13]John Mansley Robinson, *An Introduction to Early Greek Philosophy* (Boston: Houghton Mifflin, 1968), pp. 78-81.

[14]Aristotle *Politics* (trans. Benjamin Jowett) 1253a2. 25-29.

[15]Donald Kagan, rev., *Botsford and Robinson's Hellenic History* (New York: MacMillan, 1969), p. 212.

[16]*The Encyclopedia of Philosophy,* s.v., "Macrocosm and Microcosm" by Donald Levy.

[17]Ibid.

[18]Plato, *Meno,* (trans. J. Harward) 81-82.

[19]Plato, *Timaeus,* (trans. J. Harward) 36-37.

[20]W. E. Caldwell, *The Ancient World* (New York: Holt, Rinehart and Winston, 1963), p. 53.

[21]G. M. O. Grube, *Plato's Thought* (Boston: Beacon Press, 1958), p.121.

[22]Ibid., pp. 122-25.

[23]Helmer Ringgren, *Israelite Religion,* trans. David E. Green (Philadelphia: Fortress Press, 1966), pp., 245-47.

[24]Edmond Jacob, *"psuche"* in Gerhard Kittel and Gerhard Friedrich, eds., *The Theological Dictionary of the New Testament,* Vol. IX (Grand Rapids, Michigan: Eerdmans, 1974), p. 620.

[25]See Morton Smith, "Palestinian Judaism in the First Century," pp. 67-81, in *Israel: Its Role in Civilization,* ed. Moshe Davis (New York: Harper and Brothers, 1956). Smith observes that current "evidence from Palestine" indicates that Palestinian Judaism (in addition to Diasporic Judaism) "was profoundly influenced by Hellenism," as indicated by (for example) archaeological discoveries at Bet Shearim, the most famous burial ground of Rabbinic Judaism, where various Greek trappings and sentiments have been discovered (p. 68). Smith's judgment has received substantial reinforcement by Martin Hengel's definitive work, *Judaism and Hellenism: Studies in their Encounter in Palestine during the Early Hellenistic Period,* trans. John Bowden (Philadelphia: Fortress Press, 1974), 2 vols.

[26]See C. K. Barrett, ed., *The New Testament Background: Selected Documents* (New York: Harper Torchbooks,

100

1961), pp. 175-77. On the other hand, Flavius Josephus (ca. 37-100 C.E.) represents something of a contrast to Philo. Charles Guignebert, *The Jewish World in the Time of Jesus* (New York: University Books, 1959), writes that although Josephus was both Romanized and Hellenized, his "religion was much more akin to that of the Pharisees than of Philo. Fundamentally he remained a Jew—and, in certain respects, a good Jew; he was in the gospel sense, a Herodian" (p. 17).

[27] Cyrus H. Gordon in *The Common Background of Greek and Hebrew Civilizations* (New York: Harper and Row, 1962; W. W. Norton, 1965), amasses substantial evidence for an East Mediterranean foundation of both Greek and Hebrew cultures. Gordon sees the Nile Delta as the cradle of both Minoan and Hebraic cultures (p. 7), and draws a number of parallels from Near Eastern literature of the second millenium (especially the 15th-10th centuries, B.C. E.) to Homer and the Hebrew Bible. Gordon cites structural and typological similarities in ritual, sacrificial, social, military, and literary motifs between Greek, Hebrew, and other Near Eastern cultures. Examples suggesting a common Near Eastern milieu are parallels between Gilgamesh and Odysseus, and themes from Egyptian tales such as Sinuhe, the Shipwrecked Sailor, Wenamon, and the Eloquent Peasant which recur in the Odyssey and the Bible. Gordon's most startling claim is that the Minoan Linear Script A derives from a Semitic Script. Although Gordon's position underscores the *danger* of considering the Greek and Hebrew traditions in *isolation,* the possible extent of common origins remains widely debated.

[28] W. Windelband, *A History of Philosophy* (New York: MacMillan, 1935), p. 140.

[29] Robert Bellah in his article, "Religious Evolution," in *American Sociological Review,* XXIX, No. 3 (1964): 358-74, calls this "world rejection"—a characteristic which recurs in the various great historical religions.

[30] Guthrie, in *The Greeks and Their Gods,* points out that the tensions in Greece between the Aegean and Homeric cults reflect the tensions of the "religion of the soil" of the native population and the "religion of the sky" of the invaders who were "a wandering people, living by the sword rather than the plough" (pp. 52-53). Richard Rubenstein has noted that the Hebrews' invasion of Canaan produced a comparable tension between the cult of Yahweh and the cult of Ba'al. Guthrie speaks of the contract of Aegean and Homeric cults "as one between a folk whose interest is in the maintenance of uninterrupted fertility" versus "another which is absorbed in battle and conquest and dominion . . ." (p. 35).

[31] Again, it is significant to note Guthrie's description of Zeus, the god of the invading Achaeans: "Before him, man stands helpless as a creature of a lower order altogether. He is immortal, man is mortal; he is all-powerful, man is weak. He is a being entirely external to man, and to get into right relationship with him it is necessary to proceed accordingly, acknowledging his supremacy and placating him with offerings and worship. He is simply a ruler who will brook no rivals" (p. 39).

[32] Philip Wheelwright, ed., *The Presocratics* (New York: Odyssey Press, 1966), p. 20.

[33] Ibid., p. 21.

[34] E. R. Dodds, *The Greeks and the Irrational* (Berkeley: The University of California Press, 1951).

[35] Recent perspectives on cultural transcendence include: A. H. Maslow, *The Farther Reaches of Human Nature* (New York: The Viking Press, 1972), pp. 269-95; Norman O. Brown, *Love's Body* (New York: Vintage Books, 1966); Peter L. Berger, *A Rumor of Angels* (Garden City, N.Y.: Doubleday, 1969; Anchor Books, 1970); Herbert W. Richardson and Donald R. Cutler, eds., *Transcendence* (Boston: Beacon Press, 1969); William A. Johnson, *The Search for Transcendence* (New York: Harper and Row, 1974).

CHAPTER FIVE

CONSPICUOUS STRUCTURES OF CONSCIOUSNESS
FROM ALEXANDER TO THE RENAISSANCE

AS TYPOLOGICAL ANALYSIS, this chapter emphasizes structures of consciousness formative of Western world views from the emergence of Christianity to the Renaissance. This chapter must be selective, so we propose the following chart [see page 102] as a tool for understanding the unfolding of Western cosmologies. The reader may wish to expand the chart.

DIALECTICAL PROCESSES IN WESTERN CULTURE

The chart underscores the importance of history as a *psycho-social process* which follows in general a "give-and-take" dialectical course.

Civilization or human culture is a means of establishing human identity. The historical quest for identity is a dynamic and multi-faceted process; the world pictures which men project into the social or cosmic realm reflect shifting images of themselves through the corridors of time. A particular era of stability, which seems to emerge through the occasional appearance of wise leadership in a situation ripe for transition, seems to dissipate as quickly through the pettiness, narrow vision, static rigidity or vice of lesser men. The chart attempts to portray the crises which have driven men out of "sessile" civilizations or periods in search of new identity, and some of the syntheses that have emerged from such periods of ferment. The chart reflects the bias that only three of these syntheses have proved to be all-encompassing enough in every sphere of life—religion, politics, ethics, art, ideology, etc.—to be called "world" syntheses. By "world" here we do not denote the geographical bounds of these syntheses, but their inclusiveness in Western civilization. The chart attempts to isolate *militant* reactions which have recurred with regularity in our history. By *militant* we mean both military and, in some case, non-military ideological reactions. This approach is intended to set forth in bold relief the integral connection between militancy, insecurity of cultural identity, and dogmatic ideologies (often religious). The chart also illustrates how the world views of the West have ultimately failed to provide a creative cosmic niche for emerging dissident elements. The discussion of both the mechanistic and ecological world views will be reserved for later chapters.

101

DIALECTICAL PROCESSES IN WESTERN CULTURE

Western "World" Syntheses	Principle(s) of Unification	Identity Crises	Militant Reactions	Principles of Justification	New Syntheses
		Hebrew slavery in Egypt	Exodus, Conquest	Election, Revelation	amphictyony, Monarchy
		Divided Kingdom to Fall, Exile	Prophetic and Apocalyptic Vision; Maccabean revolt	Election, Covenant Promises	eclecticism; early Christianity
		Breakdown of Greek City States and failure to achieve unity	Alexander	revenge re Persia; world vision of Hellenism	Alexander's Empire; oikoumene
GRECO-ROMAN: Hellenistic Age culminating in Augustan Rome	oikoumene transformed to Roman political vision and arms	internal dissolution and external threat; Barbarians	"conversion" and mobilization of "Christian" Rome	Kingdom of God	Medieval Christendom
ROMAN–CHRISTIAN Medieval Christendom	Kingdom of God on Earth in Roman Church	Rise of Islam Plagues New Nationalism Failure of Christ to return (1000)	Crusades	Kingdom of God— "stamp out the infidel"	cross-cultural fertilization; Gothic vision to Renaissance; Exploration, etc. Copernicus
		Renaissance	Orthodoxy Religious wars Inquisition	Revelation vs. Reason	Before Enlightenment
GRECO-"CHRISTIAN" in Rationalism and Mechanical Cosmos Newton	Reason, Natural Law, World Cosmos, Deism	Politics based on divine right, aristocratic rule vs. new classes	French and American Revolutions; Romanticism, etc.	Reason, equality natural law, organism	democracy, socialism, communism
		threats to national identity; nationalism	Nazism; world revolutions;	election; national liberation, etc. (natural rights)	
ECOLOGICAL (?) world state	organic interdependence and biological unity	crisis in resources atomic threats political shifts	3rd World, Viet Nam, liberation movements	natural rights democracy	??

STRUCTURES OF CULTURE CONSCIOUSNESS:
EXCLUSIVISM AND WORLD VISION

One of the pervasive attitudes of cultural consciousness is the recurrent stance of identity viewed as a "we" versus a "them." We might conjecture that this attitude is obvious, necessary, perhaps biologically rooted. It is *obvious* because it is a widespread phenomenon not confined to Western culture. It is *necessary* because the establishing of "our" identity seems to entail reference to some others. Also, it appears to be *biologically* rooted since nature itself as we know it exists in a wonderful array of varying species of plants and animals; even "non-organic" natural phenomena seem to exhibit recurrent taxonomic patterns. Therefore the justification for discussing this mode of self-understanding is just its universality, and the particular effects which it seems to manifest in the Western psyche.

In Greek, Hebrew, Roman and Christian consciousness there are strong indications of feelings of superiority with regard to other peoples. In classical Greece the *barbaros* is contrasted with the *hellenes*. *Barbaros* originally means "stammering" or "stuttering" or "uttering unintelligible sounds." The implication of the distinction between Greek and barbarian is that non-Greek speaking peoples utter inferior and less meaningful phrases. (Indeed, Greek was considered to be *the* language of culture well into Roman times, when it was supplanted—but never really replaced—by Latin.) The linguistic roots of this distinction are significant, since (as we have seen) language is one of the primary carriers of culture. The "Babel factor" is undoubtedly a key to the attitudes of suspicion, or even disdain, which persist even in the modern era. Within ancient Egyptian civilization this mistrust or sense of superiority was apparently commonplace:

> (The ancient Egyptian) was semi-urban and sophisticated of mind and felt foreigners to be rustic and uninitiated. He was cut off from his neighbors by sea and desert and felt that he could afford a superior isolationism. He made a distinction between 'men,' on the one hand, and Libyans or Asiatics or Africans, on the other. The word 'men' in that sense meant Egyptians: otherwise it meant 'humans' in distinction to the gods, or 'humans' in distinction to animals. In other words, the Egyptians were 'people'; foreigners were not . . . The concept that only our group is 'folks,' that outsiders lack something of humanity, is not confined to the modern world.[1]

From this statement we might infer that even the concept of "humanity" is culturally defined.

Within classical Hebrew culture the "we"/"them" distinction was equally pronounced. The earliest communal identity grew out of vaguely common patriarchal ties, but more significantly, out of the bond forged by liberation under Moses from Egypt and the long wilderness trek. Of course the culminating event in Hebrew identity was considered to be the Sinaitic Covenant. Out of these historical memories emerged the concept of "election" or "chosen people." Yahweh had announced, "I will be your God and you will be my people." After the liberation, Yahweh's prestige was inflated with each successive victory: the conquest of Canaan, the coalescence of the twelve tribes, and finally the Monarchy under David and Solomon. From an henotheistic tribal deity he became the Lord of Heaven and Earth, beside whom there were no gods. And from an insignificant and heterogeneous band of slaves, the Hebrews became *the* people of Yahweh, specially commissioned to show forth His will (embodied in the Torah) to all nations.

After the classical ages of Greece and Israel, decline and defeat forced intimate contact with, and greater tolerance of, new peoples. It was during the death throes of the states of Israel and Judah that the prophets saw Yahweh as calling all peoples unto himself. Likewise, it was after the decline of the *polis,* and after decades of humiliation at the hands of Persia, that the Macedonian Alexander rallied the Greeks for his brief moment of glory. Out of the cultural ferment that followed, the concept of *oikoumene,* "one inhabited world," became the table-talk for Hellenistic intellectuals. Alexander had established Greek outposts as far south as Egypt and as far east as India. In the years that followed, Hellenism was intermingled with Babylonian, Persian, Egyptian, Syrian, Jewish and a host of other cultural and religious traditions. The second chart, opposite, illustrates the course of the *oikoumene.* Alexander Campbell speaks of an "almost scientific effort" in the new milieu to discover religious analogies. Isis and Demeter, Horus and Apollo, Thot and Hermes, Amun and Zeus were identified. Campbell remarks:

> The Greeks in Bactria and in India identified Krishna with Heracles, Shiva with Dionysus, and in the West the later Romans saw, not only in the Greek gods but also in the Celtic and Germanic, respectable counterparts of their own . . .[2]

Campbell points out that other syncretistic movements had spontaneously developed in history, but this is the first era where trans-cultural *efforts* were made. Greek philosophy and science were enriched by contact with Oriental cults and Babylonian astronomy and mathematics. The cosmologies of Aristarchus and Ptolemy which appeared during this period were to stand largely unchallenged until the time of Copernicus. Mystic traditions from India and the East stimulated the spiritual atmosphere of the age. The Hellenistic Era was a time of widespread ferment, pluralism, and confusion; but out of the cross-cultural encounters emerged the great synthetic ideologies which were to shape the future West: Stoicism, Neoplatonism, Christianity. Moreover, the science of the era has proved to be precocious. The Hellenistic Age is noteworthy for another reason: it is most like our own.

Rome, the inheritor of the Hellenistic legacy, was able to exercise the muscle of *Realpolitik* and seemed to make *oikoumene* a political reality. But the new world order proved to be finally Roman, and the old "civilized"/"bar-

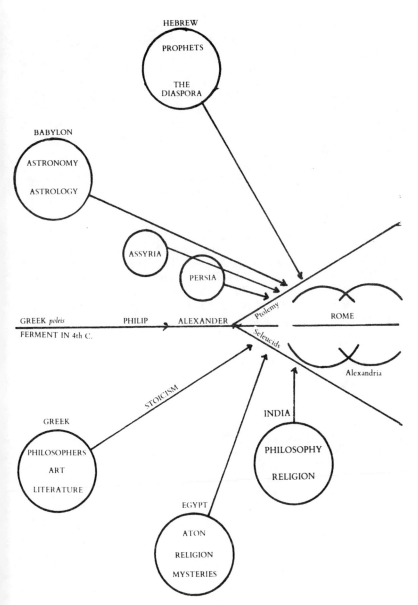

THE MILIEU OF THE HELLENISTIC *oikoumene*

barian" contrast reappeared in new garb. In Rome, "barbarian" (applicable to most peoples outside—and some inside—the Empire) became as severe an approbrium as ever it was in classical Greece, implying "wild," "fierce," "crude" or "uncivilized." Most of all, peoples living outside of what was to become the *Pax Romana,* who did not enjoy the benefits of Roman law or culture, the safety of its military and the convenience of its roads, were simply considered deprived of the essentials of real humanity.

As we turn to early Christianity, we find mixed attitudes. Jesus had seemed at times to speak of God as the Father of all men. But the proper criteria of Christian identity, and the extent of the redemptive work of Christ, were hotly contested from the death of Jesus to the critical Apostolic Assembly (ca. 49 C.E., when Gentile converts were admitted officially on an equal footing with Jewish Christians) and beyond. From Jewish apocalyptic, Christianity adopted the defensive/aggressive stance of militant particularism—polarizing believer from unbeliever, light from darkness, and God from Satan. Apocalyptic warnings of the direst character are also attributed to Jesus by the Gospels. Other influences from Judaism seemed to heighten the tendency toward particularism: the old Torah becoming new Torah in Christ, the old and new covenants, and the Wisdom/Word union applied to Christ. The Church became the New Israel, the true remnant anticipated by the prophets. However, there were some who saw other implications in the prophetic heritage. The New Covenant envisioned by Jeremiah (e.g., chapter 31) affirmed that the Law—to be written on men's hearts—was spiritual and not literal. Thus Paul could say:

> He is a Jew who is one inwardly, and real circumcision is a matter of the heart, spiritual and not literal. His praise is not from men but from God . . . For not all who are descended from Israel belong to Israel . . . it is not the children of the flesh who are the children of God, but the children of the promise who are reckoned as descendants. (Romans 2:29; 9:6-8)

Such a concept strikes at the heart of legalistic and literalistic religion. And the writer of Colossians asserted that in the Body of Christ (a concept of Rabbinic and/or Stoic origin)[3] "there cannot be Greek and Jew, circumcised and uncircumcised, barbarian, Scythian, slave, free man, but Christ is all, and in all" (Colossians 3:11). Particularly radical is the inclusion of "barbarian, Scythian, slave," the dregs of humanity for Roman society, and "uncircumcised"—which meant both "unclean" and "outside the Covenant" to Judaism. The Scythian, with his bloodthirsty customs, was considered by both Greek and Roman to be an almost sub-human species. But this universal understanding of the Christian revelation was finally eclipsed by the apocalyptic disposition to particularism.[4] In the end the distinction between the "saved" and the "damned" became the predominant legacy of the new religion, although the larger vision has never been entirely eclipsed.[5]

Once more as we consider the synthesis of the Judeo-Christian and the Greco-Roman components in the West, we are struck by a pernicious conflation. The Judeo-Christian distinction between "elect" and "damned," wedded with the Greco-Roman distinction between "civilized" and "barbarian" has evolved a culture which has generally considered itself the "believing civilized" world, and has patronized or pitied the "unbelieving uncivilized" world of non-Western cultures. Such has often been the motivating force of "Christian Civilization," from the militant Crusades to "conversions" of all sorts of indigenous peoples in the New World, Africa and the East, both by sword and by the Word. The same kind of attitude— perhaps slightly more veiled—often seems to inform Western foreign policy and diplomacy in the twentieth century. Undoubtedly, for example, much of the hostility towards communist Russia has stemmed from the fact that she has often been viewed as an "Asiatic" or at least chiasmal people—traversing the territory between East and West, between Christian and pagan.[6] The triumph and successes of materialistic communism in Russia have posed not only a political and military threat, but an uncomfortable challenge to the delicate web of "superior" identity of the Christian West. One cause of widespread anomie and confusion in Western Civilization in recent decades is the breakdown of historic cultural presumptions in the face of the dawning pride and power of divergent peoples around the world. It is very difficult indeed to continue to consider Western Civilization as God's established pattern for humanity. We all must now come to grips with the cross-cultural currents of a Neo-Hellenistic Age.

PATRIARCHY AND HIERARCHY

Patriarchal structure is deeply imbedded in Roman culture. The earliest unit of social organization was a kinship group called the *gens*.[7] But the most important social unit was the family, ruled by the absolute authority of the father—the *pater familias*.[8] The title *patres* was also given to the wealthy aristocrats who attained power among the *gentes*. From the word *patres* we derive the designation *patrician,* and "the rest of the people were called *plebs* or *plebians,* which seems to mean the filling or the mass."[9] The patriarchal family remained the central institution in Roman society, and included the sons and their wives, unmarried daughters, clients and slaves.[10] Incipient within the hierarchical structure of the family was the later authoritarianism of the Empire. Julius Caesar was first bestowed with the title *pater patriae,* and after him Augustus. And just as the father exercised life and death prerogatives within the family, so the emperor assumed these prerogatives for the Empire. With Augustus the *pater patriae* was but a prelude. Upon his death his *apotheosis* was declared, and in the tradition of Near Eastern kings, he was deified and listed among the gods. Excluding the escapades of the mad Caligula, this trend reached its height with Domitian (81-96), who assumed the title *dominus et deus,* lord and god."[11] Already in Augustus' day the expression *senatus populusque Romanus* had entered the final stage of becoming mere myth.

The triumph of monarchy in Rome was not hindered by the *ethos* of the family. The pervasive theme of Vergil's *Aeneid* is the glorified *pietas*—the loyalty owed to the proper hierarchical structures of family, country and gods. *Pietas* implies reverence, patriotism, willingness for self-sacrifice. The Empire becomes a *projection* of the family, an *extended family* under the fatherhood of the emperor. Aeneas asserts his *pietas* to his father Anchises as Troy is burning: "You think, sir, I could take one step and leave you here? Monstrous! This, from a father's lips"; so Romans would come to regard their duty to the emperor. Aeneas himself, upon the death of Anchises, becomes the new *pater* of his people, sculpted by Vergil as a prototype of Augustus.

The Roman authoritarian principle—rooted in the family and buttressed by the imperial assumption of Near Eastern kingly titles of divinity—converged with Judeo-Christian tradition in varied, but significant ways. The Hebrews had a patriarchal family structure, and the idea of Yahweh as Father evolves historically. Philo spoke of God as Father in a philosophical vein. Maximus of Tyre wrote in the second century, B.C.E.:

> God Himself, the father and fashioner of all that is, older than the Sun or the Sky, greater than time and eternity and all the flow of being, is unnameable by any lawgiver, unutterable by any voice, not to be seen by any eye. But we, being unable to apprehend His essence, use the help of sounds and names and pictures . . . yearning for the knowledge of Him, and in our weakness naming all that is beautiful in this world after His nature—just as happens to earthly lovers . . . If a Greek is stirred to the remembrance of God by the art of Phidias, an Egyptian by paying worship to animals, another man by a river, another by fire—I have no anger for their divergences; only let them know, let them love, let them recall.[12]

This striking and evocative passage illustrates that the metaphor of God as Father must have been abroad in the Hellenistic world; yet the words are those of a philosopher (though their religious value is not to be denied). We find similar references in Stoicism. Jesus speaks of God as Father in personal, existential, or even mystical tones in the Gospel of John. Yet the sudden proliferation of references to God as Father in first century Christianity must surely have not been hindered, if not specifically inspired, by the Roman honor due the *pater familias.* Although Jew and Christian alike were offended by the divine titles assumed by the emperors, the mark of patriarchal hierarchy is clearly demonstrable in the emerging Christian tradition.

Christian organization of the churches was at first loosely patterned after the Jewish synagogue with its lay preacher; but soon, influenced by the Temple priesthood and Roman hierarchy, authoritarianism triumphed. The structure of the Medieval Church reflects a Judeo-Roman rarefaction quite removed from the early community of believers. The church in the book of Acts is a far cry from the elaborate monarchial episcopate. The later use of the titles "priest" and "father"—the Roman bishop becoming the "Holy Father" or the Pope—evinces a highly-evolved stratification. We can identify at least three essential roots of the medieval hierarchy: the traditional Jewish priesthood, the Roman hierarchy resembling the authoritarian family, and the Neoplatonic "chain of being" (a topic for later discussion).

Before passing judgment on the Romans, we should consider several factors. First, in the ancient Near East authoritarianism and hierarchy were the norms, not the exceptions. Secondly, not all of the emperors of Rome arrogated to themselves divine status. C. N. Cochrane remarks that the precedent set by Augustus "imposed a nemesis" upon his successors "from which there could be no escape."[13] Tiberias begged the senate to remember that he was only a man; and the dying Vespasian remarked with grim irony, "I suppose I'm becoming a god."[14] We must conclude that there is further irony in the legacy of Rome, which at its best *was* a kind of world family. As Cochrane notes in another context:

> Amid the wreckage of empires founded on tyranny and exploitation it stood alone as the project of a world-community united by ties of the spirit. As such, it was genuinely *political;* it went beyond race, beyond colour, and, in all but a few exceptional instances, beyond religion . . . Under the aegis of Eternal Rome, Greek and Latin, African, Gaul, and Spaniard remained free to lead their own lives and achieve their own destiny . . . But, while local and racial differences continued to exist, citizens of the empire discovered a bond of community with one another on the plane of natural reason. It was on this account that the Roman order claimed a universality and a finality to which alternative systems of life could not pretend.[15]

But the world family of Rome was to become a specifically Christian family in the Middle Ages. Although the writer of Ephesians could say "I bow my knees before the Father, from whom every family in heaven and on earth is named . . . ," it became propitious to belong to one family—the Christian family—as the Jews of the Middle Ages were to discover.

LAW

As a seminal structure of Western consciousness the concept of law cannot be overestimated. Roman Law is the epitome of the predisposition to order and tradition which characterizes the Roman mind. Caldwell writes regarding the early Roman Republic:

> Controlling all Roman activities were the *mores majorum,* the customs of the ancestors. Tradition prevailed in the constitution, in law, in religion, in education, and in daily life. Discipline and conservatism were the keynotes of these customs.[16]

Roman law itself began in the early regal period under the authority of the king delegated to the pontiffs, who oversaw the *fas* or religious law as well as the emerging *jus civile* or civil law. In the fifth century B.C.E. the famed Twelve Tables were published. In this prototypical code the rules of the court were established, and the laws regulating debt, family life, property, and criminal acts were recorded.[17] Caldwell remarks that these tables "were the product of a people, literal-minded and narrow, but with a great sense of justice."[18] Eventually the influence of the Twelve Tables was virtually superseded through new interpretations and changes of customs primarily brought about through the praetors or magistrates. With Augustus, certain eminent jurists were given the right to deliver opinions. In the following years their opinions came to constitute a veritable science of law.

Roman law in its developed form consisted of three divisions. The *jus civile* or civil law was fundamentally the law of Rome and her citizens, including the statutes of the Senate, the decrees of the Princeps, the edicts of the praetors and customs from antiquity which carried the force of law.[19] The *jus gentium,* or law of the peoples, was a basically new idea, not confined to a particular state, but considered to be applicable to men of all nations.

> It was the law which authorized the institutions of slavery and private ownership of property and defined the principles of purchase and sale, partnership, and contract.[20]

The final branch of law, the *jus naturale,* developed in the Empire under Stoic influence. "Natural law" remained primarily on an ideal level—a universal concept developed in conjunction with a universal state. Cicero affirmed

> True law is right reason consonant with nature, diffused among all men, constant, eternal. To make enactments infringing this law, religion forbids, neither may it be repealed even in part, nor have we power through Senate or people to free ourselves from it.[21]

This concept of natural law influenced the *jus civile* and the *jus gentium* so that:

> The power of the father of the family was weakened; the harsh rules regarding slaves were softened; women gained control over their property; and the principle that an accused was innocent until proved guilty was firmly established.[22]

Between C.E. 529 and 535, Justinian, the Emperor of Byzantium, commissioned the famous *Corpus Juris Civilis* or *Institutes*. This codification of the law for the Empire included "an elementary treatise on the principles of the law, a digest . . . of the written opinions of the great jurists, and a code made up from the *constitutions* of the earlier emperors."[23] With new rulings appended, this code became the foundation of medieval law, and is reflected in the body of modern law. Justinian's code reflects the Roman heritage, the Stoic concept of natural law, and is dedicated "In the name of our Lord Jesus Christ."

The final Christianizing of Rome, and the Romanizing of Christianity, reflect among other things a mutual disposition towards law. We need hardly comment how important the Torah was in Jewish tradition. Christians could see in the Roman concern for justice a dim reflection of the eschatological law of God promised by Isaiah and Micah:

> It shall come to pass in the latter days
> that the mountain of the house of the Lord

> shall be established as the highest of the mountains,
> and shall be raised up above the hills;
> and peoples shall flow to it,
> and many nations shall come. . .
> For out of Zion shall go forth the law,
> and the word of the Lord from Jerusalem.
> He shall judge between many peoples,
> andf shall decide for strong nations afar off . . .
> (Micah 4:1-3)

Although Augustine believed that the City of God was eternal, and its order permanent, even the earthly city could reflect some temporal order. Augustine's conviction that he was living in the millenial period between Christ's first and second coming, and that the devil was "restrained," must have contributed to the mounting credibility of Roman law as a useful temporal device to restrain evil. In the meantime the heavenly city was calling "citizens of all nations," creating "a society of pilgrims of all languages."[24] Furthermore, as the Medieval Church grew in power and prestige, the body of canon law—reflecting the decisions of councils, creeds, theologians and popes—drew heavily from Roman sources such as Justinian.

The triumph of Roman Christianity entails the victory of what we have called "sessile consciousness." Both in the vertical structure of hierarchy and the horizontal "symmetrical" structure of law (which puts everything in its appropriate spatial relationship), the spatial, conservative disposition had triumphed. The early Christian concept of the transcendence of law by grace and by the Spirit, gave way to new patterns of external orders and rigid rules. Cicero had once remarked:

> Cato used to say that the superiority of our city to others depended upon the fact that the latter almost always had their laws and institutions from a single legislator . . . whereas our republic was not created by the genius of any individual, nor in the lifetime of one man but through countless centuries and generations.[25]

Just so, tradition, order and propriety, as well as formal law, evolved as norms of Western consciousness. Cicero also enumerated what we would call the basic nomistic principles of Western Civilization:

> As for the foundations of this social security, to be defended even at the cost of life and limb, I may enumerate them as follows: the official religion of worship and divinization, executive authority, senatorial influence, statute and customary law, the popular courts and magisterial jurisdiction, good faith, the provinces and allies, imperial prestige, military and financial strength.[26]

These principles are especially concordant with Stoicism, and we shall turn to Marcus Aurelius as representative of the embodiment of such sessile structures in the Stoic cosmic scheme.

The World Cosmos of Marcus Aurelius

Marcus Aurelius succeeded Antonius Pius in 161 C.E. Marcus was a humble man, not ambitious for power, and his *Meditations* are an excellent paradigm of the wedding of Stocism with Roman life—an expression of the Roman legacy at its best. Hallie[27] cites four elements in early Greek philosophy assumed by Stoicism: Heraclitus' doctrine of the *logos,* an all-pervasive rational principle (or law of nature), and his doctrine of change; Megarian logic; the Cynics' doctrine that nature is superior to local conventions, and their belief in the "autonomy of the virtuous man"; and Socrates' exemplification of the rational life.

Stoicism itself, "founded" by Zeno around 300 B.C.E., underwent a protracted evolutionary development; what we see in Marcus is a thoroughly Romanized Stoicism, less interested in the intricacies of logic or cosmology, more concerned with practical affairs of Roman life and ethics. Nevertheless, what Marcus does say about *cosmos* illustrates the world picture tacit in his ethical reflections. Rome itself never developed an official world picture or philosophical cosmology. The best we can do is suggest the hidden assumptions behind the ofttimes turbulent course of the Empire: the patriarchal and familial hierarchy, the legal disposition, and the *ethos* of militancy. Stoicism most closely approximates a Roman cosmology.

First of all, we see in Marcus' reflections the inimitable Stoic and Roman propensity for order. The first principle of Stoic order is the monistic unity of the universe:

> One should continually think of the universe as one living being, with one substance and one soul—how all it contains falls under its one unitary perception, how all its actions derive from one impulse, how all things together cause all that happens, and the nature of the resulting web and pattern of events.[28]

For the Stoics the cosmos is a rational whole, a perfect sphere, held together by God or the *logos* and permeated by the divine fire. A function of the world order is cyclical death and rebirth. *Change* is therefore necessary and natural—yet it is *regulated* change, itself following orderly patterns.

> Observe continually all that is born through change, and accustom yourself to reflect that the nature of the Whole loves nothing so much as to change existing things and to make similar new things. All that exists is in a sense the seed of what will be born from it, but you regard as seeds only those which are cast into the earth or the womb. But that is too unenlightened.[29]

For man there is one life to be maximized, and death, as natural, is not to be feared:

> Now, if ever, you must realize of what kind of ordered universe you are an emanation, that a time limit has now been set for you and that if you do not use it to come out into the light, it will be lost, and you will be lost, and there will be no further opportunity.[30]

> What is the nature of death? When a man examines it in itself, and with his share of intelligence dissolves the imaginings which cling to it, he conceives it to be no other than a function of nature, and to fear a natural function is to be only a child. Death is not only a function of nature but beneficial to it.[31]

Death, a dissolving into the natural elements from which one is born, is simply a part of the *order* of things.

Within the vision of world order, providence (*pronoia*) plays an important role, ruling both necessity (natural physical laws) and chance (the realm of autonomy, pervaded by omnipresent reason):

> The works of the gods are full of Providence. The works of Chance are not divorced from Nature or from the spinning and weaving together of those things which are governed by Providence. Thence everything flows. There is also Necessity and what is beneficial to the whole ordered universe of which you are a part. That which is brought by the nature of the Whole, and preserves it, is good for every part . . .[32]

Providence is indeed the guidance of *logos* throughout the cosmos, or of *pneuma* (spirit)—both world spirit and the portion in the individual, guiding each to a proper destiny:

> . . . there remains as characteristic of the good man that he loves and welcomes whatever happens to him and whatever his fate may bring, that he does not pollute the spirit established within his breast or confuse it with a mass of impressions and imaginings, but preserves it blameless, modestly following the divine, saying nothing but what is true, doing nothing but what is just.[33]

Marcus advised that one should nourish the soul with the following reflection:

> "Nothing will happen to me which is not in accord with the nature of the Whole," and second, "It is possible for me to do nothing contrary to the god and the spirit within me, for there is no one who can compel me to do so."[34]

The latter statement of Marcus Aurelius is illustrative of the paradox within Stoicism, indeed a Roman paradox, between necessity and action. Within the Hellenistic world, fate (*moira*) or necessity (*ananke*) was a veritable god. Yet both Stoicism and Roman life are geared towards the exercise of free will in the pursuit of duty. The solution for Stoicism lies within the monistic conception of a rational cosmos. Exercising reason, man *will* choose the provident course and secure peace. Yet even so, one cannot go against his fate; to do so only brings distress. World *order* therefore results in an *ethos* of duty and a peculiar life style.

The whole pragmatic life of the Stoic is defined by the knowledge that he is a microcosm of the macrocosm; the accompanying norm, reiterated endlessly, is that one should "live in accordance with nature" (*kata phusin*). Through such a life, man will achieve *apatheia* ("spiritual peace") or *euthymia* ("well being") or *eudaimonia* ("happiness of the soul"). "To live in accord with nature" is to pursue a rational life of duty and virtue, and to flee passion.

Marcus remembers with gratitude his Stoic mentors, and remarks that with their inspiration

> nothing stops me from living in accord with nature, and if I still fall short of this it is through my own fault . . . (I am thankful) that I had no sexual realtions with Benedicta or Theodotus, and that even later when erotic passion came to me, I retained my health . . .[35]

The Stoic temper is one of sobriety and endurance; distrustful of emotions, it is undoubtedly what Freud would call "repressed." But in terms of the Roman character, Stoicism fit. Caldwell[36] points out that even in the Early Republic *virtus, gravitas,* and *pietas* were the ruling virtues. *Pietas* we have mentioned; *gravitas* refers to sobriety of disposition and outlook. Marcus Aurelius speaks of "endurance and frugality," and in enumerating additional lessons learned from others he says:

> From Diognetus: to avoid frivolous enthusiasms; to distrust what miraclemongers and magicians say about charms, exorcising spirits, and the like; not to keep quails for cock-fights or get excited about such sports; to tolerate plain-speaking; to be at home in philosophy and attend the lectures . . . to write dialogues when still a boy; to want to sleep on a pallet or on hides, and other such things as the Greeks are trained to.[37]

Furthermore, Marcus speaks of being "the same man always, when in great pain, at the loss of a child, or during a long illness."[38] And another similar expression of imperturbability reads, "to show no trace of anger or any other passion,"[39] or, to "rid yourself of all aimless thoughts, of all emotional opposition to the dictates of reason."[40]

As a strongly conservative philosophy, and although accepting orderly change, Stoicism distinctly fears novelty. Marcus records that he has learned

> never to lack good taste nor to pursue novelty for its own sake . . . (or) not to be always chopping and changing, moving from place to place and from one course of action to another . . .[41]

At the same time, Stoicism has definite liberal ideals, the most pronounced of which is tolerance, based upon a cosmic commonalty of all persons. Although in public life one must necessarily encounter churlish and obnoxious people, Marcus wants always to remember that

> the nature of the wrongdoer is of one kin with mine—not indeed of the same blood or seed, but sharing the same mind, the same portion of the divine . . . I cannot feel anger against him who is of my kin, nor hate him.[42]

Finally, part and parcel of the microcosm/macrocosm monism (combined with the "extended family" concept of Roman society) is an alert social disposition, so the Stoic always pursues "what is reasonable and for the common good." For the whole world is interconnected:

> everything which shares in a common intelligent nature tends similarly . . . Among rational creatures there are communities, friendships, households, and public meetings, and in war there are treaties and truces. Among still higher beings, though they are far distant from each other, there is union of a kind, like that of the stars. Thus a rise in the scale of beings brings a common feeling even among those who are far apart.[43]

Marcus points out that this social nature runs throughout the natural world, including bees, or herds of animals. The organic tendency towards orderly groupings and symmetry has attracted renewed interest among sociologists, anthropologists, and ecologists in our own day. Marcus feels that in the human sphere

> An exile is he who flees from social principle; blind, who keeps the eye of his mind closed; a beggar, who has need of another and does not possess within himself all that is of use in life. A tumor on the universe is he who cuts himself off in rebellion against the logic of our common nature . . . He is but a splinter off the community who separates his own soul from that of all rational beings, which is one.[44]

Here again, we have a peculiar tension manifesting itself within Stoicism. On the one hand we have noted the liberality of a universal brotherhood based on nature, yet on the other the judgment that one must *conform* to the common good is a rather conservative implication.

Stoicism—originally a Greek philosophy—found a comfortable home in Roman culture where its world picture could reinforce deeply-engrained facets of Roman consciousness. Conservatism, world order, universality, dispassionate rationality, and realistic acceptance of the state of things combined with belief in the utility of the will, marks points of coalescence with the Roman mentality. Perhaps the most visible legacy of a Stoic world picture is modern-day bureaucracy. Here again we see propensities for order, dispassionate regularity and rationality, "fairness" combined with emotional detachment, change which must be effected through proper preordained (providential) channels, and fear of novelty and impropriety. Missing in modern bureaucracy is nature, and an accompanying cosmic or religious sense (though the adverb "religiously" would apply). Missing, too, is the monistic ethical complex, which in Marcus Aurelius makes the public and private spheres one.

AUGUSTINE AND THE CHRISTIAN SYNTHESIS

Born in 354 C.E. in Tagaste, North Africa, Augustine witnessed the success of Christianity in the waning Roman Empire. Augustine, who at first became a Manichaean and only in 386 adopted a Neoplatonic form of Christianity, is the most articulate spokesman for the Christian Synthesis until scholasticism. Augustine's writings, along with the great creedal definitions of the third and fourth centuries, are keys to understanding the character of Greco-Christian orthodoxy in the ensuing centuries.

As a *Christian* writer, Augustine finds the final norm of truth in the biblical history of salvation culminating in Jesus Christ. But as a *Greco-Christian*, Augustine believes that faith or belief cannot be separated from thought. For "to believe" is "to think with assent."[45] And although revelation is *prior* to reason, the "seeing" of reason, which is understanding, *completes*

faith. Augustine's byword is "believe in order that you may understand."
Thus Augustine conceives of no distinction between philosophy and
theology.[46]

For Augustine, Plato is the philosopher supreme. He affirms

> Those who are praised as having most closely followed Plato—who is
> justly preferred to all the other philosophers of the Gentiles . . . do perhaps
> entertain such an idea of God as to admit that in Him are to be found the
> cause of existence, the ultimate reason for the understanding, and the end in
> reference to which the whole life is to be regulated . . . If, then, Plato
> defines the wise man as one who imitates, knows, and loves this God, and
> who is rendered blessed through fellowship with Him . . . why discuss with
> the other philosophers? It is evident that none come nearer to us than the
> Platonists.[47]

Augustine proceeds to inform us that the Platonists have demonstrated God's
changelessness, His absoluteness, and His creative priority to all things.[48]
Thus

> Plato determined the final good to be to live according to virtue and
> affirmed that he only can attain to virtue who knows and imitates God . . .
> Therefore he did not doubt that *to philosophize is to love God* . . .[49]

Augustine notes that for Plato the "true and highest good" is God[50] and
"we prefer these (Platonists) to all other philosophers and confess that they
approach nearest to us."[51] But why are the Platonists so near to the biblical
doctrine of God? For his answer, as Philo before him, Augustine interprets
Exodus 3:14 as "I am He who *is*"—indicative of God's immutable and
unchangeable nature. Here is the classical case of misunderstanding from the
conflation of Hebrew and Platonic cosmologies. Plato's concept of static,
unchanging Being is impressed upon the Hebrew historical and existential
framework. Exodus 3:14 refers not to God's abstract Being, but to his promise
of his concrete historical presence and activity among his people. The
Hebrew text should be rendered something like "I will become what I will
become" or "I will cause to happen what I will cause to happen," in either
case indicating God's free, sovereign, and *present* hand in *history*.

In addition to the doctrine of God, Augustine is indebted to Platonic
dualism. For both Plato and Augustine, the eternal world of Truth (ideas,
forms) is superior to the changing world of the senses. Moreover, the soul is
superior to the body, and the world of spirit to the world of matter. Truth is
independent of the senses (and thus empirical verification). "Here Augustine
discovered the universality, necessity and immutability"[52] of truth. Truth
exists as *a priori* knowledge in the *Divine Mind.* Augustine defines blessedness
with this classical ring: "Man is blessed when all his actions are in harmony
with reason and truth."[53] "Law" likewise is not simply the historical
revelation of Yahweh, but exists as eternal cosmic principle.

In addition to the ontological dualism absorbed from Plato, Augustine reflects a dualism from another source—the *cosmic* dualism of his Manichaean background. Like their Zoroastrian forebears in Persia, the Manichaeans divided the cosmos into two primal warring principles, Light and Darkness. The realm of light is associated with the world of spirit; the domain of darkness with the world of matter. Augustine evinces this predisposition in his interpretation of Genesis 1:3-4, "God divided the light from the darkness; and God called the light Day, and the darkness he called Night." Augustine takes this to mean that God separated the good and evil angelic forces:

> But between that "light" which is the holy company of the angels spiritually radiant with the illumination of the truth, and that opposing "darkness" which is the noisome foulness of the spiritual condition of those angels who are turned away from the light of righteousness, only He Himself could divide . . .[54]

Again we see that Augustine has imported an alien principle to interpret this Hebrew cosmogonic myth.

Furthermore, Augustine incorporates a final dualism—the *historical* or *ethical* dualism of the biblical tradition, based on the myth of the Fall and Original Sin:

> For God, the author of natures, not of vices, created man upright; but man, being of his own will corrupted, and justly condemned, begot corrupted and condemned children. For we all were in that one man, since we all were that one man who fell into sin by the woman who was made from him before the sin . . . And thus, from the bad use of free will, there originated that whole train of evil which, with its concatenation of miseries, convoys the human race from its depraved origin, as from a corrupt root, on to the destruction of the second death . . .[55]

Augustine believes that the punishment of the first sin has resulted in the corruption of the body:

> For the corruption of the body, which weighs down the soul, is not the cause but the punishment of the first sin; and it was not the corruptible flesh that made the soul sinful, but the sinful soul that made the flesh corruptible.[56]

The historical and ethical dualism of the Christian myth is used here as a causative factor in justifying a position which is more distinctly Neoplatonic or Manichaean—the denigration of the body. In envisioning an initial fall of certain angels (and chiefly the devil himself) as the source of cosmic conflict, Augustine reiterates the Zoroastrian scheme he was taught in his Manichaean days.

We have cited only a few examples in Augustine of the effects of the Greco-Christian Synthesis. The commingling of components from discordant world views often destroys the original integrity of those world views—as we suggested in discussing the relationship of Hebrew historical guilt to Greek natural (or ontic) guilt. In Augustine we see an eclectic mixture of Persian Manichaeism, Greek Neoplatonism and Judeo-Christian biblicism. The result is similar: all this-worldly or human avenues of escape or integrity are cut off, so that Augustine can say of man's condition, apart from God's supernatural salvation:

> But man did not so fall away as to become absolutely nothing: but, being turned towards himself, his being became more contracted than it was when he clave to Him who supremely is. Accordingly, to exist in himself, that is, to be his own satisfaction after abandoning God, is not quite to become a nonentity but to approximate to that.[57]

The verdict on the condition of fallen man is acute. Man's sin not only renders him *historically* culpable, but rips loose the roots of his being from God's substantive Being, casting the fragile human self on the brink of nothingness. With the union of these divergent strands, the classical avenues of human identity and fulfillment are cut off. *Ontological dualism* robs the historicism or existentialism of the Hebrew *ethos* of potency. The *cosmic dualism* of light and darkness, or good and evil, fractures the world order as an arena of spiritual powers. There can be no "living according to nature" since nature is rent asunder. Finally, the biblical *historical and ethical dualism* pronounces *reason* and *will* ultimately unreliable. Augustine can give the rational faculty a role *post*-revelation. To be trustworthy, reason must be subsumed always under the aegis of revelation, and may be invoked only *after* belief is already enjoined.

Little wonder, then, that Augustine's "philosophy of history" should embody the end result of these dualisms. The City of God alone is the proper domain for understanding God's cosmic purposes, whereas the city of man is a source only of error and darkness. It is this legacy that shapes a good deal of European history in the Middle Ages until—contrary to Augustine's expectations—Christ does not return in the eleventh century. Then the intolerable subjugation of man's autonomous faculties begins to slacken in the rise of scholasticism and the quest for new syntheses. Of course, the picture is far more complex than we have suggested, since political struggles, wars, famines, plagues and shifting economic conditions all contributed to the course of events. However, Augustine's eclectic synthesis is largely revived in the Protestant Reformation, and remains formative in rationalistic Protestant orthodoxy until this day. Scholasticism, and especially St. Thomas's revival of Aristotle, mollified the dilemma somewhat in the Catholic tradition. With the Renaissance a new era of conflict begins, pitting the forces of reason and empirical knowledge against revelation.

ROOTS OF MEDIEVAL COSMOLOGY

The Greco-Christian Synthesis reaches its fullest expression in the medieval world picture. Authur O. Lovejoy, in his masterly treatise *The Great Chain of Being*,[58] enumerates four principles in medieval cosmology deriving mainly from Neoplatonism: the Principle of Plenitude, the Principle of Emanation, the Principle of Continuity and the Principle of Hierarchy (which Lovejoy calls "unilinear gradation").

The Principle of Plenitude stems from Plotinus' belief that Plato's eternal forms are reflected fully in temporal counterparts:

> The Absolute would not be what it is if it gave rise to anything less than a complete world in which the 'model,' i.e., the totality of ideal forms, is translated into concrete realities.[59]

Emanation is correlate to Plenitude. All of the cosmos flows forth or emanates out of the ineffable "One." For Plotinus, the "One" is known through the *nous* (the intellectual-spiritual principle) which is the image of the One, though not as sublime. At the third level exists the Soul which descends still further, creating the material order (which for Plotinus mirrors the symmetry and beauty beheld by the Soul in the pure realm of being). Individual souls enter bodies because of the appetite to create, but are immortal and ultimately separate from the body.

The third principle, Continuity, ultimately derives from Aristotle. All quantities must be continuous and contiguous, not completely separate or discrete. The phenomenal world, including all organisms, is interlinked by a series of forms. Aristotle asserts that Nature

> passes so gradually from the inanimate to the animate that their continuity renders the boundary between them indistinguishable; and there is a middle kind that belongs to both orders. For plants come immediately after inanimate things . . . (and seem) in comparison with other bodies, to be clearly animate; but compared with animals to be inanimate. And the transition from plants to animals is continuous; for one might question whether some marine forms are animals or plants, since many of them are attached to the rock and perish if they are separated from it.[60]

From this principle springs the organic interdependence of the medieval cosmos.

Finally, there is the Principle of Hierarchy. Hierarchy, as we have noted, derives cultural force from Roman patriarchal society, and philosophical substance from Neoplatonism. The single most important source of the hierarchical structure is the sixth century writer Pseudo-Dionysus. Steeped in the thought of Proclus the Neoplatonist, a man anonymous to us wrote four influential treatises entitled *Celestial Hierarchy, Ecclesiastical Hierarchy, On Divine Names,* and *Mystical Theology.* Especially from the first two of these works medieval culture drew its cosmology—a Neoplatonic hierarchy thinly cloaked in Christian terminology. This scheme was attributed to Dionysus the Areopagite, a disciple of St. Paul (Acts 17:34).

The hierarchical scheme of Dionysus dominated not only medieval cosmology, but as Lovejoy remarks "down to the late eighteenth century many philosophers, most men of science, indeed most educated men"[61] were to affirm this world picture. In it the universe is depicted as a "holy order" ordained by God, a celestial hierarchy descending by stages to the ecclesiastical hierarchy. The celestial hierarchy consists (in order of descent) of seraphim, cherubim, thrones, dominions, powers, authorities, principalities, archangels and angels. Throughout this heavenly order diffuses the radiancy of God's light, reaching its pinnacle of brilliance as it approaches the divine source. On the terrestrial level, the ecclesiastical hierarchy, likewise manifesting degrees of spirituality, descends from Jesus to three triads: chrism, communion, and baptism; bishops, priests and deacons; and monks, laity and catechumens.[62] We see in these orders the "baptized" version of Plotinus' and Proclus' cosmological pictures of the ineffable "One" which, through successively descending emanations from itself, creates the universal order.

With medieval cosmology "the world separates itself into a lower and a higher, into a sensible and an intelligible world."[63] These worlds stand in polar antithesis to one another, yet are connected by mediating links. The soul, by following the established hierarchy, attempts to wing its way out of the material world, the lowest order, up the rungs of the spiritual ladder of being towards God. This order is demonstrably explicit in the iconography and sculpture of the Romanesque cathedral. Fleming remarks

> In such a divine order, nothing could be left to chance; and all life had to be brought into an organizational plan that would conform to this cosmic scheme of things. The stream of authority, descending from Christ through St. Peter to his papal successors, flowed out from Rome in three main directions. The Holy Roman emperor received his crown from the hands of the Roman pontiff, and, in turn, all the kings of the Western world owed him homage, and on downward from the great lords to the humblest serf, all of whom had a preordained place in this great cosmic plan.[64]

The two remaining tributaries included the clerical succession from Rome through the bishops to the lower clergy, and finally monastic orders whose abbots owed their allegiance to the pope.

The imposition of this Neoplatonic cosmic scheme upon Christian Europe produced certain tensions which contributed to the later Renaissance. Whitehead claims that "faith in the possibility of science . . . is an unconscious derivative of medieval theology."[65] Although he is alluding to the assumption of the rationality of nature, the fact that the medieval cosmos was a total world picture—holistically *locating* all natural and social phenomena in a rational order—prefigures the efforts of later cosmologists to discover a single world order subject to ineluctable laws.

Moreover, borrowing an expression from Heraclitus, "the way up is the way down" or conversely, "the way down is the way up." In the era prior to the eleventh century we see a world despairing of the material order, racked by plagues and political dissolution, and anticipating the return of Christ; in the twelfth century we begin to witness a resurgence of faith which culminates in the renewed belief in spiritual possibility symbolized by the Gothic cathedral. In other words, there is a gradual emerging awareness in medieval man that he is not *trapped* at the bottom of the chain of being, but can in fact begin a gradual ascent towards a fuller humanity (based on mystical vision). If in Gothic mysticism the vision is of the *divine*, the emphasis soon shifts ground from that which is seen to the *seer*, and with refurbished belief in his own rational and spiritual capacities, Western man enters upon a new era.

THE BREAKDOWN OF THE GRECO-CHRISTIAN SYNTHESIS

In Pico's famous *Oration on the Dignity of Man* he says

> At last it seems to me I have come to understand why man is the most fortunate of creatures and consequently worthy of all admiration and what precisely is that rank which is his lot in the universal chain of Being—a rank to be envied not only by brutes but even by stars and by minds beyond this world.[66]

For Pico man's position in the scheme of things is not to be lamented but celebrated. When the world was created "as Moses and Timaeus bear witness," God, the Divine Craftsman, created man. *Moses* and *Timaeus*— perhaps here is the first reunion of these two as equals since Philo. For Pico, God's first words to man were:

> Neither a fixed abode nor a form that is thine alone nor any function peculiar to thyself have we given thee, Adam, to the end that according to thy longing and according to thy judgment thou mayest have and possess what abode, what form, and what functions thou thyself shalt desire . . . Thou, constrained by no limits, in accordance with thine own free will, in whose hand we have placed thee, shalt ordain for thyself the limits of thy nature. We have set thee at the world's center that thou mayest . . . observe whatever is in the world. We have made thee neither of heaven nor of earth, neither mortal nor immortal, so that . . . thou mayest fashion thyself in whatever shape thou shalt prefer.[67]

Man's destiny is an open question, and Pico cites with equal ease Plato, Aristotle, the Bible, Mohammed, the Pythagoreans, Empedocles, and Zoroaster. Pico is eclectic: "I have ranged through all the masters of philosophy, investigated all books, and come to know all schools."[68]

Although after the Middle Ages the Christian cosmos remained intact for most of Europe (as the subject matter, if not the form, of most Renaissance art suggests), a steady march had begun away from the secure bastion where once everyone and everything had had its divinely preordained place. The rebirth of Aristotle, first signaled by medieval Islam, once more lent credibility to the world of the senses. Averroes filtered Aristotle through Neoplatonism:

> Creation is eternal, by emanations; there is no creation in time, and hence no first man, no Adam and Eve, no Fall. Matter is eternal, and so is that mysterious Intellect of which Aristotle speaks . . . human intellects live on after death only as moments in the single Intellect of mankind. Hence there is no personal immortality, no heaven or hell, and no last judgment.[69]

Obviously such ideas are not congenial to Augustinian orthodoxy.

Lovejoy declares that "it was not the Copernican hypothesis, nor even the splendid achievements of scientific astronomy during the following two centuries"[70] that brought about the great change in cosmology. It was instead the Platonic doctrine of plenitude (which in the Middle Ages was accepted in principle and especially applied to the *biological* sphere), that now was rightfully (as Plotinus intended) extended to the whole cosmos. According to Lovejoy the implications of this extension included:

> 1) the assumption that other planets of our solar system are inhabited by living, sentient, and rational creatures; 2) the shattering of the outer walls of the medieval universe, whether these were identified with the outermost crystalline sphere or with a definite "region" of the fixed stars, and the dispersal of these stars through vast, irregular distances; 3) the conception of the fixed stars as suns similar to ours, all or most of them surrounded by planetary systems of their own; 4) the supposition that the planets in these other worlds also have conscious inhabitants; 5) the assertion of the actual infinity of the physical universe in space and of the number of solar systems contained in it.[71]

Needless to say, these assumptions were not the product of the imagination of the masses, who continued to conceptualize the universe in the old geocentric terms.

Contrary to some modern theorists, the geocentric hypothesis did not grant man a superbly exalted position. In fact

> the whole sublunary region was, of course, incomparably inferior to the resplendent and incorruptible heavens above the moon. Thus Montaigne, still adhering to the older astronomy, could consistently describe man's lowest dwelling place as "the filth and mire of the world, the worst, lowest most lifeless part of the universe, the bottom story of the house." How, then, he demanded, could a creature native to it . . . dare in imagination "to place himself above the circle of the moon and reduce heaven under his feet? . . ."[72]

In 1640 John Wilkins cited one of the objections to the Copernican hypothesis as the "vileness of our earth" which, located in the center, is furthest removed from the incorruptible heavens and is therefore the worst place in the universe.[73] Thus *geocentrism* was integral to the Christian dogma of man's humiliation, and the *heliocentric* theory, which removed man from the "vile center," thereby exalted him.

Actually, the heliocentric location of man hardly disturbed many of the Christian myths. The universe was still centered, still spherical in shape, and still securely walled in.[74] The profound significance of man in the medieval scheme was due, not so much to the shape of the world stage, but to the actions which took place on that stage. These actions could be transferred to a new stage without loss of dramatic impact. The theological contradiction between divine self-sufficiency and the "immeasurable solicitude on the part of Deity itself," where one of the persons of the Godhead could be constrained to become incarnate and secure man's salvation because of "a single natural folly of an unsophisticated pair in Mesopotamia,"[75] could be transferred to a sun-centered stage as well. Furthermore, the cosmic coefficient of man's importance in the Christian scheme included the belief that

> Throughout history lesser beings from the upper world had been busy ministrants to man, while rebel spirits had been scarcely less flatteringly engrossed in the enterprise of his destruction.[76]

Lovejoy quotes from a character in a novel by Zangwill:

> As I was looking at Signorelli's "Descent into Hell," I was thinking how vividly our ancestors enjoyed life, how important each individual soul was, to have the ranged battalions of Heaven and Hell fighting for it. What an intense sense of the significance of life![77]

The real threats to man's secure theological position include the assumption of intelligent life on other planets, or the breakdown of the finitude and symmetry of the universe. Such questions raise fundamental doubts about the unique visitation of this planet by the Son of God, or the singularity of our galaxy—that here alone is the central stage for the divine drama, etc. The militant defensiveness of the Church becomes more comprehensible when we recognize how man's cosmic position in the divine scheme seemed to be threatened by events such as Tycho Brahe's discovery of a nova (new star) in 1572, which challenged the order of the "fixed stars" (and thus the changeless order of God's creation). Bruno was burned at the stake because his "decentralized, infinite, and infinitely populous" universe (derived by simple logic from the Principle of Plenitude) seemed to be an attack upon the cosmic nature of man's salvation within the bounds of a symmetrically-ordered finite universe.[78]

Within the medieval cosmos the human race was the central focus of divine action. The actual denigration of this material world was necessary to salvation and heavenly ascent. Heliocentrism, by exalting the material order, indirectly undermined the scheme of salvation. The cosmic consciousness of the typical medieval man was "sessile" to the core: spatially rigid, hierarchical, geometrically ordered, unchanging. If for some (like Pico) a more flexible cosmic scheme offered freedom for human development, to the defenders of the established geocentric picture it was not a psychological trap, but a secure theological, cosmic and psycho-social home. The threat of anomie—the dissolution of the changeless order—must have sent secret chills of terror through the bones of comprehending churchmen. In this sense, the Renaissance does represent motile consciousness in the budding concerns for cosmic and geographical exploration, political innovation, historical reflection, etc. The Greco-Christian Synthesis—that great conceptual bulwark which had remained essentially untouched for a thousand years—began to tremble to its foundations. From henceforth a life-and-death battle with the resurgent forces of liberated reason and empiricism would mark the course of modernity.

FOOTNOTES

[1]John A. Wilson, "Egypt: The Nature of the Universe," in *Before Philosophy*, H. and H. A. Frankfort, John A. Wilson and Thorkild Jacobsen (Baltimore: Penguin Books, 1972), p. 41.

[2]Alexander Campbell, *The Masks of the Gods: Occidental Mythology* (New York: Viking Press, 1969), p. 240.

[3]The origin of the Body of Christ imagery is unsettled; its use in Colossians may be directed to counter "the Colossian heresy" which W. G. Kummel suggests may be "a form of Jewish Gnosticism combined with Christianity." See Paul Feine, Johannes Behm, and (re-edited by) Werner G. Kummel, *Introduction to the New Testament*, translated by A. J. Mattill, Jr. (Nashville: Abingdon Press, 1966) p. 240. W. D. Davies claims: "Paul accepted the traditional Rabbinic doctrine of the unity of mankind in Adam . . . that the very constitution of the physical body of Adam and the method of its formation was symbolic of the real oneness of mankind . . . Was it not natural, then, that Paul when he thought of the new humanity being incorporated 'in Christ' should have conceived of it as the 'body' of the Second Adam, where there was neither Jew nor Greek, male nor female, bond nor free." See W. D. Davies, *Paul and Rabbinic Judaism* (London: S.P.C.K., 1965), p. 57. For a typical instance of Stoic 'body' imagery, see Marcus Aurelius *Meditations* 8:34. John A. T. Robinson, *The Body: A Study in Pauline Theology* (London: SCM Press, Ltd., 1952), pp. 59-60, footnote 1, cites a number of other Stoic uses of "body" imagery. See also Robin Scroggs, *The Last Adam: A Study in Pauline Anthropology* (Philadelphia: Fortress Press, 1966). Scroggs points out that Paul's concept of Christ as the Second Adam in whom a restored or new humanity appears is definitely drawn from rabbinic eschatological conceptions. See pp. 31; 56 ff.; 70 ff.; 82 ff. However, Scroggs observes that Paul's concept of "image" differs from the rabbis (but is not unlike a concept to be found in Qumran writings), (pp. 70-71). The ethical content of "image" could reflect some Stoic influence. See also Richard Rubenstein, *My Brother Paul* (New York: Harper and Row, 1972), pp. 55 ff., 63; 129 ff. Rubenstein writes: "Paul's dream of a united mankind in which tribal and creedal differences would finally be obliterated was consistent with a compelling strain in Jewish thought . . . Nowhere is Paul more prototypically Jewish than in his strenuous pursuit of this universalist vision. Perhaps the very stringency of Judaism's definition of itself over against the "gentiles" helped to generate the vision of a unified mankind. . . One might speculate that the more particularistic a group becomes, the more likely it is to generate a universalistic ideology as a way out of its own isolation" (p. 129).

[4]See Davies' excellent summary of Rabbinic speculation concerning Adam in chapter three of *Paul and Rabbinic Judaism*. The universality of Adam's body may have provided the model for the radical vision of the unity of all men in Christ, the Second Adam. See above.

[5]As Richard Rubenstein has observed, the universality of all men in Christ already bears a new particularistic qualifier, namely "in Christ." Furthermore, as primitive Christianity emerged as a distinct sect, increasingly predisposed to institutionalization, the transference of emphasis from cosmic brotherhood to sectarian exclusivism becomes more understandable. Indeed, the ambiguity of the term "brotherhood" is instructive. A vision of cosmic brotherhood which is nevertheless predefined and bounded so as to exclude others is implicitly contradictory, since the effective expression of such a vision is the appearance of just another particularistic kinship—sectarian "brotherhood." When the early Christian vision failed to gain immediate universal acceptance, the defensive stance of the new sect subtly shifted the contours of its vision from universal brotherhood to particularistic brotherhood. The absence of the expected *parousia* is yet another pertinent factor.

[6]The concept (however historically accurate or inaccurate) of Russia's "Asiatic" character can "be traced as far back as Herodotus' description of 'Scythia,'" writes Jesse D. Clarkson, *A History of Russia* (New York: Random House, 1961), p. 4. "The West's picture of Russia was largely in terms of Siberia and the wolves, of the knout and the nagaika wielded by presumably Oriental Cossacks . . . In the 1920's the New York *Times* correspondent in Moscow regularly interpreted Russia in the light of her 'Asiatic' character, and even today there are many who think of Stalin as essentially an 'Oriental' despot." In the early twentieth century T. G. Masaryk wrote that "it must be remembered that the Russian crossing the Western frontier speaks of 'going to Europe'" (p. 5).

[7]W. E. Caldwell, *The Ancient World* (New York: Holt, Rinehart and Winston, 1963), p. 338.

[8]Ibid.

[9]Ibid. p. 339

[10]Ibid., p. 361.

[11]Ibid., p. 459.

[12]Maximus of Tyre, "Oration VIII.10," in *Hellenistic Religions: The Age of Syncretism*, ed. Frederick C. Grant (New York: Bobbs-Merrill: The Library of Liberal Arts, 1953), p. 168.

[13]Charles Norris Cochrane, *Christianity and Classical Culture* (London: Oxford University Press, 1968), p. 129.

[14]Ibid.

[15]Ibid. p. 73.

[16]Caldwell, p. 363.

[17]Ibid., pp. 429-30.

[18]Ibid.

[19]Edward McNall Burns, *Western Civilizations: Their History and Culture*, Vol. I (New York: W. W. Norton, 1969), p. 240.

[20]Ibid.

[21]Ibid.

[22]Caldwell, p. 471.

[23]Ibid.

[24]Saint Augustine, *The City of God* (trans. by Marcus Dods) XIX.17.

[25]Cochrane, p. 32.

[26]Ibid., p. 45.

[27]*Encyclopedia of Philosophy*, s.v., "Stoicism," by Philip P. Hallie.

[28]Marcus Aurelius Antoninus, *The Meditations* (trans. by G. M. A. Grube) IV.40.

[29]Ibid., IV.36.

[30]Ibid., II.4.

[31]Ibid., II.12.

[32]Ibid., II.3.

[33]Ibid., III.16.

[34]Ibid., V.10.

[35]Ibid., I.17.

[36]Caldwell, p. 363.

[37]Marcus Aurelius Antoninus, *The Meditations*, I.6.

[38]Ibid., I.8.

[39]Ibid., I.9.

[40]Ibid., II.5.

[41]Ibid., I.16.

[42]Ibid., II.1.

[43]Ibid., IX.9.

[44]Ibid., IV.29.

[45]*The Encyclopedia of Philosophy*, s.v., "St. Augustine," by R. A. Markus.

[46]Ibid.

[47]Saint Augustine, *The City of God*, VIII.4.

[48]Ibid. VIII.6.

[49]Ibid., VIII.8.

[50]Ibid.

[51]Ibid., VIII.9.

[52]Markus, p. 201.

[53]Ibid., p. 202.

[54]Saint Augustine, The City of God, XI.19.

[55]ibid. XIII.14.

[56]Ibid., XIV.3.

[57]Ibid., XIV.13.

[58]Arthur O. Lovejoy, *The Great Chain of Being* (New York: Harper Torchbooks, 1960).

[59]Ibid., p. 54.

[60]Aristotle, *Historia Animalium,* VIII.1 (sec. 588).

[61]Lovejoy, p. 59.

[62]*The Encyclopedia of Philosophy,* s.v., "Pseudo-Dionysus," by E. T. Osborn.

[63]Ernst Cassirer, *The Individual and the Cosmos in Renaissance Philosophy* (New York: Harper Torchbooks, 1964), p. 9.

[64]William Fleming, *Arts and Ideas* (New York: Holt, Rinehart and Winston, Third Ed., n.d.), pp. 155-56.

[65]Alfred North Whitehead, *Science and the Modern World* (New York: The Free Press, 1967), p. 13.

[66]Giovanni Pico Della Mirandola, "Oration on the Dignity of Man," in Ernst Cassirer, Paul O. Kristeller and John H. Randall, Jr., eds., *The Renaissance Philosophy of Man* (Chicago: University Press, 1969), p.223.

[67]Ibid., pp. 224-25.

[68]Ibid., p. 242.

[69]Paul O. Kristeller and John H. Randall, Jr., "General Introduction," in *The Renaissance Philosophy of Man,* p. 10.

[70]Lovejoy, p. 99.

[71]Ibid., p. 108.

[72]Ibid., p. 102.

[73]Ibid.

[74]Ibid., p. 104.

[75]Ibid., p. 103.

[76]Ibid.

[77]Ibid.

[78]Ibid. p. 119.

CHAPTER SIX

THE COSMIC MACHINE

THE PURPOSE of this chapter is to identify the development and character of the mechanical image of the cosmos, which has been the pervasive (though not exclusive) world picture of the modern era. We will first review other cosmic pictures which have preceded its emergence. The chart on page 128 portrays basic contours of the various Western cosmologies.

The Emergence of a Mechanical World Picture

Anaximenes attempted to account for the world order by his theory of the compression and dilation of air, the fundamental element. When compressed, air becomes dense and dark, sinking towards the center of the cosmos. Here the earth is formed. When dilated and rarefied, air becomes hotter and brighter, and because of its lightness moves towards the periphery of the universe.[1] For Anaximenes this explanatory scheme ultimately elicits a picture of the cosmos as a world organism. For the air is the principle of intelligence and justice (compensation) both in men and in the cosmos—in the microcosm and in the macrocosm. The Pythagoreans adopted Anaximenes' basic premises, but with the addition of a value judgment —*why* corruption and decay dwell in the material realm. The Pythagorean answer is ethical and religious: the compressed air is impure, the body is a prison for the immortal soul, and the realm of the upper air and the heavens is the soul's real home. Anaximenes' scheme was monistic; the Pythagoreans' is dualistic—the roots of belief in an ontological split in nature. The Pythagoreans also developed the concept of the cosmos as a mathematical and geometrical harmony, consisting of numerical ratios. As the heavenly bodies revolve, they create a grand symphony of music (the "music of the spheres" of which Kepler later speaks). Plato exhibits strong Pythagorean influence.

Aristotle followed the essential plan mapped out by Anaximenes and Pythagoras, and like Plato, conceived of the whole cosmos as a perfect sphere. His cosmos was

> a vast but finite sphere centered upon the centre of the earth and bounded by the sphere of the fixed stars, which was also the 'prime mover,' the *primum movens* of the scholastics, the originative source of all movement within the universe. Fixed in the centre of the universe was the spherical earth, and surrounding it concentrically were a series of spheres like the skins of an onion. First came the spherical envelopes of the three terrestrial elements, water, air, and fire, respectively. Surrounding the sphere of fire

PROMINENT IMAGES OF THE COSMOS IN THE HISTORY OF THE WEST

ERA	CHARACTER	MODEL	SPACE/TIME	COSMOGONY	ENERGIZING PRINCIPLE
CLASSICAL	Natural	Organism	finite, temporal	set in motion; crafted	Nature = Divine (immanence) Rationally Ordered
MEDIEVAL	Divine	Organism	finite, temporal	created	Deity creates and sustains Nature; Deity transcendent
ENLIGHTENMENT	Divine	Mechanism	finite, temporal	created	Deity creates Nature as self-sustaining machine
MODERN	Natural	Mechanism	finite or infinite	naturally occurred	Nature is a self-sustaining machine
CONTEMPORARY	Natural	Mechanism or Organism	finite or infinite; temporal or eternal	naturally occurred	Nature is the expression of cosmic energy throughout

were the crystalline spheres in which were embedded and carried round, respectively, the moon, Mercury, Venus, the sun, Mars, Jupiter and Saturn, which made up the seven 'planets.' Beyond the sphere of the last planet came that of the fixed stars, and beyond this last sphere—nothing.[2]

Following the Pythagoreans, the world order involved a dualistic split between the lighter eternal and changeless realm (out of which the cosmos emerged) and the heavier realm of decay and time at the center. Implicit within this picture of the world order as a natural organism was an ethical and religious tone. With the exception of the heliocentric view of Aristarchus of Samos (b. 310 B.C.E.) Aristotelian geocentrism predominated, expressed classically in the Ptolemaic and Neoplatonic world pictures (each of which entailed certain modifications, such as Ptolemy's epicycles).

The Judeo-Christian response to the natural organic world picture was mixed. The Pythagorean dualistic premise made the scheme adaptable to the sin-and-salvation themes. Medieval cosmology follows the Neoplatonic-Aristotelian picture (especially in the theologically-altered form propounded by Pseudo-Dionysus). Cassirer notes that:

> The task of medieval thought had consisted largely in tracing the architectonics of being and in delineating its main design . . . every phase of reality is assigned its unique place; and with its place goes a complete determination of its value, which is based on the greater or lesser distance which separates it from the First Cause. There is no room here for doubt, and in all thinking there is the consciousness of being sheltered by this inviolable order which it is not the business of thought to create but only to accept. God, the soul, and the world are the three great points on which all being hinges . . . Knowledge of "nature" is synonymous with knowledge of creation . . .[3]

Until scholasticism, little speculation regarding cosmology appeared in the Christian world. St. Augustine spoke of "the disease of curiosity" in his *Confessions,* and counselled "I no longer dream of the stars."[4] When he does speak in cosmological terms, Augustine reflects the old Hebrew and Egyptian three-tiered universe, which he derived from the mythic cosmography of the Bible.

In the later Middle Ages, with the rediscovery of Aristotle, natural cosmology ("the realm of nature") was given a place alongside revealed truth ("the realm of grace"). Because of the dualistic heritage of earth/heaven, matter/spirit, etc., this acceptance of classical geocentrism was comfortable enough for the Church.

The real problem for the Church developed, not so much from naturalistic cosmology, which was susceptible to theological interpretation, but from the epistemology of the Renaissance. For a variety of reasons, the "realm of nature" began to overtake the "realm of grace." This development accompanies the decline of the Church's authority—and in fact, her cosmic *control.* The Church had failed to prove superior to Islam in their confrontations, whether political (the Crusades) or intellectual (Islamic scholasticism preceded and influenced her Christian counterpart), A variety of other factors—plagues, famines, the disappointed hopes for Christ's return, the decline of feudalism (where the Church was the Ultimate Overlord) accompanied by urbanization, statism, and rise of the burgher class, the dissolution of Catholic unity (e.g., the "Babylonian Captivity")— all contributed to the decline of both the prestige and dominance of the Church over the minds of men. In this situation, nature and reason—almost granted equality with grace and revelation by the scholastics—made significant gains.

An attendant circumstance of the Church's receding authority was renewed cosmological speculation. The efforts of Copernicus (1473-1543), Galileo (1564-1642), Kepler (1571-1630), Descartes (1596-1650) and Newton (1642-1727), are formative of a new world view. We should note that Copernicus was a clergyman; Kepler was given to theological, Pythagorean-numerological and astrological ruminations; Descartes was preoccupied with proving God's existence; and Newton composed lengthy (albeit heterodox) theological treatises. Of these, only Galileo stirred an ecclesiastical hornets' nest.

The critical attitude which cuts loose the cosmos from its theological moorings is expressed in these words of Kepler:

> As for the opinions of the saints, I reply that the weight of Authority counts most in theology, but in philosophy it is Reason which matters. Thus St. Lactance denied that the Earth is spherical; St. Augustine admitted that the Earth is spherical, but denied the Antipodes. Today, the Holy Office admits the smallness of the Earth, but denies its motion. For me, the most sacred thing of all is the Truth; and with all respect to the Church, I have demonstrated according to my philosophy that the Earth is round, inhabited all round to the Antipodes, is of insignificant size, and is travelling rapidly among the other worlds.[5]

We discussed the implications of Copernican heliocentrism for the old dualistic view: man is now removed from the polluted center, yet the universe is still spherical and finite. Copernicus' reshuffling of the cosmic picture is far more significant culturally than the development of a celestial mechanics:

> With Freud, man lost his Godlike mind; with Darwin his exalted place among the creatures of the earth; with Copernicus man had lost his privileged position in the universe. The general intellectual repercussions of this fact are more dramatic than any consequences within technical astronomy, where one can speak of the Keplerian "revolution" but of not more than a Copernican "disturbance."[6]

Man's new position implies greater freedom (from a "corrupted" earth at the dense center), but also a greater threat. Even though the Christian scheme could be transposed into a Copernican cosmos, it would mean abandoning the integral hierarchy of the Middle Ages. Such accommodations—which have continued to the present—have caused many to question the Church's integrity: Is Christendom, loosed from a viable total cosmology, condemned to endless retreat in the face of new discovery?

If in the medieval world picture, the earth was the center—yet the repository of the base corruptible elements—the heavens were the realm of spiritual progression leading upwards to God. Understandably then, the Church would respond defensively to the Copernican hypothesis, which threatens the whole scheme, or to Galileo's penetration of the virgin heavens with a *telescope,* robbing that realm of its mystification and sanctity.* Galileo approached the sacred cosmos with empirical observation, and mathematical and mechanical calculation. Kepler, whose writings are infused with mystical concerns, formulated the critical laws of celestial mechanics: the three laws of planetary motion. It remained for Newton—himself committed to certain theological perspectives—to give the picture of the cosmic machine its classical formulation.

MECHANISM AND ATOMISM

What is a machine? We might define a machine as a self-contained, non-organic artifact which operates according to the interrelationship of its parts. In common experience machines are constructed for a wide variety of functions: e.g., production, transportation, measurement, communication, information-processing, problem-solving, labor-saving. The machine, as a self-contained, integrally-operating artifact, also has served as a model for the world. The mechanistic cosmology depicts the world as a self-contained physio-chemical system of integral parts operating according to mathematically expressible laws. The mechanistic model differs from an organic model in that *within* the system there is no place for an animating, vitalistic or divine principle, or purposeful intelligence. All organisms are reducible to physio-chemical processes. Within an organic model, mechanical functions are ultimately explicable according to some animating principle. Within the mechanical model, organic functions are reducible to mechanical functions. The theory of atomism offers an explanation for the basic constituent parts of the world machine.

Atomism, the theory that material reality is composed of minute, simple and unchangeable particles (called "atoms" from *atomos,* "indivisible"), arose in early Greece as a solution to the dilemma between the permanence or immutability of Being, which is one, and the temporality or flux of the sensory order, which is many. Leucippus and Democritus (whose lives spanned the late sixth through the mid-fifth centuries, B.C.E.) asserted that

*A contemporary—if somewhat trite—parallel is the plaint uttered after the first astronauts reached the moon, that it would never again hold the same fascination for lovers. Interestingly enough, the astronauts themselves responded to their experience with an almost mystical sense of reverence and awe.

reality consists of both the "full" and the "void" (each of which is legitimately existent). The material world is essentially a mixture of these two principles; hence material bodies are changeable and divisible as long as there is void in them, or until they have been subdivided to the point where "full" and "void" are completely separate—the "full" existing as changeless, indivisible, and numerically infinite particles called "atoms." According to Democritus, the variety of the sensory world could be explained by the *quantitative* difference among atoms: "sour" is caused by atoms which are bulky, jagged, and many-angled; "bitter" arises from atoms which are curved and smooth, but crooked and small in size, etc.[7] Heavy and light depend on the configuration of atoms and the amount of void.[8] Colors, odors, sounds have no substance in themselves, but derive from the arrangements of atoms. The world order itself "came to be" by means of a vortex motion which separated and ordered things by mere chance.[9] Moreover, Democritus asserted that there were an infinite number of world-orders, and mankind emerged "from water and slime . . . like worms, without a maker and for no reason."[10] The chance configuration of atoms is responsible for all that is. Whatever the more unrefined aspects of the original theory (such as "bulky, jagged and many-angled" atoms), atomism is foundational to our modern world view. An atomic theory in a mechanical model functions as a non-vitalistic or purely materialistic explanation for all things.

With the exceptions of Epicurus and Lucretius whose physical theories are drawn from Democritus, because of Plato and Aristotle atomism exercised little influence until the modern age. In the seventeenth century the atomic theory was again a topic of discussion, but it remained for John Dalton (1766-1844) to illustrate how chemical results buttress the atomic picture. Dalton envisioned the atomic structure of compound particles:

> Dalton himself in *A New System of Chemical Philosophy* stressed the great importance of "ascertaining the relative weights of the ultimate particles, both of simple and compound bodies, the number of simple elementary particles which constitute one compound particle, and the number of less compound particles which enter into the formation of one more compound particle."[11]

After Dalton, the atomic theory developed rapidly.

In the nineteenth century mounting evidence for the existence of atoms, such as Brownian movements and the spectra of black radiation, culminated in the discovery of the radioactive disintegration of elements by Becquerel in 1896. In the twentieth century, the *sub*atomic world has shattered the fundamental assertion of the indivisibility of atoms. Indeed, we now recognize that

> Subatomic particles can be classified in broad families according to kinds of interactions they participate in, or, as it is often put, according to the kinds of forces they "feel." The forces considered are the four fundamental ones

that are believed to account for all observed interactions of matter: gravitation, electromagnetism, the strong force and the weak force.[12]

All particles except the photon are classified according to their response to the strong force and the weak force. These forces refer to the rate at which interactions take place among subatomic particles. Particles that feel the strong force are called hadrons; those that do not feel the strong force but react to the weak force are called leptons. These particles, and constituent members of the families, are symbolized by mathematical numbers and equations.[13]

> In the twentieth century physics has probed the nucleus within, and has broken up the nucleus into its constituent particles. Those particles are now interpreted as being composites of more basic entities, the quarks. It is not unreasonable to imagine that we shall someday penetrate the quark and find an internal structure there as well. Only the experiments of the future can reveal whether quarks are the indivisible building blocks of all matter, the "atoms" of Democritus, or whether they too have a structure, as part of the endless series of seeds within seeds envisioned by Anaxagoras.[14]

Thus the quest for Democritus' "atom" still goes on. Remarking on this quest for "indivisible components"—the true atoms—Werner Heisenberg notes that

> The "thing-in-itself" is for the atomic physicist, if he uses this concept at all, finally a mathematical structure; but this structure is—contrary to Kant—indirectly deduced from experience.[15]

The relevance of atomism to a mechanical cosmos is severalfold. First of all, atomism provides a quantitative and purely mechanical explanation of the cosmos. All things are reducible to quantifiable basic constituents. Secondly, as opposed to "more anthropomorphic" explanations of the source of the world order—such as spirit, consciousness, God, etc.—atomism provides "less anthropomorphic" models: the abstractions of mathematical formulae. In fact, as Heisenberg comments above, the "thing in itself" of the modern atomic physicist is quite divorced from direct experience, and is in fact solely a "mathematical structure." If at first glance atomism, by breaking down the world into seemingly solid components, seems antithetical to idealism, the fact is that mathematical structures as Plato recognized are every bit as removed from our experience as his ideal world of forms.* In our discussion of language, we were exposed to the danger of the ontological fallacy; we find this danger recurring here in terms of the symbolic "language" of mathematics. It is assumed that "atoms" or subatomic particles are "things." Newton, who was the great framer of the mechanistic world picture, illustrates well how the atomic theory reifies the world:

> Newton contended that it "seemed probable" to him that "God, in the beginning, formed matter into solid, massy, hard, impenetrable, moveable particles, of such size and figures, and with such other properties, and in

---

*The forms at least are perceptible as "faint shadows" in the sensory world; but how can we encounter the shadows of mathematical formulae?

such proportions of space, as most conduced to the end for which he formed them"; and that "these primitive particles, being solids, are incomparably harder than porous bodies compounded of them; even so hard, as never to wear, or break in pieces."[16]

Newton's world is reducible to ontological solid parts, which are nevertheless known only as abstractions! The process of attributing ontic presence and substantiality to abstractions is called by Alfred North Whitehead "the fallacy of misplaced concreteness,"[17] the error of mistaking the Abstract for the Concrete.

Perhaps a cultural illustration will demonstrate the relevance of the abstract cosmos of mechanism and atomism. In the medieval world picture, the Neoplatonic-Christian Synthesis created an immense hierarchical and symmetrical structure of the cosmos in which everyone and everything (including all social and organic functions) had its proper spatial location. In a bureaucratic structure, loosed from theological legitimation, hierarchical and symmetrical schemes become mechanical processes in which persons, functions, and relationships are dispatched as disembodied abstractions or atomic units. In this example the richly dramatic "architectonics of being" of the Middle Ages are reduced to calculative functional abstractions in a mechanical cosmos.

Typical Expressions of Mechanism

Descartes signals the singular (though shifting, ever novel) role of reason in the Modern Age with his fundamental axiom—that which cannot be doubted—"I think, therefore I am." From this initial premise, born of doubt, Descartes exhibits an unshakeable faith in the capacity of reason to penetrate the structures of the universe. Following the Pythagorean-Platonic tradition, Descartes believed that the tools of reason—mathematics and geometry— could be employed in the analysis of the entire realm of nature. Cassirer remarks that, for Descartes:

> There is no barrier between the realm of clear and distinct concepts and the realm of facts, between geometry and physics. Since the substance of physical body consists in pure extension, knowledge of this extension, that is, geometry, is master of physics. Geometry expresses the nature of the corporeal world and its general fundamental properties in exact definitions and proceeds from these by an uninterrupted chain of thought to the determination of the particular and the factual.[18]

Reason, following geometrical principles, is granted a pervasive role by Descartes, but we have not yet entered the realm of *experimental* science. Science is still an *a priori* axiomatic task; the intellect and the cosmos are viewed as self-sufficient and autonomous structures. In his *Conversations on the Plurality of Worlds,* the Cartesian Fontenelle compares the behavior of a philosopher to that of a mechanic. Cassirer summarizes the gist of Fontenelle's arguments:

. . . nature, in the spectacle it constantly presents, has so carefully hidden its mechanism that it has taken us centuries to come upon its mysterious springs of action. Not until modern times was man permitted to look behind the scenes; science sees not only phenomena themselves, but also the clockworks which bring them about . . . "I esteem the universe all the more," writes Fontenelle, "since I have known that it is like a watch. It is surprising that nature, admirable as it is, is based on such simple things."[19]

For Fontenelle, the analogy of the universe to a mechanical instrument—the watch—does not detract from its beauty; seemingly in line with the Greek conceptions of harmony, the mechanical image reflects the fine geometry of the cosmos. Fontenelle sees no qualitative threat in a rational penetration of nature.

In the same vein, Descartes, following the general path mapped out by scholasticism, argues from his own consciousness to the existence of God. However, the autonomous intellect and autonomous nature—conceived in this mechanical fashion—could not long support theistic or even deistic presuppositions. The fate of Descartes' distinction between *res extensa* (the physical world of extended substance) and *res cogitans* (the mental or spiritual world of thinking substance) is illustrative of the collapse of all such dualisms in the West. The mechanical cosmos has no need of *res cogitans* and can account for rational functions in purely somatic terms. The later Cartesians Holbach and Lamettrie were cognizant of this discrepancy, and argued that man would become liberated from superstitions concerning God, freedom, and immortality, when the world was recognized as a naturalistic machine.[20] Frederick the Great, in examining Holbach's System of Nature, responded with a critique typical to this day:

> After the author has exhausted all evidence to show that men are guided by a fatalistic necessity in all their actions, he had to draw the conclusion that we are only a sort of machine, only marionettes moved by the hand of a blind power . . . If everything is moved by necessary causes, then all counsel, all instruction, all rewards and punishments are as superfluous as inexplicable; for one might just as well preach to an oak and try to persuade it to turn into an orange tree.[21]

The ultimate threat of the cosmic machine—as perceived here—is that the social order is robbed of legitimations for ethical and behavioral norms. Whether or not this perception has been justified, Frederick's anxiety anticipates the sense of anomie which has besieged the modern age.

Frederick's fears were not shared by all. For Thomas Hobbes (1588-1679), influenced by Galileo's mechanics, the physical laws of motion and geometry provide a direct analogy for understanding the human mind and the state.[22] Hobbes asserted

> For seeing life is but a motion of limbs . . . why may we not say, that all *automata* (engines that move themselves by springs and wheels as doth a watch) have an artifical life? For what is the *heart,* but a spring; and the *nerves,* but so many *strings;* and the *joints,* but so many *wheels,* giving motion to the body.[23]

The methodology of science is the methodology of explaining man and the cosmos. Cassirer remarks that for Hobbes, in constructing a science of the state, "nothing else is necessary than to carry over into the field of politics the synthetic and analytic method which Galileo applied in physics."[24] Political structures, like physical structures, must be broken down into their component parts if we are to understand them. Bronowski and Mazlish write:

> Hobbes and Locke were animated by the same view of nature. They saw the world as made up of bodies in motion, which were arranged in an orderly pattern and followed well-defined causal laws. Their view of the world was reflected in their view of human society. Through their thoughts run what we may call the atomic view of man and his social relations. They really thought of human societies as starting from a mass of atoms, and they were trying to discover what we might call the "gas laws" of human conduct.[25]

In Hobbes *Leviathan* the old macrocosm/microcosm scheme appears afresh. The state is "an artificial man" concerned with self-preservation. Just as the body needs a single directive center in the human brain, so the state needs a single directive head in an absolute sovereign. Reflecting the Roman and Stoic heritage, both Hobbes and Locke speak of *natural law*. However, in contrast to the Stoics, Hobbes in particular does not envision the cosmos organically, but mechanically. Even though the state is like a body, the body itself (as the prior quotation indicates) is merely a machine.

Although Hobbes and Locke share the basic presuppositions of a mechanical world picture, in Hobbes the mechanical analogy is more rigidly applied. For Hobbes the state is more like a machine directed by a single power source. Hobbes' version is deductive—moving from the mechanical whole to the proper operation of the parts. On the other hand, Locke's starting point is empirical; at birth the mind is a blank tablet (*tabula rasa*). Locke is more atomistic. The mind starts in a kind of void (like Democritus' atoms), and upon encountering a world of others begins to acquire impressions and ideas. The state comes about through the coalescence of equal free men who agree on a social contract.[26] For Locke the state of nature is like the state of Democritus' atoms: free-floating bodies in the cosmic void. However, for Locke the state of nature is equally a state of *reason*, unlike Hobbes' view of a natural condition of brutish men warring with one another. Hobbes pictures the state as an artificial invention:

> Nature . . . is by the art of man (able to) . . . make an artificial animal . . . For by art is created that great Leviathan called a commonwealth, or state, . . . which is but an artificial man . . . [27]

On the contrary, Locke derives the state from natural law, and it is contracted for the sake of protecting men's natural rights. Hobbes presents us with a secularized and mechanized version of the medieval theological hierarchy. Locke presents us in part with a modernized interpretation of Roman Law and Stoicism filtered through a quasi-scientific methodology. The reappraisal of the classical *cosmos* as a mechanical rather than an organic order is a change of critical proportions, and informs us not only of a basic difference between the classical and modern understandings of the state, but of a fundamental difference in the model of *human being* itself.

The full-scale mechanical model of the cosmos is the creation of Sir Isaac Newton (1642-1727). With the publication of his *Principia*, the cosmology which was to dominate Western thought until the early twentieth century was established. In his Three Laws of Motion physical systems are treated as "masses in motion," affecting each other by "forces" (which are defined in terms of the spatio-temporal relations of masses and the constants associated with those masses). These laws are:

  I. Every body continues in its state of rest, or of uniform motion in a right (i.e., straight) line, unless it is compelled to change that state by forces impressed upon it.

 II. The change of motion is proportional to the motive force impressed; and is made in the direction of the right line in which that force is impressed.

III. To every action there is always opposed an equal reaction; or, the mutual actions of two bodies upon each other are always equal, and directed to contrary parts.[28]

Newton also proposed his laws of Absolute Space, Time and Motion "in which bodies could truly, rather than merely relatively, be said to be in motion."[29] Newton regarded space as "a physical reality, stationary and immovable," and though there was no means of demonstrating this premise, he "clung to it on theological grounds."[30] Newton's universe can be described as

> A universe permeated with an invisible medium in which the stars wandered and through which light traveled like vibrations in a bowl of jelly . . . It (the Newtonian world picture) provided a mechanical model for all known phenomena of nature, and it provided a fixed frame of reference, the absolute and immovable space, which Newton's cosmology required.[31]

Newtonian mechanics have proved to be of immense practical significance. Yet in light of the Einsteinian Revolution, Newton's abstractions and absolutes appear to reflect a subtle residue of mythopoeism; i.e., Newton attributes actual substance to descriptive symbols (e.g., "force," "space," "motion," "time") which represent modes of relationship or interaction. The mechanical model—of great utilitarian value—acquires ontological status and thus is liable to Whitehead's "fallacy of misplaced concreteness."

In twentieth century physics "space" and "time" are not "things." The spatio-temporal continuum describes the relative context of physical bodies with regard to one another as they are in motion. By contrast, Newton's world is a closed mechanical system. As Heisenberg says:

> Newton begins his *Principia* with a group of definitions and axioms which are interconnected in such a way that they form what one may call a

"closed system." Each concept can be represented by a mathematical symbol, and the connections between the different concepts are then represented by mathematical equations expressed by means of the symbols.[32]

Newton's world picture is an *a priori* structure which, once accepted, provides internal consistency according to absolute laws posited of an idealized state of nature. In general, this system adequately describes the physical phenomena of everyday life. However, in the spheres of microphysics (the atomic and subatomic domain) and macrophysics (the astro-physical domain) Newton's laws, which describe "an eternal structure of nature, depending neither on a particular space nor on particular time,"[33] are no longer adequate. In these spheres bodies described are not in a relative state of rest, but are in fact moving at immense speeds with regard to one another. In quantifying and abstracting the natural world, mechanical description can never fully represent the concrete entities or relationships found in that world. Although the new physics also employs mechanical abstractions, it attempts to acknowledge contextual considerations and the *relative* value of mathematical generalizations. The field of *mechanics* remains fundamental to physical theory; but it is no longer clear that a *mechanical world picture* is sufficient to describe the rich diversity and mystery of the physical world itself.

Bearing in mind these limitations, we return from the cosmic sphere to the cultural sphere. In *The Wealth of Nations* (published in 1776) Adam Smith laid down the foundations of a mechanical theory of labor. His *laissez faire* economy again suggests the atomic theory, for in it men are depicted as isolated units of competition and self-interest. In Smith's mechanical process the providential ordering of the Divine Mechanic is still visible. "By pursuing his own interest" the individual "frequently promotes that of the society more effectually than when he really intends to promote it."[34] Indeed, Smith believes that "he is in this, as in many other cases, led by an invisible hand to promote an end which was no part of his intention."[35]

Perhaps another illustration of Whitehead's "fallacy of misplaced concreteness" is Smith's depiction of labor as a commodity, rather than an activity.[36] By this view, as Marx was to observe in the following century, the laborer himself is in danger of becoming a mere commodity. Smith's understanding of the division of labor added to the assumption that man is a mere "machine of production." Smith remarked:

> The man whose whole life is spent in performing a few simple operations, of which the effects are perhaps always the same, or very nearly the same, has no occasion to exert his understanding or to exercise his invention in finding out expedients for removing difficulties which never occur. He naturally loses, therefore, the habit of such exertion, and generally becomes as stupid and ignorant as it is possible for a human creature to become.[37]

Smith not only anticipated in these words the technological dehumanization of the worker, he also intoned:

> Human society, when we contemplate it in a certain abstract and philosophical light, appears like a great, an immense machine whose regular and harmonious movements produce a thousand agreeable effects.[38]

Smith thus pictures society as an orderly structure of nature to which man must adjust himself harmoniously, if not mechanically. Contrary perhaps to his intentions,[39] Smith's theories, along with changes wrought by the Industrial Revolution, contributed to the mechanizing of society as well as the cosmos.

A final and illuminating facet of the mechanistic world view is the rise of deism. The earliest known use of the term "deist" was by the Calvinist Pierre Viret, who in 1564 wrote of certain unidentified intellectuals who opposed both atheism on the one hand, and the christological doctrines on the other. Commonly endorsed beliefs among seventeenth century deists included, as first set forth by Lord Herbert of Cherbury (1583-1648):

1) That there is one God;
2) He ought to be worshiped;
3) That virtue and piety are the chief parts of divine worship;
4) That man should be sorry for his sins and repent;
5) That there are rewards and punishments in the here and hereafter.[40]

In general the deists affirmed rational religion and free will, and denied biblical miracles, biblical idolatry and biblical authority. Famed deists in England included Charles Blount, John Toland, Anthony Collins and Matthew Tindal; in France and Germany, Voltaire, Rousseau and Kant; in America, Franklin, Jefferson, Washington and Thomas Paine.[41]

However, the deism significant to the mechanical world picture is not the deism of these men, but a later form of deism in the eighteenth and nineteenth centuries which asserted that God, the First Cause, created the world and established immutable laws by which it is governed. The world operates as a self-sustaining machine created by God. Two images described the relationship between God and world. God is depicted as a clock-maker, who created a precision instrument which operates on its own without the intervention of the craftsman, except perhaps for occasional repairs. Or God is said to be like an absentee landlord to whom rent is due, but who only rarely looks in on the affairs of his tenants. In either case, God has left behind his rationally-apprehensible laws for man's benefit and direction.

The later deism acknowledges the mechanistic world view of the new science, but attempts to retain God both as Ultimate Cause and as the Source and Norm of Law, Order and Morality. Furthermore, God is the source of reason, through which this knowledge is attained.

In *The Protestant Ethic and the Spirit of Capitalism*[42] Max Weber points out how the Reformation provided legitimation for the *ethos* of capitalism: especially Luther's doctrine of divine calling, Calvin's emphases on divine transcendence and worldly "proof" of one's election, and a Protestant ascetism which underscores sobriety, hard work and opposition to pleasures of the flesh.[43] Weber's thesis illuminates how Protestant doctrine is to be reconciled with the worldly realities of profit, success, the division between labor and management, etc.

It could be asserted that the real hidden religion of the modern Industrial Age is deism. Although this is an over-generalization, if we examine how deism functions it is not hard to see deistic beliefs in capitalist assumptions lying beneath the polite deference to denominational dogmas and ritual. We might formulate this hidden creed as follows:

1) God is the Sovereign Creator of Order, and His Laws are rational and clearly obvious throughout society and the cosmos;

2) All proper authority, rationality, morality, and order derive from God's Laws;

3) God does not interfere with the Laws He has established; He takes a *laissez faire* approach to the world; God favors the *status quo* (which derives from His Laws);

4) Although God is responsible for man's ultimate salvation, in the here-and-now man is responsible for his own salvation;

5) The chief end of Religion is *morality* and morality is a personal, private affair, the social implications of which are sobriety, honesty, frugality, deference to authority, and hard work;

6) Some men attain to power and wealth naturally, and with God's blessing (or predestination); others are ordained to the role of "faithful servants" (workers); (or) power and wealth are the rewards of God for hard work, and subservience is the punishment for laziness.

God may be absent by degrees in the hidden deism of the mechanical cosmos. Atheism can retain the *ethos* of the above creed, but leave God out of the picture. A more evangelical form of the above creed would acknowledge the need for conversion, Bible study, etc., as long as God remains chiefly the Establisher of Order and the Securer or Provider of Eternal (other-worldly) Salvation; perhaps by prayer and faithfulness God may even be enjoined to appear secretly by His Spirit to stir the recalcitrant hearts of workers to recognize the true blessings of capitalism. In this example we are moving away from a strict deism, but that is precisely the point. Deism as an overt institutional religion could never overcome the strongly entrenched orthodoxy of the churches. However, as a tacit faith of the Machine Age, deism (with various modifications and accommodations to traditional religion) may have triumphed as the secret creed of millions. Most laymen are not theologically sophisticated, and the task of equating *laissez faire* deism with other-worldly pietism may not be nearly as difficult as it would first appear.

The secret triumph of deism may be more understandable if we compare the medieval and mechanical world pictures. In the medieval world view the hierarchical arrangement of society and the cosmos, as well as its proper "orders," are established by analogy with the Neoplatonic chain of being (which becomes the chain of command of the Christian God). With the rise of the middle class, the appearance of mercantilism, and the radical re-arrangement of the social order (which is no longer controlled by the church), medieval culture disintegrates. With the rise of statism and the innovations in science and industry, the modern age emerges.

However, the orderly *cosmos* which is necessary for social cohesiveness could not be abandoned. *Reason* (reborn in the scholastic effort to patch up the sinking ship of medieval Christendom) became the new mode of legitimating the social order. The *object* of reason is the rationally discernible world order. The *effects* of reason are the deduced principles by which the cosmos and society should operate. With the mechanistic hypotheses of science—and in particular the compelling model set forth by Newton—the pattern of the rational order now seemed self-evident. The lost cohesiveness of medieval society could be recaptured by picturing the world and society as a gigantic machine, operating efficiently through hierarchical and geometrical inter-relationships of its parts. Even God could be retained as the Designer (and Ultimate Point-of-Reference) of the machine. But whether God is allotted a role or not, the machine is essentially secular, since it is self-functioning. Nonetheless legitimation for morality, authority, order and tradition can be found in *reason*—the canons of which serve rather like an operating manual for the machine. Since it is conveniently abstract and remote, deism is natural, though optional, to the mechanistic cosmos. The medieval cosmos, robbed of its divinity, seemed robbed of its life (since the organic was divinely energized). But the mechanical world picture, unable to restore organic wholeness (which in its autonomous form was lost in classical times by the convergence of dualisms in Christianity), could at least restore order and rationale to the world via its cohesive model.

REASON AND MECHANISM

In the history of the West the use of the term "reason" has varied greatly, from its autonomy in classical Greece and Rome to its subjugation to revelation in the Christian Synthesis, to its restored dignity, signaled by scholasticism and emergent in the modern era. Ernst Cassirer points out that from the seventeenth to the eighteenth centuries a significant shift in the meaning of reason occurs. In the great philosophical systems of the seventeenth century reason is generally treated as an *a priori* principle of the cosmos itself. In the eighteenth century it is transformed into a tool of analysis (without necessarily denying all of its former nuances). "The new logic . . . is rather the 'logic of facts.' The mind must abandon itself to the abundance of phenomena and gauge itself constantly by them."[44] The mind is now in the service of phenomena. The new spirit is both analytical and synthetic:

> It is only by splitting an apparently simple event into its elements and by reconstructing it from these that we can arrive at an understanding of it . . . The structure of the cosmos is no longer merely to be looked at, but to be penetrated . . . We must, of course, abandon all hope of ever wresting from things their ultimate mystery, of ever penetrating to the absolute being of matter or of the human soul.[45]

These words recall the atomistic and mechanical spirit. Just as the heavens lost their sacred mystery through the probing of the astronomer's telescope, so now reason in its mechanical or instrumental function penetrates the structures of nature, dissecting it into its component parts; synthetically, reason is to restructure the parts into a lawfully operating mechanism.

Reason, therefore, is not so much a characteristic of nature—its organic attribute—as it is a tool of analysis acquired by man. Cassirer's summary of the new functions of reason[46] may be outlined in four steps: 1) solid facts based upon observation constitute the starting point; 2) analysis aims at discovering the interdependence of these data; 3) from analysis general principles emerge; 4) these principles do not constitute a new absolute system (as in the seventeenth century), but relative points of departure for new discoveries. The seventeenth and eighteenth century legacies of reason contribute to the great institutional structures of the modern era. We might suggest that modern technology seems to be more the child of eighteenth century analysis, whereas bureaucracy seems more the product of seventeenth century *a priori* hierarchical and mechanical systems. Thus reason can function in *two* mechanical modes, as an internal deductive *a priori* principle (*esprit de systeme,* "the spirit of the system"), or as an external inductive analytical tool (*esprit systematique,* "a systematic spirit"). Voltaire argued for the latter use

> We must never make hypotheses; we must never say: Let us begin by inventing principles according to which we attempt to explain everything. We should rather say: Let us make an exact analysis of things . . . Where we cannot utilize the compass of mathematics or the torch of experience and physics, it is certain that we cannot take a single step forward.[47]

In fact both uses of reason have proved indispensable to modern science.

THE INDUSTRIAL REVOLUTION

In 1769 James Watts secured the first patent for his steam engine. Though industry had already made great strides by this time, it was still primarily centered in the home. In the latter eighteenth century—especially in England—the factory system began to emerge. Bronowski and Mazlish observe that

> the essential change which the Industrial Revolution brought was not in machines but in method. The Industrial Revolution was only incidentally a change in industrial techniques; it was more profoundly a change in industrial organization . . . The cardinal change which the Industrial Revolution brought was to move many of these industries from the home into the factory . . . Before 1760, it was standard to take the work to

villagers in their own homes. By 1820, it was standard to bring everyone into a factory to have them work there.[48]

The change from home to factory cannot be attributed to any single factor. Economic changes in investment and credit, new methods in agriculture, urbanization, a burgeoning middle class—all contributed to this cultural shift.

The Industrial Revolution created a new kind of culture and identity for a vast number of people. From a theoretical and intellectual system the mechanistic cosmos becomes a cultural way of life. Not only is industry dependent upon the machine, but the successes and profits of industry necessitate the subjugation of the laborer to the machine, and persons acquire a machine-like function. Thus a new identity accompanies the rise of the factory system. The thinking implicit in the emergent technology is atomistic and mechanical. Each of industry's components, whether human or mechanical, is envisioned as a discrete unit, abstract and separate—yet interrelated in a carefully predefined causal system. Berger, Berger and Kellner argue in *The Homeless Mind* that the style of work in industry involves the machinelike functions of mechanisticity, reproducibility, participation, and measurability.[49] That is, the worker—a machinelike component whose functions can be reproduced by others—is a "cog in the wheel" of a larger structure; and his work is quantifiable or measurable. (The implicit mechanical world view of bureaucracy and technology—explicit incarnations of the Newtonian cosmos—will be described in chapter eight.)

REACTIONS TO MECHANISM

We should expect that such a fundamental change in world view (with the triumph of the mechanical model) should not go unchallenged. We will examine only two of the many reactions to mechanism, but will suggest a third for later discussion.

One of the most penetrating attacks on the economic system which accompanies the mechanical cosmos is Karl Marx's classical discussion of "alienated labor." Although this discussion is not primarily an assault upon the mechanical world view, its implications constitute a formidable critique of that world view. Marx begins by asserting that the fundamental components of capitalism—private property, greed and competition, the separation of labor and management, the money system—all conspire in an integral (and we might add mechanical) system to dehumanize man. First of all, the product of the worker's labor is valued in terms of money—an external and abstract standard. In fact the more the worker produces, the greater money value he has created over against himself, and thus the cheaper his own life has become. Marx asserts that "the object produced by man's labor—its product—now confronts him in the shape of an alien thing, a power independent of the producer."[50] As the world of things which exists in its own right (apart from the human world) increases, the human world is devalued. Marx feels that there is an analogous situation here to religion:

> The more man puts into God, the less he retains in himself.* The worker puts his life into the things he makes; and his life then belongs to him no more, but to the product of his labor. The greater the worker's activity, therefore, the more pointless his life becomes.[51]

In the mechanistic cosmos, the component parts are viewed as atomistic *things*—not as integral organic parts. Just so, the mechanical system reifies man as a thing.

Not only is the worker alienated by creating a product over against himself, but the worker becomes a slave to things. In fact, the greater facility with which the worker fits into the mechanical process, the more he becomes defined by that process. Not only the product, but the process itself alienates:

> the work he performs is extraneous to the worker, that is, it is not personal to him, is not part of his nature; therefore he does not fulfill himself in work, but actually denies himself; feels miserable rather than content, cannot freely develop his physical and mental powers, but instead becomes physically exhausted and mentally debased.[52]

Marx's words here are similar to Adam Smith's, cited previously. Marx concludes that "only while not working can the worker be himself; for while at work he experiences himself as a stranger . . . His labor is not voluntary, but coerced . . ."[53] In fact, the worker's identity is so threatened by this process, that he "feels freely active only in his animal functions—eating, drinking, procreating . . ."[54]

A further implication of the mechanized world of the worker is his relationship to nature. Unable to remain in constant and vital contact with air, light, animals, plants, stones, man is cut off from his own organic nature. Furthermore, nature itself is manipulated and dissected by mechanical industry. The expression *"raw materials"* is indicative of the subversion of nature by the mechanical process. "Raw materials" signifies that nature has become a conglomeration of *things*—abstracted and reified—not a living, integral organic process. Marx's vision is prophetic of contemporary ecology.

A final, and most destructive, facet of the labor process (as Marx sees it) is an assault on human nature's *species being,* or social being. The creation of a world of things results in a material mediation between man and man. Men become evaluated by other men not as persons, but as commodities, as property-holders or propertyless workers or peasants. The end result of the mechanized capitalistic economic system is the reduction of humanity to mere machines of production.

Marx's critique must be weighed in terms of its historical location in the mid-nineteenth century before the appearance of legal safeguards to protect

---

*The shift from medieval culture to capitalism implies a shift from God to Mammon as the "Other" to be worshiped.

the worker, and before the labor union movement negotiated shorter work weeks, minimum wages, etc. Changes have occurred in the capitalistic system. But we must still question whether these changes are mere external adjustments or genuine internal and philosophical modifications. In chapter eight we shall cite recent studies of technology and bureaucracy which indicate that the mechanistic cosmos is alive and well in today's institutions.* Marx, interestingly enough, never dealt with bureaucracy.

Some of the same objections raised by Marx to the mechanical cosmos are evident in Romanticism. Romanticism—a rich and varied term—in this discussion refers to a type of world view which stands in polar contrast to mechanism. Romanticism invokes aesthetic canons of critique—as opposed to Marx's humanistic socio-economic analysis.

Often considered as species of Romanticism are the movements of religious revivalism and pietism. Revivalism especially appealed to lower-class masses, offering a "balm in Gilead" when this life seemed nothing more than the bleak routinization of mechanical labor. Pietism, akin to revivalism in its emphasis upon *feelings,* was generally more mollified and sophisticated (as Schleiermacher's *On Religion: Speeches to its Cultured Despisers* illustrates). Pietism offered an alternative less radical than the "pie in the sky." A pious spirit could be cultivated in the here-and-now.

Commonly identified emphases of Romanticism include the return to nature, the value of emotion or passion, mysticism, individualism, etc. Each of these stands in polarity to the mechanical definition of man (or his "condition"): nature versus machine, emotional attunement and involvement versus dispassionate abstraction, mysticism versus empirical objectification, and individual uniqueness versus atomistic anonymity. Schleiermacher, in speaking of piety, echoes sentiments often expressed by Romantic literature:

> The contemplation of the pious is the immediate consciousness of the universal existence of all finite things, in and through the Infinite, and of all temporal things in and through the Eternal . . . Religion . . . is to have life and to know life in immediate feeling, only as such an existence in the Infinite and Eternal . . . Wherefore it is a life in the infinite nature of the Whole, in the One and in the All . . .[55]

Leaving out the terms "pious" and "religion" Schleiermacher speaks broadly for the Romantic spirit.

It is well known that, accompanying Romanticism was something of a Gothic revival and glorification of the Middle Ages. This bears comment since the processes which robbed the medieval cosmos of its mystification and sacral content are the same processes which created the mechanical picture of the world. In particular, Romanticism objected to the autonomy and cold

---

*And the reader might note: technology and bureaucracy are also trans-cultural phenomena, appearing worldwide in the modern age. Is there an underlying "cosmology" common to all appearances of these institutional structures?

abstractions of reason—over against which it set the truth-apprehending and organic value of intuition. Speaking in the Romantic spirit, Richard Wagner could personify Revolution as the "e'er rejuvenating mother of mankind"[56] (a naturalistic image), or Sir Walter Scott could advocate return to authentic folk traditions rooted in nature and historical customs.[57] Thus romanticism embodies no one program of action, but in an important sense represents a *reaction to* the mechanized world of science and technology. We would not deny the significant creativity of Romanticism, but we would suggest that its eclecticism and individualism evidence no unifying principles or goals (except in the broadest sense); and therein may lie the clue to its demise as a so-called "movement," though the Romantic *spirit* continues to stir afresh from time to time (e.g., in the late 1960's).

One final "reaction" (or naturally emergent dialectical opposition) is the revolution in physics from the late nineteenth century to the present, in which the foundational premises of the old Newtonian cosmos have proved no longer adequate. Although Newton's principles have buttressed the development of science and technology on a number of levels, as "absolutes" they have proved inadequate. The new cosmology will be discussed in later chapters. Here we simply enumerate some of the discoveries contra-Newton: the Michelson-Morley experiments and the loss of the "ether," Einstein's relativity theories, Heisenberg's "uncertainty principle," new penetrations into the world of the atom, and the new historical orientation of the sciences.

In its more extreme forms mechanism is perhaps the most graphic example of sessile consciousness. Not only is the world dissected in spatial terms and reconstructed in geometrical and hierarchical abstractions, but also it is *loosed* from its roots both in organic nature and history—the twin *processes* which infuse the world with life and novelty. It is then no wonder that the heritage of mechanism is paradoxical: as that which creates the most highly structured and predictable *orders* it is also that which has thrust Western culture into (perhaps) the greatest anomistic vacuum it has ever known. These implications should become clearer in the following section of our study.

FOOTNOTES

[1] John Mansley Robinson, *An Introduction to Early Greek Philosophy* (Boston: Houghton Mifflin, 1968), pp. 42-43.

[2] A. C. Crombie, *Medieval and Early Modern Science,* Vol I (Garden City, N.Y.: Doubleday Anchor, 1959), p. 75.

[3] Ernst Cassirer, *The Philosophy of the Enlightenment* (Princeton: Princeton University Press, 1951), p. 39.

[4] Jean Charon, *Cosmology* (New York: McGraw-Hill, 1970), pp. 51-52.

[5] Ibid., p. 103.

[6] *The Encyclopedia of Philosophy,* s.v. "Copernicus," by Norwood R. Hanson.

[7] Robinson, P. 200.

[8] Ibid., p. 201.

[9] Ibid., p. 208.

[10] Ibid., pp. 213; 216.

[11] *The Encyclopedia of Philosophy,* s.v. "Atomism," by Andrew G. M. van Melsen.

[12] Sidney D. Drell, "Electron-Position Annihilation and the New Particles," *Scientific American* 232 (June 1975): 50.

[13] Ibid.

[14] Ibid.

[15] Werner Heisenberg, *Physics and Philosophy* (New York: Harper Torchbooks, 1962), p. 89.

[16] W. H. Werkmeister, *A Philosophy of Science* (Lincoln: University of Nebraska Press, 1940). p. 287.

[17] Alfred North Whitehead, *Science and the Modern World* (New York: The Free Press, 1967), pp. 51; 58.

[18] Ernst Cassirer, p. 51.

[19] Ibid., p. 50.

[20] Ibid., p. 67 ff.

[21] Ibid., p. 71.

[22] W. H. Greenleaf, "Hobbes: The Problem of Interpretation," in *Hobbes and Rousseau: A Collection of Critical Essays,* ed. Maurice Cranston and Richard S. Peters (Garden City, N.Y.: Anchor Books, 1972, pp. 1-36, identifies three types of interpretation dominating Hobbes studies. The *traditional* interpretation portrays Hobbes as a materialist who applies the mechanical precepts of naturalistic science to political theory. The second approach to Hobbes, the *natural law* interpretation, cites the scholastic and Stoic natural law tradition as being of equal—if not greater—significance than mechanistic science. This interpretation underscores Hobbes' ethical strain as reflecting an ultimate allegiance to the God who established the laws of nature. The third approach to Hobbes, the *individualist* or *nominalist* interpretation, denies the ultimacy of either of the former positions, citing rather Hobbes' peculiarily modern or classically nominalist character. Both the second and third interpretations may not take full cognizance of Hobbes' express scientific intentions, but in any case Hobbes' naturalistic orientation must be tempered by considerations of both other recurrent strains and also his socio-historical location. C. B. Macpherson, *The Political Theory of Possessive Individualism* (New York: Oxford University Press, 1962), also stresses the socio-historical location of Hobbes.

   See also Hannah Arendt, *The Origins of Totalitarianism* (New York: Harcourt Brace, Harvest, 1951-73), p. 141, on Hobbes: "This new body politic was conceived for the benefit of the new bourgeois society as it emerged in the seventeenth century . . . The Commonwealth is based on the delegation of power, and not of rights . . . In regard to the law of the state . . . there is no question of right or wrong, but only absolute obedience, the blind conformism of bourgeois society."

[23] J. Bronowski and Bruce Mazlish, *The Western Intellectual Tradition: From Leonardo to Hegel* (New York: Harper Torchbooks, 1962), p. 197.

[24] Cassirer, p. 19.

[25] Bronowski and Mazlish, p. 203.

[26] Macpherson, p. 256, argues concerning Locke, that: "The notion that individualism and 'collectivism' are the opposite ends of a scale along which states and theories of the state can be arranged, regardless of the

stage of social development in which they appear, is superficial and misleading. Locke's individualism, that of an emerging capitalist society, does not exclude but on the contrary demands the supremacy of the state over the individual. It is not a question of the more individualism, the less collectivism; rather, the more thorough-going the individualism, the more complete the collectivism." In the same regard, we can see how the models or imagery of both atomism and mechanism are relevant to an understanding of modern "bourgeois" (and perhaps also Marxist) institutions.

For an alternate perspective on Locke, see Norman O. Brown, *Love's Body* (New York: Vintage Books, 1966), who suggests a Freudian encounter between primal father (absolute monarch) and sons (social contract, equal rights), in a psychoanalytic interpretation of Locke's significance, pp. 4-31.

27 Bronowski and Mazlish, pp. 204-05.

28 *The Encyclopedia of Philosophy*, s.v. "Newtonian Mechanics and Mechanical Explanation," by Dudley Shapere.

29 Ibid., p. 495.

30 Lincoln Barnett, *The Universe and Dr. Einstein* (New York: Bantam Books, 1973), p. 40.

31 Ibid., p. 41.

32 Heisenberg, p. 93.

33 Ibid.

34 Adam Smith, "An Inquiry Into the Nature and Causes of the Wealth of Nations," in *Great Books of the Western World*, Vol. 39, ed. R. M. Hutchins (Chicago: Encyclopaedia Britannica, Inc., 1952) p. 194.

35 Ibid.

36 Bronowski and Mazlish, p. 348.

37 Adam Smith, *The Wealth of Nations*, 2 vols. (London: Everyman's Library edition, 1954), II: 263-4.

38 Adam Smith, "The Theory of Moral Sentiments," in *Adam Smith's Moral and Political Philosophy*, ed. Herbert W. Schneider (New York: 1948), p. 39.

39 Out of fairness to Smith, it must be observed that he would not have approved the use to which his theories were put. Roland Stromberg, *An Intellectual History of Modern Europe*, 2nd ed. (Englewood Cliffs: Prentice-Hall, 1975), pp. 171-72, observes that Smith himself valued a simple frugal life and indicated substantial sympathy for the plight of both farmers and laborers. The mechanical model was meant to guarantee the freedom of individuals whose actions automatically would serve the collective welfare of society by means of the "invisible hand."

40 *The Encyclopedia of Philosophy*, s.v. "Deism," by Ernst C. Mossner.

41 Ibid.

42 Max Weber, *The Protestant Ethic and the Spirit of Capitalism* (New York: Scribner's, 1950).

43 David Little, *Religion, Order, and Law: A Study in Pre-Revolutionary England* (New York: Harper Torchbooks, 1969), discusses the struggle in England between Anglicanism and Calvinist Puritanism. This struggle is of critical relevance in another stage of the secularization of the medieval sacred cosmos. Little identifies the conflict as one of basic structures of authority and legitimation wedded to conflicting social interests. Anglicanism defended the old order and its traditional hierarchy attached to the crown. Puritanism, allied to rising bourgeois interests (which would culminate in the Industrial Revolution), envisioned a new order first visible in the church, and then in society. Little writes that "In contrast to Stoic and humanist conceptions, Calvin subordinates natural law to the sovereignty of God. There is no law above or outside God: 'God is above the order of nature'!" (p. 40). It is not too radical a step from this position to that of the *deists*, where God establishes the self-sufficiency of a world machine. For Calvin, political authority is derivative of the divine order, and as long as it reflects the divine order, commands absolute obedience. Yet when human orders do not accord with the divine order, they cease to be constituents of God's order and resistance is appropriate (p. 46). Calvin's view of conscience is pertinent here. Moreover, Little observes: "We have here the basis for a 'new aristocracy' or new elite, whose credentials are not birth, wealth, or position, but voluntary obedience and functional responsibility. Because "pure Christians" are related to true order, to God's order, they assume a privileged place . . . they become a new model for society . . ." (p. 74). One representative of this veritable new world view, Thomas Cartwright, followed Calvin in stressing the voluntary obedience to God's command as issuing in a proper social order (p. 87). In fact, it is the believers' "ability to consent freely to right order" that "distinguishes them as the Body of Christ" (p. 88). Although Cartwright decried social distinctions in the Body of Christ, he saw the nobility and the

gentry as more predisposed to piousness. Cartwright defined God's calling in terms of economic functions (pp. 95-96). Little observes: "Implied here is a withering away of the state and consequently, a devaluation of the state (and of the law) as the source or expression of ultimate earthly order" (p. 104). The ramifications of this study for modern bourgeois and democratic society and institutions should be obvious (as well as the shift of imagery to a mechanical world picture).

See also: Michael Walzer, *The Revolution of the Saints: A Study in the Origins of Radical Politics* (Cambridge: Harvard University Press, 1965), and Herbert W. Schneider, *The Puritan Mind* (Ann Arbor: The University of Michigan Press, Ann Arbor Paperback, 1958).

[44]Cassirer, p. 9.

[45]Ibid, pp. 10, 11; 13.

[46]Ibid., p. 21.

[47]Voltaire, *Traité de Metaphysique,* chs. III and V.

[48]Bronowski and Mazlish, pp. 308-09.

[49]Peter L. Berger, Brigitte Berger, and Hansfried Kellner, *The Homeless Mind* (New York: Vintage Books, 1974).

[50]Karl Marx, "Alienated Labor" in Eric and Mary Josephson, eds., *Man Alone: Alienation in Modern Society* (New York: Laurel Books, 1972), p. 95.

[51]Ibid.

[52]Ibid., p. 97.

[53]Ibid.

[54]Ibid., p. 98.

[55]Friedrich Schleiermacher, "Speeches on Religion to its Cultured Despisers," in John B. Halstead, ed. *Romanticism* (New York: Harper and Row, 1969), p. 141.

[56]Richard Wagner, "The Revolution," in Halsted, *Romanticism,* p. 233.

[57]Sir Walter Scott, "Dedicatory Epistle, *Ivanhoe,"* in Halsted, *Romanticism,* p. 247.

SECTION III

COSMOLOGY AND MODERN CONSCIOUSNESS

CHAPTER SEVEN

COSMOLOGY AND POLITICAL MYTHOLOGY

AS IN PAST chapters our intent is to establish a typological framework, the understanding of which will help illumine the implicit models which we employ in the construction and valuation of our social cosmos. The following discussion is divided into two parts. The first describes mythical structures of legitimation, community, and teleology (society's "goal") employed in the framing of political theories seminal to modern Western societies. Our discussion naturally must be both selective and (hopefully) representative. As such we refer the reader to footnotes intended to provide a partial index of more complex issues beyond our present aim of identifying mythical structures.

The second section explores the mythical roots of two forms of modern fascism—Nazi Germany and Mussolini's Italy. Somewhat contrary to other Western ideologies, fascism owes its ideological expression more to contemporary propagandists than to major philosophical theorists such as Locke or Marx. Thus our discussion of fascism will focus upon mythical structures of legitimation of its official apologists.

ILLUSTRATIVE MYTHIC STRUCTURES IN THE MODERN WEST

Mythic Sources of Legitimation and Authority

From whence does the political cosmos spring? Apart from the complex interrelationship of geographical, economic, racial, socio-historical and related factors, we legitimate our political *nomoi* (laws, customs—the formal loci of authority) through mythic structures.

One of those structures frequently recurring in early modern political theory is the so-called "state of nature." Hobbes, Locke, and Rousseau all appeal to this phrase, and there is some hint of a similar theme in the early Marx.[1] For Hobbes "the state of nature" was an essentially negative judgment—a mythical condition of man comparable to a state of civil war, the natural concomitant of the absence of stable political authority.[2] Hobbes' civil state thus becomes the mythical counterpoint for keeping such a chaotic condition at bay. For Rousseau (1712-1778) "the state of nature" is an equally mythical,[3] primitive condition of man, where idyllic conditions prevail and man's true humanity is unfettered. John Locke (1632-1704) seems to conceive of "the state of nature" in terms closer to Hobbes.[14]

Locke sketched a landscape of this imagined state against which he proposed the derivation and functions of political authority:

> To understand political power right, and derive it from its original [source], we must consider what state men are naturally in, and that is, a state of perfect freedom to order their actions and dispose of their possessions and persons as they think fit, within the bounds of the law of nature *without asking leave or depending upon the will of any other man.*[5]

Locke characterizes this state as "a state of equality, wherein all the power and jurisdiction is reciprocal."[6] Would not such freedom lead to chaos? Anticipating this objection, Locke asserts that the "state of liberty is not a state of license," since it derives from the law of nature established by God to assure life, health, liberty and property. The first function of government therefore is to protect these primal rights,

> that all men may be restrained from doing hurt to one another, and [that] the law of nature be observed, which wills the peace and preservation of all mankind.[7]

The particular emphasis upon *property* rights is not Locke's innovation, but was already part of the justification of the Roman state. As Cicero says,

> The primary concern of those responsible for the conduct of public affairs . . . will be to make certain that every man is secure in his possessions . . . For, though nature herself prompts men to congregate together, nevertheless it is in the hope of protecting what they have that they seek the protection of cities.[8]

As Cochrane points out, Cicero conceived of property as an "extension of personality."[9] Thus private property is a reflection of human nature. Thomas Jefferson reflects Locke's assumption in the opening words of the Declaration of Independence:

> We hold these truths to be *self-evident,* that *all men are created equal,* that they are endowed by their Creator with certain inalienable Rights, that among these are Life, Liberty and the pursuit of Happiness . . .

These words echo the naturalistic presuppositions of Stoicism: since all nature is pervaded by the *logos* (reason), each man possesses the *logos spermatikos* (seminal reason) and therefore all men are brothers. Jefferson's reference to the Creator is deistic in tone, accentuating the inherent naturalism of the human condition. We might summarize the Lockeian legacy[10] to democracy in these propositions: a) "Rights" derive from a superior source (nature or nature's God); b) the Law is prior to any government in time, and human authority should always derive from it; c) the chief end of government is to protect these rights; d) the right to resist illegitimate power derives from the premise that the laws of civil society must only supplement, but not *alter,* the Laws of Nature. These assumptions, though modified to fit the modern bourgeois state, reflect the socio-cosmos of Roman classicism, and especially

Stoicism. The main source of legitimation is nature, which as a harmonious and rational whole imbues its parts with this same character. Locke and Jefferson seem to perceive the deistic God in terms greater than a mere mechanical functionary, or Aristotelian First Cause. Indeed, their deity definitely reflects biblical personalism. God is therefore acceptable to the orthodox who can interpret Him in their own way. As the impact of mechanism became more pronounced upon the modern world, "natural rights" became descriptive of the functioning world machine; and the individualism (implicit in the concept of natural rights) became by measure a more radical atomism. Natural rights, which were to become the basis for community, if conceived atomistically could also militate against community.

Jean Jacques Rousseau (1712-1778) also singled out the primacy of the state of nature. Rousseau's vision of this original state seems more like a secularized version of the Genesis Myth of the Fall than a restatement of classical ideas. Man in his innocence is a good creature—happy, healthy, and unfettered by the bonds of civilization. But the primal beauty of humanity is corrupted by civilizing forces such as agriculture, metallurgy, and (most of all) the distinction between "mine" and "thine" that creates private property with its greed and egoism. The critical divergence between Locke's and Rousseau's "states of nature" anticipates the difference between modern capitalism and communism in the assessment of private property. Rousseau believes private property infects man with the disease of social pride and greed; in Locke private property is *part* of man's "natural state." Here we have variant mythologies—divergent structures of consciousness—both deriving from a quasi-similar starting point! Locke and Rousseau depict "man in a state of nature" with contrasting portraits. Locke's rational ideal evokes the image of a Stoic statesman contemplating the cosmos. Rousseau's first man is a "noble savage"—a kind of secularized Adam; or in terms of modern myth, perhaps a courageous and generous-hearted Tarzan.

Rousseau's state of nature is transformed into the civil state via a social contract in which individuals voluntarily submit themselves to the "general will." The general will, another mythical structure, ostensibly arises from the free association of intelligent human beings seeking to overcome the tyranny of individual wills. The general will reflects the ancient Greek principle of macrocosm/microcosm. Rousseau says that the state or the nation "is nothing but a legal person the life of which consists in the union of its members."[11] But the general will itself attains the status of complete sovereignty:

> Just as nature gives each man an absolute power over all his limbs, the social pact gives the body politic an absolute power over all its members; and it is the same power which, directed by the general will, bears, as I have said, the name of sovereignty . . . So we see that even as a private will cannot

represent the general will, so too the general will changes its nature if it seeks to deal with an individual case; it cannot as a general will give a ruling concerning any one man or any fact.[12]

Although Rousseau envisioned the general will as genuinely *representative* of the will of the people, his principle has been abused[13] in the service of totalitarianism.

In the *name* of the people many offenses have been committed *against* the people. The "general will" or "the people" can easily become a disembodied abstraction—a secularized divine will hierarchically and arbitrarily ruling over the many. John Stuart Mill expresses this danger:

Society can and does execute its own mandates; and if it issues wrong mandates instead of right, or any mandates at all in things with which it ought not to meddle, it practices a social tyranny more formidable than many kinds of political oppression . . .[14]

Of course Mill's argument may be invoked to counter governmental regulations, social welfare, or federal intervention in behalf of minority interests. The question then becomes not only how the general will is determined and maintained, but also how particular wills, whose interests are jeopardized by the general will, are effectively safeguarded. For example, the *utilitarian* rule of Bentham—"the greatest happiness for the greatest number"—sounds like a reasonable and convincing safeguard, but its mechanical application may result in the oppression of those not included in the "greatest number." The problem of the relative authority and execution of a "general will" recurrently haunts political theories of every ideological genre.

Various utopian myths for securing the happiness of the greatest number have appeared in the past two hundred years. The American Constitution attempts to mollify the absolutist danger by its representative system marked by a balance of power (or "checks and balances") between legislative, judicial, and executive branches of government. Yet a radically-altered economic base, the expansion of population from a small integral set of New England states to a vast super-state, and the unwieldy overlap of federal and state bureaucracies suggest a few of the complexities which belie the deceptive simplicity of the stated ideal. Indeed the population factor alone in many modern states appears an unavoidable chasm between government and the "people" conceived as its ultimate point of reference.

The utopian Saint-Simon (1760-1825), influenced by his study in physics, imagined a society created by both physical and social scientists. Such a society would be hierarchical, unabashedly mechanical and scientific—an endeavor run by social engineers. Taking a very modern (and utilitarian point of view) Saint-Simon bemoaned:

The scientists, artists, and artisans, the only men whose work is of positive utility to society, and cost it practically nothing, are kept down by the princes and other rulers who are simply more or less incapable bureaucrats

> . . . society is a world which is upside down. The nation holds as a fundamental principle that the poor should be generous to the rich, and that therefore the poorer classes should daily deprive themselves of necessities in order to increase the superfluous luxury of the rich. The most guilty men, the robbers on a grand scale, who oppress the mass of citizens, and extract from them three or four hundred millions a year, are given the responsibility of punishing minor offenses against society . . .[15]

Saint-Simon did not see science and humanitarian concerns as mutually exclusive. But Saint-Simon's vision, though later influencing Marx, culminates in a society based on a new "scientific" myth where:

> the spiritual power is in the hands of *scientists,* the temporal power in the hands of *property-owners;* the power to nominate those who should perform the functions of the leaders of humanity, in the hands of *all;* the reward of the rulers, esteem.[16]

Saint-Simon's prescription (excepting his reward for rulers as "esteem" only), may be more prophetic of the so-called modern "welfare state." Like Rousseau's general will, Saint-Simon's hierarchical structure appeals to "the people," and also like Rousseau reflects a kind of secularized Christian vision. As opposed to the priestly power of the medieval church, there is the priestly power of science; as opposed to the temporal power of the great feudal lords, there is the temporal power of property owners; instead of a Neoplatonic chain-of-being, there is in its place a scientifically-established bureauracy.

Saint-Simon's contemporary, Charles Fourier (1772-1837), acknowledged openly the union of divine and scientific mythical structures. In his eccentric plan society was to be organized into phalanxes of 800 persons, placed together scientifically and operating communally. Fourier believed that this arrangement was divinely revealed to him.

The last great utopian scheme was devised by an industrialist, Robert Owen (1771-1858). Directly anticipating Karl Marx, Owen disparages private property, religion, marriage, and money. Like Saint-Simon and Fourier, Owen transfers man's salvation from God to science. He proclaims:

> *Scientific* arrangements will be formed to make wealth everywhere, and at all times superabound . . . It will be equally evident that the unwrought materials to produce manufactured wealth exist in superfluity, and that *scientific* aids may now be constructed to procure and work up these materials without any disagreeable, unhealthy, or premature manual labor, into every variety of the most useful and valuable productions.[17]

If Owen sees scientific planning as necessary to the material structure of society, the moral structure derives from a "state of nature" which does not necessitate, but rather nullifies human legislation:

> It will be obvious, even to children, thus *rationally* educated, that all *human laws* must be either *unnecessary,* or *in opposition to Nature's laws,* they must create disunion, produce crime incessantly, and involve all transactions in inextricable confusion . . . In this New World, the sympathies of human nature will be tightly directed from infancy . . . The impurities of the

present system, arising from *human laws opposed to nature's laws, will be unknown.*[18]

George W. F. Hegel (1770-1831) also attempted to incorporate a scientific perspective in his system of historical idealism. Hegel believed that reason could discern the dynamics of history and discover the structure of the state most naturally suited to the historical process. According to Herbert Marcuse, Hegel's philosophical system is "the last great expression" of a cultural idealism which "renders thought a refuge for reason and liberty."[19] Yet, Marcuse continues, Hegel abandons "the traditional aloofness of idealism from history."[20] Reason will engage the real, and the universal must account for the particular. Hegel's myth reflects Aristotle in this regard.

In his own day, Hegel believed that European "civil society,"[21] reflecting the Western traditions of Roman natural law and Christian "conscience," was mainly attuned to *private rights* and *private morality* (pervasive concerns of Enlightenment bourgeois individualism).[22] This individualist bias could be overcome only in the *state,* which is an *ethical community.*

Three "bonds" hold the state together. The first bond is the "common subjection" of its members "to a supreme and independent public authority," which "acts through statutes, but sometimes through prerogative orders which, like statutes, have universal legal validity within the confines of the state."[23] This is the *political* bond. The second, or *civil* bond stems from individuals acting in self interest who initiate "a nexus of relations, which though regulated by law, is in no way a direct product of the legal order."[24] Marriage or corporations exemplify such relations. The third or communal bond is the *ethical* bond, which lends the state its unique character. This bond includes sharing "the same concepts, principles or ideals of the good life, which have been handed down from generation to generation," and such "spiritual" factors as "common language, culture, religion or national consciousness."[25] It is ironic that the very crowning character of the state— its ethical dimension—later becomes perverted as a key myth of the Third Reich.[26] Hegel himself considered the "spiritual factors" to be of secondary significance in constituting the ethical community.[27]

What *kind* of political structure would embody Hegel's "rational" vision? He believed that constitutional monarchy avoided the extremes of both democracy and autocracy. Even classical democracy seemed to fall short of Hegel's idea. As Shlomo Avineri observes:

> The polis is thus an entity which despite its apparent beauty enslaves the individual, and the democratic nature of its structure only accentuates the individual's total absorption in the political system. The alternative to this form is, according to Hegel, the modern constitutional monarchy, which is based on the rule of law and the freedom of the individual who identifies with, and at the same time differentiates himself from, the state.[28]

Individuality is mediated through the monarch, who symbolizes subjectivity, and whose prerogative expression "'We command,' is thus pure subjectivity willing itself."[29] Thus individualism is preserved, and is even one of the sources of strength of the state;[30] but its occurrence does not contradict the cohesion of community. Pelczynski writes:

> The task of keeping 'civil society' within its proper bounds as one 'moment' of the ethical whole thus ultimately devolves on the political organization of the 'ethical community.' This organization has to be responsive to the legitimate claims of 'particularity' and 'subjectivity,' yet independent and strong enough to resist their excessive pressure and escape the danger of being dominated by them.[31]

For Hegel, protection of the state from domination by bourgeois interests, and assurance of its constitutionality, required a hereditary (as opposed to an elective) monarchy:

> The monarch's exclusive prerogatives over the executive, the civil service and the armed forces, and his right to veto the Estates' legislative proposals, are all explicable by Hegel's eagerness to prevent their domination by the forces of 'particularity' and 'subjectivity,' and by his belief that only the monarch's ultimate personal control can guarantee that they all remain first and foremost organs of the 'ethical community.'[32]

The *muthos* of constitutional monarchy as the most *rational* form of government has had limited historical influence. Nonetheless, Hegel considered his models to be scientific in that they were designed to account for historical processes and the actual situation of men.

Citing Hegelian idealism as his counterpoint, Karl Marx (1818-1883) formulates the single most influential political myth of modern times. In the *German Ideology* (1845-1846) Marx and his supporter, Friedrich Engels, express radical opposition to the abstract character of Hegel's rational legitimations. The only authentic legitimation of political theory is the situation of "real individuals, their activities and the material conditions under which they live, both those which they find already existing and those produced by their activity."[33] Marx and Engels claim that "scientific" *praxis* has triumphed in these words. Man as existing is the "first premise of all human history."[34] The scientific reality of man's existence is social existence.

Insofar as Marx reflects the classical Greek ideal of the *polis*, as well as Feuerbach's assertion that man *by nature* is a "species being," society is envisioned not as artificial, but as a natural, material expression.[35] Marx and Engels wish to ground the social structure solidly within the real, everyday experience of men:

> The production of ideas, of conceptions, of consciousness is at first directly interwoven with the material activity and the material intercourse of men, the language of real life . . . Men are the producers of their conceptions, ideas, etc.—real, active men, as they are conditioned by a definite development of their productive forces . . . Consciousness can never be

anything else than conscious existence, and the existence of men is their actual life process . . . In direct contrast to German philosophy which descends from heaven to earth, here we ascend from earth to heaven.[36]

In opposition to both Hegel and to traditional Western society, Marx rejects any hierarchical principle of legitimation. If we examine Marx's assaults on capitalist society we discover that his first concern is to affirm concrete *humanity* in contradistinction to both the traditional hierarchical and the new mechanical cosmic myths. Marx inveighs against the remnants of medieval Christendom which alienate modern man. Religion itself (which, like Feuerbach, Marx interpreted anthropologically), postulating a belief in God, creates an alien will which stands over against man and alienates him from himself. Secondly, the class structure is even worse than the feudalism from which it historically derives. The modern worker, unlike the serf, is alienated from the land and excluded from direct personal participation and gratification in the process and products of his labor.

Furthermore, Marx depicts the material results of the labor system of capitalistic economics in grim terms. The laborer is alienated from the product of his labor. He is devalued by the creation of a world of things over against himself. He is alienated from other men since relationships are valued through the mediating abstraction of money or capital. He is cut off from nature. But worst of all, he is alienated from his own humanity. And yet man—especially the worker who is in such a condition—is the pivotal point of reference of Marx's appeal. For Marx, a new mythic structure, the "classless society," is to be effected by the agency of the proletariat, entailing a transformation of the human condition. The creation of a new socio-economic order is the creation of a new humanity.[37] The actual social and material condition of man must remain the locus of authority for Marx.

Thus far we have observed various sources of legitimation underlying the modern state: Nature, the General Will, Reason and History, Material Reality or the actual historical condition of man. In all cases the legitimating norms reflect some interpretation of major loci of the Judeo-Christian or classical traditions. Marx's materialism reflects the classical presuppositions of Greek atomism (the subject of his doctoral dissertation),[38] if not a secularized Hebrew historicism. The "classless society" draws upon imagery of Christian universalism.

This penchant to recall historical archetypes is a pervasive expression of political thought. Men cannot live without mythical structures. The structures of hierarchy and mechanism recur in a variety of institutional or ideological settings. On July 31, 1955, Chairman Mao uttered these typical words: "We must have faith in the masses and we must have faith in the Party. These are two cardinal principles. If we doubt these principles, we shall accomplish nothing."[39] Here the general will is embodied in the will of the Party, and the will of the Party reflects its hierarchical structure:

> We must affirm anew the discipline of the Party, namely: 1) the individual is subordinate to the organization; 2) the minority is subordinate to the majority; 3) the lower level is subordinate to the higher level; and 4) the entire membership is subordinate to the Central Committee.[40]

With slight modifications, the above statement could be a typical utterance of a corporate or ecclesiastical bureaucrat.

On the other hand, Russell A. Kirk, a spokesman for American conservatism lays down these six canons of conservative thought:*

> 1) Belief that a *divine intent* rules society as well as conscience, forging an *eternal chain* of right and duty which links great and obscure, living and dead. Political problems, at bottom, are *religious* and *moral* problems . . .
> 2) Affection for the proliferating variety and mystery of *traditional life,* as distinguished from the *narrowing uniformity* and *equalitarianism* and *utilitarian* aims of most radical systems . . .
> 3) Conviction that civilized society requires *orders* and *classes. The only true equality* is *moral* equality . . .
> 4) Persuasion that *property* and freedom are inseparably connected, and that economic levelling is not economic progress . . .
> 5) Faith in *prescription* and distrust of "sophisters and calculators." Man must put a control upon his will and his appetite, for *conservatives know man to be governed more by emotion than by reason. Tradition* and *sound prejudice* provide checks upon man's anarchic impulse;
> 6) Recognition that *change* and reform are not identical, and that *innovation* is a devouring conflagration more often than it is a torch of progress.[41]

Kirk's creed, too, with slight modification, might fit quite well into an apologetic for medieval society based on the Neoplatonic chain-of-being. Kirk further attacks these innovations of modern thought: 1) defining man as a socio-political animal (actually a classical position); 2) seeing man primarily as a rational being (also a classical position); 3) the belief that all men are created equal and are endowed by nature with equal rights (asserted by Stoicism); 4) a classless society (early Christian universalism); 5) social ownership of property; 6) innovation. Although Kirk's hidden agenda seems to be debunking Marxism and liberalism, he equally challenges key mythical referents of the Declaration of Independence. Kirk also singles out notions of man's perfectibility, unlimited progress, challenges to tradition (especially the welfare movement), and political or economic egalitarianism as contrary to the "conservative model" for society. It may be observed that Kirk is hardly "conserving" classical traditions which are conveniently depicted as "innovations."

To underscore the broad variety of competing frames of authority, and the diverse uses of the structures of traditional Western thought, we cite the contemporary political scientist, Zevedei Barbu. According to Barbu's

---

*Kirk's canons are excellent illustrations of what we have called sessile consciousness.

interpretation, "democracy" is far removed from the conservatism of a Kirk. Far from being established once and for all as an eternal mode of truth, democracy is a dynamic frame of mind. Barbu's "frame of mind" contradicts the assertions of Kirk at certain critical junctures:

1) One of the basic traits of the democratic frame of mind can be described as the feeling of *change* . . . a state of *permanent transformation* and *readjustment of forms* . . . the first category of the democratic frame of mind . . . (also):
2) . . . the feeling that the *growth* of society is determined *from within* . . .
3) . . . a feeling of the *instability* and *relativity of power and authority* . . .
4) . . . an attitude of confidence in reason . . .[42]

For Barbu, states which would claim the rubric "democratic" must derive from "consent of the governed." Thus they must accept cosmological pluralism and competing frames of reference. Barbu's "democracy" is referred to an entirely different set of mythical norms (which we have called motile).

Individual and Community

One of the most common sources of legitimation is "the People." "The People" seems to refer self-evidently to the *community* of the governed, but this definition cannot be automatically assumed. In early Greece *demos* meant "poorer people," and democracy was defined as the rule of the poor over the rich (*demos:* "the common people" + *kratein:* "to rule").[43] This is a mythical root for the communist rule of the proletariat or working class. But "the People" is an elusive euphemism, and the "rule of the People" perhaps self-contradictory (in that ultimate democracy would not be a "rule" at all, but the unanimity of all in every decision). In the classical Athenian pattern, *democracy* entailed the opportunity for "the People" to influence directly the policies of government, or to have their *interests* represented.[44] In Marxist theory "the People" ("the proletariat") are at first *not* the holders of the reins of society; "after the Revolution" all people are to become workers—a "universal class" in which the old bourgeois economic bases are broken down.[45] The instruments of production belong to the *state,* which ostensibly becomes the *trustee* of the people or the personification of their interests. We see that "the People" is a very nebulous concept reflecting a wide variety of possible mythical referents. Who are "the People" of modern society, and what is their *ethos* (character, style, self-concept)?

Is "community" a natural or artificial state of humanity? According to Locke, the state of nature is fundamentally individualistic—a state wherein man may act "without asking leave or depending upon the will of any other man."[46] Locke himself identifies ways in which "the state of nature" is lacking:

There wants an established, settled, known law, received and allowed by common consent to be the standard of right and wrong . . . There wants a known and indifferent judge, with authority to determine all differences according to the established law . . . there often wants power to back and support the sentence when right, and to give it due execution.[47]

Thus, though not necessarily in a state of hostility, people in a state of nature would be isolated, since no common "law" would bind them together. *The state* is a necessary counterpoint to this mythical structure. Rousseau's concept of a "state of nature" is not so different from Locke's at this point:

Since no man has any natural authority over his fellows, and since force alone bestows no right, all legitimate authority among men must be based on covenants.[48]

Rousseau depicts the social contract as an agreement of free individuals who coalesce for popular majority rule and parliamentary representation. But the glimmer of a romantic aura surrounding the isolate individual—the noble savage (who in actual anthropological studies lives in a closely knit and most often highly rigid social unit), never disappears from Rousseau's vision. For even in the life of community Rousseau cautions

To renounce freedom is to renounce one's humanity, one's rights as a man and equally one's duties. There is no possible *quid pro quo* for one who renounces everything; indeed such renunciation is contrary to man's very nature; for if you take away all freedom of the will, you strip a man's actions of all moral significance.[49]

Mythical conceptions and the personal experiences of their creators seem historically interrelated. The lives of Locke and Rousseau reflect a variety of personal factors conspiring to reinforce a strong individualism. Both were (more or less) of bourgeois backgrounds. Locke was quite influenced by modern physics, and anticipated behaviorism with his theory of knowledge. Ideas, impressions accumulate on the initially "blank slate"; and just as atoms coalesce to form molecules and compounds, so impressions coalesce to form ideas and thought. Locke's tacit atomism is reflected in his theory of individuals and the state.[50] Rousseau emerged in an environment still dominated by Descartes, whose entire philosophical system rested upon the primal consciousness of the individual: *cogito ergo sum.* Rousseau's background and temperament compelled him towards a prolonged personal and emotional struggle towards recognition by, and some security within, the community. His vision of the individual who in a natural state is a noble, self-sufficient being (perhaps unappreciated by the civilized world), and who in the social contract attains higher ethical awareness and achievement, may well mirror his own journey from rustic troubadour striving for new sophistication and acceptance, to the Paris *salons.*[51]

The individual/community polarity and the idea of the social contract also reflect established structures of the Christian myth. In the biblical tradition, we see the polarity recurring. The first man is the lonely Adam who has for his companions only the beasts and God himself, until Eve is created. Noah stands alone as he prepares the ark of salvation for the world. Abraham leaves the advanced society of Ur as a wanderer in search of a new land. Moses, raised in the sophistication of the Egyptian court, must become an isolated shepherd among the hills of Midian to prepare for his mission. The biblical prophets appear as stark solitary figures arising to confront corruption of the Hebrew societies. Jesus, though followed by the twelve, remains enshrouded in mystery and a certain remoteness. At the trial or hanging on the cross his singular figure looms over the whole course of Western history. The biblical "contract" or "covenant" between God and man follows the mission of a Moses or a Jesus; at its core, it is *not* an agreement between men, but a dispensation of God. But the divine covenant both in classical Israel and in medieval Christendom did not sustain the political process forever. Thus in the modern West it is replaced by a strictly social covenant among "freely participating" persons. For in social contract theory, individuals are always prior to the state or society,[52] and the rights of the individual must remain the supreme *muthos*.

If community—and especially the *state*—are conceived as artificial impositions upon "individuals," it is not difficult to see how a mechanical model of the state triumphs; i.e., if it is assumed that unfettered "individualism" is *ultimately* the natural state, then "institutional life" will by necessity assume some air of a mechanical artifact. In this case individualism only exacerbates structural abstractions implicit within a bureaucracy.

Alternatives to democratic political theory also underscore the quest for a structure capable of easing the individual/community tensions. Jeremy Bentham (1748-1832) is in many ways the modern Epicurus. His *utilitarian rule* is a *quantitative* and *atomistic* assessment of society based on the norms of "pain" and "pleasure" for the greatest numbers.

> To *multiply* pleasures, to *diminish* pains—such is the whole business of the legislator. Their *value* should be well known, therefore. Pleasures and pains are the only *instruments* that can be employed . . . If we examine the *value* of a pleasure considered *in itself*, and with relation to *one single individual*, we shall find it to depend on four circumstances: 1) its *intensity*; 2) its *duration*; 3) its *certainty*; 4) its *proximity* . . . etc.[53]

But John Stuart Mill (1806-1873), influenced by Bentham, protests of the danger of the "tyranny of the majority":

> The "people" who exercise the power are not always the same people with those over whom it is exercised; and the "self-government" spoken of is not the government of *each by himself*, but of each by all the rest.[54]

On the other hand, recent theorists, although recognizing the coercive nature of political constraint, have warned us of the dangers to society of unbridled individualism (and its mythical rationalizations). T. H. Green (1836-1882) especially warns of the danger of such individuals forming alliances for selfishness and greed:

> The civilization and freedom of the ancient world were short-lived because they were partial and exceptional. If the ideal of true freedom is the

maximum of power for all members of human society alike to make the best of themselves, we are right in refusing to ascribe the glory of freedom to a state in which the apparent elevation of the few is founded on the degradation of the many, and in ranking modern society, founded as it is on free industry, with all its confusion and ignorant license and waste of effort, above the most splendid of ancient republics.[55]

Green's point has been dramatically underscored in recent days by the mounting awareness of the crises of pollution and energy, and the precariousness of the general ecological balance. Society's frequent recalcitrance in ignoring these crises illustrates the tenacity of deeply entrenched mythical structures.

Likewise, Leonard T. Hobhouse (1864-1929) assails the tendency to extreme *laissez faire* individualism in modern democratic society. He writes that "mutual aid is not less important than mutual forbearance, the theory of collective action no less fundamental than the theory of personal freedom."[56] Hobhouse recalls the socio-political nature of man in an organic society which

means that, while the life of society is nothing but the life of individuals as they act one upon another, the life of the individual in turn would be something utterly different if he could be separated from society.[57]

John Dewey (1859-1952) echoes the trend to mollify unqualified individualism supposedly deriving from natural law:

The fundamental defect [of earlier democratic liberal philosophy] was lack of perception of *historical relativity*. This lack is expressed in the conception of the *individual as something given*, complete in itself, and of liberty as a *ready-made possession* of the individual, only needing the removal of external restrictions in order to manifest itself. The individual of earlier liberalism was a *Newtonian atom* having only external time and space relations to other individuals, save that each social atom was equipped with inherent freedom. These ideas . . . formed part of a philosophy in which these particular ideas of individuality and freedom were asserted to be *absolute and eternal truths;* good for all times and all places.[58]

Here Dewey has pointed out a critical defect in the abstract philosophical myths (atomism, mechanism, absolutism) which fail to consider history or the dynamics of socio-political change. In this regard Dewey's observations sound a little like Marx's critique of Hegel.[59] However, for Dewey, the liberal imperative differs from orthodox Marxism (which stamps its own predetermined scheme upon history).[60] Dewey extrapolates from the positivistic concerns of science:

The commitment of liberalism to experimental procedure carries with it the idea of continuous reconstruction of the ideas of individuality and of liberty in intimate connection with changes in social relations.[61]

In Dewey, like Barbu, we can perceive a fundamental shift in the conception of democracy: we can no longer posit an ideal or eternal abstract law, unalterable by, and fundamentally divorced from, historical process. Dewey illustrates how the methodology, if not the content, of modern science has helped reshape the world picture of modern society. That society is now more likely to be depicted as an empirically-perceptible dynamic process.

One of the recurrent criticisms leveled against contemporary states is the charge of repression of individual liberties. Without enjoining this issue in terms of concrete case histories, we can review the pertinent mythic structures which define the individual's role vis-a-vis society.

We alluded to Rousseau's concept of the *general will,* as well as his myth of the *noble savage.* There is of course a strong tension between this desirable natural individualism and the more ethical social state which becomes the bearer of the general will. There is an even greater tension between the idea of individual rights and a general will. Democracy has read Rousseau more in terms of the former, fascism and communism more in terms of the latter. In any case, Rousseau illustrates the inevitable tensions between the rights of the individual and those of the community.

Saint-Simon, who advocated a new hierarchical and elitist society run by scientists, nevertheless concerned himself with the fate of the "have-nots," and appealed to the prophetic tradition of the Judeo-Christian myth:

> What is the nature and character, in the eyes of God and of Christians, of the power which you wield? What is the basis of the social system which you endeavor to establish? What measures have you taken to improve the moral and physical condition of the poor? You call yourselves Christians, and yet you base your power on material force; you are still the successors of Caesar, and you forget that true Christians have as the final goal of their efforts the abolition of the power of the sword, the power of Caesar, which by its nature is essentially transitory . . . Remember that Christianity commands you to use all your powers to increase as rapidly as possible the social welfare of the poor![62]

Saint-Simon never suggests that society can escape orders and hierarchies; he is rather pleading that its *muthos* be more ethically informed.

Saint-Simon's contemporary, Charles Fourier, envisions his plan for a communist utopia as coming to him by divine revelation. His workers' phalanxes are to be comprised of eight hundred persons each; the placing of persons is to be determined scientifically (in the twentieth century, Fourier might advocate computer analysis for this task). Fourier is explicit in identifying the "evils of individualism" in industry, e.g., "wage labor=indirect servitude," paternalism, waste, unemployment, competition and the contradiction of individual and collective interest.[63] In a similar vein, Robert Owen visualizes a kind of millenial worker's paradise. He proposes that

> We, therefore, as the disinterested friends of all Classes of all Nations, recommend to all Governments and People, that the old prejudices of the world, for or against class, sect, party, country, sex, and color, derived solely from ignorance, should be now allowed, by the common consent of all, to die their natural death; that standing armies of all nations should be disbanded in order that the men may be employed in producing instead of destroying wealth; that the rising generation should be educated from birth

to become superior, in character and conduct, to all past generations; that all should be trained to have as much enjoyment, in producing as in using or consuming wealth, which, through the progress of science, can be easily effected; that all should freely partake of it; and that, thus, the reign of peace, intelligence, and universal sympathy, or affection, may, forever, supersede the reign of ignorance and oppression.[64]

But Marx is the most unambiguous in suggesting a "realistic" program of how such a community must be understood. Contrary to Fourier, it does not derive from religious principle. For the *early* Marx, the real basis of community is found primarily not even in the solidarity of the proletariat (in his later writings the revolutionary vehicle for transforming capitalism), but rather in human nature itself. Like Feuerbach (and the classical Greek conception of *polites*), man is conceived as a species being, a social being—a being "in community" or "in relationship." But in his growing antipathy to abstract statements about human *nature,* Marx envisioned "community" not as an ideal, but as the material locus of the socio-economic life of man, which can be observed, measured and evaluated. In this regard Marx's emphases seemed to shift from humanism to social science. He wrote that the premises of materialism

> are men, not in any fantastic isolation or abstract definition, but in their actual, empirically perceptible process of development under definite conditions . . . Where speculation ends—in real life—there real *positive science* begins: the representation of the practical activity, of the practical process of development of men . . .[65]

However, in this century Joseph Stalin seems to transform Marx's concrete science[66] into an abstract formal science:

> . . . the science of the history of society, despite all the complexity of the phenomena of social life, can become as precise a science as, let us say, biology, and capable of making use of the laws of development of society for practical purposes.[67]

Yet in any case, Marxist theory ostensibly derives *community* from human nature and its empirical, material, and scientifically apprehensible condition in the world.*

Particularism, Universalism and Teleology

Every political ideology posits some mythical point of departure where man is depicted as leaving behind either some inferior or some primitive social condition to implement an ideal community. The *arche* ("beginning") may be an original "state of nature" or the present enslavement of the worker in modern mechanistic or capitalistic society, or some other social counterpoint. The thesis that we should look for the end in the beginning— for the *telos* ("goal," "end") in the *arche*—is suggestive. For example, if man is "free" and "equal" in an original state of nature, we would assume that the

---

*However, we would remind the reader of the inherent "mythicizing" tendency of language itself, regardless of the theoretical framework employed. See Chapter two.

ideal community should honor these norms. If the worker is enslaved in an unjust capitalistic economy, we should look for an obverse goal of some worker's paradise. The self-concept and self-legitimation of a people is often to be found in the harmony or polarity between *beginning* and *end* as comparative mythical points of reference.

The goals of "democracy" may seem to many fairly self-evident. Just as "all men are created equal" and "are endowed by their Creator with certain inalienable rights," we assume that the securing of these rights, including "life, liberty and the pursuit of happiness" is the fundamental goal of democracy. However, the *terms* of this idealistic conception are hopelessly abstract. As we begin to ask for further exposition, it becomes clear that "equality, life, liberty and the pursuit of happiness" are not substantive, ontically objectifiable and empirically translucent, states. The *hidden agenda* becomes not the mythic *ends,* but the concrete *means* by which the ends are implemented (and therefore actually defined). In this case "the means are the bearers of the ends." In America the slogans "equality, life, liberty and the pursuit of happiness," for example, are roughly equated with "republican" government and free enterprise.

Indeed, considering the transformations in modern post-industrial societies, the designation of a society as "democratic" becomes problematic.[68] For example, propelled by Social Darwinism, nineteenth century imperialistic "democracy" (a contradiction in terms) envisaged its mythic goal as self-dissemination (or expansion) to the "underprivileged" peoples of the world:

> Take up the White Man's burden—
> Send forth the best ye breed—
> Go bind your sons to exile
> To serve your captives' need;
> To wait in heavy harness,
> On fluttered folk and wild—
> Your new caught, sullen peoples
> Half-devil and half-child . . .
>
> Take up the White man's burden—
> Ye dare not stoop to less—
> Nor call too loud on Freedom
> To cloke your weariness
> By all ye cry or whisper,
> By all ye leave or do,
> The silent, sullen peoples
> Shall weigh your Gods and you.[69]

If Rudyard Kipling's paternalistic sentiments[70] are shared overtly by few today (most particularly not by those "sullen peoples" who have weighed our Gods, and found them wanting), they nevertheless dramatize a fundamental missionary zeal which has characterized or disguised much activity of the "democratic" "Christian" West. The source of this attitude is to be found in the peculiar coalescence of democratic theory, Christianity and capitalistic economy, which produces an uncanny series of mythic tensions (which like positive and negative magnetic poles, have energized the expansion of the West).

We have already cited Max Weber's work elucidating the ties between the Protestant sense of calling or election and economic frugality and prosperity. If Barbu deems democracy fundamentally a state of mind geared to transformation, growth, the relativity of authority, and confidence in reason, the traditional frame of mind of ostensible "democratic" societies has seemed more intent upon transforming the world into its own sessile image— convincing "backward" peoples of the moral superiority of our "freedom" (which often in the past implied the conversion of other "pagan" persons to Christianity). The hidden tensions resident in these attitudes emanate from the juxtaposition of Judeo-Christian and Greco-Roman structures. The Judeo-Christian sense of moral superiority and historical calling and mission is in essence particularistic, since the "universal" vision entails in actuality the triumph of a *particular* world view over all competitors.

The Greco-Roman sense of intellectual and aesthetic superiority (at least in some of its forms) allows for the universality of reason and the educability of all men to a rational mode of life. Yet this cosmic sense of reason could often bear the tacit assumption that there is only one actual expression of rationality, truth, etc.—e.g., the Roman Empire. Again, with the wedding of the two traditions, the West has been imbued with a two-fold sense of superiority, both historical-ethical and intellectual-aesthetic. The tensions between the two traditions—and perhaps frustrations created by a "split" consciousness—have called forth herculean efforts to create synthetic myths or legitimations (e.g., Hegel). Ontological anxiety has fueled the triumph of Western Civilization: the anxiety between revelation and reason, between history and nature, between *Homo religiosus* and *Homo profanus* (or *Homo organicus*). In each case the polarities have become parallel modes of legitimation, and have driven the West forward at an obsessive-compulsive pace which has finally reached a crisis point. The split has widened and the forces of tension now have a wedge driven between them: the emergent identities of the "other" peoples and nations all over the world in South America, in Africa, in Asia, in the Far East—most of whom, in the interest of asserting their own indigenous cosmoi, have not fit neatly into classical and Christian world pictures. Moreover, Marxist revolutionary movements (which have won more victories among these peoples than Western democracy) perhaps have faced more realistically the cold fact that imposing a particularistically-conditioned pseudo-universalism on people of widely divergent cultures and values is both unfeasible and indeed impossible.*

---

*However, indegenous movements such as the Islamic Revolution in Iran, have showed greater potency than either the West *or* the Soviets had anticipated.

Prior to Marx, Utopian visions in the West wrecked upon the reef of historical reality. The musings of a Saint-Simon, a Fourier, a Robert Owen, or a score of others, may have left a legacy for later socialist and Marxist mythologists. Owen's plea for civil rights, the death of racism and sexism, disarmament and world economic and political cooperation continue to sound as a clarion call in the long night of our worldwide pluralistic factionalism. But at least in one regard, if not in others, Marx was surely right: we must start with the material reality of the human condition. If the world is to attain some sort of unity, it will not be because of a sudden worldwide awakening to ethical vision, but rather because of pressing necessity and the relentless god, Expediency. As in the case of the Civil Rights Movement in the U.S. in the sixties, laws creating actual *rights* may precede the gradual diffusion of new attitudes and popular pious rationalizations. However, we must remember that without the vision or the myth, no one would have worked to enact those laws.

Why has the Marxist vision been so successful on a worldwide scale?[71] Marxism, more than any prior political philosophy, has appealed to the masses of people in their actual situation: "workers of the *world* unite." At least as mythic principle Marx's "classless society" promises the proletariat: 1) freedom from taxonomic and mechanistic slotting; the socially-deprived acquire an identity and a community; 2) freedom from the alienating aspects of private property; for Marx, property belongs to the community with the state as its trustee; 3) freedom from the destructiveness of competition; 4) a legitimation and meaning for historical existence; the Dialectic illustrates the unfolding of history in its movement towards universal community; the worker becomes part of this community by taking up the cause of the Revolution. In one way or another each of these components is to be found in the *muthos* of primitive Christianity (especially as depicted in Acts). Unlike primitive Christianity, to implement its vision Marxism has openly advocated the accruing and proper use of political and military *power*. Stalin remarks:

> ... the masses become welded into a new political army, create a new revolutionary power, and make use of it to abolish by force the old system of relations of production, and firmly to establish the new system.[72]

The religious force of Marxism has often been cited. The camaraderie of a people welded together through suffering and liberation has its archetype in the Egyptian bondage and the Exodus event out of which the people of Israel emerged. The appeal to the breaking down of class structures and the dream of a universal community parallels the New Testament image of the Body of Christ, in which "there is neither Jew nor Greek, circumcised nor uncircumcised, slave nor free, male nor female." Finally, the eschatological appeal of a New Earth based upon the triumph of the Elect (the workers) over the unbelieving world (the bourgeoisie) and the demonic forces (capitalism) is a powerful "religious" vision. The strength of Marxism, then, has been not only its tapping of the "grass roots" of society—the masses of the world—but also its inherent identity-creating mythology or world view with its emotive "religious" flavor. The weakness has been the ease with which *means* have overshadowed *ends:* totalitarianism and thinly-disguised fascism have too often succeeded the popular base. The "general will" ceases to be the will of "the people" and becomes the will of the Party bosses. Yet this "free world" critique of Marxism does not take into account two factors: 1) Soviet Russia and China, like the West, face the same pluralism, nationalism and successful insubordination of "Third World" forces, and adjustments are necessary; 2) Marxist theory—directed specifically towards the oppressed and calling upon *them* to marshal their own resources—is more generally adaptable to provincial concerns than a preconceived bourgeois model of freedom and prosperity, which for many years capitalist countries sought to stamp upon the "downtrodden masses" of the world.

To simplify—and perhaps oversimplify—the picture: classical democracy has been marketed with an hierarchical supremacy resembling medieval Christendom—attempting to mold the masses by an Eternal Order stamped down upon them from top to bottom. This cosmic vision has crashed upon the bedrock of material and social reality. This rigid sessile mold has been unable to contain the turbulent and creative torrents of motility—of "revolutionary" consciousness striving for new world location and new identity. But Marx, challenged by the dynamism of Hegel's historical vision, inverted the Dialectic and imbued the communist myth with a sense of concrete social location and material realism. Thus communism has sought to transform the world by working from the bottom up—in hopes that the top will topple and the rest will level out. Admittedly hierarchism has invaded the communist world. But hierarchism is not ultimately justified by Marx's world picture, and the resiliency of Marxism may be its own realism. In fact it is just that realism which indicates that there can be no idealized communist model which can ever be stamped upon all peoples. Apart from military force, "communism" will triumph only in synthetic and pluralistic forms, not through the monolithic rigidity which still infects communist world leaders. Moreover, if "democracy" triumphs—it, too, must assume more flexible, adaptable and indigenous forms. Democracy is not without its motile elements. Its great internal strengths are representative and constitutional government, modes of redress, balance of power ("checks and balances"), freedom of speech and freedom of the press. In accordance with our own norms, we would do well to affirm the myth-making capacity or self-determination and freedoms of all "other" peoples, through not imposing our definitions upon them.

Political prophecy is a risky business, but it does not take great genius or foresight to recognize that the world of tomorrow must implement new myths of synthesis, compromise, and local flexibility, promoting the integrity of a pluralistic world. It seems unlikely that any purely sessile abstraction can win the day in the multifarious political milieu of modernity. The last political myth we shall examine—totalitarian fascism—has surely tried.

THE MYTHICAL COSMOS OF FASCISM

The term "fascism" derives from the Latin *fasces*. The *fasces*—a bundle of thin rods bound together with an ax among them—was carried by Roman magistrates as a symbol of Roman imperial power and unity. This mythic symbol appropriately describes the mythical esprit de corps which the official apologists of Italian and Nazi fascism attempt to create. Italian and Nazi fascism embody in dramatic and tangible form a kind of "fascist mind-set" which recurs perhaps more subtly in contemporary fascist regimes. The "Axis" form of fascism can be interpreted as a thoroughgoing religious cosmology thinly disguised in secular clothing. In significant respects it represents a rebirth of the medieval vision. The ensuing exposition of the fascist myth intends to accentuate further the evocative and effective impact of mythic cosmologies in Western politics, and in particular those which most suggestively awaken historical archetypes nostalgically embedded within our consciousness.

Hierarchy and Authority

When the bishop of Rome assumed increasing powers in the latter days of the Roman Empire, the prestige of his office—propelled by the centrality of Rome itself and its own symbols of world domination—steadily mounted. Furthermore, as Christianity became the official religion of the Empire, and as the Neoplatonic hierarchical cosmology was enlisted by theologians to legitimate ecclesiastical claims to temporal authority, the stage was set for the integral world view of the Middle Ages.

The examination of fascist propaganda suggests that their world vision is set forth as an answer for the demise of the medieval Christian cosmos which had once stabilized Europe. Whether, or to what extent, that stability is merely fanciful, no effective cosmology has since taken its place. It is not as though the fascist theoreticians always consciously aped the medieval tradition, yet in some instances this seems to be the case.

Fascism envisions a single, powerful and intelligent leader who, like a supreme pontiff, has unquestioned authority. The fascist leader appears as a kind of secularized divine monarch or secularized high priest whose words are veritable "revelation," and who—though the source of the law—is himself for all intents and purposes "above the law." The fascist leader is the national *hero,* who is to embody the will and character of the nation. Mario Palmieri writes in 1936:

Fascism holds, in fact, that the State must be a social, political, economic, moral and religious organism built as a *pyramid* at whose *vortex* is the *national hero*, the greatest man of his time and his nation, and leading to this national hero by an uninterrupted series of continuously widening powers arranged in *hierarchies*. The hierarchy becomes thus the very essence of Authority and the hierarchical arrangement of society its truest expression in the world of man.[73]

The hero not only stands at the pinnacle of the hierarchy, but like Carlyle's prototype, becomes a messianic figure—an incarnation of the divine:

A hero is he who can pierce with the *mystic light* of an *inner vision* to the very heart of things; he who can rediscover the greatest and most profound of all truths: viz., that beyond this realm of fugitive appearances there lies, *immutable* and *eternal*, what Fichte called the *"Divine Idea of the World"*. . . To acknowledge that a man *in our midst*, a man of *flesh and bone*, with our vices and our virtues, with our strength and our weaknesses . . . is truly a hero . . . we must ask of him first of all, and above all, that through his speech, his actions, his influence, his example, his whole life, in short, he live the very message he is delivering to us.[74]

It is true that this is a mere man of flesh, but he is led by the spirit into the "realm of timeless and absolute Reality" achieved at the cost of "difficulty, abnegation, martyrdom, death."[75] This representative man has a mission very much like the "suffering servant" of Second Isaiah, chapter 53:

Surely he has borne our griefs
 and carried our sorrows;
yet we esteemed him stricken,
 smitten by God, and afflicted.
But he was wounded for our transgressions,
 he was bruised for our iniquities;
Upon him was the chastisement that made us whole,
 and with his stripes we are healed.
(Isaiah 53:4-6)

The appellation of such a messianic role[76] for Hitler is implied in these words of Herman Goering in 1934:

Hitler's mission is of importance for the *history of the whole world*, because he took up a war to the death against Communism . . . The German people has arisen and Germany will again be healthy. For that we have *the guarantor* who is Adolf Hitler, the Chancellor of the German people and the protector of their honor and freedom.[77]

By the late thirties, Hitler's "divine mission and calling" are crystallized in the eyes of man. Ernst Hueber writes in 1939:

The Fuehrer is the *bearer* of the *people's will;* he is *independent* of all groups, association, and interests, but he is bound by laws which are inherent in the nature of his people . . . He transforms the mere feelings of the people into a conscious will . . . The Fuehrer unites in himself *all* the sovereign *authority* of the Reich; all public authority in the state as well as in the movement is derived from the authority of the Fuehrer . . . The authority of the Fuehrer is *complete* and *all-embracing* . . .[78]

With the absolute will of the people and complete authority invested in himself, the Fuehrer is free "to go against the subjective opinions and convictions of single individuals."[79] The specific religious nature of Hitler's authority is illustrated by the following Nazi poem recited by German school children:

> About thee stand thy people, oh my Fuehrer,
> And when, in kindness or in wrath, thou sqeakest,
> Thou art, by God's decree, the voice this people finds.
> In thee do they both form and will assume—
> Thou art the law in them. In thy vast planning
> The fathers' purest dreams are made come true.
> Still in a thousand years our grandchildren
> Down roads of thine will travel, down thy streams.[80]

This language—couched in liturgical form—reflects dogmas of a sovereign will ("in kindness or in wrath"), predestination ("by God's decree"), mystical identity ("In thee do they both form and will assume—Thou art the law in them"), and millenial vision ("a thousand years"). The structures of consciousness of Christian doctrine are deeply rooted in the Western mind. Hitler understood from an early date the mandate of his messianic role. These words, spoken in 1935, bear a sentiment he reiterated often: "Nothing is possible unless one will commands, a will which has to be obeyed by others, beginning at the top and ending only at the very bottom."[81] The hierarchical structure is clear: the reappearance of the old Neoplatonic ladder in quasi-secularized form.

The creation of the Nazi myth evinces less evidence of specific traditional continuity than the fascist regime in Italy. The reasons for this are undoubtedly manifold. One line of interpretation would suggest that Germany (unlike England, France, and America whose national identities were established by revolution) had but recently emerged as a unified nation, only to suffer severe national humiliation after World War I. Thus drawing upon ideas which circulated in Germany since the late nineteenth century, Hitler's "new myth" inspired the flagging psyches of the German people. To be successful, the "new myth" must plumb the reservoir of powerful archetypes and blend them into a catalytic alchemic potion.

In Italy the mythical structures were historically conspicuous. First, there is Rome. Palmieri writes:

> Fascism means, in fact, the return to Order, to Authority; the return to the Roman conception of human Society, (a) conception of which those centuries of oblivion could obscure but never efface. Fascism is, in other words, intimately connected to Rome . . .[82]

Out of Rome spring two authoritarian traditions, which are to be tapped by fascism:

> Twice in the past, from Rome, a Universal Idea has sent a message of harmony and unity to divided, warring and ailing mankind . . . The triumph of Order, of Authority, of equal Justice under Law, saw the Empire of Augustus and of Trajanus give to mankind for the first and only time in human history the life-enhancing blessing of political unity. The

triumph of the Catholic Idea of salvation in Christ and through Christ and His Church, saw the Empire of the Church give to mankind the life-inspiring blessing of spiritual unity. *The Triumph of the Fascist Idea of subjection of all individual life to the life of the Whole will see a new Empire rise . . . Fascism may finally furnish man with the long sought solution of the riddle of life.*[83]

In any case, though the myths differ according to context in Italy and Germany, their basic structure remains the same—absolutist, hierarchical, authoritarian—and the accompanying consciousness conveys the blind allegiance due religious revelation.

Community: The Spiritual Body

Just as fascism creates a new hierarchical "chain of being" in its authoritarian structure, so too the fascist "community" is envisioned as a spiritual body, an organic unity, like the Body of Christ. But just as the Body of Christ was fixed in the visible realm of the medieval Roman Church, so too, fascism is eminently *Realpolitik*—the Kingdom of God on earth. As we have seen, the Nation achieves a mythical status in which the "general will" demands the absolute subservience of every individual will. No sacrifice is too great—no price too costly to pay. As the saints and the martyrs are completely compliant to the will of God expressed through an ecclesiastical hierarchy, and as the Crusaders took up lance and sword in behalf of the Word, so, too, fascism demands of believers ultimate obedience and ultimate commitment.

Benito Mussolini (1883-1945) defines clearly the separation between the "spiritual" and physical worlds, with the apogee of spirituality attained by identifying with the State:

> Thus Fascism could not be understood in many of its practical manifestations as a party organization, as a system of education, as a discipline, if it were not always looked at in the light of its *whole way of conceiving life*, a *spiritualized* way. The world seen through Fascism is *not* this material world which appears on the surface, in which man is an individual separated from all others and standing by himself, and in which he is governed by a natural law that makes him instinctively live a life of selfish and momentary pleasure. The man of Fascism is an individual who is nation and fatherland, which is a moral law, binding together individuals and the generations into a tradition and a mission . . . it is a spiritualized conception, itself the result of the general reaction of modern times against the flabby materialistic positivism of the nineteenth century.[84]

Fascism does not allow for a dichotomy between private life and life as a citizen. If the State is the realm of spirituality, and if there is no division between material and spiritual existence, then it follows that the State is the focal point of all experience and values. Such is the world view behind such words as "Fascism is a religious conception in which man is seen in his immanent relationship with a superior law and with an objective Will" which "raises him to conscious membership in a spiritual society."[85]

Mussolini even contends that fascism does not consider *happiness* to be possible on this earth, and that one must step aside from the realm of temporality and change to attain spiritual life.[86] But the State bears the marks of eternity, and is "the universal ethical will" and "the creator of Right."[87] As "the highest and most powerful form of personality," the State "takes over all the forms of the moral and intellectual life of man" and is "the educator and promoter of spiritual life."[88] If we simply substitute the word "Church" for "State," we have a manifesto of the constitution and function of the over-arching universe of medieval Christendom. Giovanni Gentile calls the State "a wholly spiritual creation" and Palmieri writes that "henceforth the State is . . . a living entity, it is the *highest spiritual entity* of the political world . . . that organism of which the single *individual* is an integral, although accidental and infinitesimal part."[89] Given our belief in the sacredness of the individual, we may wonder how the individual can be "an *integral*"—"though *accidental* and *infinitesimal* part," or how can Mussolini assert "the irremediable, fruitful and beneficent inequality of men."[90] Fascism secularizes the medieval conception of the Body of Christ. The individual, who in the body is "integral and organic," paradoxically becomes humbly insignificant at the bottom of the chain of being.

In Nazism, the *Volk* (the mythicized "people" who supposedly embody a unified will), the State, and the Party form an organic unity (and here is one of the fascist tendencies of communism). But the will of the whole is embodied in the Fuehrer. Hueber defines "the People" as follows:

> The political people is formed through the uniformity of its natural characteristics. *Race* is the natural basis of the people . . . As a political people the natural community becomes conscious of its solidarity and strives to form itself, to develop itself, to defend itself, to realize itself. "Nationalism" is essentially this striving of a people which has become conscious of itself toward self-direction and self-realization, toward a deepening and renewing of its natural qualities . . .[91]

Under the aegis of "nationalism" the myth of "the People" (and their "racial solidarity") is born. But the completely subordinate role of the individual to the state is clear (though thinly masked by the euphemisms of organic imagery):

> There are *no personal liberties* of the individual which fall outside of the realm of the state and which must be respected by the state. The member of *the people, organically connected* with the whole community, has replaced the isolated individual; he is included in the totality of the political people and is drawn into the collective action.[92]

Just as Italian fascism presupposes an holistic integration of the material and spiritual spheres within the supremacy of the state, so Hueber continues

> There can no longer be any question of a private sphere, free of state influence, which is sacred and untouchable before the political unity. The constitution of the nationalistic Reich is therefore *not* based upon a system of inborn and inalienable rights of the individual . . . The legal position represents the *organic fixation* of the individual in the living order.[93]

The *ethos* of fascist community is an unabashed totalitarianism packaged in the enticing wrappings of organic identity. One of the more critical implications of this order is the forfeiture of individual *responsibility* (with the forfeiture of individual will and rights) to the state. The results of this capitulation are brutally apparent in the sweeping disclaimers of the Nazis at Nuremberg—as well as the sad expressions of helpless ignorance of the German people when confronted by the occupying Allies with Nazi atrocities.

Revelation and Eschatology

Just as in the case of medieval Catholicism, the fascist world view is established by revelation, in whose service reason is enlisted for the purposes of systematic rationalization and internal consistency. There are at least four areas of "dogma"—four "fundamentals"—which testify to this quasi-theological perspective.

First of all (as we have noted), the mythical hero or Leader of the people must be the very incarnation of God's revelation, one who is predestined to a messianic role. Palmieri writes of the fascist hero:

> Finally, sincerity and courage must be accompanied by belief, belief in one's own *destiny*, belief in the role which one is destined to play on the stage of life, belief in one's own powers if the world is to be actually and effectively changed through one's own efforts. Underlying this magic *trinity* of *sincerity, courage* and *faith*, there must always exist within the soul's deepest recesses a *mystic power* of immediate knowledge of the truth through the supreme gift of intuition, if the action of a man must share in the *finality* of an *act of God*. Once we find all these qualities within the soul of one man . . . we have found a man entitled to our admiration, a true hero . . .[94]

To legitimate this role, Palmieri appeals not to reason, but to faith—and belittles the doubters and skeptics:

> But our skeptical brethren—*little* men *without vision, without faith, without belief*—ask for pragmatic proof of this right to our admiration, *if not to our worship*. Such proof is evidently not needed by those who can recognize the hero when they see him, but is sorely needed by those . . . blind to the reality of the unseen.[95]

Palmieri's words seem to ring with an apocalyptic urgency similar to the warning of the unknown writer of II Peter 3:3: "scoffers will come in the last days" (questioning the doctrine of Christ's second coming). Men must have "eyes to see" to recognize the true messianic qualities of the fascist hero.

Secondly, fascism carries its own scheme of salvation which is effected in a new spiritual cultus (again reminiscent of medieval Christendom):

> . . . if man, *to achieve salvation*, must be led anew to *visualize* and *worship a deeper reality* than the immediate and closely bound world of the self, there is *one way only* to lead him to the goal . . . through the renewed *cult* of the Family, the Church, the Nation and the State, the cult will give anew *a meaning to life*; with this cult life will again find a purpose; through this cult life will finally reach its far off, magnificent goal which is nothing less than *the spiritualization of man*.[96]

The religious implications are explicit: salvation and the spiritual life are to be found in the ritual fulfillment of cultic duties. "Family," "Church" and "Nation" ascend in a graduated scale which culminates in "State"—the real focal point and pinnacle of authority—the Kingdom of God on earth. Only by the negation of his will for this kingdom does the individual realize his worth:

> *All* the recognition of a man's *worth* is expressed in the *place* he occupies in the *hierarchy: all* the *functions* of a man's social and political life are *contained* in the functions he must fulfill as a member of the *hierarchy*.[97]

The spatial rigidity of sessile consciousness and its hierarchical arrangement are again evident. Commitment to this rigid scheme guarantees the believer a sense of exact "space" and "place" and therefore secures his identity. Typical of a religious definition, "freedom" becomes the servile submission of the will to the higher authority:

> In the Fascist conception, to be free, means to be no more a slave to one's own passions, ambitions or desires; means to be free to will what is true, and good and just, at all times . . . means, in other words, to realize here in this world the true mission of man.[98]

Palmieri's definition recalls Paul's words to the Galatian church:

> For you were called to freedom, brethren; only do not use your freedom as an opportunity for the flesh, but . . . be servants of one another . . . For the desires of the flesh are against the Spirit, and the desires of the Spirit are against the flesh.   (Galatians 5:13,17)

But the fascist subjection of the individual will to the state, though secular in substance, is couched in sacred language. The call to ascetic self-sacrifice strikes at the heart of Christian consciousness, and the appeal to revelation legitimates the otherwise secular content (and indeed often blasphemous contours) of a life blindly surrendered to this higher authority.

A third facet of dogma, springing out of the revelatory claims of the fascist hierarchy, is "religious" law. This connection is most dramatically substantiated by the actual "Fascist Decalogue" or Ten Commandments, issued in 1934:

1. Know that the Fascist and in particular the soldier, must not believe in perpetual peace.
2. Days of imprisonment are always deserved.
3. The nation serves even as a sentinel over a can of petrol.
4. A companion must be a brother, first, because he lives with you, and secondly because he thinks like you.
5. The rifle and cartridge belt, and the rest, are confided to you not to rust in leisure, but to be preserved in war.
6. Do not ever say, "The Government will pay . . . " because it is *you* who pay; and the Government is that which you willed to have, and for which you put on a uniform.
7. Discipline is the soul of armies, without it there are no soldiers, only confusion and defeat.
8. Mussolini is always right.
9. For a volunteer there are no extenuating circumstances when he is disobedient.
10. One thing must be dear to you above all: the life of the Duce.[99]

Although these Ten Commandments were issued for the military, they illustrate the authoritarian and legalistic presuppositions of fascism, including such age-old maxims as "might makes right," "never question higher authority," "our country is always right" (or "our country, right or wrong"), "warfare is inevitable," etc. Such simplistic truisms are part and parcel of the fascist mentality which defines the world as a preconceived, closed system where everything and everyone is dispatched into a proper niche (a genuine "compartmentalizing" of the world). Such a system is most easily legitimated by a religious or quasi-religious appeal, since empirical or rational (analytic) foundations are impossible.

A final and most demonic effect of the fascist system is the division of the world into "believers" and "unbelievers"—or more significantly—"the Elect" and "the Damned." Such a polarity stems naturally from the revelatory foundations of the system, where no opposition can be tolerated and yet where the existence of *an enemy,* a scapegoat, is necessary for the functioning of the system. The identification of an hostile "other" feeds the sense of uniqueness, confirms the "calling" or "election," provides peoples over against which "our identity" and "our mission" can be understood. If all were brothers, there could be no simple external categories which would make some "superior" to others. It is a germane and telling fact that the particular dichotomy of "saved" and "damned" seems to be most pervasive in historical or cultural milieus where psycho-social helplessness threatens and anomie prevails: e.g., Post-Exilic Judaism, the oppressed classes or peoples constituting early Christianity, Western Europe prior to the Crusades or prior to the Reformation; or more recently, Italy and Germany in the early twentieth century.

Is it accidental that it was in first century Palestine, where the Jews for over five hundred years had watched a succession of foreign overlords, that the vision of God's divine intervention in Christ—which was to transform the restive course of history by making this its central point—was born? Likewise, is it accidental that in war-weary and depression-wracked Germany, the year 1930, Alfred Rosenberg should write:

> The "meaning of world history" has radiated out from the north over the whole world, borne by a blue-eyed blond race which in several great waves determined the spiritual face of the world . . . A *new faith* is arising today: the myth of the blood, the faith, to defend with the blood the divine essence of man. The faith, embodies in clearest knowledge, that the Nordic blood represents that *mysterium* which has replaced and overcome all the old sacraments . . .[100]

In 1924, Adolf Hitler writes in *Mein Kampf* of a rising distinction between "them" and "us"—a distinction which, in the years to come, was to delineate the "saved" from the "damned" (including the Jews, the communists and later "all the others"). Hitler inveighs against the mixing of the races, a practice which he feels is responsible for sapping the strength of Western civilization in general, and Germany in particular. The "Aryan," Hitler says, is "the Prometheus of mankind," the one out of whom "springs the divine spark of genius at all times," the one who is responsible for the triumph of man in the evolutionary process.[101]

But the enemy of the Aryan was to be all too easily located. Richard Rubenstein, who traces the long course of anti-Semitism in Germany from the Middle Ages to the Nazi death camps, points out that the structures of Christian consciousness in Germany had long ago predetermined who "the enemy" was to be:

> The medieval myths of the Jew as Christ-killer, from which were derived the secondary myths of the Jew as Anti-Christ, Devil's spawn, Satan, sorcerer, magician, cannibal, and murderer, pointed to the existence of a demonic power equal to the task of sapping Germany's strength, of secretly causing her defeat, and of gloating in the triumph of the victors.[102]

It is ironically the people who gave birth to the concept of election who now must bear the brunt of its intolerance.[103] Typical of statements of anti-Semitism from Hitler's *Mein Kampf,* is:

> The mightiest counterpart to the Aryan is represented by the Jew . . . In the Jewish people the will to self-sacrifice does not go beyond the individual's naked instinct of self-preservetion . . . If the Jews were alone in this world, they would stifle in filth and offal; they would try to get ahead of one another . . . Hence the Jewish people, despite all apparent intellectual qualities, is without any true culture . . .[104]

The tiresome list of Hitler's anti-Semitic epigrams could be multiplied many times over, but the point is that an enemy had to be created to serve as counterpoint to the myth of election. Thus it was necessary that Hitler should specifically establish that the Jews were not simply a "religion," but a "race":

> The Jew has always been a people with definite racial characteristics and never a religion; only in order to get ahead he early sought for a means which could distract unpleasant attention from his person . . . Due to his own original special nature, the Jew cannot possess a religious institution, if for no other reason because he lacks idealism in any form . . . On this first and greatest lie, that the Jews are not a race but a religion, more and more lies are based in necessary consequence . . .[105]

Hitler's cognitive gymnastics are not accidental features of his denigration of the Jew. Rather it is absolutely essential that the Jew should be conceived as an opposite *race* to fuel the flames of the Aryan myth. Furthermore, Hitler's perjorative comment about the lack of *Jewish idealism* penetrates to the heart of a genuine threat to the Nazi system. Idealism—in its "purest" form—presupposes a system of truth that is *independent* of *historical* contingency. But Judaism is *the* outstanding historical faith (insofar as Christianity, in its typical orthodox form, has subjugated historicity to an idealized theological system; furthermore, Christianity's historicism is derivative from its Jewish origins). There could be no reconciliation between the ahistorical idealistic mythology of Nazism and the historical faith of Judaism. Christianity on the other hand, (especially in its medieval form) had evidenced time and again its malleability for union with political myths. Perhaps it was just the historical resiliency and continuity of Judaism that contrasted so sharply with the threatened extinction of German identity and continuity at the close of World War I. Moreover, in the face of historical anomie, Germany was left without the option of appealing to historical precedent, and therefore turned to the realm of myth (which nevertheless could be imbued with quasi-historical roots).

It should be clear that fascism, both in its overt formulations and in its covert implications, is a religio-political philosophy evincing an ahistorical disposition and feeding on the security penchant of sessile consciousness. Within the framework of its basic presuppositions, which are comparable to "revealed truths," reason *is* operative in a deductive supportive role as "scholastic" expositions of the substance, duties, rewards and ramifications of fascism. Fascism operates like a religion, and for this reason the "fascist mind" in politics implies a blind religious acceptance and obedience, impervious to criticism and empirical facts to the contrary. The greater danger of fascism in our century is probably to be understood in this regard (as a political "mind-set").

With the eclipse of the last workable overarching world view in the Middle Ages, the tides of pluralism have slowly risen and now engulf the modern world. The sweet recollection of a "time when . . ." everything and everybody occupied its secure place in a neat cosmic hierarchy (identified with the medieval cosmos or any mythical period) will continue to haunt modern man until or unless he discovers a new viable universal cosmos, or learns to live with greater flexibility, appreciation of variety, and acceptance of the inevitability of his historical existence. Furthermore, we can only hope that the course of fascism in this century may teach us the costly consequences of any idealistic myth which demands conformity, and is grasped desperately and emotively in the hopes of salving the acute threat of our mortality. Nature is *living* just because it *is* a dynamic *process*, even as its recurrent taxonomic patterns are suggestive of meaningful order and stability. The motile is as necessary to life as the sessile, and only where both operate integrally is holism achieved.

FOOTNOTES

[1] At the first in his "Theses on Feuerbach" Marx draws from Feuerbach the description of man as a "species being"; in his later writings Marx moves away from any suggestion of a natural or substantial definition of man in favor of conceiving him in terms of his concrete socio-economic location. See Karl Marx, "Theses on Feuerbach" in *Writings of the Young Marx,* translated and edited by Loyd D. Easton and Kurt H. Guddat (Garden City, N.Y.: Anchor Books, 1967), pp. 400 ff.

[2] C. B. Macpherson, *The Political Theory of Possessive Individualism* (London: Oxford University Press, 1964), writes that "Hobbes's state of nature or 'natural condition of mankind' is not about 'natural' man as opposed to civilized man but is about men whose desires are specifically civilized; the state of nature is the hypothetical condition in which men as they now are, with natures formed by living in civilized society, would necessarily find themselves if there were no common power able to overawe them all" (pp. 18-19).

[3]Rousseau's conception of the "noble savage" suggests that his vision of "the state of nature" was not solely mythical.

[4]Macpherson notes that Locke "specifically puts into the state of nature, money, the consequent inequality of possession of land, and the supersession of the initial spoilage limit on the amount of land a man can rightfully possess." Thus for Locke, the state of nature already implies conflict. Macpherson continues, "it must be remembered that Locke's state of nature is a curious mixture of historical imagination and logical abstraction from civil society" (p. 209). James G. Clapp, "John Locke," in The Encyclopedia of Philosophy, writes, "Although Locke sometimes wrote as if the state of nature were some period in history, it must be taken largely as a philosophical fiction, an assumption made to show the nature and foundation of political power . . ."

[5]John Locke, An Essay: Concerning the True Original Extent and End of Civil Government in Great Books of the Western World, Vol. 35, ed. Robert M. Hutchins (Chicago: Encyclopaedia Britannica, Inc., 1952), p. 25.

[6]Ibid.

[7]Ibid., p. 26.

[8]Charles Norris Cochrane, Christianity and Classical Culture, (London: Oxford Univrsity Press, 1968), p. 45.

[9]Ibid., p. 46.

[10]This summary of the Lockeian legacy identifies the position drawn from Locke, but of course does not explore some of the intricacies of Locke's own discussion, which is to be found in his Second Treatise, chapters XV to XIX.

[11]Jean-Jacques Rousseau, The Social Contract, tr. and introduced by Maurice Cranston (Baltimore: Penguin Books, 1968), p. 74.

[12]Ibid., pp. 74 and 76.

[13]An example of this tendency is in Heinrich von Treitschke's Politics. Von Treitschke quotes Rousseau: "Rousseau has aptly said, in one of the few maintainable passages of his Contrat Social, 'La volonte generale n'est pas la volonte de tous.'" This is, "The general will is not the will of all." See Heinrich von Treitschke, Politics, tr. B. Dugdale and T. de Bille (London: Constable and Company, Ltd., 1916). On the other hand, Stanley I. Benn writes, "for democrats in the tradition of Rousseau, men achieve moral fulfillment only as participants in the collective self-governing process, helping to give expression to the 'General Will' for the 'Common Good'; failure in this constitutes failure in one's moral duty as a citizen." ("Democracy," Encyclopedia of Philosophy.) These instances illustrate divergent uses for which Rousseau's concept has been employed.

[14]John Stuart Mill, On Liberty, (New York: Bobbs-Merrill, The Library of Liberal Arts, 1956), p. 7.

[15]Henri de Saint-Simon, Social Organization, The Science of Man and Other Writings, ed. and tr. Felix Markham (New York: Harper and Row, Harper Torchbooks, 1964), p. 74.

[16]Ibid., p. 11

[17]Robert Owen, "An Address from the Association of All Classes of All Nations to the Governments and People of All Nations," in The Book of the New Moral World (Glasgow: H. Robinson and Company, 1837).

[18]Ibid.

[19]Herbert Marcuse, Reason and Revolution: Hegel and the Rise of Social Theory (Boston: Beacon Press, 1960), p. 15.

[20]Ibid.

[21]Z. A. Pelczinski, "The Hegelian Conception of the State," in Hegel's Political Philosophy, pp. 1-29 (Cambridge: Cambridge University Press, 1971), p. 10.

[22]Ibid., pp. 7-8.

[23]Ibid., p. 14.

[24]Ibid.

[25]Ibid., p. 15.

[26]Hannah Arendt writes in The Origins of Totalitarianism that the "concretization of ideas had first been conceived in Hegel's theory of state and history." That is, such ideas as "common language, culture,

religion or national consciousness" were to be worked out "in the process of history in which ideas could be concretized only in a complicated movement." However, the perversion of Hegel's vision came about through "the vulgarity of mob leaders" who "hit upon the tremendous possibilities of such concretization for the organization of masses. These men began to tell the mob that each of its members could become such a lofty all-important walking embodiment of something ideal (as in Pan-Slavism and Pan-Germanism) if he would only join the movement. Then he no longer had to be loyal or generous or courageous, he would automatically be the very incarnation of Loyalty, Generosity, Courage." Arendt depicts the results of this transformation: "The particular reality of the individual person appears against the background of a spurious reality of the general and universal, shrinks into a negligible quantity or is submerged in the stream of dynamic movement of the universal itself. In this stream the difference between ends and means evaporates together with the personality, and the result is the monstrous immorality of ideological politics. All that matters is embodied in the movement itself; every idea, every value has vanished into a welter of superstitious pseudo-scientific immanence" (p. 249).

27Pelczynski, p. 15.

28Shlomo Avineri, *Hegel's Theory of the Modern State* (Cambridge: Cambridge University Press, 1972), p. 112.

29Ibid.

30Pelczynski, p. 16.

31Ibid., p. 23.

32Ibid., p. 25.

33Karl Marx and Friedrich Engels, *The German Ideology: Parts I & III*, ed., with an introduction by R. Pascal (New York: International Publishers, 1947), p. 7.

34Ibid.

35Beyond his early *Theses on Feuerbach*, Marx makes it increasingly clear that he does not conceive of some essential "human nature," but assumes that we must speak of man always in terms of his concrete socio-economic and historical existence (as for example in *The German Ideology: Parts I & III*, written with Friedrich Engels). See *The German Ideology*, p. 7.

36Ibid., pp. 13-14.

37Karl Marx and Friedrich Engels, "Manifesto of the Communist Party," in *Great Books of the Western World*, vol. 40, pp. 415-34 (Chicago: Encyclopaedia Britannica, Inc., 1952), p. 424, write: "The proletarians cannot become masters of the productive forces of society except by abolishing their own previous mode of appropriation, and thereby also every other previous mode of appropriation . . . All previous historical movements were movements of minorities, or in the interest of minorities. The proletarian movement is the self-conscious independent movement of the immense majority, in the interest of the immense majority."

38Marx received a doctorate in 1841 from the University of Jena for a thesis on Epicurus and Democritus. See Neil McInnes, "Karl Marx," *The Encyclopedia of Philosophy*.

39Mao Tse-Tung, *Quotations from Chairman Mao-Tse-Tung* (Peking: Foreign Language Press, 1967), p. 3.

40Ibid., p. 255.

41Russell Kirk, *The Conservative Mind from Burke to Santayana* (Chicago: Henry Regnery Co., 1953), pp. 7-8.

42Zevedei Barbu, *"Democracy and Dictatorship"* (New York: Grove Press, 1956).

43*Encyclopedia of Philosophy*, s.v. "Democracy," by Stanley I. Benn.

44See Donald Kagan, rev., Botsford and Robinson's *Hellenic History*, fifth ed. (New York: Macmillan, 1970). The fifth century *ecclesia* or popular assembly embraced in theory all male citizens over eighteen years of age, most of whom (with the exception of those in military service) regularly attended (p 192). On the other hand, the issues before the Assembly (which could indeed pass laws and decide on matters of foreign policy, etc.,) were initiated by the Council of Five Hundred (the *boule*, chosen by lot from citizens over thirty years of age) which exercised administration through the *prytanies* (ten smaller groups of fifty members each, each of which successively held office for thirty-six or thirty-seven days) (p. 194).

45Karl Loewith, *From Hegel to Nietzsche: The Revolution in Nineteenth-Century Thought*, tr. David E. Green (Garden City, N.Y.: Anchor Books, 1967), writes, "The proletariat is the 'universal class,' representing no particular limited interests. When it liberates itself, it will mean the end of the private human existence of the bourgeois as well as of private property and private capitalistic economics: in short, all distinction

184

between the private and public spheres. This distinction will be replaced positively by the universality of a mode of existence which is common to all, a community with communal ownership and a communal economy. Marx's ideal of democracy is the *polis* which has been transformed into a *cosmopolis*, a society of free men, whose individual member is not a bourgeois, but a *zoon politikon*" (p. 313).

⁴⁶John Locke, p. 25.

⁴⁷Ibid., pp. 53–54.

⁴⁸Rousseau, p. 53.

⁴⁹Ibid., p. 55.

⁵⁰J. Bronowski and Bruce Mazlish, *The Western Intellectual Tradition: From Leonardo to Hegel* (New York: Harper and Brothers, 1962), write: "Hobbes and Locke were animated by the same view of nature. They saw the world as made up of bodies in motion, which were arranged in an orderly pattern and followed well-defined, causal laws. Their view of the world was reflected in their view of human society. Through their thoughts run what we may call the atomic view of man and his social relations. They really thought of human societies as starting from a mass of atoms, and they were trying to discover what we might call the 'gas laws' of human conduct . . . The method in Locke's psychology and political science was the same— reduction to the simplest parts and conditions" (pp. 205, 211).

⁵¹Romain Rolland, "Jean-Jacques Rousseau," in *French Thought in the Eighteenth Century*, presented by Romain Rolland, Andre Maurois and Edouard Herriot (New York: David McKay Company, 1953), p. 9, says, "He had passed his first thirty years in a happy and sleepy atmosphere as a little Swiss tramp, which life had made him, into a truant schoolboy, regardless of social restraints and laws. He was thus all the more sensitive to the moral and almost physical repression of the artificial world of letters and court-life in Paris. At first, frightened and stifled, he had repressed his feelings of suffering, revolt and disgust. But these feelings were accumulating. And now they had exploded! With one stroke, he uncovered the social evil— the corruption and iniquity of society. And the tremendous response to his first cry revealed a mission hitherto unsuspected by him."

⁵²*The Encyclopedia of Philosophy*, s.v. "Social Contract," by Peter Laslett.

⁵³Jeremy Bentham, "Principles of Legislation," in *Communism, Fascism, and Democracy: The Theoretical Foundations*, ed. Carl Cohen (New York: Random House, 1972), p. 447.

⁵⁴Mill, p. 6.

⁵⁵T. H. Green, "Liberal Legislation and Freedom of Contract," in *The Works of Thomas Hill Green*, Vol. 3 (London: Longmans, Green and Co., 1888).

⁵⁶Leonard T. Hobhouse, *Liberalism* (New York: Henry Holt and Company, n.d.), p. 124.

⁵⁷Ibid., pp. 125–126.

⁵⁸John Dewey, "The Future of Liberalism," *The Journal of Philosophy* 32 (April 25, 1935): 9.

⁵⁹Jean Hyppolite, *Studies on Marx and Hegel*, tr. John O'Neill (New York: Basic Books, 1969), writes that "it is often remarked that Hegel spiritualized action where Marx materialized it. Marx himself believed this to be the substance of his critique of Hegel. But I think there is some evidence for the argument that Hegel and Marx are engaged in a similar critique of alienation . . . Marx began his critique of Hegel with an attack on the Hegelian conception of the State. Marx attacks the Hegelian State as a *cultural universal* on the ground that it only *abstractly* mediates the separation between the private interests of the bourgeoisie, summarized in the doctrine of Natural Rights, and the nature of man supposedly outlined in the doctrine of Rights . . . (pp. xv and xvii). Marx's first and extensive critique of Hegel was published in the *Franco-German Annals*. Hyppolite asserts that it is the "disequilibrium between the Idea and historical reality which emerges as the first result of Marx's study" (p. 106). Marx "in turn" seeks "for the root of the Idea in a historical reality—the proletariat—whose dynamic content Hegel had tried arbitrarily to limit and fixate . . . " As Hyppolite notes, Marx did not have available Hegel's critical early works, for the "dialectical" element in Hegelian thought in fact is opposed to this kind of fixation (p. 108). "Marx's entire critique of Hegelian Idealism is contained in the reversal of its inverted conception of the State. The truly concrete subject, the bearer of the predicate, is *man as social being*, who belongs to what Hegel called bourgeois society, and the State, which Hegel mistakenly took for the Subject, as Idea, is in fact a predicate of man's social nature. The Idea—in reality, the product of man's social activity—appears in Hegel as the authentic subject which results in 'a mystery which degenerates into mystification,' as Marx puts it" (p. 112).

[60]Hippolyte remarks that "Marx is not immune to the notion of a final state of life in which the real subject of history—and the whole problem lies in knowing just what is the real subject— transcends itself immanently" (p. 113). Jean-Paul Sartre, *Search for a Method*, tr. Hazel E. Barnes (New York: Alfred A. Knopf, 1963), describes especially the transformation of Marxism in the U.S.S.R., "the economic planning imposed by a bureaucracy unwilling to recognize its mistakes became thereby a violence done to reality. And since the future production of a nation was determined in offices, often outside its own territory, this violence had as its counterpart an *absolute idealism. Men and things had to yield to ideas—a priori;* experience, when it did not verify the predictions, could only be wrong" (pp. 22-23). Sartre also writes of Marxism in general, "The Marxist approaches the historical process with universalizing and totalizing schemata. Naturally the totalization was not made by chance. The theory has determined the choice of perspective and the order of the conditioning factors; it studied each particular process within the framework of a general system in evolution . . . " (p. 25). Yet Sartre's "progressive" rendition of Marxism (p. 133 ff.) would hold a certain dynamism in common with Dewey. Richard Bernstein, *Praxis and Action: Contemporary Philosophies of Human Action* (Philadelphia: University of Pennsylvania Press, 1971), writes: "Paradoxically, Dewey . . . is the closest and furthest away from Marx. *Au fond,* Dewey was a reformer. He was deeply skeptical of the demand for revolution as understood by Marx. Dewey's advocacy of liberal amelioration would have been seen as the greatest threat to genuine revolutionary *praxis,* and I have no doubt that Marx would have attacked Dewey in the same ruthless manner in which he attacked all 'true socialists.' The dialectic that can take place between Marx and Dewey is the political dialectic of our time. On the Marxist side, there is the sharp criticism that liberalism can be self-defeating and sanction what it seeks to change. From a Marxist point of view, reformist liberalism of Dewey's variety doesn't get at roots and fails to appreciate the extent to which conditions of political economy as they now exist in advanced capitalist societies (including the state capitalism of many so-called Communist countries) continues to perpetuate alienation and exploitation of man . . . The crisis that we are now confronting in America in race relations, in the crumbling of our cities, in the failures of our school system, in the realization of how impotent government controls are in the face of increasing pollution, are indications of inability of reformist liberalism to come to grips with the social problems and crises that confront us all. But on the side of Dewey and the pragmatists, we cannot forget how easily a demand for absolute humanism and human emancipation can turn into its opposite—absolute totalitarianism . . . Here I think that the pragmatists can be helpful. For they had a more thoroughgoing understanding of what must be the norms of objective, self-correcting inquiry. Epistemologically and practically, they have been aware of how any theory, hypothesis, or doctrine, can all too easily pass into dogma" (pp. 80-81).

[61]Dewey, loc. cit.

[62]Saint-Simon, pp. 114-15.

[63]F. M. Charles Fourier, "The Mistakes of Industry," in *Selections from the Works of Fourier,* trans. Julia Franklin (London: Swan Sonnenschein and Co., 1901).

[64]Owen, loc. cit.

[65]Marx and Engels, p. 15.

[66]The difference between Marx and Stalin is a point of much debate among various Marsists. In Jean-Paul Sartre, *Search for a Method,* for example, we find a critical distinction between *"living Marxism,"* which is "heuristic"; and even though "its principles and its prior knowledge appear as regulative in relation to its concrete research," nevertheless in Marx himself "we never find *entities." "Marxist voluntarism,"* on the other hand, has reduced "analysis" to the act of "getting rid of detail," of "forcing the signification of certain events," of "denaturing facts" or "inventing a nature for them in order to discover it later underneath them." The heuristic principle—'to search for the whole in its parts'—has become the terrorist practice of 'liquidating the particularity.'". Sartre thus clearly distinguishes between this orthodox Marxism, which he asserts has become *"a voluntarist idealism,"* and a dynamic *living Marxism* (pp. 26-28). Sartre continues his description of the orthodox or ideological position, "Our abstract Marxist . . . will affirm the constant progress of materialism; then he will describe a certain idealism—analytic, mathematical, slightly tinged with pessimism—which he will finally offer us as a simple riposte, already defensive, to the materialistic rationalism of the rising philosophy" (p. 54). Thus according to Sartre's analysis, Marx's conception of social science would represent something far more concrete and experimental than Stalin, whose position reflects fairly rigid *a priori* principles. On the other hand, Bernstein, *Praxis and Action,* remarks, "We can, from the vantage point of scholarly objectivity, say that the crimes committed in the name of "orthodox" Marxism are the greatest perversion of the letter and spirit

186

of Marx's work, that the Marxism represented by a Stalin is an absolute distortion of Marx. But such a claim, which is all too common today, tends to be naive about those elements in Marxism which allowed for such a perversion and misinterpretation. I recognize that we cannot condemn Marx for the barbaric practices carried out in his name. But I believe that we must be sensitive to those elements in Marx's own thought which have allowed for this perversion" (p.81).

[67] Joseph Stalin, *Dialectical and Historical Materialism* (New York: International Publishers, 1940), p. 20.

[68] "Democratic—if the term should be used at all—had by America's "Age of Imperialism," for example, acquired a heavy baggage of qualifiers. William H. Marnell, *Man-Made Morals: Four Philosophies That Shaped America* (Garden City, N.Y.: Doubleday, 1966; Anchor Books, 1968), writes: "A chemical analysis of the American Philistine of the nineteenth century would reveal in his thinking, molecules of utilitarianism fused with molecules of classical economics, coalescing with carefully selected molecules of the Calvinistic creed and molecules from the Declaration of Independence and other documents from the Age of Reform carefully and completely wrenched out of context." "The American Philistine, however, achieved his full development" only with the "fusion of social Darwinism . . ." "As a believer in social Darwinism he will believe that the *laissez faire* to which he subscribes as a utilitarian is part of an inexorable and unalterable law of nature leading onward and upward on the evolutionary principle, but leading individuals onward and upward at varying speeds and to varying heights which are determined by their individual abilities . . ." (pp. 244-45). Social Darwinism, with a selective reading of Christian and democratic sources, became the prime legitimation of imperialism. Richard Hofstadter, in his classical study *Social Darwinism in American Thought* (Philadelphia: University of Pennsylvania Press, 1944; Boston: Beacon Press, 1955), writes: "While Darwinian individualism declined, Darwinian collectivism of the nationalist or racist variety was beginning to take hold . . . At a time of imperialist friction there was nothing to stop the advocates of expansion and the propagandists of militarism from invoking these very shibboleths of group survival, or from transmuting them into a doctrine of group assertiveness and racial destiny to justify the ways of international competition. The survival of the fittest had once been used chiefly to support business competition at home; now it was used to support expansion abroad" (pp. 202-03). Some of the problems of the use of the term "democratic" are discussed by Stanley I. Benn, "Democracy," in *The Encyclopedia of Philosophy*. Should the term—as *demos* suggests—apply to the rule of the poor over the rich? Or in the Athenian style, does democracy necessitate personal participation in policy-making? Or *representative* government? Is there such a thing as "popular sovereignty?" Do "the people" have a "will"? Does democracy imply the safeguarding of individual rights and the protection of minorities? Is the Marxist charge that bourgeois democracy "cannot equalize political power where economic power is unequal" just? These are some of the questions which must be addressed in discussing "democracy."

[69] Rudyard Kipling, "White Man's Burden," in *The Modern World: 1848 to the Present*, ed. Hans Kohn (New York: MacMillan, 1968), pp. 129-30.

[70] Underlying Kipling's poem, writes Richard Hofstadter, was also "Haeckel's Biogenetic Law, that, since the development of the individual is a recapitulation of the development of the race, primitives must be considered as being in the arrested stages of childhood or adolescence—'half devil and half child,' as Rudyard Kipling has said" (p. 193). Psychologist G. Stanley Hall felt that "the child-like character of the backward peoples entitled them to tender and sympathetic treatment by their phylogenetic 'elders' . . ." (Ibid.)

[71] Richard Bernstein, *Praxis and Action,* gives a somewhat different, but highly useful account of the strengths of a (non-"orthodox") Marxism (see pp. 305-310). Bernstein understands Marxism primarily "as a basic orientation, a way of asking new sorts of questions, and a set of insights that make us sensitive to conflicts and contradictions within existing society, and as posing for us deep and disturbing challenges" (p. 308). Bernstein asserts that the heart of Marx's thinking is "'a radical anthropology' which seeks to overcome the dichotomies that have plagued modern thought and life: the dichotomies between the 'ought' and the 'is,' the descriptive and the prescriptive, fact and value" (p. 307).

[72] Stalin, p. 44.

[73] Mario Palmieri, *"The Philosophy of Fascism,"* (Chicago: 1936).

[74] Ibid.

[75] Ibid.

[76] Actually such a role is hinted at much earlier in Hitler's career. On July 6, 1926, Joseph Goebbels wrote: "Weimar. Hitler spoke. About politics, the Idea, and organization. *Deep* and *mystical*. Almost like a *gospel*.

One shudders as *one skirts the abyss of life with him.* I thank *Fate* which *gave us this man."* See Joseph Goebbels, *The Goebbels Diaries,* ed., trans. with an Introduction by Louis P. Lochner (Garden City, N.Y.: Doubleday, 1948), p. 8.

[77] Herman Goering, *"Germany Reborn,"* (London: George Allen & Unwin, Ltd., 1934).

[78] Ernst R. Hueber, "Constitutional Law of the Greater German Reich," in *National Socialism* (Washington: U.S. Government Printing Office, 1943).

[79] Ibid.

[80] Will Vesper, "Poem to Hitler," tr. Carl Cohen, in *Communism, Fascism, and Democracy: The Theoretical Foundations,* p. 378.

[81] Adolph Hitler, "Obedience Uber Alles," in *Hitler's Words: the Speeches of Adolf Hitler from 1923 to 1943,* ed. G. Prange (Washington: Public Affairs Press).

[82] Palmieri, loc. cit.

[83] Ibid.

[84] Benito Mussolini, "The Doctrine of Fascism," in *The Social and Political Doctrines of Contemporary Europe,* Michael Oakeshott (New York: Cambridge University Press, 1950), p. 164.

[85] Ibid., p. 165.

[86] Ibid., pp. 165–66.

[87] Ibid., p. 167.

[88] Ibid., p. 168.

[89] Palmieri, loc. cit.

[90] Mussolini, p. 172.

[91] Hueber, loc. cit.

[92] Ibid.

[93] Ibid.

[94] Palmieri, loc. cit.

[95] Ibid.

[96] Ibid.

[97] Ibid.

[98] Ibid.

[99] Anon., "The Fascist Decalogue," in *The Social and Political Doctrines of Contemporary Europe,* p. 180.

[100] Alfred Rosenberg, "The Myth of the Twentieth Century," in *National Socialism* (Washington: U.S. Government Printing Office, 1943).

[101] Adolf Hitler, *Mein Kampf,* trans. Ralph Manheim (Boston: Houghton Mifflin, Sentry Edition, 1971), p. 290.

[102] Richard L. Rubenstein, *After Auschwitz: Radical Theology and Contemporary Judaism* (New York: Bobbs-Merrill, 1966), p. 29.

[103] Hannah Arendt, *The Origins of Totalitarianism* (New York: Harcourt Brace, Harvest, 1973), p. 242, writes "That the pan-movements' fanaticism hit upon the Jews as the ideological center, which was the beginning of the end of European Jewry, constitutes one of the most logical and most bitter revenges history has ever taken. For of course there is some truth in "enlightened" assertions from Voltaire to Renan and Taine that the Jews' concept of chosenness, their identification of religion and nationality, their claim to an absolute position in history and a singled-out relationship with God, brought into Western civilization an otherwise unknown element of fanaticism (inherited by Christianity with its claim to exclusive possession of Truth) on one side, and on the other an element of pride that was dangerously close to its racial perversion . . . For tribal nationalism is the precise perversion of a religion which made God choose one nation, one's own nation . . . The hatred of the racists against the Jews sprang from a superstitious apprehension that it actually might be the Jews, and not themselves, whom God had chosen, to whom success was granted by divine providence. There was an element of feeble-minded resentment against a people who, it was feared,

had received a rationally incomprehensible guarantee that they would emerge eventually, and in spite of appearances, as the final victors in world history."

[104] Hitler, pp. 300–302.
[105] Ibid., pp. 306–307.

CHAPTER EIGHT

THE MYTHICO-RELIGIOUS COSMOLOGY
OF TECHNOBUREAUCRACY

THE FOLLOWING chapter is unique in two ways that bear initial comment. First of all, it consists of two parts. The first of these is a short story, or a kind of parable or fable intended to reflect the quasi-religious cosmology of modern bureaucracy. This medium of expression is not only a change of pace, but also is designed to capture some of the personal dynamics of the issues at hand.

The second section of the chapter describes what appear to be constants of a world view underlying what we shall call "technobureaucracy." This neologism is not to burden the reader with further jargon, but is proposed to convey a critical assumption; namely that bureaucracy and technology reflect, by varying degrees, approximately uniform world views derived from similar archetypal structures of consciousness. This perspective is the second unique facet of the chapter, in that the author is not aware of an exactly comparable assumption (although Berger, Berger and Kellner seem to approach this stance at times in *The Homeless Mind*).[1] "Technobureaucracy" assumes that bureaucracy and technology each disclose both an hierarchical scheme which seems most like a secularized medieval world picture, and, mechanistic assumptions like the world view of Enlightenment science. Bureaucracy perhaps draws more visibly upon the former, and technology upon the latter. The second section of this chapter emphasizes the *technological* dimensions, whereas the first mythically engages *bureaucracy*.

A BUREAUCRATIC FABLE
(Or How a Perfectly Ordinary Young Man Experiences the Beatific Vision)

I need hardly confess to some embarrassment in writing this account, because I am a practical man, and never considered myself religious or a seer or anything. In fact, for months after I got my job at Gabriel Enterprises I used to think the most divine thing on earth was pretty Cindy Sue—the little secretary who seemed to bounce to the rhythm of the Xerox Mastermind— the next most beautiful thing on earth, which I was hired to operate.

Actually I was very proud of my job as Computer Controller II in the Division of Central Boxing. After all, I had just graduated from the University, and thank God, had had enough sense to switch my major from English Literature to Computer Sciences—I think it was the summer quarter after my sophomore year when I finally made up my mind.

Anyway, starting out at eleven-five was not a bad break, and I knew that some day I would meet the girl of my dreams and just settle down to a quiet life in one of those pretty brick houses with trees (I believe in trees and I think my house is different because it has a really unusual green roof and sidings and awnings). Anyway it was Cindy Sue who was to be the other part of my dream—that is until I found out how narrow my dream had been all along.

After eight months at my job Cindy Sue and I got married, and for a long time afterwards I thought I was the luckiest man in the world. We moved into that house I mentioned (which was particularly nice because of being on a dead end). I don't want to be too personal here, since I'm writing to tell about my visions. But since from what I hear, revelations and conversions often come at difficult times, I should point out that after a year Cindy Sue and I were not doing too well. She worked until she got pregnant. And after that she seemed to get feeling worse and worse. I tried to tell her it was just the pregnancy, but I was too tired when I got home from G.E. to sit there and argue or listen to her cry. And to add to it all, I began to look around me at my job.

There I was, stuck away in building E, not even *close* to where management *really* was. Mr. Devon, who was Computer Controller for all the divisions, only came round twice a week—and I began to wonder what kind of place I was in, anyway. And yet it seemed like finding another job I'd just have to start over again in some obscure corner, and here at least I had experience, and people liked me. But this was when the real crisis came—I was wondering how I could *ever* get out of this rut . . .

Before telling you about my vision, I want to say a little about my religious background, or lack of it, since I want you to understand how remarkable this vision really was. I grew up in Louisville, Kentucky. Actually my Mom was from Ohio and my Dad was from Arkansas. My Dad worked as a senior draftsman at a local engineering firm, and Mom used to be a private secretary for a lawyer. But she gave that up when I was just a kid. My family were moral people, but not really religious. My Dad was what I think you would call a "lapsed Catholic"—he wouldn't go to church for anything and the only time he mentioned God or the saints was when he was drunk—I think you know what I mean.

My Mom was a fairly regular Methodist—and especially when I was about eight to twelve years old she would drag me to church with her. But after that I balked, and finally in a couple of years she leveled off to about once a month.

The only really religious person in my family was my aunt Freida—my Dad's sister out in California. She had thought about being a nun until she met Uncle Fred, an airline pilot, and once when she came to visit she told Mom I was growing up a little pagan—and made me recite some prayers from a little green book.

Anyway, to get back to the vision. One night I had just finished watching a Reds game, and was lying in bed half awake thinking about Cindy Sue's bitchiness and my isolation as a Computer Controller II in the Central Boxing Division in building E. Suddenly I saw this strange light dancing on the bedspread by Cindy Sue's (who was asleep) feet. I felt a little faint and thought I was getting tired and this was a headlight or something, reflecting through the curtain from the street. But then this *figure* appeared—a man dressed up really nicely in a blue suit and a spiffy tie—but there was something eerie and old about him. Yet somehow I wasn't scared. I knew down inside that he had come to answer my problems. The figure was silent and I sat there wondering if I was just dreaming. I pinched myself and could feel it.

Finally I got up the nerve and asked him, "Who are you?" And he says, "St. Bonaventure." And I said, *"who?"* And he repeated, "St. Bonaventure."

I'm still not sure that this was the St. Bonaventure of history, who was (as I found out later in the dictionary), a *medieval* saint. But I guess whoever it was, was definitely God's servant or angel, and he was to appear to me several more times and change my life forever.

I said, "What do you want?" And he replied, "I have come to you in your time of need, to reveal to you a secret hidden for ages—a secret known only to a few men who never really tell anybody else: the secret behind all *success*. Someday, my son, you will become president of Gabriel Enterprises."

Well I really couldn't believe this. I was dumbfounded.

St. B. (as I shall call him) continued, "I will reveal to you in four successive visions—on nights of my choosing—the hidden meaning of Gabriel Enterprises, and the way of ascent up the ladder to the president's office."

I listened intently. I should say a word about what I did during and after these visions. Mainly I just listened with all my mind to St. B.—and every once in a while asked a question. After he finished, he would just vanish—instantly, just like that. Then I would beat it to the den to write down everything he said. I think his presence must have lingered awhile each time, since I think the words I am reporting here are almost verbatim. I'm going to recount each vision here, and then at the end I'll summarize what they all did for me.

First Vision (Continued)

"The first principle, my son, is the principle of *eternal essence*. As a greater saint than I once said, 'The first essence has no need of a model; there is no other model but itself.'[2] Do you understand these words?"

"Uh, no . . ."

"The *Eternal Essence,* my son, is the begetter of all the *divine ideas,* the *patterns* of all being, the *eternal archetypes.* These are begotten out of the terrible and beautiful arbitrariness of the Divine Being, from whom all things flow. Do you understand?"

"Well, no I . . . what, er, how does this all fit in with me?"

"The meaning, my son, is the *Order!* The *Order* of Gabriel Enterprises proceeds from the decisions made in heaven by God. It is established once and for all times—eternal, immutable and perfect. The Divine Blueprint is stored away in the vaults of the heavenly chambers. No mere man may challenge or change the *Eternal Order.* Your role is to learn of its existence. To contemplate its perfection. To study it up and down, and through and through! I have revealed, to you, O child of God, what is the *Divine Order!"*

With these words St. B. vanished, and just for a lingering moment I saw—in a flash—a huge diagram; and suddenly, intuitively, I *knew* where I was! The picture was inexact, but months later, when studying the G.E. Manual I found the actual picture of what I had seen in my vision—the corporate structure of Gabriel Enterprises!

For weeks I pondered these words. At first I felt elated, happy. I felt I knew my place again, but then the old doubt began to creep back in—had I just dreamed up this vision? I began to wonder.

It was on a Tuesday night when St. B. appeared again. Like before, I was half awake, thinking about a fishing trip. I hadn't been fishing for over six weeks and I really wanted to go back to that little mountain stream . . . But my thoughts were scattered by the sudden appearance of St. B.—he gave me a start! He was wearing the same blue suit, but I think his tie was different—it looked like a Paisley print. Following are the words of the second vision.

Second Vision

"Good evening, my son. And now, while I am with you, hear the words of my oracle. Tonight I will speak to you of knowledge, and of faith and reason. You have understood that there is a *Divine Order,* now I will tell you more.

"The *Patterns* of all things are laid down by a Higher Authority. Faith precedes reason, and reason precedes knowledge. Through faith you know of the Divine Order. Hold fast to that faith, my son! But you are given an *Intellect.* A gift of divine grace—by it *understanding* may be attained— illumination will follow. Do you understand?"

"I think a little better this time."

"Knowledge springs from the intellect *working upon* the *images presented to it* and illumined by God.[3] These are the words of a greater saint than I. Do you

understand? You must make your intellect an active thing—God himself has given you your own particular mind to come to understanding, to know the *Divine Abstractions*. Do you know where to find these abstractions—are the blinders removed from your eyes that you may see?"

"Can you . . . tell me more?"

"Yes! To the seeking soul, divine illumination will not be withdrawn! For *certain* knowledge, the intellect has to be *ruled* by *immutable* and *eternal rules, not* by its own state, but by those which are *above it* in eternal truth!"[4]

I confess, I had never received such a challenge. At first I was glued to his every word—yet somehow inside I felt inferior, unworthy. I saw visions of the Great Corporate Manual of G.E.—I wondered if in it there were statutes of judgment, of eternal fire . . .

"Your mind is wandering, my son! Pay attention! Follow my words and there will be no judgment. Only advancement—only salvation!

"Your own mind *has no ideas*—You must understand that it is blank. Only a blank tablet may be filled with writing. Only an empty vessel, with the grace of God! Yet you *may* know all things—does this sound like a contradiction? It is not—it is a divine paradox.

"Listen now. By *contuition*—this word is a divine secret—by *contuition* you may know all things as God knows them! But enough for now. You grow weary. Contemplate my words, and I shall return again in due time."

I must confess that these last words left me baffled. I thought about them for weeks—and every time I was just on the verge of *knowing* what St. B. meant, it slipped away. Like the word on the tip of your tongue. But I did know that he was right. My mind was empty. Only later was I to realize the real force of these words. But for now I tried to fill it by studying—at every chance I got—the *Order,* the *Rules,* the *Manual.*

One day Mr. Devon came in, and he made some comment about J. Robert Bynnings, the Chairman of the Board of G.E. He thought it would be way above my head. But he was amazed—or maybe startled, when I quoted the "corporate words" of J. Robert Bynnings—historically uttered some eight years ago at the seventy-fifth anniversary meeting of the Board of Directors:

> Gentlemen, in this great country given to us by God, we have established an enterprise. Ours are the blessings of freedom, of competition, of material rewards. This great corporation embodies the precepts of Order. God set up laws to govern his universe. And so, we too, follow laws which are just and fair—yet established once and for all. The patterns of our corporation, under advice from the Board and the sound authority of our President, will continue to lead us forward into a new era of prosperity.

Some two months passed before St. B. appeared again. But I was feeling more confident, and not long after I spoke to Mr. Devon, a vice president had called me in to commend me for my work, and hinted that I might get a raise.

The next vision was somewhat different from the rest. It was Thursday night. Cindy Sue had fallen asleep an hour ago. While reading the G.E. Manual, I had dozed off. Suddenly, I was awake, and there was St. B., this time in a green pin-stripe suit with a grey necktie.

Third Vision

"May the Divine Light rest upon you, my son. We are pleased with your diligence, and your faith! I promise you again—and do not forget these words—someday you shall be president of G.E.!

"Tonight I will reveal to you the *Mystery of Creation*. All Creation flows out from God. This, we call *emanation*. All beings, by a process both eternal and immutable, spring from the creative *Mind of God* through a chain of *intermediary causes* of *continually diminishing perfection*.[5] Do you understand?"

I felt small. "I think . . . maybe so."

"The whole of the cosmic *machine* was *produced* in time *from nothing*, by *one principle* only who is *supreme* and whose power, though immense, still arranges all according to weight, number and measure.[6] This, my son, is the trinity of creation: *weight, number* and *measure*. Each soul is weighed, numbered and measured, and fit into its proper slot. This is the glory of *creatio ex nihilo*—do you understand?

"The whole created order is a material means of bringing the soul to God[7]—the ascent of the soul—do you understand?

"Listen, my son, and I shall speak to you an eternal truth, revealed by a greater saint than I:

> Secondary beings imply a first; dependent beings imply an independent being; contingent things imply some necessary being; the relative implies an absolute; the imperfect, something perfect; participated beings imply one unparticipated being; if there are potential beings, then pure act must also exist; composite things imply the existence of something simple; the changeable can only exist with the unchangeable.[8]

Do you understand?"

My whole body shook with excitement; I was having some kind of mystic experience. I suddenly felt like I knew who I was and where I belonged—and that someday I could be something more! Could have my own being!

"That is all for now, my son. When I leave you, look intently and you will see something beautiful." St. B. vanished in a flash.

Out of the glow of the evaporated presence I saw another vision. An ancient cathedral arose, huge, dark and majestic. It looked kind of like the old gym at Central High (where I went) before they tore it down and built the new one. But this building was covered with huge doors and columns and things. Especially, above the doors, there were all kinds of carvings or sculptures, guarded by gargoyles.

As I gazed at this strange sight I suddenly just knew I was supposed to look at the sculptures above the big door in the middle. These carvings were arranged in a big semicircle, yet coming down from the top of the circle to the bottom, in neatly separated compartments. This, I knew, was the *Divine Order* that St. B. had talked about.

At the very top of the circle was a sun-like carving with rays coming out of it. I had to squint, but I saw clearly a vision of the face of God! On pondering him further, he looked strangely like J. Robert Bynnings—only with a long beard, and more ethereal.

Around J. Robert . . . that is, around God, there hovered the heavenly host, angels which I think they call cherubim or seraphim or something. Only these angels looked different. I looked more closely and the angels were all hovering over a long table, which came out from God as if he were at the head. The angels all had briefcases. One of them looked a little like St. B.

Immediately below this heavenly court was the figure of Christ, seated in a dignified manner with his arms opened up, as if gesturing to me. Christ was dressed up in a suit just like St. B.; his manner was stern, but friendly. As I looked into the face of Christ I was really surprised, because he too looked like J. Robert Bynnings. I glanced up at the sun—and there was no more face there! I looked back at Christ, and the likeness was remarkable, only Christ had a halo over his head.

Around his outstretched arms there were eight neatly separated and equal compartments arranged in a semicircle. Below him, but rising up above his belt line, was St. Peter—I knew this was St. Peter because in one hand he held a big key, and in the other a copy of the Heavenly Book. I stared at St. Peter; and his features looked just like Marvin Flemming, the President of G.E. Yet as I watched, slowly they were transformed before my eyes—and just for a moment I thought I saw myself in St. Peter— Only I hope not, for I was old and harsh and drawn. The eight compartments each contained a saint with different symbols. I don't remember the symbols, but they were, I knew, the eight divisions of G.E. and the eight vice presidents.

Underneath St. Peter and Christ and the eight compartments were other people, orderly-arranged. Yet somehow they looked all alike. There were bishops and lesser priests, I guess, and at the bottom a thousand faceless souls standing at attention. One of the priest-like figures looked like Mr. Devon, and for the second time I thought I saw myself for just an instant—a tiny face just above the souls at attention, who must have been the peasants or office boys or whatever.

At this point the vision ended as abruptly as it began. In the following days I knew I had seen not only the divine purpose behind G.E., but had caught a glimpse of the purpose of the whole universe. St. B.'s words stood out in my mind: the trinity . . . weight, measure, number . . . and I knew I was being weighed and measured and numbered. The last vision came within ten days. It was night again, and St. B. appeared as before.

Fourth Vision

"This is the last time I will appear to you, so listen carefully, my son. You have seen the Divine Order, and you know your place in it. You have heard the voice of promise. But now I will show you *The Way.* You must be alert.

"You are created in the image of God—you, like He, are a Trinity: of memory, intelligence, and will. *Memory* is the Father principle, the source of all and the Eternal Essence. *Intelligence* is the Son principle, the Divine Reason that knows and loves the Father, or the Eternal Patterns. *Will* is the Spirit principle, the breath that pervades your body and causes you to act. Do you understand?

"I have told you before that you are empty—your mind is blank. But it is slowly becoming filled with the knowledge of the Divine Order. I have spoken to you of *contuition*—and now you shall know. *Contuition* is seeing each part of the Order like God sees it. It is looking as if through His eyes. Do you begin to see?

"From his magisterial chair in heaven Christ teaches us interiorly.[9] Christ is the Model for humanity. St. Peter derives his authority from Christ, and proclaims Christ's will on earth. Hear on.

"Only St. Peter is next to Christ, and Christ is God's emanation. How can *you* then, my son, a mere man, a weak worm, rise to the knowledge of God? But you have within you the trinity of *memory, intelligence,* and *will,* and through these you may think God's thoughts after Him and act as if Christ were in you.

"And now, my son, the last words I shall leave you are these. There are *six stages of ascent* to the chair of St. Peter and before the throne of Christ.[10] Hear now. Mark. Absorb. This is your salvation. But first know, at each stage you are thinking God's thoughts—thoughts of the Divine Order. The way before you is the Way of Contemplation.

"First, you must use your *Will.* This is the key to the first two stages— the first two degrees of ascent to God. My son, the world around you is a world of *sense*—meaningless people, weighed, measured and numbered. Running about like unknowing and unknown shadows in a wintry grove.

"To rise above the world of sense you must use your *will power,* but first you must understand, you too must sense; you must *feel.* You must feel the insubstantiality of the world of senses. You must comprehend the anonymity of many souls—their numb routines and their hidden passions. But remember, these faceless throngs are God's people, too. But do not linger long, or this plane will ensnare you.

"Next you must turn to your *inner* world and the imagination and passions of your soul. Follow your thoughts in their insipidness, their dull regularity. See how you are distracted by silly secretaries in the day, and television by night. Here above all, you must not linger. For you have begun to contemplate the Divine Order, and you have sensed the beauty of the

Hierarchy. Exercise the divine will within you. Let the Spirit discipline your thoughts and turn you from distractions both exterior and interior. Are you with me?"

"Yes, I think so."

"Next you must use your *intelligence* in your contemplations. To mere reflection must be added shrewd logic, calculation, analysis and reason. To *will power* must be added *rational activity*.

"The third level is the knowledge of your gifts—your natural faculties in God's image. This is the level of *self-confidence*—the power of positive thinking. This *thought,* combined with the discipline you have gained will carry you to the rank of General Computer Controller for All Divisions. Remember, this is the *Son,* Christ the *Logos* in you. He is the Exemplar who is pleasing to God in all things.

"The fourth level is the level of God's grace, and the renewal of the soul. Your discipline and your will, your positive thinking and your intelligence, the Spirit and the Son, have brought you Divine Favor, and you shall move up yet another rung in the Divine Ladder. You shall become *one* of the eight vice presidents. Be patient my son, and heed my words. This shall come to you before you are gray. And remember at all times your Divine Nature, your Bible (the Manual), and God's grace.

"And now, listen to my words, for you shall begin the final ascent. The key to the last two planes of Being is to add the principle of the Father to the principles of the Spirit and the Son. *Memory* must be added to will and intelligence. You must now *remember* the thoughts of God which are always the same, and reflect upon the Divine Order *as a whole.* You must remember that the *Divine Being* is in *you*—and that God is Being. He is the Absolute. He alone is Uncreated and Self-subsistent—the One, the Source of all things, the Alpha and the Omega. Learn to think God's thoughts after Him. You must become God's *memory*—you must see the *whole* as He sees it. And then—and then only, my son—you shall become president. In those days grayness shall have spread from your temples, and balding will be well-advanced.

"But there is one final stage of ascent—the last step to perfection: the contemplation of the blessed Trinity. God is not only One, but Three: Father, Son and Spirit. His Being emanates from the top throughout the entire substructure. Here you shall know that the perfect Abstraction, the perfect Impersonality and the perfect Spirit are One in God. Here *memory* will pass into *communion,* and your mind, your will, your very Being shall partake of the blessed Trinity.

"Here is the Holy of Holies—the mystery of all G.E. As God's Abstracted Body, It shall become you and you shall become It. This step I cannot explain further; words fail even me. It is a great mystery. You shall learn of it when you are well advanced in years.

"And now my son, I say goodbye to you forever. Heed my words and you shall succeed." St. B. vanished abruptly, and I was never to see him again.

As I reflect on these last revelations of St. B., I have been with G.E. now for six years. I am now General Computer Controller for All Divisions, and St. B.'s prophecies have begun to be fulfilled.

I was divorced two years ago, but I don't mind. Now I can study the Manual more and more at night. I almost have it completely memorized. I am trying to learn to think Mr. Bynnings' thoughts after him—and I hear it whispered by some that I sound like a tape recording of him. That makes me very happy.

Under me are six Computer Controller II's, and programmers and secretaries. But when I become Vice President in my division, I shall strictly enforce the Manual and not tolerate the way everybody is so lax. All of my energies are directed towards this effort. I am learning to heed St. B.'s instructions, though I think it will take me many years to understand them all.

Sometimes when I am alone at night, I fancy myself seated alone in the dark cathedral of my vision. I can feel the spiritual presence in the silence; and those solemn massive columns, the empty altar and the eerie shadows, lie so still.

And then I turn my eyes to those great carvings. The minute figures all in a row, standing at attention. The bigger figures of priests and bishops, all arranged in neat compartments. And St. Peter standing there under Christ, holding the key and the Manual. And if I stare long enough at the figure of Christ, I fancy myself being drawn to him. I can sense my body being sucked up onto that throne and it feels like my flesh is turning to stone.

Homo Faber and the Orthodoxy of Technobureaucracy

The image of *homo faber,* "man the maker," is a unique synthesis of two converging world views in the West: Christian orthodoxy, and the atomistic, materialistic and mechanistic cosmos which we have called "the world machine." Technology and modern bureaucracy are the key institutional artifacts of the ideological wedding of these two traditions. What are the common modes of ideological functioning of our modern techno-bureaucratic world, and what are its mythic roots?

As Sam Keen suggests, "Man must make a structure of ideas within which to dwell, no less than he must construct a city to insure rational and orderly satisfaction of his needs."[11] In a real sense *ideas* are just as much artifacts* as social, institutional and physical structures which are first conceived in thought. Following Plato, ideas are the primal artifacts, the blueprints of cultural expression. But contra-Plato, ideas are also dialectically-spawned artifacts of the cultural process—synthesis as well as

---

*From the Latin *ars, artis,* "art" or "skill," and *facere,* "to make."

thesis, product as well as program. Even so, the ideology of the technobureaucratic world is both product and program, a unique synthesis and a blueprint of our future (unless we return to the drawing board).

Furthermore, it might be helpful for the present to abandon the evocative, but often misleading, distinction between "artificial" and "natural." Everything that man has ever made—or will make—involves the use of *natural* components, including synthetics, plastics, atomic bombs, or even sub-atomic particles created for a fleeting instant in a bubble chamber. The real differentiation is perhaps between extra-human nature and human culture, which is a special case of nature. One reputed sin of technology—its "artificiality"—might better be depicted as the reckless tipping of the scales of the whole of nature by the special case of human culture. The techno-bureaucratic world is a special form of human culture which has particularly contributed to such an imbalance.

Technology (from *techne,* Greek for "art" or "skill"), is a functional coefficient throughout the history of human culture. Moreover, there is an ideological, as well as semantic, relationship between *techne* ("art" or "skill") or technology, and aesthetics (from *aisthetikos,* "perceptive"), and cosmology (from *kosmos,* variously "world," "world order," and even "beauty" or "harmony"; and *logos,* the "word," "reason"—or loosely—"structure" of the cosmos). Simply stated, technology reflects a certain perception of the world—a certain "aesthetics" or "cosmology."

The modern technology of *homo faber*[12] is in part a secular derivative of two biblical passages—Genesis one and John one.

> And God blessed them (male and female), and God said to them, "Be fruitful and multiply, and *fill the earth* and *subdue* it; and *have dominion* over the fish of the sea and over the birds of the air and over every living thing that moves upon the earth. (Genesis 1:28)

> In the beginning was the *Word* [*logos*], and the Word was with God, and the Word was God . . . *all things were made* through him, and without him was not anything made that was made . . . And the Word became flesh and dwelt among us . . . (John 1:1-3,14)

In Genesis man is commissioned as lord over nature. The biblical intent of this injunction was to underscore the *responsibility* of man as a benevolent monarch upon whose shoulders was to rest the welfare of his kingdom. However, coupled with the recalcitrance or hostility of nature consequent to the "Fall" (in Genesis three), the divine appointment to lordship has been construed as a carte blanche for the unbridled exploitation of the natural world.

Furthermore, Judeo-Christian apocalyptic writings have propagated the expectation of a new earth, the arrival of which is contingent upon the destruction of the old, present earth. Romans 8:20,21 discloses the "futility" of nature at present awaiting future redemption of the sons of God. It is no wonder that Western consciousness has often exhibited a "devil-may-care" attitude towards the fate of the plant and animal kindgoms, the soil, the seas, and the air. After all, according to certain biblical passages, *God* himself has *cursed* the earth, and who are we to defy divine providence?

The second passage, the Johannine account of the divine *logos*, buttresses the technobureaucratic attitude towards the world. The *Word* is depicted as the *Maker* of all things, which implies* that nature, as the creation of the divine *logos*, is subject to his *control* and *manipulation*. In the Greco-Christian Synthesis the *logos* is interpreted in the light of such concepts as the Platonic Demiurge and the Neoplatonic hierarchy of being (in which the earth is inferior or under demonic control); hence the *logos* loses its Johannine personalism ("The Word became flesh and dwelled among us"), and becomes an *abstraction*. The *Word* becomes equated with *thought* (*orthodoxy* means "right thinking"). The power of the Word then becomes the power of rational planning and manipulation. The *logos* becomes a blueprint and the world is the logical artifact of the Word.

The orthodoxy of technobureaucracy is its cognitively-derived tendency to *plan*, to *control*, and to *manipulate*. The patriarchal divinity of Protestant orthodoxy establishes an intricate and exact system of belief and piety which exhibits the same *mechanisticity*[13] (or smooth machine-like regularity of function) as technology or bureaucracy.† The God of orthodoxy, although disguised in age-old personalistic metaphors, is in reality as functionally absent as his derivative counterpart, the Absent Clockmaker of deism. Like Newton, both deities have chosen arbitrary starting points for positing *a priori* absolutes upon which are built immense, logically-tight, intraconsistent and intricate, rational and mechanical systems. God *controls* and *manipulates* every facet of human life and behavior by his law. In orthodoxy "law" is equated with the Bible, but is often euphemistically cushioned by reference to "grace" (administered by Christ or the Holy Spirit). Created in God's image and possessing Christ in his heart, from legalistically-justified premises the orthodox Christian in a position of power can legitimate control and manipulation of others; in a subordinate position it is incumbent to accept the divine mandate of being so controlled or manipulated.

It is not coincidental that within orthodoxy, *freedom* is construed as absolute *dependence* upon God's will and his grace; one must accept whatever a beneficent providence (external to one's self) will bring. Both technology and bureaucracy—with or without pious legitimations—operate generally according to similar legalistic, patriarchal and dependency-creating premises.

---

*See also Colossians 1:16,17.

†This belief system is most evident in American fundamentalism, which often has included among its ranks stalwarts of capitalism and industry such as H. L. Hunt and R. G. LeTourneau.

Berger, Berger and Kellner enumerate four elements in the "style of work" of technology.[14] These include *mechanisticity* (discussed above), *reproducibility, participation,* and *measurability.*

Reproducibility (or perhaps better, *replicability*) means that every act within the work process can be duplicated by the same or another worker. Just so, protestations to the "uniqueness of the believer and his gifts" notwithstanding, the orthodox pattern of piety ordains preestablished roles and expectations of behavior which should be replicated in every believer according to his/her situation (e.g., functions of church officers, domestic structures of husband, wife and children, the patterns of morality, etc.).

Participation (or perhaps better, *componentiality,* used by the Bergers and Kellner to describe "cognitive style"), indicates the subservient role of the individual as a *part* of a larger *whole* (the organization or sequence of production, or equally, the entire bureaucratic structure). In orthodoxy, the individual is part of the Body of Christ; but the Body of Christ in practical terms becomes the local church with its rigid dogmas and lifestyle. The ostensible "individualism" of personal conversion is misleading, since rigid interpretations and expectations are attached to such an experience. Where emphasized, it is a kind of dramatic union card which makes one "O.K." as part of the ranks of true believers.

Measurability (or *quantifiability*), means that the tasks of the worker are considered generically isolable in terms of quantitative value. In orthodoxy the status of one's piety is measured by such quantifiable data as "having a conversion," the regularity of Bible study, prayer, and church attendance, and (though somewhat covertly) the amount of money donated to the local church. Even the "steps" of salvation achieve formulary status in some circles, e.g., recognition of sin, repentance, prayer, and testimony or confession, etc. For orthodoxy, piety is possible without cosmic faith (which, trusting the integrity of the cosmos as a whole, affirms a creative participatory role in human affairs, geared towards the highest fulfillment of spiritual potential in every person). In the scenario of orthodoxy, as in the secular world of technobureaucracy, the "Divine Mechanic" is the great soul-juggler. Persons are quantifiably dispensable (according to their usefulness) to realms of "light" or "darkness." If persons meet certain measurable standards of propriety (e.g., reciting appropriate "creedal" words, registering accepted opinions regarding religious or political issues, "keeping up appearances," generally conforming and avoiding "stirring up trouble" or controversy), they are favored, honored, given raises, promoted, or saved. However, if they betray doubt concerning cherished beliefs, suggest changes beyond superficial adjustments, dress or act "differently," or "keep bad company," they are likely to be demoted, passed over, talked about, or designated for "firing" (either *from* the job or *in* the eternal flames).

Moreover, technobureaucratic and religious orthodoxy share a belief in the power of the *Word,* since truths are primarily propositional or formulary. Thus, for *homo faber* words are tools to *manipulate, define* and *control.* It is important that everything and everyone must be properly defined, labeled, categorized and compartmentalized. As Sam Keen suggests

> Symbols are no longer words somehow saturated with the ultimate power that informs all things, the *logos,* but are instruments which may be turned to any purpose man desires. Symbols do not reflect reality—they create it; thus the word is still creative of all meaning, but now it is the human word. Words have replaced *logos* as the creative agent.[15]

The disposition towards verbal manipulation reflects a concatenation of the primitive and the modern. As in mythopoeism, words have power. As in (Korzybski's) Aristotelianism, words have substance. The addition of mechanism grants words atomistic or componential status. With these converging strands, verbalization becomes a means of power, control and categorization. Words *a priori* create reality. Words are literally tools of power which can be used to play upon the superstition or credulity of the unreflective.*

The point is that both technobureaucracy and religious orthodoxy share a scholastic, creedal, and legalistic belief in words. Not out of experiential revelation either natural or divine, but out of arbitrary human decision the bounds of meaning and truth are preestablished in a mechanical verbal framework. And woe betide the one who *challenges* their ostensible "divine" origin; for titles, roles, functions, definitions, and compartments, as well as opinions and utterances of propriety, are sacred "things." Words are both sacred and profane. The latter, which include all matters not relegated to the former, may be used with relative freedom (e.g., normal conversation regarding family, food, football). But in the area of the sacred, orthodoxy creates an arbitrary mechanical system, and technobureaucracy depends upon an arbitrary, functional orthodoxy.

In orthodoxy (especially fundamentalism) the Word has never become flesh. It has remained an abstraction—a tool of manipulation, power, and legitimation, just as God has remained an aloof patriarch in spite of all pietistic claims to the contrary. In addition, the remedial "Jesus" or the "blessed Holy Spirit" become insidious alter-egos, functioning either for internal compensation or external control. The course of one's life—which is not autonomous but other-directed, is thereby referred to a beneficient providence which "works for the good in all things."

Technobureaucracy operates with a similar style of consciousness: the atomistic componential individual, the harmonious meshing of components in their proper niches, and the abstracting of persons qua persons in favor of

---

*In this regard, the modern world owes a significant debt to logical positivism (whatever its excesses) which has clearly demonstrated the critical importance of anchoring words in experiential reality where their symbolizing value may be tested, verified and understood.

expected roles and designated functions; all is legitimated by a preconceived structural system into which everything must fit. With the loss of real uniqueness, the individual (typically portrayed as the little cog in the great wheel) concomitantly loses the integrity of experience. Time and experience are spatialized by being forced into rigid preestablished interpretive frames. The motile flux of experience becomes an illusion explicable in terms of eternal sessile archetypes. As Keen suggests, "*homo faber* is active not to occupy time but to find *salvation.*"[16] *Salvation* is the desire of everyone wedged into a system of absolutes, just as surely as *release* is the desire of every prisoner. Yet this statement must be qualified. For we read occasionally of an elder prisoner finally released, but wanting to return to prison—the one security known; so too, many partisans of modern institutional orthodoxy become so conditioned and so numbed *to* their condition, that they imagine themselves truly saved.

A further ramification of *homo faber* (and his institutional machines and mechanical ideologies) is the attendant inversion of artisan and artifact. *Homo faber* becomes *homo fabricatus,* "man who is made" or "fabricated man"—man the product of the cosmic machine.

> On the assembly line man becomes only another part of the machine, and a poor one at that—always breaking down and hampering the efficiency of the process by allowing grief, joy, or fatigue to invade working hours. . .[17]

In the systems of both orthodoxy and technobureaucracy, humanity is expected to conform to a mechanical ideal of perfection. Behavior which does not measure up is generally tolerated, but besieged by a proper dose of guilt- and inferiority-inducing admonitions. "Grace" (or economic necessity) restores the ailing sinner to the divine production line. Of course one who strays too far from the fold, or errs too grievously—whether apostate or union agitator—is beset by demonic influence and must be censored or fired.

What happens to human self-concepts in such systems? Many understand this external imposition of pre-packaged identity, and initiate appropriate compensatory measures. Yet even here the dominant cultural image may win a subtle triumph. As Sam Keen points out, the highly advertised *homo ludens* ("man the playful one") is often a pathetic and thinly-disguised mask of *homo faber.*[18] The widespread popularity of the playboy/playgirl models may be understood in part as the flip-side of the workboy/workgirl images of the mechanical universe. Keen identifies "two foci of play: consuming and romantic sexual activity,"[19] each of which reflects an underlying world view of orthodox consciousness.

> Both the advertisements and the "Playboy Advisor" make it clear that the game of consuming has rules that must be rigidly followed. The playboy must be an expert on the latest styles in clothing, automobiles, wines and all luxury appliances; he must know whether to stir or to shake a martini . . . Moral concerns do not create any anxiety . . . but the possibility of being discovered "in bad taste" creates the specter of shame—how embarrassing

to quote the wrong authors, serve the wrong wine, be caught with old-fashioned "repressive" views on sex, or the like . . .[20]

The rigid *ethos* of attitude and lifestyle reveal the same conformity and mechanical requirements as the factory, the bureaucracy, or orthodox cult. In extreme ascetic views sex is distinctly evil outside of—and strictly functional ("procreative") within—marriage. The playboy/playgirl motif manifests a secret asceticism in its functional view of sex. For here sex is not an authentic expression of the self engaging the whole person, but is rather a means to an end. As Keen says, *homo faber* used "his genitals as 'tools' to forge out an identity," and is besieged by "how-to-do-it" manuals laying down rules for an intricate mechanical "game."[21] Spontaneity and holism are impossible for asceticism (with its rigid rules of abstinence and warnings against the flesh) or for playboyism (with its mechanical code of expectations and behavior).

A further mythical orientation of both technobureaucracy and Christian orthodoxy is the focus upon the *possible* at the expense of the *actual,* or a denigration of the present (this world) in favor of the future (a world-to-come). Orthodoxy, and more particularly fundamentalism, tends to anticipate a future divine intervention in human affairs to alleviate the demonic influence or power over this present world. Human fulfillment in the present is available only in fragmentary fashion; it must be postponed for the most part to the future life. Furthermore, one must strictly control and restrain present wishes and desires, fears and anxieties, for a life disciplined to future salvation.

Within the technobureaucratic purview, the present is similarly restrained and controlled in the interest of working towards goals to be realized in an imagined future. In its extreme Utopian form, as Keen points out, the vision includes: perfectly executed megacities, economic and consumer welfare, abundant leisure, highly sophisticated communication and transportation systems, space travel, stable populations and stable food production, the elimination of poverty, disease and famine, the control of emotions, effortless mechanical learning techniques, and even some day, the triumph over death ("the last enemy").[22] In the case of both the sacred and the secular future visions, mortality, worldliness, and present struggle are regarded as evils to be eliminated, not as blessings to be enjoyed.

A final similarity of religious and technobureaucratic orthodoxies is the fear of *novelty.* Such a fear is a coefficient of sessile consciousness and the desire for eternal security—either theological or economic. Keen describes this fear in terms of the clashing of the Nietzschian Apollonian and Dionysian consciousnesses. In speaking of what we have termed the "Greco-Christian Synthesis" he says

It soon produced a new legalism, traditionalism, and orthodoxy which itself forbade novelty. No new ephiphany could occur, because Christ was the definitive intrusion of the divine into history, and thus the Christian community lived by remembrance of things past and hope for things to come, but with little expectation that any present moment was radically open to the Divine.[23]

Although technobureaucracy may engage in limited methodological experiments in the quest for greater efficiency, the only real innovations are new labor-saving devices or machines, not significant renovations of the *a priori* and arbitrary premises of the institutional structure itself. Technology may continue to create awesome new devices for the mechanizing of culture, but as of yet there is no evidence of any widespread examination of its essential world view. However, the forces of historical necessity (e.g., energy, ecology, clean air) may perhaps precipitate such an examination. For the present, bureaucracy, technology, and orthodox religion seem to be thriving prodigiously within the framework of sessile consciousness, where, to reiterate, time is spatially quantified and measurable, and reality is strictly compartmentalized to fit basic cosmological presuppositions. There are many indications that this "holding game" cannot last indefinitely; worldwide economic, religious, and political pluralism, and more indirectly the altered consciousness awakened by new cosmologies, all challenge the immobility of traditional assumptions.

AN OBJECTION TO THE HOMO FABER MODEL

The historical data usually marshaled for identifying man as *homo faber* seems to have been misconstrued, according to Lewis Mumford.[24] Stone artifacts of primitive cultures perhaps have been granted disproportionate significance, since it is the *stone* artifacts which are physically durable as opposed to largely-unknown articles of fabric, paper, pottery, etc. (whose purposes may have been aesthetic, religious, or non-utilitarian). Mumford suggests that man's brain has "more mental energy to tap than he needed for survival."[25] In fact

> at every stage man's technological expansions and transformations were less for the purpose of increasing the food supply or controlling nature than for utilizing his immense actual resources and expressing his latent potentialities in order to fulfill more adequately his own unique superorganic needs.[26]

Although human beings have achieved a certain level of sophistication, they are not unique in using tools or building. Mumford further proposes that the invention of language "was incomparably more important to further human development" than elementary tool-making.[27] Man *is* in fact *homo sapiens;* he is the "mind maker":

> Opposed to this stereotype [*homo faber*] is the view that man is preeminently a mind-using, self-mastering animal; and the primary locus of all his activities is his own organism.[28]

But old biases die hard. When the art of the Altamira caves was first discovered, it was labeled a hoax because "the leading paleo-ethnologists" refused to acknowledge that Ice Age hunters "had either the leisure or the mental inclination to produce art . . . that showed powers of observation and abstraction of a high order."[29]

Mumford observes that the Greek form for "technics" refers equally to both industrial production and symbolic art. "Technics at the beginning was broadly life-centered, not work-centered or power-centered."[30] Only about five thousand years ago did man begin to invent a "monotechnics" which was "devoted to the increase of power and wealth by the systematic organization of workaday activities in a *rigidly mechanical pattern.*"[31]

Modern technology then, was born with the invention of the "megamachine"—Mumford's term for regimenting humanity as an integral mass- (and often slave-) labor force for projects such as pyramid-building and temple-construction. In Egypt, according to Mumford, the eclipse of the god Osiris by Atum-Re represents a change in culture and cosmology. Osiris "symbolizes the older, life-oriented technics," whereas

> Atum-Re, the sun-god, who characteristically created the world out of his own semen without female cooperation, stands for the machine-centered one. The expansion of power, through ruthless human coercion and mechanical organization took precedence over the enhancement of life.[32]

Modern technology begins by mechanizing persons—turning the many into tools of manipulation and control for the exaltation and honor of the few. Mumford proposes the human "megamachine" as the most sophisticated technological innovation until the mechanical clock.

The patriarchal system from which the "megamachine" historically derives its legitimation is critical to the cosmological structure of modern technobureaucracy:

> The Nuclear Age conception of "absolute power" and infallible intelligence, exercised by a military-scientific elite, corresponds to the Bronze Age conception of Divine-Kingship; and both belong to the same infantile magico-religious scheme as ritual human sacrifice.[33]

In such a scheme persons are not intelligent homeostatic organic occurrences, nor is community a biocultural expression. (Much less is there a role for implicit spiritual value within all human life.) Individuals and society are understood atomistically, materially and mechanically. Sam Keen suggests that this mechanical hierarchy is largely responsible for the "spiritual schizophrenia" of modern *homo faber* "in which there is an oscillation between omnipotent and impotent feelings and expectations."[34] This schizophrenia is a thinly-veiled counterpart of the age-old "master/slave" dichotomy of the "megamachine," and perhaps a clue to the sadistic-masochistic syndrome that seems so prevalent in modern society. The most brutal crimes of modern technobeaurocracy occurred in Nazi Germany, where an hierarchical and patriarchal quasi-religion triumphed. Richard Rubenstein dramatically underscores the point:

> As adults, the quantifying rationality of modern society affords men many opportunities to treat others as dead objects rather than live persons. The tendency to treat the human as inanimate is inherent in the necessities of technical civilization. For most of us, the tendency is regrettable and unavoidable. For the Nazis, it became an end in itself. This characteristic . . . was exemplified in the death camps, the stench of the corpses and the use of people as raw material to be turned into feces, which was the chief industry of the camps.[35]

The full horror of this technological genocide was unknown to the public until after the War, when it was revealed that the Jews were systematically slaughtered for "industrial" use: body fat was used for soap; gold teeth for bank deposits; skin for lampshades; and general remains for fertilizer.[36] These atrocities are the prime historical incident in modernity of the demonic insanity which can prevail when a fiercly-exclusive and arbitrary "ortho-doxy" is wedded to the depersonalizing abstractions of the cosmic world machine.[37] We have pointed out the primitive roots of such absolute systems. Mumford says "To the extent that our megatechnics ignores these fundamental insights into the nature of organisms and human personalities, it is *prescientific* in its attitude toward the human personality."[38]

The sickness and frustrations which abound in much of the modern technobureaucratic world disclose its anachronistic cosmology of sacred absolutes. Emptied of sacred legitimation and therefore emptied of sacred meaning, this cosmos is not thereby freed of its rigid and perfectionistic norms. The widespread, blasphemous disregard for the sacredness of human life (e.g., three major wars, psychotic mass slayings, worldwide terrorist attacks) sets in bold relief the critical failure of outmoded absolutist cosmologies* to stem the destructive tide of the human "Id."

The urgent need for a new ethical cosmos tests the fiber of Mumford's faith in man as truly *homo sapiens*. But we must agree with him that world culture demands a "dismantling of the megamachine, in *all* its institutional forms . . . with a redistribution of power and authority to smaller units, under direct human control.[39] "In all its institutional forms" must include not only industry and government, but education, religion, and other giant institutions which reflect—either overtly or covertly—the ideology of the megamachine. But such a task requires new insights into the cosmos—insights available in part by extrapolations from the significant data of ecology and cosmology in recent years. Within the present context we will enumerate further examples of how biological, mythical and historical roots have converged in modern culture in the cosmos and ethos of technobureaucracy and its ideological kin.

---

*Such cosmologies are not confined to the "Christian" West, as the resurgence of fundamentalist Islam testifies.

208

A MYTHICAL CHART OF THE TWO HEMISPHERES OF THE BRAIN AND WESTERN CONSCIOUSNESS

Left Hemisphere	Right Hemisphere
	COGNITIVE FUNCTIONS
logical	analogical
analytical	synthetic
linear, sequential	synchronistic
propositional, abstract	emotive, concrete
language	image-ination, intuition
hierarchical, geometric	radial, symmetric
Aristotelian thought and	Heraclitean thought and
the aesthetics of substantive	the aesthetics of dynamic
space-time	space-time
	SEXUAL ORIENTATION
masculine, aggressive	feminine, receptive, protective
man versus nature	harmony
man versus man	nurturing
warfare	sensuous
technology	exploring
action	wonder
homo faber	*homo ludens*
"inquisition," "analysis,"	"intuition," "synthesis,"
"probing": the masculine	"nurturing": the feminine
sexuality—authentic if	sexuality—authentic if
not rape, violation	not stifling, smothering
danger: cold, impersonal,	danger: maudlin sentimentality;
danger: rugged isolation	danger: mindless dependence
	MYTHICAL TENDENCIES
Amun Re	Osiris and Isis
Apollo	Dionysus
Warlike images of Yahweh	Mother Goddesses, Ba'al
the Christ of orthodoxy	the Christ of the New Testament
state cults	mystery religions
spatial, sessile	motile, temporal
gnosis—orthodoxy—manipulation	*pneuma*—communion—community
institutional	gnostic
atomistic, mechanistic	organic
patriarchy, hierachy,	democratic, egalitarian,
authoritarian	participation

Judeo-Christian	*Greco-Roman*	*Judeo-Christian*	*Greco-Roman*
alienation	abstraction	mysticism	aesthetics
asceticism	reason	communion,	nature
		sacrament	

209

Homo Faber, Cerebral Hemispheres and a Case for Feminism

The foregoing chart constitutes an attempt to provide one mythical model for the analysis of Western consciousness. It is not to be taken literally. Although exploration into the functions of the two hemispheres of the brain made by Gazzaniga and Sperry[40] in the sixties would suggest some empirical evidence for the dichotomies depicted by the chart, our model undoubtedly oversimplifies and is subject to revision and qualification (perhaps as further research results are established). The chart may be of some utility in understanding current struggles within Western culture.

From the standpoint of apparent functions of the two hemispheres,* Western Civilization seems to be built upon the functional hypertrophy of the left lobe of the brain. Perhaps there is no better exemplar of this thesis than the technobureaucratic institutions of modern society. The triumph of the mechanical cosmos and technology represents the apex of logical, analytical, sequential and geometric functions. Bureaucracy appears as a mechanized and secularized counterpart of the Neoplatonic cosmology of the Middle Ages. Its spatial hierarchy of ascending orders, its carefully defined spheres of jurisdiction, function and role, and its tendency towards orderliness and compartmentalization of knowledge and persons (called by the Bergers and Kellner the "taxonomic propensity") are illustrative. Mechanization and secularization entail anonymity, atomisticity, neutrality, and mechanical quantifiability of persons within the institutional frame. The "aesthetics" of these institutions is clearly Apollonian—though in a particularly sterile and colorless form as the stark functionalism of much modern architecture illustrates. In the extreme, technobureaucracy seems to exhibit the complete atrophy of right hemispheric concerns. Life processes are emptied of all vital emotional, eccentric, intuitional, or cultural (cultivated) value. The clear effects upon *much* of Western Civilization are the widespread love of material *things* and the accompanying reification of persons (as Marx warned long ago).

In lieu of the model of the two cerebral hemispheres, perhaps we can gain particular perspective and appreciation of the feminist protest of recent years. Feminism accentuates the need for rectifying our (literal) mental imbalance and cultural schizophrenia. Any argument speciously suggesting that women, often excluded from certain aspects of left-hemispheric culture for several thousand years, are "intellectually inferior," may be countered by the assertion that men are "mentally inferior" as regards the functioning of the right lobe of the brain. Sex roles appear to be largely cultural in origin, not primarily products of the genetic code. If young children of both sexes

---

*The left hemisphere is usually associated with logical, analytical, propositional, and linguistic, cognitive functions; the right hemisphere with intuition, fantasy, creativity, holistic "background" perception, etc.

have not yet gravitated towards the functions of one lobe or the other, it would appear that the bifurcation of the sexes is primarily a derivative of both our linear, logically-biased educational focus, and also culturally-assigned sexual role expectations. Real sexual differences seem to be more hormonal than intellectual, though a vast area of research remains open in this field.

In any case, feminism registers an appropriate protest to the masculine and left-hemispheric imbalance of our society.[41] *Homo faber* is an inadequate model of human nature if for no other reason than it virtually excludes half of the human self. In the quest for new models of *human being*, it is essential and timely to recognize that such a model must fully incorporate right-hemispheric (traditionally feminine) human functioning. Nurturing as well as aggression; psychic, intuitive and creative capacities as well as logic; organic interdependence as well as social independence, must be properly accounted for. Moreover, the hostility and misunderstanding among nations, as well as at times between the sexes, will be greatly mollified if the two sexes develop their latent capacities, to balance out—and where necessary for health and freedom, to cancel out—old cultural roles. (Women, for example have not been the prime perpetrators of warfare.)

A Brief Excursus on one Source of Left-Hemispheric Militancy, Mechanism and Masculinity in Western Culture

We outlined the similar structures of consciousness between Greco-Chistian orthodoxy and technobureaucracy. It would not be difficult to illustrate how the intolerance and defensive-aggressive stance of orthodoxy (coupled with political power) have precipitated violence and military conflict for well over a thousand years. We need only cite the history of Christianity from Constantine through the Crusades, the Inquisition, orthodox witch- and heresy-hunting, the religious wars of Europe, and the conflict still aflame between Catholics and Protestants in Ireland. A further example is the alliance in contemporary America between blind patriotism ("our country right or wrong"), orthodoxy ("for God and country"), and the "military-industrial complex." "Communism"—conceived as a monolithic united worldwide whole—is still regarded as the veritable force of Antichrist by many Americans.

The origins of the militant alliance of orthodoxy and patriotism is complex, and would require investigation into a diverse array of historical factors.* However, in the early years of Christianity one particular struggle sheds light upon its evolution from a small peaceful fellowship to a militant worldwide Church.[42]

---

*Militancy in Christianity has many sources, e.g., Roman imperialism, Jewish apocalypticism, etc.

Apart from occasional intense persecution in the first three centuries of Christianity, the most severe external battle (the battle with gnosticism was primarily internal) which the Church fought was with Mithraism. Mithra the Tauroctonous ("Bull Slaying") came very close to triumphing over Christ first in Rome, and then in Western history. Although institutionally Mithra was finally defeated, ideologically he may have won a secret victory.

Appearing in both the *Vedas* and the *Avesta*, Mithra was a very ancient god,[43] and from the first a warlike combatter of evil.[44] Although not originally prominent in the Zoroastrian pantheon, Mithra gained prestige by his popularity with Persian monarchs (such as Artaxerxes) and other Near Eastern kings. Thus Tauroctonous Mithra appears on the obverse of a number of coins in the ancient world. Over a period of several hundred years there developed around Mithra a cult which became (like the Judeo-Christian tradition) a bearer of Zoroastrian doctrines. Mithraism also reflected the general conflation of Babylonian and Persian traditions and the eclecticism of the Hellenistic *oikoumene*. Mithra, who was at an early date identified with the Sun, assumed characteristics of both the Babylonian *Shamash* and the Greek *Helios*.

According to Plutarch, Mithraism was introduced in Rome in the century before Christ. By the end of the first century C.E., Mithraism was being disseminated throughout the Empire. Mithra's militant character created great popularity among the Roman army.[45] For two centuries Mithraism was more successful in missionary endeavors than Christianity; shrines to Sol Invictus—"the Invincible Sun"—have been discovered throughout the territory once held by the Old Empire. Many reliefs depicting the Tauroctonous Mithra still exist.

The character of Mithra—as a rival of Christ—is significant. The Tauroctonous Mithra reliefs show a cosmogonic myth of Mithra slaying the Bull.[46] From the slain animal spring the wheat and the vine and domestic animals. The Bull itself was granted divine status.[47] Psychoanalytically and archetypically, the bull is often a symbol of male sexuality and aggression (note the importance of the bull in Picasso's etchings and his famed canvas *Guernica*). In some reliefs Mithra has the bull by the horn, and the expression "grasping the bull by the horns" still connotes the aggressive tackling of a problem or a dilemma. The horn itself can be taken as a phallic symbol, as can the torches of the twin torchbearers often depicted with Mithra on the reliefs. Mithra is a god well-suited to Roman power and hegemony, for he is a god who inhabited "places where war and commerce were constantly conducted."[48] Initiates into Mithraism were inducted into the cult by the *taurobolium*, or bathing in the blood of a bull. It was believed (as is typical of mythopoeic consciousness) that a share in the strength of the animal and participation in his immortal divine status were thereby assured. For the adherents of Mithraism "life is a battle."[49] Cumont writes

They did not lose themselves . . . in contemplative mysticism; for them good dwelt in *action*. They rated *strength* higher than gentleness, and preferred *courage* to lenity. From their long association with barbaric religions, there was perhaps a residue of *cruelty* in their ethics. A *religion of soldiers*, Mithraism exalted the *military virtues* above all others.[50]

Furthermore, Mithra was a god "eternally young and vigorous" who pursued his enemies without mercy; he was "always awake, always alert," and could never be surprised.[51]

Mithraism, like Neoplatonism, envisaged the cosmos as divided into different zones: seven successive spheres (each associated with a planet) for the journey of the soul to heaven (the realm of the fixed stars).[52] In each sphere the soul was freed of some vice—e.g., the passions, vital energy, the intellect, dreams—so that upon penetrating the eighth heaven it was naked and stripped of all worldliness, prepared to bathe in the light of the gods.[53]

Mithraic brotherhoods and communities, which offered salvation to initiates of all social ranks, were organized into "colleges" patterned after "the constitutions of the municipalities or towns."[54] In addition to priests there were officers elected to manage temporal affairs. These officers bore such secular titles as "trustees," the "first ten," "presidents," "curators," "attorneys," and "patrons."[55] The Mithraic congregations were organizationally interconnected and apparently met in general assembly.[56] Women occupied an inferior role in Mithraism.[57] Mithraism reached its apogee of power "toward the middle of the third century."[58]

Mithraism exemplifies—as poignantly as any ancient religion—the supremacy of masculinity, patriarchy, militancy and hierarchical organization within (and legitimated by) religion. Until the conversion of Constantine, Mithraism seemed destined to become the official cult of Rome.[59] The triumph of Christianity was at the cost of absorbing some of the spirit and method of its rival. For after all, as legend has it, Constantine was told, "under this sign (the chi-rho) *conquer.*" Mithraism enjoyed a brief revival under Julian the Apostate (331-363). Upon his death Christianity was restored to its official status and, often resorting to terrorism and execution,* went about systematically stamping out its enemy. Christian orthodoxy, intent upon victory over its bellicose rival, resorted to the devil's methods for stamping out the devil's own henchmen. Henceforth, the devil's militancy was to become sanctified by the Church. The secret triumph of Mithraism was the transformation of Christianity into a militant faith. There are of course other factors responsible for the Church's transformation, including its sufferings during the years it was an "outlaw" religion in the Empire.

The Christian tradition owes to Mithraism (in whole or in part) Sunday, December 25th (the birthday of the Sun), the extreme ascetic ethics of monasticism, military orders, etc.[61] Both religions practiced baptism;

---

*The chained skeleton in the condemned Mithraic temple of Lorraine evidences these tactics.[60]

celebrated a symbolic Lord's Supper; believed in heaven and hell, good and evil, and divine forces doing battle with demonic spirits.[62] Both Mithra and Christ were mediators between the celestial father and men, and both belonged to a trinity.[63] Both indeed taught salvation secured by blood sacrifice, and participation of believers in eternal life. How many of the dogmas of medieval orthodoxy may have derived in part from Mithraism may never be settled. What is certain is that after its encounter with this sect of soldiers, Christianity was never the same.

The Christianity of the New Testament is in certain fundamental respects a different religion from the orthodoxy that triumphed in Rome, and whose dogmatic structures still persist in secular form in technobureaucratic institutions of modernity. Perhaps feminism, which may help redress Western cognitive imbalance, could also help the Church purge subtle remnants of an aggressive orthodoxy which still bears the stigmata of a long dead rival.

FOOTNOTES

[1]Peter Berger, Brigitte Berger, and Hansfried Kellner, *The Homeless Mind* (New York: Vintage Books, 1974).

[2]Gordon Leff, *Medieval Thought: St. Augustine to Ockham* (Baltimore: Penguin Books, 1958), p. 195.

[3]Ibid., p. 195.

[4]Ibid., p. 204

[5]*The Encyclopedia of Philosophy*, s.v. "St. Bonaventure," Allan B Wolter.

[6]Ibid.

[7]Ibid.

[8]Ibid.

[9]Ibid.

[10]Herbert Musurillo, "Bonaventure's 'The Soul's Journey to God,'" *Thought: A Review of Culture and Idea* 46 (Spring 1971): 110-13.

[11]Sam Keen, *Apology for Wonder* (New York: Harper and Row, 1969), pp. 121-22.

[12]Such imagery seems to reflect very basic components of human culture. Hannah Arendt, *The Human Condition* (Chicago: The University of Chicago Press, 1958), in an enlightening discussion regarding the emergence of *homo faber*, observes: "Fabrication, the work of *homo faber*, consists in reification. Solidity, inherent in all, even the most fragile things, comes from the material worked upon, but this material itself is not simply given and there, like the fruits of the field and trees . . . Material is already a product of human hands which have removed it from its natural location . . . (p. 139). Arendt assumes that the act of fabricating automatically entails violence against nature, by manipulating and objectifying it. Such an assumption suggests a dichotomy between culture and nature which seems (in this context) thought to be inevitable. It is just such a dichotomy that ecology seeks to overcome.

[13]Berger, Berger and Kellner, p. 26.

[14]Ibid.

[15]Keen, p. 122.

[16]Ibid., p. 124.

[17]Ibid., p. 125.

[18]Ibid., p. 140 ff.

[19]Ibid., p. 141.

[20]Ibid., pp. 141–42.

[21]Ibid.

[22]Ibid., pp. 125–36.

[23]Ibid., p. 159.

[24]Lewis Mumford, "Technics and the Nature of Man," in *Technology and Culture: An Anthology*, ed. Melvin Kranzberg and W. H. Davenport (New York: New American Library, 1972), p. 200 ff.

[25]Ibid., p. 204.

[26]Ibid., p. 205.

[27]Ibid.

[28]Ibid., p. 206.

[29]Ibid., pp. 206–07.

[30]Ibid., p. 208.

[31]Ibid.

[32]Ibid.

[33]Ibid., p. 213.

[34]Keen, p. 118.

[35]Richard L. Rubenstein, *After Auschwitz: Radical Theology and Contemporary Judaism* (New York: The Bobbs-Merrill Co., 1966) p. 39.

[36]Ibid.

[37]Richard L. Rubenstein's analysis of the rationale behind the bureaucratic machinery employed in the methodical and systematic elimination of the Jews by Nazi Germany is most pertinent here. See *The Cunning of History: Mass Death and the American Future* (New York: Harper and Row, 1975). Rubenstein writes: "Protestantism violently rejected the Catholic attempt at reenchantment. Its insistence on the radical transcendence of the one sovereign Creator and his utter withdrawal from the created order was far more thoroughgoing than the earlier Jewish attempt at disenchantment. Martin Luther proclaimed that the world was so hopelessly corrupted by sin and so totally devoid of the saving presence of God, that the Devil is in fact Lord of this world. The Protestant insistence that man is saved by faith alone *(sola fidei)*, rather than works, separates man's activities in the empirical world from the realm of divinity with a remorseless logic to which biblical Judaism had pointed but did not reach . . . The land of the Reformation was also the land where bureaucracy was able to create its most thoroughly secularized, rationalized, and dehumanized "achievement," the death camp . . . God and the world had to be so radically disjoined that it became possible to treat both the political and the natural order with an uncompromisingly dispassionate objectivity . . . it is the biblical tradition that has led to the secularization of consciousness, disenchantment of the world, methodical conduct (as in both Protestantism and capitalism), and, finally bureaucratic objectivity" (pp. 29 and 31). Cf. also chapter 4, "The Health Professions and Corporate Enterprise at Auschwitz" (pp. 48–67).

[38]Mumford, p. 213.

[39]Ibid.

[40]Richard D. Konicek, "Seeking Synergism for Man's Two-Hemisphere Brain," *Phi Delta Kappan* (September 1975): 37–39.

[41]Of course, as Richard Rubenstein has pointed out, feminism may also be an expression of envy for masculine prerogatives. But in any case, with greater research into the cultural and/or biological bases of sexual differences we will hope for a more balanced understanding. See Richard Rubenstein, *The Religious Imagination: A Study in Psychoanalysis and Jewish Theology* (Boston: Beacon Press, 1971), pp. 43–57.

[42]It is difficult to say how much of a caricature or how much of a reality the expression "small peaceful fellowship" entails. For example, Luke's description in the Acts of the Apostles tends to gloss over divisions within the early community which are represented more realistically by Paul. Moreover, it is equally difficult to discover whether some of Jesus' militaristic words, such as the apocalyptic passages in the

synoptics, are legitimate reflections of his teaching, later interpolations by his more defensive followers, or both. Of course certain other New Testament books, such as the Thessalonian letters, II Peter, Jude and Revelation, clearly contain typical expressions of vindictive apocalypticism.

[43]Franz Cumont, *The Mysteries of Mithra* (New York: Dover, 1956), p. 1.

[44]Ibid., p. 4.

[45]Ibid., pp. 36–40.

[46]Ibid., p. 137.

[47]Ibid.

[48]Ibid., p. 78.

[49]Ibid., p. 140.

[50]Ibid., pp. 141–42.

[51]Ibid., p. 143.

[52]Ibid., p. 144.

[53]Ibid., p. 145.

[54]Ibid., p. 168.

[55]Ibid., pp. 168–69.

[56]Ibid., p. 194.

[57]Ibid., p. 173.

[58]Ibid., p. 200.

[59]Ibid., p. 204.

[60]Ibid., pp. 190–91.

[61]Ibid.

[62]Ibid.

[63]Ibid.

CHAPTER NINE

MAN THE MICROCOSM

WORLD VIEW is a reflection of self-definition. Ludwig Feuerbach, in his classical treatise *The Essence of Christianity*, concluded that all theology is anthropology. The human is projected into the divine. John Priest has asserted that "all cosmology is anthropology."

Man must construct the cosmos through his own biological and cultural equipment. At this fundamental level all knowledge, all language, all thought is anthropological. The real question remains, to what extent (if any) humanity is able to extrapolate itself from the specificity of the "human condition" and to see the world through "other eyes." In other words, to what extent is our perception of nature and the cosmos solely a reflection of our peculiar location (which we ourselves have defined)?

Kingdom	Animalia (Animals)
Phylum	Chordate (Chordates)
Class	Mammalia (Mammals)
Order	Primates(Primates)
Superfamily	Homioidea (Hominoids)
Family	Homininae (Hominines)
Genus	Homo (Man)
Species	sapiens (Modern Man)[1]

Perhaps one of the great tasks or challenges for future *psycho-analysis* (including all who are engaged in the analysis of the human psyche) is the discovery of the extent to which individual emotional and cultural location, including self-image, affects "world analyses." To what extent have all thinkers projected themselves into their cultural or cosmological world pictures? Are we forever ensconced or imprisoned within a solipsistic labyrinth with no exits? This depends upon to what extent man *is* an isolable entity.*

In the following discussion we will compare some of the conceptions of "human being" vying for our allegiance in contemporary Western culture. Within our limited scope, we will not engage in the important task of thoroughgoing historical analysis. Furthermore, some of the issues raised here will be considered in a different light in the final chapters.

In surveying competing world views of our age, the most significant question in weighing their relative merits may be how each defines man. How

---

*Conceiving of man as an isolable entity is a peculiarly Western habit. Eastern, Native American, and a variety of indigenous cultures conceive of human beings as organically integral to nature.

is the question "who am I?" or "who are we?" answered? One significant clue is the way in which the subject is broached. Is the critical question, "who am I in my private experience?" or "what is man?," generically? Obviously the two questions are mutually interdependent, yet the raising of one as opposed to the other is an immediate indication of vital cosmological presuppositions. How the question is raised suggests a correlative question, namely "what is the chief datum of human self-definition: my private experience, divine revelation, society, nature . . . ?"

Moreover, the particular way in which "human being" is conceived is vital to the way in which the natural and communal environments are understood and valued, and to the future which humanity imagines for itself.

Orthodox Man

The most pervasive and influential model of man in the West remains the Judeo-Christian tradition, especially in its orthodox form. We have suggested how the dogmas of the Greco-Christian Synthesis survive in secular—as well as in traditional sacred—form. In both the sacred and secular versions human self-definition is considered generically—and the chief datum is humanity's relationship to some preestablished ideal—whether God, divine perfection, a static and mechanical model, or a reified Superego.

Man as *imago dei* is endowed with divine gifts of intellect, emotions, will, and spiritual sensitivity. Yet the image is clouded, arrested, or perverted by the influence of "original sin." In classical Israel man is a struggling, weak creature beset by historical and temporal guilt. With the incorporation of the apocalyptic scheme, first Judaism and then early Christianity began to betray profound distrust of the present world. With the ensuing input of Platonic idealism with its ontological split, the salvation once available to man through repentance and this-worldly faithfulness was crippled. Since this sphere—and the body which belongs to it—are thus relegated to moral corruption and demonic control, the possibility of present worldly integrity is impaired. The emergent self-image of man, in itself and apart from divine grace, is impotent, since strength, salvation and ultimate hope all stem from a radically-other order. Polarities are the only options: damnation/salvation, guilt/repentance, this world/the eternal world, physical/spiritual, etc. Thus attendant upon a Greco-Christian orthodoxy is schizophrenia (in the literal, not clinical, sense—a "split mind"). The present horizontal, existential world bows before a future, vertically-impinging mythological order. Yet right-hemispheric wonder, though preserved in liturgy and communion, plays no real role in theological formulation (in its left-hemispheric, propositional mode).

How does man, informed by such values, envision his relationship to nature and community? We have traversed this ground. Man and nature are divided. Man is lord and manipulator of the natural world. Divisions and alienation exist among men as well. The only natural solidarity of humanity is solidarity in guilt and sin. Community is not a natural expression, but a supernatural creation contingent upon divine grace and human conformity.

Obviously the situation we have described does not occur in monolithic fashion within the history of Christendom. There are indeed many variations on a theme. However, the significance of the *orthodox* perspective (in addition to the fact that many still adhere to its literal churchly form) is that the essential *structures of consciousness* in the secular world reflect, *not* the avant garde or the heterodox in Christian tradition, but orthodox modes of self-definition and world-conception. *Attitudinally,* such exemplars as mind-body duality, divisions of the "saved" and "damned," manipulation of the natural world, apocalyptic distrust of history, and most significantly for self-awareness the sense of guilt and isolation, all illustrate the influence of the covert orthodoxy (albeit secular) of both institutions and persons in the modern West.

EXISTENTIAL MAN

"Existential man," as a general nomenclature, is a convenient demarcation only. The widespread use of "existentialism" as representative of a more or less uniform school of thought is erroneous.[2] On the other hand, to reflect upon the meaning of the concrete existence of man—as opposed to speaking abstractly of some *a priori* "human nature"—is at least in part a shared stance of a number of significant thinkers (who may differ critically with regard to other matters). If "existential" denotes such a reflection, then it may designate the concerns of a diverse array of thinkers both past and present. In the present context we admit to a loose delineation which serves as an "umbrella" term for related perspectives approaching persons in their concreteness and specificity.

The modern Christian sage, Soren Kierkegaard (1813-1855) manifests strident antipathy towards bourgeois society. A vigorous antagonist of institutional Christianity and the abstractions of scholastic theology, Kierkegaard never quite escapes the grasp of certain orthodox "structures of consciousness." In his quest to discover how one might be a Christian in hypocritical bourgeois society, Kierkegaard shares the traditional Pauline disdain (expressed, for example, in I Corinthians) for all forms of "worldly" wisdom. Moreover, Kierkegaard assumes the biblical judgment of the harshness and despair of the human condition, and envisions the only ultimate means of escape as an act of faith.

The Church has become a mere worldly guise. True Christianity must abandon all "pagan discourse" which, in redefining biblical terms so that they "mean anything and everything," has become mere "toothless twaddle."[3] Kierkegaard ridicules abstract speculation[4] in a manner we might first assume is a return to biblical historicism; but history—insofar as it entails a continuity of tradition—is displaced by the pristine present.[5] United with the church in spiritual bankruptcy is the socio-political world. In Kierkegaard's eyes, the human condition must be understood in a psychological and existential purity beneath institutional facades. (True to his own convictions, Kierkegaard strove for purity in a life of relative isolation.)[6]

In Kierkegaard the apocalyptic becomes personal. Only out of polarized consciousness—an anxiety of the ego contemplating its *falseness within* its historical and cultural setting[7]—is salvation possible. The resultant severe individualism[8] assails both community ("The very maximum of what one human being can do for another in relation to that wherein each man has to do solely with himself, is to inspire him with concern and unrest");[9] and the cosmos ("for ethical maturity consists in apprehending one's own ethical reality as infinitely more important than any understanding of the world-process").[10] Only a recognition of one's Job-like insignificance in the activity of worshipful self-deprecation will avail:

> Precisely because there is an absolute difference between God and man, man will express his own nature most adequately when he expresses this difference absolutely. *Worship* is the maximum expression for the God-relationship of a human being, and hence also for his likeness with God, because the qualities are absolutely different. But the significance of worship is, that God is absolutely all for the worshiper; and the worshiper is again one who makes the absolute distinction.[11]

Guilt is not failure according to historical or cultural norms, but it is existential, for "the essential consciousness of guilt is the first deep plunge into existence."[12]

Karl Barth echoes Kierkegaard's despair of worldliness:

> We go off and build the pitiable tower at the Babel of our human righteousness, human consequence, human significance. Our answer to the call of conscience is one great makeshift, extending over the whole of life, a single gigantic "as if" (als ob)! And because and as long as we are willing to think, speak, and act "as if"—*as if* our tower were important, as if something were happening, as if we were doing something in obedience to the conscience—the reality of the righteousness after which we hunger and thirst will elude us.[13]

Barth, like Kierkegaard, deplores the liberal pride of Enlightenment man, arrogating himself by a claim to self-knowledge apart from divine revelation. For Kierkgaard, man before God is naked, with neither nature nor community[14] to give him succor. It is not accidental that Kierkegaard is disinterested in the natural world: the age-old material/spiritual duality is implicit within his thought. Furthermore, Kierkegaard departs from the mainline of Christian tradition as regards the significance of community or the Body of Christ (which is of radical importance within the New Testament tradition). In this sense Kierkegaard is the radical Protestant in extreme. To base one's Christianity upon confession of faith or baptism is tragic-comic, and

> In relation to Christianity . . . objectivity is a most unfortunate category; he who has an objective Christianity and none other is *eo ipso* a pagan, for Christianity is precisely an affair of spirit, and so of subjectivity, and so of inwardness.[15]

At this point Kierkegaard clearly severs the orthodox ties; even so the glimmers of a long tradition of the isolate ego alone before God linger on. As Augustine said, "in these three things no true-seeming illusion disturbs us; . . . I am most certain that I am, and that I know and delight in this."[16] From Augustine through Descartes and Kierkegaard to modern existential thought there is the recurrent line of subjectivism[17] which haunts the West and appears in various secular guises, including capitalism and romanticism.

Finally, Kierkegaard's subjectivism is dramatized in his conception of salvation, or man's mode of transcending his ego predicament. Here the inherent circularity of a thinly-veiled solipsism dramatically emerges.[18] Kierkegaard's counsel on becoming a Christian is that one must—on a strictly *internal* level—make a qualitative "leap of faith" in Jesus Christ. The rites of the Christian community may serve as a deterrent or a hindrance to such a decision; for when "there is no outwardness to distract the attention," the genuine inwardness of such a choice is less hindered.[19] Kierkegaard does concede that the external rites, etc., may serve as "the watchman that arouses the sleeper";[20] here he is cautious, and in any case seems oblivious to the Pauline sense of "we"—of a "*people* of God," or a Body of Christ, or of any cosmic struggle confronting the individual. His intense disgust with the Danish state church (Lutheran) only serves as an historical emotional referent for a doctrine fundamentally purely arbitrary: one must choose simply because one must choose. Existentialism never quite escapes the Kierkegaardian solipsistic dilemma. Perhaps we may say that it is just in his personal arbitrariness[21] that Kierkegaard serves as the greatest inspiration for his future "disciples."

Kierkegaardian existentialism, if not consistently, at least recurrently, completes the cycle of schizophrenia which is nascent within orthodoxy. If man apart from divine grace stands naked and alone, then how much more naked and how much more alone when grace itself is withdrawn from the scene. There is no need to retrace the well-worn paths of the so-called "Death of God" from Nietzsche to the popular movement of the sixties. However, the chief implication of God's absence and/or death—whether conceived as welcome release for man's freedom, or an "awful" and "terrifying" freedom in the face of cosmic anomie—is man's aloneness.

This isolation, a popular theme of modern literature and culture, is succinctly and poignantly characterized in the title of Sartre's play, *No Exit,* or graphically dramatized in Edvard Munch's eerie canvas "The Scream." Isolation afflicts many individuals in more extreme forms of technobureaucracy, where an arbitrary hierarchy exists apart from any divine or cosmic legitimation, or any rational or naturalistic frame of reference.

Only madmen seem to dare the *reductio ad absurdum* or logical consequence of total solipsism—namely that the ego is trapped within its own illusions; and that time, history, nature, or relationships—indeed all reality external to the self—is unknowable or absurd. Nonetheless existentialism finds such "absurdity" lurking about in a diverse array of cultural settings in the West. Cultural expressions of subjectivism are manifold.

Edmund Husserl (1859-1938), whose concern is the establishing of a new philosophy of being, advocates a subjectivist methodology reminiscent of Descartes. The entire phenomenological world is to be "bracketed" so that only the ego remains. Husserl felt that through this process a "transcendental ego" would emerge through which "pure consciousness" or "absolute being" would be apprehensible.[22]

Karl Jaspers approaches this concept in his elevation of authentic *Existenz* of the nonobjective self behind the phenomenal self of culture.[23] Man's culturally ensconced ego is abandoned within a life of finite decisions which, since never justified nor substantiated by any transcendent datum, creates uncertainty and automatic guilt. Yet in Jasper's *Philosophical Faith and Revelation,* a late work in which he seeks a philosophical-theological dialogue, he asserts that man's freedom is a gift of Transcendence; but this knowledge only expands the dimensions of guilt:

> In the world I say, 'I am free; therefore I am guilty.' In view of Transcendence I say, 'I am unfree, and yet I am guilty.' I am 'unfree' because my freedom itself, in which I come to be guilty, depends upon Transcendence.[24]

Thus man is impaled on both horns of the dilemma; in the context of my finitude in the world, or in the context of my creaturehood as God's gift, I am guilty. Jaspers here echoes Kierkegaard.

Elsewhere, Jasper's view of "human being" seems to depart from the moroseness of Kierkegaard, while maintaining a Kierkegaardian base. In his *Nature and Ethics,* Jaspers identifies a three-fold understanding of the nature of man.[25] First, human nature as *empirical existence* is the subject of scientific enquiry, and yields data for anthropology, psychology and sociology. Here, Jaspers asserts, we deal with ourselves as tools. Such knowledge is useful, but if taken too seriously is illusory. Secondly, human nature is conceived in terms of the *essence of man*—the innate, the eternal, the *imago dei*—known by illumination. In this context Jaspers appraises Kant's dictum of the *categorical imperative*—assaying one's acts as if they were to become universal norms. The danger here is casuistry, or the ineptitude of the universal to define adequately every particular. Moreover, man's life is a process, and cannot be treated in terms of a teleological absolute. Finally, human nature—as yet *undetermined*—may be understood in terms of *possibility* or "becoming." In this view man's nature is at base undefinable and open. Kierkegaard's "leap" becomes for Jaspers (more sensibly) "decision."

Jaspers is willing to concede that nature (empirical man) and essentialist models of human nature are in a limited sense instructive. Authentic existence is to be found in the third model—the "open" model which leaves one free to choose one's own self-definition. But in his rejection of the adequacy of the categorical imperative, and in his general skepticism regarding the form of institutional community in the Christian church,[26] Jaspers is on sound Kierkegaardian ground. Furthermore, in his later exploration of "philosophical faith" Jaspers seems to follow Kierkegaard in the direction of dialogue with biblical religion.[27] However, beyond his encounter with a more traditional Judeo-Christian model of man, Jaspers' philosophical stance requires openness. Both Jaspers' academicism and his clarity set him apart from Kierkegaard, whose emotionally-charged piercing aphorisms sometimes meander in tedious obscurity.

Martin Heidegger (b. 1889), Jaspers' younger contemporary, has alternately awed, baffled and outraged the philosophical world. Many consider him the most influential, creative (albeit opaque), and seminal thinker who has emerged under the rubric of "existentialism." Although Heinemann refers to Heidegger as the "Jekyll and Hyde of contemporary philosophy,"[28] Heidegger has persisted in a single quest throughout his career: a search for an indubitable base for ontology.[29]

Heidegger's first concern is the perennial philosophical question, "What is being?" In his first introduction to *Being and Time* he begins with "The Necessity for Explicitly Restating the Question of Being."[30] But as the section's title suggests, Heidegger's intended approach is radically different from that of traditional Western metaphysics. Being cannot be conceived abstractly. Contrary to his teacher Husserl, Heidegger regards man's *awareness* of the actual world as presupposing his involvement in that world. Even if the question of Being is only dimly conceived, one's "vague average understanding of Being is still a fact"[31]—a fact which is part of his worldly experience.

In addition, Heidegger is not content with the classical *cogito ergo sum*. Behind Descartes' assertion, Heidegger in his existential analytic inquires what "are the modes of awareness that *make possible* such confrontations of the self."[32] In the quest for a basic ontology Heidegger wishes "to analyze the self that is the source" of all categorizing,[33] for "only through the self-reflective consciousness of human existence" can Being be approached.[34] For Heidegger, the study of Being and the study of man are inseparable. But Heidegger is not creating a general anthropology of human nature, since all philosophy is a subject-oriented activity. All Being must be understood in terms of my particular being—an investigation which Heidegger later acknowledges is a necessary—but apparently not final—task on the road to discovering Being.[35]

Perhaps the designation "existentialist" for Heidegger—a label he himself rejects[36]—may be partially justifiable by reference to his distinctions between *Sein* and *Das Seiende*, translated somewhat misleadingly by Macquarrie and Robinson as "Being" and "existent," respectively. As Gelven points out, *Sein*, literally "to be," should most often be read that way; Heidegger's ontological inquiry is primarily concerned with the concrete and subjective meaning of "to be."[37] On the other hand, the quest to understand *Das Seiende* (which should perhaps be translated "being"—as an objective entity) is an *ontic* inquiry.[38] As Gelven notes, for Heidegger "any scientific inquiry about an entity is ontical, makes use of categories, and is factual. Whereas any philosophical inquiry about what it means to be is ontological, makes use of existentials, and is factical."[39] Gelven continues:

> *Being is not an entity.* This may be so obvious that it escapes us; and yet it is of central importance for the development of the analysis to come . . . its meaning is more obvious: 'to be' is not itself a thing or being. There is no such *thing* as a 'to be.' When I ask What it means to be, I am not asking *about* a thing.[40]

Heidegger himself helps us at this point:

> The 'essence' of Dasein lies in its existence. Accordingly those characteristics which can be exhibited in this entity are not 'properties' present-at-hand of some entity which 'looks' so and so and is itself present-at-hand; they are in each case possible ways for it to be, and no more than that.[41]

By *Dasein* Heidegger implies both ordinary human existence and also the peculiar etymological sense of Dasein: "to be here" (as opposed to "there").[42] "The whole point about Dasein is that it itself can wonder about itself as existing."[43] For with Dasein, as Gelven observes:

> We are not studying an object, but a *process.* How do we know that such a process actually occurs? Because we ourselves *are* a process, the process of life and existence.[44]

Dasein's tendency, however, is to reify itself as a "thing." Heidegger affirms:

> The kind of Being which belongs to Dasein is rather such that, in understanding its own Being, it has a tendency to do so in terms of that entity towards which it comports itself proximally and in a way which is essentially constant—in terms of the 'world.'[45]

Heidegger's comments about Dasein should not be taken as general comments about human nature, but rather as reflections on a processual field—not a thing, or even a self-contained subject. Dasein thus entails *possibility:*

> Furthermore, in each case Dasein is mine to be in one way or another. Dasein has always made some sort of decision as to the way in which it is in

each case mine. That entity which in its Being has this very Being as an issue, comports itself towards its Being as its ownmost *possibility*. In each case *Dasein is its possibility*, and it 'has' this possibility, but not just as a property, as something present-at-hand would.[46]

When we recall Gelven's translation of *Sein* as "to be," we are again aware of the importance of reading *Dasein* in terms of becoming, process, or possibility—and not as a static accomplished factual entity.

How does Heidegger's analysis relate to man's self-definition in the world? We must remember that Dasein does not mean man in general.[47] Each Dasein, according to Heidegger, "at the outset" faces its "undifferentiated character"—its everyday, average existence.[48] Dasein must take a stand towards this ordinary, culturally-ensconced, mode-of-life. Here Heidegger introduces the terms "authentic" (*eigentlich*, from *eigen*, "own") and "inauthentic" (*uneigentlich*). Gelven explains:

> if one is aware of the etymology, the argument has a great deal of power. What Heidegger means by "authentic" is the awareness of one's *own* self; by "inauthentic," the awareness of the self merely as others see it, or perhaps to see one's self as having a meaning or essence that is prior to and hence "other" than one's existence.[49]

Inauthenticity is to lose sight through culture of the self, to think of the self in substantial terms. Authenticity, which is not an ideal but a process, is a mode of awareness with ramifications both for the self and others.

> Heidegger argues that the primordially given "I" or self is always and already part of a world; and indeed, a world in which other persons are likewise given . . . even in an innocent walk along a field I expose my primordial sharing of the world with others. For by not trampling the crops I recognize their service to another Dasein, the farmer. Such consideration of the farmer's right and use of his land itself is not what Heidegger means by the existential Being-with (or "to-be-with: *mit sein*). Being-with is that *a priori* dimension of the self which makes consideration of the farmer's right possible.[50]

Thus authenticity for Heidegger entails not only an awareness of one's own process-oriented Dasein, but also an awareness of equally valid Daseins of other persons. Here Heidegger's subjective stance assumes a particular social role of intrasubjectivity.

However, if Heidegger's analysis of individual Dasein has distinctive social implications, it seems somewhat lacking in certain other contextual considerations. For example, as his hotly-debated collaboration with National Socialism may suggest, Heidegger seems to have little political awareness. His Being-with category does not seem comparable to Marx's concept of man as species-being. Moreover, at least in *Being and Time*, Heidegger seems to assume a *homo faber* stance which suggests little awareness of nature as an ecosystem:

> In equipment that is used, 'Nature' is discovered along with it by that use— the 'Nature' we find in natural products. Here, however, 'Nature' is not to

be understood as that which is just present-at-hand, nor as the *power of Nature*. The wood is a forest of timber, the mountain a quarry of rock; the river is water-power, the wind is wind 'in the sails.' As the 'environment' is discovered, the 'Nature' thus discovered is encountered too.[51]

As we examine Heidegger's claim to have penetrated to the roots of the question of 'what it means to be,' a paradoxical picture emerges. Certain of Heidegger's themes—though couched in original phraseology—seem to support Whitehead's sentiment that the history of Western philosophy is a footnote to Plato. Assumptions including the dichotomy between cultural and authentic modes of life, the social nature of human life, and man as *homo faber* are obviously not Heidegger's inventions. These very themes—the inauthenticity of cultural self-definitions, an apolitical conception of man's social nature, and the *homo faber* attitude towards nature—could be seen at least in part as secularized expressions of biblical motifs. On the other hand, Heidegger's thoroughgoing and ingenious development of the conception of Dasein as a processual field—and not as a predetermined essence—seems somewhat analogous to contemporary physics' interpretation of space-time.

Disavowed by Heidegger and Jaspers, Jean Paul Sartre (b. 1905) has carried existentialism out of the cloister and into the marketplace. Sartre particularly commands our respect because of his personal involvement in the struggle for justice, exemplified in his active role in the Resistance in World War II. When Sartre contrasts *etre en soi* ("being in itself," objectified being, "thingness") to *etre pour soi* ("being for itself," human subjective self-consciousness), we feel that there are concrete referents for his philosophizing. By contrast, as Heinemann says, Heidegger approaches the essentialist "monomorphic fallacy"—the confusion of words and essences.[52] Especially in his fiction, Sartre's existentialism evokes fleshly reality, and not (as is often paradoxically the case) a disembodied ideal.

Sartre's fiction is illustrative of his attempt to underscore the concreteness of human being. For example, in *The Reprieve* Sartre attempts to translate (and perhaps transform) Heidegger's abstract reflections about nothingness into the inner musings of the young professor, Mathieu Delarue. Delarue reflects upon the desolate freedom of his life, and the absence of some revelation for which he has so long hoped. As he stares down from the Pont-Neuf at the black waters of the Seine, he feels "I am nothing; I possess nothing . . . freedom is exile, and I am condemned to be free."[53] Mathieu *decides* against suicide, and so affirms his freedom in the face of Nothing (although a decision *for* suicide would have confirmed equally his freedom). The value of Sartre's story is that it captures more vividly the emotive dimensions of existentialism—the sense of anomie where "Nothing" is not so much a metaphysical category as a historical-cultural reality. Perhaps Sartre serves as midwife for what is merely a fetus in Heidegger—the effect of cosmological anomie on human self-definition and awareness. Sartre is able to capture more poignantly the sense of tragedy in the human condition—a sense obscured by the tedium of obtuse academic treatises.

Furthermore, Sartre's concept "being-for-others" plainly establishes that relationships are integral to human being. Sartre's own literary and political careers illustrate his concern *to live*, as well as *to talk*, philosophy. With Sartre, existentialism becomes a genuine world-stance—if not world view—in that it is *ethos* as well as *cosmos*, and *praxis* as well as *theoria*. This becomes all the more the case in Sartre's alliance with a liberal Marxism, where it seems that the "being for others" is now given socio-economic moorings.

As a final and diverse interpretation of man from a general "existential" framework we turn to Nicolas Berdyaev (1874-1948). Berdyaev, like Jaspers, is concerned with the philosophical/theological dialogue. Yet Berdyaev's model of human being exudes an overt religious air. Berdyaev sees himself more as an heir to Pascal and Kierkegaard,[54] and contrasts his position to the secular orientations of Heidegger and Sartre. Berdyaev accuses Heidegger of secularizing Christian consciousness: "Being (for Heidegger) is fallen and guilty in its very structure. This is catholic theology without God."[55] In particular, according to Berdyaev, Heidegger reflects the *Ungrund* of Boehme without apprehending its spiritual core. Furthermore, Berdyaev sees Sartre's *neant* as "a corruption of being" and says "his philosophy is one which belongs to the end of an age rather than to the beginning."[56] Both Heidegger and Sartre, Berdyaev believes, are spokesmen of the decadence of old models, and their talk of freedom is merely empty prattle.[57] Apart from his spiritual core, man is left in an untenable accidental position.

Berdyaev's own alternative is a philosophico-theology based upon the Christian doctrine of the Holy Spirit (which Berdyaev—like the second century Marcion—takes in an open-ended antinomian sense). Berdyaev feels that the Church has downplayed the role of the Spirit because of the threat of "the weakening of hierarchical authority,"[58] which could be legitimated more readily by analogy to the authoritarian Father-Son imagery. In his emphasis upon the Spirit Berdyaev taps the key source of motility in the biblical tradition, rightly identifying the strongly sessile frame of the ortho-dox dogmas of God the Father and Jesus Christ.

Thus revelation is a subjective experience of the Spirit—dynamic and continuously unfolding. Its objectification in static dogmas falsifies its living nature. It is in his subjectivism that Berdyaev most closely approximates the existentialist view of man. But Berdyaev's perspective, though sharing in the indeterminateness and subjectivism of existentialism ("The objectified world is not the true and real world . . . Only the subject is ultimately real, 'existential,' and only the subject is capable of knowing reality"),[59] departs from a strict existentialism in its prophetic, visionary and universalist tones. Like Joachim of Fiore, Berdyaev sees the Trinity as representing unique facets of history in its unfolding. But for Berdyaev, the era of the Spirit is not strictly chronological, though he does envision it as an era of universal human transformation, "an era of the sense of community, an era of social and cosmic transfiguration."[60] Perhaps like the "already/not-yet" dialectic of Jesus' depiction of the Kingdom of God, Berdyaev's era of the Spirit is already present in "transcendental man" (in whom the freedom of the new era has taken root). Berdyaev's concept recalls Jesus' parting promises of the coming presence of the Spirit who shall lead men "into all truth." Berdyaev's anthropology presupposes the nascent divinity in every man:

> The image of God is in every man. Every man possesses the dignity of a person, even if this person is inhibited or not manifest in him.[61]

"Transcendental man" is the divine presence within every man "outside the division into subject and object."[62]

Though not equivalent to human "nature" (since the word *nature* connotes something static and established), "transcendental man" includes the spiritual ground which is manifest in all creativity, love, and greatness within history. "Transcendental man" is therefore this-worldly and immanent, following an incarnational model. History, in which "transcendental man" is manifest, is "always a disillusionment for human personality and it always wounds it very deeply. To a notable degree history is the history of crime . . ."[63] As Hegel said, history is the history of tragedy, and for Berdyaev the history of the *ir*rational. Solely as historical being, human being is not really free. Only as one realizes his "transcendent" dimension does freedom emerge. One becomes through conscious decision a *maker* of history, and not merely a careless victim. For just as history "is alien to me as objectivization," it is also "near akin to me, it is indeed my own."[64] Both in its objectivization and in its trans-subjective createdness, history cuts across isolate subjectivism. Here Berdyaev assaults the orthodox dogma of predestination which denies the real validity of historical *process* and human *choice*.[65]

By recognizing the universality of the Spirit in all men, Berdyaev's interpretation extends Christian insights into human being—as an historical being reflecting the divine image—beyond the limitations of orthodoxy.

Although Berdyaev's analysis exposes the historical breakdown of orthodox structures, it is not always clear how he would have us recognize, apart from mystical insight or arbitrary choice, the Spirit's presence. Herein lies the paradox of an existential-mystical vision. In affirming the Kierkegaardian maxim of the subjectivity and concreteness of truth, Berdyaev's only link to universality is the idea of the Spirit, which exposes him to the critique of retreating into an inner chamber of an abstract and sequestered mysticism. We are left with the unresolved polarities of the particular and the universal, and of the concrete and the abstract.

In considering the significance of an existential model of man, it must be remembered that those philosophers most often labeled "existentialist" cannot be artificially manipulated so that they appear to affirm a uniform understanding of human life. However, certain broad trends of perspective emerge.

First of all, the emphasis upon individual responsibility for one's own destiny is critical. The existential analysis of humanity's cultural and ontological situation—portraying man adrift upon an incomprehensible sea where no land is in view—is not intended as hopeless capitulation. On the contrary, the responsibility of life rests squarely upon each individual.

Yet existential analyses may fail to command cosmological respect on several counts. For example, the ontological status of Nothingness, whatever its evocative value may be, is in fact an abstraction with no empirical reference point. As a metaphor for cultural anomie and its emotive implications, "Nothingness" merits a certain respect. But the concrete terrors of human being, such as warfare, famine, disease, loneliness, ageing, death, etc., seem far too specific to be so abstracted. *Angst* appears not in a vacuum, but eidetically within man's location in nature and culture. *Death,* which remains unknown for man, is not thereby automatically *Nothingness.* To envision death as Nothingness betrays a bias in the analysis of life processes. If man is indeed a physio-chemical, psycho-somatic whole, death cannot entail *literal* Nothingness, since even the elements of the body continue to exist in some form. Present empirical evidence seems to point to a single energy source for *all of life* in its physical, emotional, psychic, or spiritual forms. Death means *transformation, not* annihilation. We may not *care* for the something which may follow (which may thereby seem to merit the emotive label "Nothing");[66] but there is nevertheless *something* and not Nothing, however unknown or inadequate that something may appear to be.

Secondly, existential analyses—which indeed stress the historicity of human existence—lack in general a concrete sense of the socio-cultural location of human being. Sartre's "conversion" to Marxism represents the most thorough intellectual translation of existential concerns into the concrete *praxis* of socio-political life. The commendable call to "decision"— underscored in some form in most existential models—should be kept in dialectical balance with the *contextuality* of human being. Whatever choice one may make, contemplation and implementation belie any "pure"existential situation by thrusting the individual into an arena of historical and cultural precedent. It is naive to assume that the decisions under consideration are essences within some timeless panorama of our minds; they are already products as well as processes, historical moments as well as private ones. Whether I choose the "leap of faith" in Christ, the life of philosophizing, or political activism, etc., there are many who have gone before, many who are present, and many who will follow. Every individual within the cosmic scheme is *novel* and *unique.* Every individual is *also* "within the cosmic scheme."

Finally, a pivotal criticism of the "existential condition" is its implicit egotism. Alan Watts portrays the peculiar anomaly of the Western sense of the ego, which is unknown both to nature and to other cultural world views:

The sense of "I," which should have been identified with the whole universe of your experience, was instead cut off and isolated as a detached observer of that universe . . .[67]

Watts asserts that "the sense of ego is at root a discomfort and a bore . . ."[68] The constant need of Westerners to escape the "self" indicates that there may be something *un*natural about the "self"-concept from the start. We again witness the residue of Christian consciousness—the isolation of the individual as a guilty, finite being, trapped within time, in need of "salvation." Perhaps the loss of "salvation" is what makes individual responsibility—which *can* be conceived quite positively and organically—such an onerous task in certain popular depictions of the existential condition.

EVOLUTIONARY MAN

Sir Julian Huxley (b. 1887), the renowned English biologist, advances a markedly different view of man. Although evolutionary thought is the major vehicle of Huxley's concept, he by no means succumbs to naturalistic reductionism. Evolution itself, according to Huxley, consists of three subprocesses: cosmic, biological, and psychosocial.[69] On the cosmic level, evolution proceeds at a very slow pace. Biologically, as we know life on earth (and tend to extrapolate for life elsewhere in the universe), evolution operates through self-reproduction and self-mutation of organic matter.[70] Psychosocial evolution refers to the cultural productions and transformations of the human mind.

As Huxley surveys the history of biological evolution, he sees the development of structural organization "from the precellular to the cellular and the multi-cellular"[71] until we reach higher vertebrates, along a scale of increasing complexity of physiological integration and homeostasis. Through the ages various organisms have dominated. The emergence of the psychosocial level has brought dominance to man. "Progress" for Huxley is not an idealistic catchword. In fact, evolution entails dead ends and blind alleys as well as vital movements forward. "Progress" is rather a point of reference and value for humanity, deriving its *ethos* from our psychosocial nature and its *telos* from an ecological homeostasis of the *wholeness* of human concerns and culture. Man himself becomes a *partner* in the cosmic evolution localized on this planet. "Progress" involves collective action, "the only motive on which all men or nations could agree, and the only basis for transcending conflicting ideologies."[72] Furthermore, progress centers in man's psychosocial nature, necessitating both "psychosocial technology, including the production of ideological machine-tools like concepts and beliefs for the better processing of experience," and "psychosocial ecology," which aims "at a right balance between different values, between continuity and change, and between the evolutionary process . . . and the resources with which we have to operate."[73]

Huxley identifies both material-quantitative resources (food, energy, mines, industry, etc.), and psychological-qualitative resources (solitude, landscape beauty, "marine and mountain adventure," wildlife, etc.).

The individual also plays an important role in Huxley's scheme:

> But in Evolutionary Humanism, unlike some other ideologies, the human individual has high significance. Quite apart from the practical function which he performs in society and its collective enterprises, he can help in fulfilling human destiny by the fuller realization of his own personal possibilities. A strong and rich personality is the individual's unique and wonderful contribution to the psychosocial process.[74]

Thus the individual can serve as a kind of microcosm of the evolution of humanity by developing to the fullest his or her own uniqueness. Huxley believes that the main tool of development for both the individual and the race is the mind. Therefore, the function of a formal world view, which is approximately what Huxley has in mind when he speaks of a belief system or a "noetic integrator," is vital. Such a belief system must use the most accurate knowledge available to man, yet not neglect the sacred or the holy, or aesthetic values.[75] Beliefs not only shape our reality, but determine the way in which we construct our practical destiny through addressing problems like population, the use of resources, and the antagonisms among differing political blocks.[76]

A prime example of the need for new belief systems, according to Huxley, is the legacy of traditional Christian orthodoxy for man's self concept. For example, supernaturalism leads to the humiliation of man and the propitiation of God; the idea of heaven denigrates life on this earth; the doctrines of the fall, original sin, and damnation are debilitating to human freedom; and the exclusivism of the doctrines of salvation and inspiration leads to intolerance for other beliefs and science.[77] Huxley continues:

> Above all, belief in an omnipotent, omniscient and omnibenevolent God leads to a frustrating dilemma at the very heart of our approach to reality. For many thinking people, it is incompatible with our knowledge of nature and history and with the facts of evil, suffering, and human misery.[78]

Huxley offers instead a perspective similar to Feuerbach's equation of anthropology and theology, where religion can be "an applied spiritual ecology"[79] and

> Religious concepts like God, incarnation, the soul, salvation, original sin, grace, atonement, all have a basis in man's experiences of phenomenal reality. It is necessary now to analyze that basis of reality into its component parts, and then to reassemble these elements, together with any new factors that have come to light, into concepts which correspond more closely to reality and are more relevant to present circumstances.[80]

Huxley believes that it will be possible for man "to reformulate such ideas as Divine Law, obedience to God's will," and the like, "in an evolutionary terminology consonant with existing scientific knowledge."[81] Furthermore, "the reappraisal of religious experience must be a part of something much larger—a thorough investigation of man's inner world, a great project of 'Mind Exploration' which could and should rival and surpass 'Space Exploration' in interest and importance."[82]

A second significant advocate of an evolutionary theory of man is Julian Huxley's friend and colleague, the paleontologist and Jesuit philosopher, Pierre Teilhard de Chardin (1881-1955). Teilhard has written widely of man, both in a purely scientific vein and in terms of his Christian commitments. Teilhard reminds us of a critical contextual consideration, vital to any verdicts concerning human nature and destiny:

> After all, half a million years, perhaps even a million, were required for life to pass from the pre-hominids to modern man. Should we now start wringing our hands because, less than two centuries after glimpsing a higher state, modern man is still at loggerheads with himself? Once again we have got things out of focus.[83]

Human life must be placed in the context of the evolutionary process of the whole organic order. Within this holistic context, somewhat liberated from cultural presuppositions, we can gain certain basic hints regarding man's location and purpose.

As Teilhard examines the movement of the evolutionary process, there are two principles which seem to emerge: increasing complexity and increasing consciousness. As we move from sub-atomic to vertebrate structure, matter assembles itself in increasingly-complex arrangements which exhibit a progressively-mounting drive towards "consciousness." Consciousness is the result of what Teilhard calls "centeredness"—where the concentration of these complex arrangements forms self-contained homeostatic systems.

Consciousness on a human level is the highest example of this process of centeredness or "involution," and provides us with the most important clue to the direction of evolution. The emergence of human reflection—of Descartes' "I think, therefore I am" (*cogito ergo sum*)—is the process of noogenesis culminating in a new cosmic layer, the *noosphere*, or sphere of human consciousness. Like Huxley, Teilhard envisages man as occupying a unique worldly position. Though in his present state man is just a step along the way towards a more highly evolved future, he is nevertheless the frontier of evolution on this planet.

The future of the noosphere is considered by Teilhard on two levels. On a merely scientific level the two principles, increasingly complex centeredness and increasing consciousness, are leading inevitably towards a higher level of human consciousness, a new point of convergence which he calls the "Omega Point." On a second level, as a Christian philosopher Teilhard envisions the entire process of evolution as energized by God's Spirit. The Omega Point of future consciousness is the eschatological goal of creation, the Christocentric expression of the biblical promises that God shall become all-in-all.

As Teilhard surveys human culture in this century, he cites what he believes to be faint, though presently aberrant, signs of this new consciousness. The first of these, which Teilhard does not regard as inherently evil, includes the processes of socialization and collectivism. Informed by a mechanical cosmology, in their present form collectivist movements pervert the larger meaning of community.

> At no previous period of history has mankind been so well equipped nor made such efforts to reduce its multitudes to order. We have 'mass movements'—no longer the hordes streaming down from the forests of the north nor the steppes of Asia, but 'the Million' scientifically assembled. The Million in rank and file on the parade ground; the Million standardised in the factory; the Million motorised—and all this only ending up with Communism and National-Socialism and the most ghastly fetters. So we get the crystal instead of the cell; the ant-hill instead of brotherhood. Instead of the upsurge of consciousness which we expected, it is mechanisation that seems to emerge inevitably from totalisation.[84]

The all-important factor which they ignore, according to Teilhard, is personalization. Order apart from personalization, and mechanization apart from consciousness, betray a fatal misunderstanding of the life process.

Contrary to Alan Watts, Teilhard does *not* commend the devaluation of the ego.[85] The ego itself is a sign of future convergence or consciousness. Teilhard certainly does not recommend mass egotism, but he does assert that a healthy ego, integrated and exhibiting homeostatic centeredness, gives some indication of an even higher level of consciousness for the future. Thus the movement of the noosphere in authentic personalistic collectivism does not portend the negation of the ego, but rather its transcendence into something more, *not* something less. Teilhard asserts that

> All our difficulties and repulsions as regards the opposition between the All and the Person would be dissipated if only we understood that, by structure the noosphere (and more generally the world) represent a whole that is not only closed but also centered.[86]

In fact, space-time itself is of a convergent nature. If consciousness is the centeredness of space-time, then at some future (Omega) point a new involution will occur, and a higher or superior form of consciousness will emerge:

> Seen from this point of view, the universe, without losing any of its immensity and thus without suffering any anthropomorphism, begins to take shape: since to think it, undergo it and make it act, it is *beyond* our souls that we must look, *not the other way round*. In the perspective of a noogenesis, time and space become truly humanised—or rather super-humanised. Far from being mutually exclusive, the Universal and Personal (that is to say, the 'centered') grow in the same direction and culminate simultaneously in each other . . . It is therefore a mistake to look for the extension of our being or of the noosphere in the Impersonal. The Future-Universal could not be anything else but the Hyper-Personal—at the Omega Point.[87]

Both Teilhard and Huxley remind us that to understand the human phenomenon adequately, we must consider a larger context than our historical-cultural heritage (limited, among other things, by the relative novelty of scientific history, anthropology, psychology, and sociology). Some would argue that Teilhard and Huxley do not take seriously enough human failures; but we must recognize that Teilhard and Huxley are uniquely endowed to see both man's failures and successes in the broader spectrum of the evolutionary process. Whether or not science will continue to provide empirical verifications for all of Huxley's and Teilhard's speculations, remains to be seen. But *any viable* analysis of the human condition *must come to terms with* the evolutionary data available to us. Sweeping prognostications concerning the human phenomenon, such as those in which existentialism has often indulged, are empty and futile apart from consideration of man's cosmic location. They must be weighed in the light of analyses such as Teilhard's and Huxley's, although we are not thereby bound to their conclusions. Interested readers might wish to pursue similar biologically-informed perspectives, such as those of Theodosius Dobzhansky and Rene Dubos.

PSYCHOLOGICAL MAN

Sigmund Freud—as much as any single individual in the last two centuries—has incisively challenged traditional models of man. Trained in Victorian science and preoccupied with the Victorian psyche, Freud also is an expression of his culture, plumbing depths of hidden reservoirs of consciousness and culture, drawing forth visions both mundane and terrifying.

Assuming all behavior is goal-directed and purposeful, Freud attempted to decipher antecedent influences for such varied and long-neglected data as dreams, hysteria, obsessional behavior, various types of neurosis, etc. At the same time, he sought to chart the human psyche and to create a meaningful and working model for its analysis. In particular, Freud was fascinated by sexual etiology, which seemed to provide insights into little-understood facets of childhood behavior, dream imagery, compulsive or obsessive behavior, and the like. As we examine Freud's analysis, we shall attempt to identify the presuppositions which inform it.

For many years Freud sought to refine his depiction of the conscious/unconscious split. Finally, he offered his famous tripartite "map of the psyche" as a more concrete representation of psychic functions. However elementary or overly neat Freud's model might appear at first glance, he apparently never intended it to become a sacred cow, but rather a tentative probe in the quest for accurate description. Yet in Freud's own writings he appears to lapse into substantialist ways of thinking about man's psyche.[88]

First in *The Ego and the Id,* and later in "The Dissection of the Psychical Personality," substantialist phraseology recurs.[89] In *The Ego and the Id* Freud defines the ego as an *entity*.[90] In his later lecture he suggests that the ego "is in its very *essence* a subject," which can nevertheless "take itself as an object, can treat itself like other objects."[91] Freud's language may be misleading if he is speaking merely of personality *function*, which is not an essence. Yet the ego, which Freud constantly depicts as observing, analyzing, and criticizing itself, seems to be some *thing* which we possess or which possesses us. To speak of the ego as the executive *function* of the personality, balancing the demands of both internal self and world, represents the ego more as a function of the whole person than as an isolate "thing." Freud's model was seemingly not intended to be granted reified status, but his language often appears to betray an ontological disposition. For example, Freud speaks of the *split* occurring within the ego of mental patients as analogous to a *fracture* in the *structure of a crystal*. Such an image, albeit the language of analogy, seems to suggest that the ego has a rigid, substantial structure.[92] We have used the term "structure of consciousness" to represent the general space-time orientation of thought and identity within personality and culture. Freud at times speaks of the structures of the psyche almost as if they were visibly stamped upon the hemispheres of the brain.[93]

Furthermore, Freud describes the super-ego as an *agency* "which observes and threatens to punish;" for it has become "sharply divided" from the ego and "displaced into external reality."[94] Here the super-ego appears to occupy a quasi-divine status, or at least is relegated to a position of virtual autonomy. As such, the super-ego exhibits the following functions: conscience or the voice of conscience; internalized expectations and judgments of parents, educators, or society; the ego-ideal; the super-ego is also the referent of self-observation and analysis. By *ego-ideal*, Freud means "that by which the ego measures itself, which it emulates, and whose demand for greater perfection it strives to fulfill."[95] An overly-severe super-ego leads to "melancholia" or depression.[96] On the other hand, a weak super-ego seems to result in a drive to uninhibited satisfaction of the appetites,[97] especially characteristic of "liberated" manic behavior. We would describe these two extremes of behavior in terms of radical sessile or motile consciousness, respectively.

Freud's language may tell us as much about long-standing cultural assumptions as about Freud himself. His language often sounds like a transferral of the hierarchical cosmos into the domain of the psyche. Freud's analysis should not be declared artificial if, in fact, it clearly portrays the structural disposition of the traditional Western psyche. What the tripartite structure may suggest is not the "natural" condition of the psyche so much as the psyche of traditional culture. Here we approach a very important issue— namely, is there *a* natural structure for the psyche? Is not the psyche so integrally wedded to culture that "its" natural condition is indeed a mirror of the psycho-social structures of world view?

For example, Freud asserts that

> Thus a child's super-ego is in fact constructed on the model not of its parents but of its parents' super-ego; the contents which fill it are the same and it becomes *the vehicle of tradition* and of all the *time-resisting judgments of value* which have propagated themselves in this manner from generation to generation.[98]

Here is an important clue—for perhaps Freud should be understood as much as a social analyst as an analyst of the psyche. Peter L. Berger and Thomas Luckmann remind us of the dictum of Weber: We must "consider social facts as things."[99] Freud seems to follow the dictum that we must consider psychic facts as things, and implicitly as *social* things.

The super-ego as the *vehicle of tradition* is compatible with Berger and Luckmann's perpetual dialectic of the social process. The *externalization* of the social order appears in the institutional, ideological, and cultural world into which an individual is born; this world is apprehended by each of us as *objective* to the self *(objectivation)*. In the process of *internalization* social structures are incorporated into one's own psyche and identity. Freud seems to represent the psycho-social process in very similar terms:

> The past, the tradition of the race and of the people lives on in the ideologies of the super-ego, and yields only slowly to the influences of the present and to new changes; and so long as it operates through the super-ego it plays a powerful part in human life, independently of economic conditions.[100]

As we approach the third "zone" of Freud's model of the psyche, the cultural character of his picture seems even clearer. The *id* is the largely unconscious domain, or "the dark, inaccessible part of our personality" wherein lies the repository of psychic (libidinal) energy and instincts, drives and passions.[101] Freud says, "To adopt a popular mode of speaking, we might say that the ego stands for reason and good sense while the id stands for the untamed passions."[102] Here in particular Freud's tripartite division should perhaps be understood as much culturally as psychically.

If we return to the early centuries of Christianity, first in gnosticism, and more completely in the later synthesis of biblical imagery with Neoplatonic philosophy, the psychic structure of the individual (including the body) mirrors the hierarchical cosmic structure as microcosm to macrocosm. The spiritual warfare of Spirit and flesh has both psychological and cosmological dimensions. Just as gnosticism reflected the language and structure of the ancient hierarchical scheme, so Freud's model discloses a similar structure (perhaps with the addition of the mechanical imagery of early modern cosmology). Compare:

Gnosticism: Cosmos and God	Individual	Freud
God	*pneuma* ("spirit")	Super-ego
Logos (Cosmic Reason)	*psyche* (imbued with	
Nous (The Intellect)	*logos and nous*)	
Aeons or Emanations		Ego
The Material World	*soma* (and *sarx*)	Id

Freud himself speaks of "our God, *Logos*," as over against the Judeo-Christian God.[103] In terms reminiscent of Paul's description of the individual's struggle with the world, the flesh, and the devil, Freud speaks of the ego's "three tyrannical masters," the external world (the source of "realistic anxiety"), the super-ego (the source of "moral anxiety"), and the id (the source of "neurotic anxiety"). The ego is "hemmed in on three sides, threatened by three kinds of danger . . ."[104] The resemblance of Freud's triad to the world, the flesh, and the devil is transparent. The "world" and the "flesh"—if demythologized and defined in secular terms—seem quite similar to the *external world* and the *id*. However, the "devil," who has both psychic and cosmic dimensions, must share his functions between the *id* and the *super-ego* (a concept more comparable to the God of theism).[105]

To underscore the cultural location of Freud's model of the psyche, we recall the recent discoveries of the functions of the right and left hemispheres of the human brain. According to the ostensible functions of the two lobes, Freud's hierarchy of super-ego—ego—id must be turned somewhat on end. The ego corresponds much more closely to left-hemispheric functions; the id to right-hemispheric concerns. The dominance of left-hemispheric or ego functions must in part be understood in terms of cultural and historical factors. The rise of the ego as well as left-hemispheric dominance seem to reflect changes of consciousness in the West—from the gradual decline of mythopoeism to the gradual triumph of the Greco-Christian Synthesis (reaching its secular apogee in the modern mechanical cosmos). We would not reduce Freud's brilliant model to a mere referent of culture. We do suggest that this model charts the dominance of sessile structures of consciousness of modern man, as well as the restless (and generally repressed) motility of the id. The fact that for Freud, the "ego and conscious, repressed and unconscious do *not* coincide,"[106] should warn us that we must refrain from any facile equations.

The right lobe may be figuratively atrophied, but it is not dysfunctional. If, as Freud says, "the ego's relation to the id might be compared with that of a rider to his horse,"[107] modern culture threatens to throw the rider and turn the horse loose in the suburbs. We are faced not only with redefining the ego (so that it may reflect a homeostatic balance between right and left hemispheres), but also with casting down the god *logos* from its Neoplatonic throne to occupy a more humble and realistic postition. Freud identified both dreams and religion as modes of "wish fulfillment," and particularly challenged the value of the latter. Moreover, he affirmed that culture is necessarily built upon the repression of the instincts and the id, being in fact the product of the systematic sublimation of these functions. Freud has rendered us a great service as long as we grasp the historical-cultural, and not necessarily universal, dimensions of his judgments. In so doing, and informed by a greater understanding of the organic functions of the "two brains" (including dreams, fantasy, creativity, etc.), we may begin the slow and tentative task of redefining the shape of the psycho-social psyche for the future.

Carl Gustav Jung, a former disciple of Freud, broke from his mentor in 1914 to propound his own images of the human psyche. If Freud's model of the human psyche may be understood as a psycho-social analysis of Western man vis-a-vis Western culture, Jung's model at first glance seems an attempt to probe beneath cultural facades of personality to its more universal dimensions. However, we may question whether Jung's readjustments are not in themselves often equally culturally-determined. In fact, we may raise the recurrent question of whether or not all such models are variants of inevitable cultural themes. Though both Freud and Jung are modern mythmakers, one way of emphasizing their distinctive differences might be this: if Freud demythologizes the mysterious frontiers of the traditional psyche through the exposure of *eros* and *thanatos* by *logos,* then Jung remythologizes the psyche, peopling it with new gods and demons.

Apart from his useful, though pedestrian, observations concerning extraverted and intraverted personality types, Jung's most significant contribution is his alternative model of the psyche, developed both in dependency upon, and in rejection of, Freud's. We will examine its basic contours.

First of all, Jung distinguishes between the *ego* and the *self.* The *ego* is *conscious,* "the complex factor to which all conscious concepts are related" or "the subject of all personal acts of consciousness."[108] The *self* is basically unconscious, in fact the center of the unconscious and the potential center of psychic unity. The ego itself "rests on the *total field of consciousness*" and also "on the *sum total of unconscious contents.*"[109] For Jung, "the ego is never more and never less than consciousness as a whole."[110] Thus the ego, though dependent upon the unconscious, is considered to be largely excluded from it. The whole personality is more than the ego; it is ideally centered in the *self* which "cannot be fully known."[111]

Two psychic catastrophes threaten the relation between ego and self. If the ego is assimilated by the self, "the image of wholeness then remains in the unconscious."[112] For Jung there is a necessary dichotomy between the ego and the self, in order that the ego may maintain its sense of "absolute space and absolute time" in the interest of satisfying its role in culture; whereas the self is imbued with a "psychically relative space-time continuum."[113] Here it seems as though the ego belongs to the Newtonian cosmos, but the self to the Einsteinian cosmos. Such an equation may fit in quite well with the cultural emergence of the modern ego (and perhaps its inevitable transformation).

The second danger, according to Jung, is the assimilation of the self by the ego. In this case the individual ignores reality and the conscious world in favor of a world of fantasy. We would describe the first dis-ease as the triumph of rigid sessile consciousness, and the second as the victory of motility. In terms of the symbolic functions of the twin hemispheres of the brain, the triumph of the ego is the triumph of the left lobe; the triumph of the self (at the expense of the ego) is the victory of the right hemisphere. (We might ask whether in mythopoeism the right hemisphere is dominant with no signs of dis-ease; or, as seems more likely, mythopoeism achieves a workable balance between the two lobes, since it is also legitimately "empirico-logical thought"). For Jung the healthily-functioning self, which represents wholeness as symbolized by the mandala or by Christ, cannot be relegated merely to right-hemispheric functions.

Jung's concept of the *collective unconscious* and its archetypes further expands the frontiers of the inner psyche. The *shadow* archetype is in many ways comparable to Freud's *id*. Representing the dark side of the personality, the shadow is essentially emotive in nature, appearing as an autonomous and often possessive force within the psyche.[114] Jung's designation of the shadow as an archetype seems to explain the doubtful assertion that emotion "is not an activity of the individual but something that happens to him"[115] (owing to the relative autonomy of the shadow archetype). Although the shadow image may hinge on some functional validity, again (like some of Freud's language) it seems to betray a tendency towards substantialism. Jung notes that the most autonomous and resistant aspects of the shadow are *projected* into the outer world in terms of another person (or perhaps an ethnic group, etc.). This projecting mechanism seems to underscore the functional character of the shadow, and to indicate that the individual does indeed control its function, albeit on an unconscious level. The shadow may be properly at home in the right hemisphere of the brain.

Further archetypes of the unconscious include the *animus,* the hidden male within woman (and the structure of which is determined by dominant male images in a woman's life), and the *anima,* the hidden female within man (whose structure, conversely, is determined by dominant female images within a man's life). Jung associates the anima with Eros, which renders man like a child, hoping "to be caught, sucked in, enveloped and devoured,"[116] as well as protected and nourished. On the other hand, the animus "corresponds to the paternal Logos just as the anima corresponds to the maternal Eros."[117] Jung asserts that

> In man, Eros, the function of relationship, is usually less developed than Logos. In women, on the other hand, Eros is an expression of their true nature, while their Logos is often only a regrettable accident.[118]

At this point Jung might well be accused of chauvinism, and such a statement exhibits the tendency we have already seen of imposing relative cultural values upon the psyche with a certain substantialist vigor. Cultural archetypes become *a priori* archetypes of the mind, veritable Platonic eternal forms (upon which they are partially modeled).

In fact anima and animus, not to mention logos and eros, bear a striking resemblance to the functioning of the two hemispheres of the brain, which not only regulate differing bodily functions, but seem manifest at least symbolically in the peculiar dominance of certain values within the world view and *ethos* of culture. We do not wish to oversimplify, or to belittle the value of Jung's archetypes *in* cultural and psychological analysis. But we do need to explore the relative cultural or psychic location of such concepts (which are not subject to full empirical verification). It is just through the juxtaposition of such concepts to empirical referents such as the two hemispheres of the brain, that we may be able to draw more productively upon Jung's categories.

In certain ways Jung's analysis seems more adaptable to empirical referents than Freud's.[119] His call for psychic wholeness certainly parallels the seeming biological urge to achieve a balance between the two lobes. Undoubtedly Jung's model of mythic structures will continue to yield fruitful insights into the relationship between culture, cosmology, and psyche. On the other hand, Jung's writings seem to exude a certain opaqueness that we do not find in Freud, who is usually the model of perspicuity. Perhaps we may clear away some of the haze that seems to surround the archetypes by comparing them to both biological and cultural analyses.

MAN: A PRISMATIC VISION

If all of our models of human being are, like our knowledge itself, conditioned by our cultural location, we may assume that no single perspective will do justice to the human image in its historical past or future upon the world stage. To approach the fabled "human condition" via a psychological, philosophical, sociological, or religious route *alone,* produces truncated vision, and unwarranted generalizations and extrapolations from local eccentricities to the species as a whole. Eclecticism alone provides the necessary route to holism beyond the narrow limitations of any single focus. Moreover, eclecticism helps to expose hidden links between models which may, at first glance, appear entirely disparate. In the discussion that follows we will outline what we consider to be a few key componential factors which must be considered in any future model of human being.

Teilhard and Huxley (as well as modern biologists and ecologists) inform us that man is a *biological creature**—part of the *evolutionary* process. As such humanity occupies a significant, though not exclusive, place in the organic world. Although as *homo faber*—yet more significantly as *homo sapiens*—man is on the frontiers or cutting edge of evolution in its local planetary form, he cannot (if only for his own survival) ignore the healthy functioning and balance of the planet as a whole. The earth is not merely an

---

*In this regard we consider also questions of human sexuality. Humanity's sexual nature is not a separate category, since it entails socio-cultural and psychological, as well as specifically biological, considerations.

external environment; it is in a very real sense an extension of man's body. The future of human culture is dependent upon a realistic appraisal of the possibilities and limitations of the ecosystem. Furthermore, all judgments which either ignore, belittle, or contradict evidence of the evolutionary process, must be reexamined.* For example, neither optimistic nor pessimistic prognostications of man's destiny merit consideration apart from their possible feasibility or validity with regard to the evolutionary time scale (including cosmic evolution). Humanity is young, perhaps adolescent, maybe even an infant. This perspective does not guarantee survival; it does suggest that we should be given time to grow up.

Secondly, man is a *mental creature*. Our wording is deliberate. The mental dimensions must not be limited to one hemisphere alone. A human is not solely intellect or ego—indeed not solely *cogito ergo sum* (we might just as well say "I dream therefore I am"). Imagination, fantasy and intuition, the numinous as well as the rational, both the emotional and the volitional, are equally part of man's *mental* nature. As Julian Huxley has suggested, a priority of the greatest importance for human survival is a thoroughgoing, heretofore unparalleled, investigation and exploration of man's "inner space." The models of Freud and Jung (and similar models) are useful. Behaviorism deserves our respect for isolating *a* critical mode of biological and mental functioning in stimulus-response. But the great task of discovering the full functioning capacities of the brain's two hemispheres, and of the *dynamic interplay* between the brain and the socialization process, has really just begun. In addition, certain mental capacities such as telepathy and altered states of consciousness—long relegated by myopic and perhaps frightened men of science to the realm of occult nonsense—are now well-established though little understood *facts*, and may well hold (if not *the* key) at least *a* key to man's future evolution.[120] Such phenomena deserve full billing in the serious investigation of man's "inner space." Likewise, the functioning of *belief* as a *precipitate* of ideas, institutions, emotional states, physical health, and even the shape of artifacts and environment, is a reality which needs both extensive and intensive analysis.

Thirdly, man is a *socio-historical creature*. Because of previous allusions to Marx we excluded him from the foregoing discussion. But Marx must be credited for underscoring the vital importance of man's nature as a *species being*. In particular, his counsels accentuate the role of economic, political, and class structures in human self-identity. *Belief* has its social dimensions as well. The sociology of knowledge, a budding discipline geared to analyzing the functioning of belief in the social process, is particularly instructive. With anthropology and mythology, the sociology of knowledge is useful for historical as well as contemporary understanding of belief in a wide variety of

---

*At the same time it must be cautioned that our understanding of evolution itself must remain open to future data and modifications.

cultural settings. Certainly the conventional specialized disciplines of historical and political analysis, or the sciences, provide continuing frameworks of reference. The socio-historical dimensions of human being require interdisciplinary perspectives. Even psycho-analytic and ecological interpretations of history—when considered as adjuncts to the larger context—are quite viable tools. The field of ethology, pioneered by Konrad Lorenz for the study of animal behavior (especially in its social dimensions), should provide a useful check and comparison to observations concerning human social nature.

Finally, man is a *transcendent creature*.[121] Transcendence is not to be separated from man's biological, psychological, or socio-historical dimensions, and yet it suggests that man's nature as a *whole* is more than the sum of the parts. Even if man's organic, mental, and socio-historic expressions have been thoroughly analyzed, classified and categorized, not all has been said. Transcendence means two things. First, humanity must be considered holistically; the eclectic parts must be integrally incorporated (though not artificially twisted) into a holistic—yet open-ended—model. Secondly, this model (we believe) finds its propelling center, its creative source of energy, in the numinous. There is no one or right way to express transcendence. "Holiness" appears in art and music and relationships as well as ethics, in nature as well as religion. Yet neither art nor music nor relationships nor ethics nor religion are automatically or necessarily expressions of holiness or transcendence. In whatever its expressions, transcendence is a quality of human life that leads to a dynamic balance of wholeness and creativity: wholeness in fully-functioning psychosomatic and social beings; creativity in open-ended, processual and novelty-inducing vitality. The source of transcendence is both within and beyond. It meets one at the depths of one's intimate being, yet flows from vast cosmic reservoirs both unknown (or little known) and fantastic in their dimensions and implications. Transcendence should be celebrated through humane and life-affirming ethics and religions, which are broad enough in scope and deep enough in spirit to allow for a functional plurality of persons and life-styles; transcendence should be expressed through continuous creation and perpetuation of the "rights" (of life, health, freedom, sustenation, growth, and joy) of every individual and of the entire ecosystem. Transcendence is not limited to the foregoing expressions and is possible in every phase of culture and private life where health and integrity are maintained. The diagram on the opposite page is a symbolic model of humanity's nature, including transcendence.

This is only a tentative and heuristic device. However, we may clarify its structure. As Teilhard suggests, and as modern psychotherapy confirms, man must have a center. In whatever ways it is most vitally enacted, centeredness is the fundamental expression of transcendence, individual uniqueness, and wholeness. Centeredness also means integrity — or striving

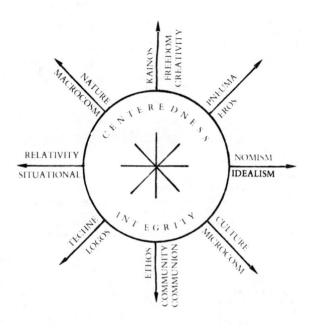

for wholeness (acting as a whole, full person) in all of life. The center is a pulsating source of energy—a creative font of dynamic process. The model suggested, a model of radial symmetry, is not a crystalline static structure, but an oscillating explosion-implosion sphere. Hurled into space, drawing in and giving back to the cosmos in a kaleidoscopic, artistic multi-dimensional array of lights, colors, forms, patterns, sounds, and waves of energy, each individual expresses and extends, intensifies, partly defines and creates the beauty and meaning of all that is, through dynamic and constructive interplay with its cosmic environs.

244

FOOTNOTES

[1]James L. Christian, *Philosophy: An Introduction to the Art of Wondering* (San Francisco: Rinehart Press, 1973) p. 335.

[2]Richard Schacht, *Hegel and After: Studies in Continental Philosophy Between Kant and Sartre* (Pittsburgh: University of Pittsburgh Press, 1975), provides an enlightening perspective concerning the term "existentialism." Schacht notes that "existentialism" is commonly used to identify an ostensible world view which includes such positions as atheism, relativism, absurdity, or nihilism, radical human freedom and responsibility, solipsism, etc., (pp. 230-231). Although affirming that such a world view undoubtedly enjoys a certain popularity in the modern West, Schacht suggests that it is *not* representative of the thought of the philosophers (such as Kierkegaard, Heidegger, Jaspers, Sartre, etc.) to whom it is usually applied (ibid.). Schacht differentiates "existentialism" (which he feels is most applicable to the thought of Sartre and Camus) from *Existenz*-philosophy—meaning the philosophy of one who is concerned with the analysis of *Existenz* (p. 237)—a term Schacht applies, with reservations, to Jaspers, Heidegger, Sartre and Kierkegaard. (See p. 238.) Schacht also introduces another term, "philosophical anthropology," which he refers to thinkers such as Max Scheler, Helmuth Plessner, Arnold Gehlen, and more loosely, to Claude Levi-Strauss and Ernst Cassirer. Although Schacht is right in exposing the careless and naive use of "existentialism," it seems uncertain that his alternative terminology will prove more useful.

[3]Soren Kierkegaard, *Concluding Unscientific Postscript*, trans. David F. Swenson and Walter Lowrie (Princeton, N.J.: Princeton University Press, 1968), p. 325.

[4]Karl Loewith, *From Hegel to Nietzsche: The Revolution in Nineteenth Century Thought*, trans. David E. Green (New York: Holt, Rinehart and Winston, 1964; Garden City, N.Y.: Anchor Books, 1967), p. 146, writes that after disappointment with Hegel and Schelling, "there runs through Kierkegaard's works a more or less explicit polemic against philosophy's claim to comprehend reality through reason."

[5]Loewith observes that "Kierkegaard . . . seeks to recapture the beginning as though eighteen hundred years of Christian history had never taken place; his goal is once more to be contemporary with the 'absolute humanity' of primitive Christianity which—humanly speaking—is 'inhuman'" (p.315).

[6]"Throughout his life he remained an outsider, at the utmost limit of bourgeois society, because he could not bring himself to engage in a profession and 'settle down with the finite' through marriage"(Loewith, p. 246). As Loewith indicates, Kierkegaard's rebellion—like Marx's—is an attack on the bourgeois world. Kierkegaard feels that "The blame for the whole present state (1848) of the European world must be borne by a 'conceited, semi-educated bourgeoisie, demoralized by the flatteries of the press,' which supposes that as the 'public' it can rule" (p 247). In Hannah Arendt, *Between Past and Future: Eight Exercises in Political Thought* (New York: The Viking Press, 1968), p. 28, Kierkegaard, Marx, and Nietzsche "were the first who dared to think without the guidance of any authority whatsoever; yet, for better or for worse, they were still held by the categorical framework of the great tradition." Thus Kierkegaard is at the first an individual without authority; his leap into a pristine faith—emptied of traditional content—removes him yet further from tradition, though strangely bound to it.

[7]"Kierkegaard's particular concern was not human equality, but Christian individuality in contrast to the 'crowd' . . . (he) was concerned with the alienation of man, but not within the world—rather within contemporary Christendom which had declared its solidarity with the world and with the state" (Loewith, p. 157).

[8]"Kierkegaard's polemical notion of real existence is directed not only against Hegel, but also as a corrective against the demands of the age. Individual existence, limited to itself, is (1) the only reality par excellence in contrast to the system; the latter includes everything on an equal footing, leveling differences (between being and nothingness, between thought and being, between universality and individuality) down to the even plane of indifferent being. It is (2) the reality of the individual in contrast to the historical universal (world history and the generation, the crowd, the public, and the age), which has no concern for the individual as such. It is (3) the inward existence of the individual in contrast to the external superficiality of circumstances. It is (4) a Christian existence before God, in contrast to Christianity made superficial in the spread of historical Christendom. And it is (5) above all, with all these characteristics, an existence which decides either for or against life as a Christian" (Loewith, p. 149).

[9]Kierkegaard, p. 346.

[10]Ibid., p. 348.

[11]Ibid., p. 369.

[12]Ibid., p. 473.

[13] Karl Barth, "The Righteousness of God," from his *The Word of God and the Word of Man* (Boston: Pilgrim Press, 1928), rpt. in W. Warren Wagar, ed., *Science, Faith and Man* (New York: Harper and Row, 1968), p. 49.

[14] Although Kierkegaard shared with Marx a hostility for bourgeois society, "Marx's target is the alienation of man from himself produced by capitalism, Kierkegaard's is the alienation of the Christian from himself produced by Christianity . . . Kierkegaard protested passionately against this (Marxist) idea of social existence because he saw 'in our time' every kind of association—whether in the 'system,' in 'mankind,' or in 'Christendom'—as a leveling force. 'It is out of the question that the idea of socialism and the community should become the salvation of the age . . .'" (Loewith, pp. 150, 156).

[15] Kierkegaard, p. 42.

[16] Saint Augustine, *The City of God* (trans. by Marcus Dods) XI.26.

[17] Richard J. Bernstein, *Praxis and Action* Philadelphia: University of Pennsylvania Press, 1971), however, warns against taking Kierkegaard's "Truth is Subjectivity" maxim—spoken through the mouth of Johannes Climacus—too seriously. According to Bernstein, "Kierkegaard himself was acutely sensitive" to the temptation which has seduced many existential philosophers who have sought to build a 'new' philosophy on Kierkegaard's (especially Climacus') claims" (p. 98). If Bernstein is correct, we must still assume that the subtle misreading of Kierkegaard has exerted a wider influence than a more accurate grasp of his real intentions. Bernstein's discussion is especially valuable in elucidating Kierkegaard's ironic technique and in explicating the major issues of Kierkegaard's dialogue with Hegel.

[18] Bernstein observes: "What I find so distressing about existentialism is the logic of its dialectic—the existential solipsism and nihilism that threatens it. This nihilism threatens to undermine precisely that which they have so dramatically sought to underscore . . . I believe that Kierkegaard saw this, and that this is the clue to understanding the morbidity, hopelessness, and black despair of his latest journal entries" (p. 312).

[19] Kierkegaard, p. 341.

[20] Ibid.

[21] Kierkegaard's "personal arbitrariness" is a function of his daring "to think without the guidance of any authority whatsoever" (Arendt, p. 28). Without recourse to man's socio-political nature (like Marx), or other traditional frames, Kierkegaard could only look within himself. But still imbued with the traditional Western sense of the isolated ego, Kierkegaard's "leap" of Christian faith could claim no external supportive referents. We would agree here with Bernstein's judgment: "I do not think that the nihilism that threatens to undermine existentialism is an 'accidental' or 'incidental' conclusion of the existential dialectic . . ." (p.312). For if the individual can never be conceived mediately, but only immediately, then there are no external referents. Bernstein suggests that "We need to incorporate the Hegelian and Marxist insight that there are historical ways in which the existing individual can be 'mediated,' that there are forms of alienation and exploitation that can be overcome. Marx, and especially Hegel, saw that any dialectic of the existing individual which cuts him off from the social character of his individuality is doomed to failure" (pp. 312-13).

[22] F. H. Heinemann, *Existentialism and the Modern Predicament* (New York: Harper Torchbooks, 1958), p. 53.

[23] *The Encyclopedia of Philosophy*, s.v. "Karl Jaspers," by Peter Koestenbaum.

[24] Karl Jaspers, *Philosophical Faith and Revelation*, trans. E. B. Ashton (London: Collins, 1967), p. 237.

[25] Karl Jaspers, "Nature and Ethics," in *Moral Principles of Action*, ed. Ruth Nanda Anshen (New York: Harper and Row, 1952), rpt. in *Science, Faith and Man*, pp. 127-30.

[26] Jaspers, *Philosophical Faith and Revelation*, pp. 346-63.

[27] Ibid.; Heinemann, p. 76.

[28] Heinemann, p. 90.

[29] Ibid., p. 91.

[30] Martin Heidegger, *Being and Time*, trans. John Macquarrie and Edward Robinson (New York: Harper and Row, 1962), p. 21.

[31] Ibid., p. 25.

246

[32] Michael Gelven, *A Commentary on Heidegger's 'Being and Time'* (New York: Harper Torchbooks, 1970), p. 9.

[33] Ibid., p. 11.

[34] Ibid., p. 13.

[35] In his "Preface to the Seventh German Edition" of *Being and Time,* Heidegger writes, "While the previous editions have borne the designation 'First Half,' this has now been deleted. After a quarter of a century, the second half could no longer be added unless the first were to be presented anew. Yet the road it has taken remains even today a necessary one, if our Dasein is to be stirred by the question of Being" (p. 17).

[36] Schacht in *Hegel and After* writes, ". . . Heidegger and Jaspers . . . and the French philosopher Gabriel Marcel are vehement in their rejection of the label ('existentialist'). And they are quite justified in rejecting it, considering the significant differences between their views and those of Sartre and Camus and their followers" (p. 232).

[37] Gelven, pp. 18–19.

[38] Ibid.

[39] Ibid., p. 20. J. L. Mehta, *The Philosophy of Martin Heidegger* (New York: Harper Torchbooks, 1971), writes: "The distinction between existenziell and existenzial is basic in Heidegger. The former term refers to the ontic, the factual and the experienced, whereas the latter refers to its ontological and transcendental condition and significance . . . For Heidegger . . . the factual, existing man is the basic fact and the source of all projects of the understanding. The 'facticity' of man consists in this that the possible ways in which he can understand himself and the world presuppose, and are limited by, the actual historical situation in which man at any time happens to be and the particular tradition he happens to inherit. This is the meaning of the 'hermeneutics of facticity' . . ." (pp. 8, n. 16 and 22–23).

[40] Gelven, p. 21.

[41] Heidegger, p. 67.

[42] Gelven, pp. 22–23.

[43] Ibid., p. 23.

[44] Ibid., p. 24.

[45] Heidegger, p. 36.

[46] Ibid., p. 68.

[47] Gelven, pp. 29; 50–51.

[48] Heidegger, p. 69.

[49] Gelven, p. 47.

[50] Ibid., p. 66.

[51] Heidegger, p. 100.

[52] Heinemann, p. 105.

[53] Jean-Paul Sartre, *The Reprieve,* trans. Eric Sutton (New York: Vintage Books, 1973), p. 364.

[54] Nicholas Berdyaev, *Truth and Revelation,* trans. R. M. French (New York: Collier, 1962), p. 109.

[55] Ibid.

[56] Ibid., p. 111.

[57] Ibid.

[58] Ibid., p. 145.

[59] Nicolas Berdyaev in Heinemann, p. 158.

[60] Berdyaev, *Truth and Revelation,* p. 145.

[61] Ibid., p. 155.

[62] Ibid., p. 19.

[63] Ibid., pp. 82–83.

[64] Ibid., p. 84.

[65] Ibid., p. 125.

[66]Of course the dissolution of the organic unity would seem to suggest "nothingness" for that unity.

[67]Alan Watts, *The Book: On the Taboo Against Knowing Who You Are* (New York: Vintage Books, 1972) p. 109.

[68]Ibid., p. 123.

[69]Perry Le Fevre, *Understandings of Man* (Philadelphia: Westminster Press, 1966), p. 30.

[70]Ibid.

[71]Ibid., p. 31.

[72]Sir Julian Huxley, "Evolutionary Humanism," from *The Humanist Frame* (New York: Harper and Row, 1961), rpt. in Wagar, p. 97.

[73]Ibid.

[74]Ibid., p. 98.

[75]Le Fevre, pp. 38-39.

[76]Ibid., pp. 39-41.

[77]Huxley, p. 88.

[78]Ibid., p. 89.

[79]Ibid., p. 92.

[80]Ibid., p. 93.

[81]Ibid., p. 94.

[82]Ibid., p. 96.

[83]Pierre Teilhard de Chardin, *The Phenomenon of Man* (New York: Harper and Row, 1965), p. 225.

[84]Ibid., pp. 256-57.

[85]Ibid., p. 258.

[86]Ibid., p. 259.

[87]Ibid., p. 260.

[88]If Freud did not intend his tripartite model of the psyche to be taken as substantialist, he was perhaps predisposed to substantialist modes of thought by his tacit commitment to a philosophical point of view similar to the Helmholtz School. Daniel Yankelovich and William Barrett, *Ego and Instinct: The Psychoanalytic View of Human Nature—Revised* New York: Random House, 1970), write, "for more than a quarter of a century, from 1873 to 1902—and in his most intellectually formative years to boot—Freud was closely associated with, and directly influenced by, Brucke, Breuer, and Fliess, all of whom maintained steadfast allegiance to the thought of Helmholtz. It would have been extraordinary if Freud had not assimilated the mode of thought that prevailed in this milieu. Nor was it merely a matter of personal relationships. The climate of thought, which the Helmholtz School represented, seemed at the time unassailable. The later discoveries within physics itself that were to change the thinking of physicists in our own century had not yet arrived; in the middle of the nineteenth century the Newtonian mode of thought had achieved such triumphs that it seemed the universally binding model for all science, that of man as well as nature. If there were to be scientific explanations of any subject matter, then these explanations must be in accord with that model. And what is that prescribed mode of explanation? It requires first that any complex phenomenon be reduced to elementary components, particles or atoms as the case may be; and then, in order that the movements of these elementary particles be calculable, they must be governed by the law of inertia . . . It is now possible to see out of what intellectual background Freud's concept of the "mental apparatus" emerges. It is nothing less than a psychological surrogate for the Newtonian postulates of inertia and conservation of energy" (pp. 47-48). According to Yankelovich and Barrett, Freud's Newtonian orientation is not only visible in the early abortive *Project for a Scientific Psychology,* which "insists that explanation must always proceed by *reduction to elementary entities"* (pp. 49-50), but also in *The Ego and the Id* (1923) where Freud supplements his topographical (*topos:* "place") approach with a *structural* analysis (p. 53). "When viewed closely, the formulations of *The Ego and the Id* bear a striking resemblance to his first metapsychological paper—the *Project* of 1895" (p. 55). Here Freud chooses a model where "the mental apparatus" of the psyche "is a thoroughly Newtonian engine, and the supposed laws by which it is governed are markedly similar to Newton's laws of motion" (p. 56). According to Yankelovich and

Barrett, this mechanical, substantialistic model of Freud's constitutes a "curious regression" from his genetic model of 1905, and creates "glaring difficulties" for the psychology of the ego up to the present day. "The heart of those difficulties can be found in the conflict between a developmental point of view and that of a Newtonian mechanism" (ibid.). Calvin Hall, "*A Primer of Freudian Psychology* (New York: Mentor Books, 1954), speaks of ego, id, and superego more in terms of processes, but nowhere actually addresses this question (see pp. 22-35).

[89] The model first clearly set forth in 1923 in Freud's *The Ego and the Id*, trans. Joan Riviere and rev. and newly ed. James Strachey (New York: W. W. Norton and Company, 1962), is succinctly discussed in his 1933 lecture "The Dissection of the Psychical Personality," *New Introductory Lectures on Psychoanalysis*, newly trans. and ed. James Strachey (New York: W. W. Norton and Company, 1964). Freud's analysis in the latter source is somewhat shorter (23 pages as opposed to 46 in *The Ego and the Id*, English editions), but also seems to be somewhat more cogent.

[90] Freud, *The Ego and the Id*, p. 13.

[91] Freud, *New Introductory Lectures on Psychoanalysis*, p. 58.

[92] Ibid., p. 59.

[93] In *The Ego and the Id* Freud writes "The ego is first and foremost a bodily ego; it is not merely a surface entity, but is itself the projection of a surface. If we wish to find an anatomical analogy for it we can best identify it with the 'cortical homunculus' of the anatomists . . ." (p. 16). Or in speaking of consciousness, Freud says that it is "the *surface* of the *mental apparatus*," "a function to a system which is *spatially* the first one reached from the external world—and spatially not only in the functional sense but, on this occasion, also in the sense of anatomical dissection" (p. 9).

[94] Freud, *New Introductory Lectures on Psychoanalysis*, p. 59.

[95] Ibid., p. 65.

[96] Ibid., p. 60.

[97] Ibid.

[98] Ibid., p. 67.

[99] Peter L. Berger and Thomas Luckmann, *The Social Construction of Reality* (New York: Anchor Books, 1967), p. 18.

[100] Freud, *New Introductory Lectures on Psychoanalysis*, p. 77.

[101] Again Freud's substantialistic language may becloud the cultural function of the id. For example in *The Ego and the Id* he defines the id as follows:"I propose to take into account by calling the *entity* which starts out from the system Pcpt. and begins by being Pcs. the 'ego,' and following Groddeck in calling the *other part of the mind*, into which this *entity* extends and which behaves as though it were Ucs., the 'id'" (p. 13). Freud's analogy of the struggle between the ego and the id underscores the impression of two warring entities: "Thus in its relation to the id it is like a man on horseback, who has to hold in check the superior strength of the horse; with this difference, that the rider tries to do so with his own strength while the ego uses borrowed forces" (p. 15). Freud's language often entails personification, which also contributes to the impression of substantialism, for example "The id . . . has no means of showing the ego either love or hate" (p. 49).

[102] Freud, *New Introductory Lectures on Psychoanalysis*, p. 76.

[103] Sigmund Freud, *The Future of an Illusion*, trans. W. D. Robson-Scott (New York: Anchor Books, 1964), pp. 88-89.

[104] Freud, *New Introductory Lectures on Psychoanalysis*, p. 77.

[105] David Bakan, *Sigmund Freud and the Jewish Mystical Tradition* (New York: Schocken Books, 1965), writes: "If God is identified with the superego, then the corresponding antagonistic image is the Devil, who dwells in hell. As we have indicated earlier, in the psychoanalytic relationship the analyst is at one and the same time the representative of the superego as well as a tolerant, understanding father figure. Now what is the Devil, psychologically? The answer is eminently simple, on one level. *The Devil is the suspended superego*. He is the permissive superego. The Devil is that part of the person which permits him to violate the precepts of the super-ego. Roheim in his discussion of Freud's paper on demoniacal possession says: 'The dream is a refutation or rebuttal of an attack made upon the Ego by the Super-ego. The pact with the Devil is

therefore really a pact with the Super-Ego not to help human beings in getting these things but to stop preventing them in doing so'" (p. 211).

[106] Freud, *New Introductory Letters on Psychoanalysis*, p. 70.

[107] Ibid., p. 77.

[108] Carl G. Jung, *Psyche and Symbol: A Selection from His Writings*, ed. Violet S. de Laszlo (New York: Anchor, 1958), pp. 1-2.

[109] Ibid., p. 3.

[110] Ibid.

[111] Ibid.

[112] Ibid., p. 23.

[113] Ibid.

[114] Ibid., p. 7.

[115] Ibid.

[116] Ibid., p. 10.

[117] Ibid., p. 15.

[118] Ibid., p. 13.

[119] Jung's series of dichotomous pairs, such as *ego* and *self*, *logos* and *eros*, *anima* and *animus*, seem more readily adaptable to the brain's dual hemispheric structure than Freud's semi-hierarchical tripartite *superego/ego/id* model. However, as we have suggested, Freud's model may more accurately portray the actual functioning *ethos* of cultural and institutional structures in the West.

[120] See chapter twelve.

[121] The assertion that man is a *transcendent* creature, though not universally affirmed, is nevertheless widely held. *Transcendence* can mean various things. The following works represent recent attempts to define or redefine transcendence: A. H. Maslow, *The Farther Reaches of Human Nature* (New York: The Viking Press, 1972), esp. pp. 269-295. Norman O. Brown, *Love's Body* (New York: Vintage Books, 1966); Peter L. Berger, *A Rumor of Angels* (Garden City, N. Y.: Doubleday, 1969, Anchor Books, 1970); Herbert W. Richardson and Donald R. Cutler, ed., *Transcendence* (Boston: Beacon Press, 1969); and William A. Johnson, *The Search for Transcendence* (New York: Harper and Row, 1974).

CHAPTER TEN

THE NEW COSMOLOGY

. . . in the midst of all stands the sun, for who could in this most beautiful temple place this lamp in another or better place than that from which it can at the same time illuminate the whole? Which some not unsuitably call the light of the world, others call the soul or the ruler. Trismegistus calls it the visible God, the Electra of Sophocles, the all-seeing. So indeed does the sun, sitting on the royal throne, steer the revolving family of the stars.[1]

Thus spoke Nicholas Copernicus (1473-1543), the great cosmologist who initiated the heliocentric revolution. His words reveal a stance which straddles two universes. One foot steps ahead towards a universe of solar systems and galaxies—a cosmos vast beyond the wildest reaches of our comprehension. Yet the other foot rests behind, firmly planted in the comfortable security of a mythopoeic anthropocentrism, where the sun remains a deity—the center of a humanly conceived divine order.

The assaults upon the comforting stability of a geometrically neat and "local" universe have come slowly; in fact, the full consciousness of the new world picture has yet to dawn upon the great majority of contemporary humanity. In 1572 in the constellation Cassiopeia a *nova* ("new star") flared brilliantly, then slowly faded. While some were heralding its appearance as the return of the Bethlehem star to announce the second coming of Christ, Tycho Brahe (1546-1610) observed this novel visitor until it finally disappeared from view, all the while measuring its location and intensity.[2] The new star (believed today to have been a *supernova,* an exploding star) was perhaps the first modern harbinger of the apocalyptic promise of "new heavens and a new earth." But paradoxically contrary to the expected biblical cataclysm, this apocalypse was to dawn almost imperceptibly, with few dramatic moments, yet nonetheless radically rearranging the old fixed order of the cosmos for all time to come. However, Tycho himself was unaware of the fuller implications of this fiery omen.

Johannes Kepler (1571-1630), a devotee of Pythagorean mysticism, is another figure straddling two worlds. On the one hand he bequeathed to posterity his famed three laws of planetary motion, while on the other he constructed an aesthetically-pleasing, but fanciful, mechanical model of the cosmos, geometrically and mathematically exact and proportionate.[3]

With Kepler's contemporary, Galileo Galilei (1564-1642), the world was thrust yet another step towards a radically new world picture. The events of Galileo's life, as has been often observed, presage a protracted life-and-death battle between two grand traditions—Greek science and Christian theology. Galileo's construction of a telescope—the instrument by which he discovered mountains and craters on the moon (assumed by his contemporaries to be a perfect sphere of crystal) and four satellites orbiting Jupiter (challenging not only geocentrism, but also a strict heliocentrism)—may be taken as a symbol. The telescope, anticipating the extension through technology of man's sensory powers of observation and measurement, is the sword of science raised to challenge the sword of God's word. The first bout seemed to go to the armies of God, for in 1633 Galileo was convicted of:

> believing and holding the doctrines—false and contrary to the Holy and Divine Scriptures—that the sun is the center of the world, and that it does not move from east to west, and that the earth does move and is not the center of the world: also that an opinion can be held in support of this, after it has been declared and decreed contrary to the Holy Scriptures.[4]

Sir Isaac Newton (1624-1727) not only stands as a genius who laid the groundwork of modern physics and astronomy; he is also the last great apologist for a cosmology of absolutes, where the laws of the physical universe as the laws of God are considered to be transparent—simple and immutable—and objectively apprehensible to man. Newton formulated the laws of inertia, momentum, and action-reaction, as well as the law of universal gravitation. Furthermore, he postulated the laws of Absolute Space, Time, and Motion on the one hand, while dabbling in biblical prophecy and theology on the other. His world machine was to be enlisted in the service of proving the existence of the divine mechanic. Newton wrote:

> This most beautiful system of the sun, planets, and comets could only proceed from the counsel and dominion of an intelligent and powerful Being . . . This Being governs all things . . . as Lord over all . . . The Supreme God is a Being eternal, infinite, absolutely perfect . . . He endures forever and is everywhere present; and by existing always and everywhere, *he constitutes duration and space* . . . In him are all things contained and moved, yet neither affects the other; God suffers nothing from the motion of bodies, bodies find no resistance from the omnipresence of God.[5]

Here is the key to Newtonian absolutes—God himself "constitutes duration and space." Thus when Newton speaks of "absolute, true, and mathematical time," which "of itself, and from its own nature, flows equably without relation to anything external" (which is also called "duration"), and "absolute space" which "in its own nature, without relation to anything external *remains always similar and immovable,*"[6] there is a hidden agenda. The creation, perfection, geometrical static harmony, and substantiality of nature are direct expressions of its rootedness in the Divine Being, whose perfections Newton describes in the foregoing passage.

The Newtonian absolutes, like the absolutes of revelation infallibly construed, create an insurmountable dilemma for man—a dilemma which was to spell the breakdown and inversion of the Newtonian starting point. The point is really quite simple: man in his finitude must begin with his own spatio-temporal and empirical location; *a priori* absolutes—even if they exist—are unknowable to him. We are creatures of historical context—which translated into mathematical terms is a central assumption of Einstein's two theories of relativity. Moreover, "space" or "time," or "space-time" are anthropomorphic myths, not thereby untrue; on the contrary, they are vehicles of world-building, producing quite tangible results. But the worlds we have built have changed many times, and we must not err by attributing universal status to a particular occurrence. Universal laws are assumed to exist (as modern physics considers the universe to be homogeneous and isotropic), but we may only experience them as particulars, and they must be translated afresh to meet new contextual realities.

In 1718 Newton's colleague Halley ascertained that Sirius, Arcturus, and Aldeberan, three brilliant stars, did not conform to the position established by Hipparchus some two thousand years earlier.[7] Again the fixed heavens were threatened with motion. But the man who was to shake the static order of the heavens once and for all was William Herschel (1738-1822), a man of immense patience (who succeeded in making a telescope to satisfy his purposes only after two hundred abortive efforts) and tenacity. In 1781 Herschel discovered Uranus, and followed this *coup* with a series of startling discoveries, including not only the existence of various other star systems similar to our "Milky Way," but also gaseous nebulae and binary stars. (As late as 1920 Heber D. Curtis of Lick Observatory and Harlow Shapley were debating the location of the sun in the Milky Way and whether or not the Milky Way is the whole universe, or just one among many "island universes." These issues were not resolved for some time.)[8]

It is not surprising that William's son John Herschel (1792-1871) followed his father in blazing a trail for a new world picture. John challenged a simplistic atomism which depicted the atoms clashing together like billiard balls. He suggested that contingency was the most obvious aspect of the universe, and challenged contemporary men of science to come to terms with the implications of sun spot changes, the shapes of nebulae, and geophysical climatic changes.[9] The Herschels were quiet revolutionaries, yet their work was integral to the dissolution of the old local and static cosmos.

The winds of change were blowing with a steadily mounting intensity. In 1842, the same year that Charles Darwin settled at Down in Kent to begin his writing, Christian Doppler, the Austrian mathematician, demonstrated that light waves show a change in frequency depending upon the velocity of their source relative to an observer.[10] From this new observation, the "Doppler Effect," it could be demonstrated beyond all question that the "fixed" stars were not "fixed" at all, but hurtling through space at unimaginable speeds. Jean Charon describes this principle:

> The effect is very similar to that which we find with a whistling train; the whistle is high-pitched when the train is approaching, and when the train begins to recede the note of the whistle drops. The light coming from the stars behaves in an analogous manner. If the star is moving towards us, the spectral lines are shifted to the violet or short wave end of the spectrum; if the star is moving away, the shift will be to the red or long wave end of the spectrum.[11]

In 1868 William Huggins discovered that, according to the Doppler Effect, the star Sirius was receding from us at a velocity of fifty kilometers per second.[12] By 1917 V. M. Slipher had announced that out of fifteen spiral nebulae galaxies examined, thirteen were receding at a mean velocity of six hundred kilometers per second.[13] In 1930, the American astronomer Hubble formulated a law which states that "the speed of recession of a galaxy is linked with its distance from us; the more remote the galaxy, the quicker it is moving away."[14] In other words, the universe now appears to be literally "flying apart" at phenomenal speeds of up to 150,000 kilometers per second.[15] We live in a rapidly expanding universe.

Our present understanding of our cosmic location differs radically from the cosmos of Copernicus or Newton, or that of most educated men fifty to seventy-five years ago. Donald Menzel offers the following model of our solar system to give us some sense of perspective.[16] If the solar system were proportionately reduced by five billion times, so that one million miles equal one foot, the following picture would emerge. The sun appears the size of a basketball, with the earth a grain of wheat revolving about it some 100 feet away. Venus and Mercury, the sizes of a grain of wheat and a mustard seed respectively, rotate some 70 and 40 feet about the sun. Mars, a mite larger than Mercury, orbits at 160 feet. Jupiter, approximately the size of a golf ball, is 500 feet from the sun, and Uranus and Neptune, both pea-sized, revolve some 2000 and 3000 feet away, respectively. Menzel notes that as we survey our solar system we are struck by a great emptiness. The next near star is a double star, some 4000 *miles* away from our model sun. Inspired by Mark Twain's *Captain Stormfield's Visit to Heaven,* Menzel constructs a further model of the universe itself. On a second scale, letting $\frac{1}{16}$ inch equal one light year (the distance that light, traveling at 186,000 miles per second, traverses in one year—approximately 6,000,000,000,000 miles into space), Menzel represents the entire universe as a spherical volume roughly the size of the earth. If we could enter the volume it would at first glance appear entirely empty. As a matter of fact, only with a microscope of extraordinary power could the stars be seen at all. The largest would be one-millionth of an inch across, the smallest about the size of an atom. Further examination would detect that

Stars are by no means scattered uniformly throughout the enormous volume. They form groups, or clusters, several hundred feet in diameter, something like giant swarms of gnats. The stellar population is concentrated in these regions, with vast realms of nothingness in between. Some of these groupings of stars are irregular in shape. Others are round and flat, like a pie plate. Each group contains hundreds of millions and sometimes as many as a hundred billion stars, with the model stars spaced, on the average, a few tenths of an inch apart. Again, what impresses us most is the emptiness of space and the vast distances between stars and groups of stars. Stellar traffic lanes are decidedly uncrowded. The chances of two stars accidentally colliding is almost infinitesimal.[17]

To approach the more immediate universe on a "normal" scale,[18] we find that our Milky Way galaxy, some 100,000 light years from rim to rim, contains one (Menzel) to two (Shapley) hundred billion stars. Stars vary widely in size from one hundred times the diameter of our sun to those smaller than the planet Jupiter. Moreover the stars range from brilliant white and blue "hot" stars to "cooler" red stars. Our sun is of median size and brightness. About one-third of all stars are *double*, with two members revolving around a common center of gravity. There are indeed star clusters of even more members, such as the familiar Pleiades (approximately 120 or more stars), or globular clusters composed of thousands of stars. Our galaxy contains such clusters, and is itself a spiral nebula, typical of billions of galaxies in the universe. Our disk-shaped galaxy rotates, and it takes 2,000,000 centuries for our sun to finish an orbit of one cosmic year. As we look into our Milky Was we discover a "long, dark rift" which astronomers believe to be huge clouds of dust—material which has not yet condensed into stars. The distance between galaxies is enormous, assumed to be some 100,000 to 1,000,000 light years on the average. Galaxies themselves are found in clusters in some places, and we now estimate at least 10,000,000 other galaxies within our visual range.

Not only does the enormity of our universe boggle the mind, but the picture of its dynamic activity and extreme peculiarity (e.g., quasars, pulsars, and black holes) has completely shattered the secure and manageable universe variously defined by humanly apprehensible absolutes from ancient mythopoeism to Newton's mechanical model and beyond. Harlow Shapley writes:

> The displacement of the sun and earth from positional importance, the sudden relegating of man to the edge of one ordinary galaxy in an explorable universe of billions of galaxies—that humiliating (or inspiring) development is or should be the death knell of anthropocentrism. It should incite orienting thought by modern philosophers and theologians, and perhaps it has and will.[19]

Insofar as we have regarded man as the focal point and final end of the universe, Shapley is surely right, especially since by *conservative* estimation, there are in the known universe some "ten billion planets suitable for organic life something like that on earth."[20] On the other hand, we can never forget that we are presently limited to our human understanding and framework.

The loss of traditional cosmic anthropocentrism does jar the integral relationship between the cosmos and culture still assumed to exist long after Newton. Newton's own model attempted to establish the interrelationship between cosmic and human orders—both the products of divine ordination. With the upheaval of the old cosmos, in one sweeping gesture are toppled the traditional cosmic underpinnings of hierarchical theological, social, and political systems—not to mention tacit analogies between cosmic and ethical absolutes. Some scientists attempt to avoid these implications by claiming that, as a strictly scientific endeavor, cosmology is independent of social, religious and ethical questions. Some theologians, seeking to preserve orthodox tenets and to avoid the charge of obscurantism, have likewise laid out two spheres of truth (the spheres of nature and grace established for this purpose by Thomas Aquinas). More extreme reactions include the fabled "Flat Earth Society" of London, which disavows all evidence of modern astrophysics and space travel as a hoax perpetrated for political purposes.

Finally, the Presocratics who first proffered the macrocosm/microcosm relationship may have been wiser than we suppose. In the final chapter we will approach new possibilities for a macrocosm/microcosm picture harmonious with the new cosmology. Presently we return to ramifications of the new cosmology.

New Laws—New Perspectives

Albert William Levi asserts that three scientific revolutions have been at the root of the metaphysics of the Western world. The first revolution, that of the Ionian nature philosophers, produced three great cosmological systems: the system of Aristotle, emphasizing "form" and "matter"; the system of Democritus—the primal atomic theory; and the system of Plato, based on mathematical relations. The second great revolution was that of the seventeenth century philosopher-physicists, Galileo, Newton, and Descartes, who "found the rationality of nature to consist in its susceptibility to mathematical treatment."[21] The dominant image of the cosmos which emerged from the work of these men is the world *machine*, "whose parts function harmoniously and regularly with calculable mathematical precision."[22] Finally, the Western world is still in the throes of the third great revolution, the revolution of the new cosmology, the chief dimensions of which are embodied in relativity and quantum theories.

Relativity presupposes the work of Fizeau, Michelson, Fitzgerald and Lorentz, but Einstein is its chief formulator. The quantum theory stemmed initially from the work of Max Planck, but has been developed by Max Born, Schroedinger, Niels Bohr, Heisenberg, de Broglie and Dirac.[23] Both relativity and quantum theory are critiques of former absolutes (and attempts to free the laws of nature from strict anthropocentric frames). Relativity reinterprets Newtonian space and time; quantum challenges a simplistic atomism of matter and energy. Relativity deals mainly with the *macrocosm,* including galactic and extra-galactic measurements and perspectives. Quantum theory relates to the *microcosm*—the atomic and subatomic worlds as they appear to us through our measuring devices and experimental framework.[24] Both relativity and quantum theory have raised critical epistemological questions concerning the status of man as knower in his cosmic location. Physicists today are still searching for a "unified field theory" which will encompass both the macrocosmic and microcosmic domains, including the reinterpretations of space-time, substance, and causality.

Before examining the specific shape of relativity theory and quantum theory, it would be helpful to consider the practical question of man's relationship as an observer to the physical world. Just as Berkeley asserted that all qualities are channeled through the senses and are dependent upon the perceiving mind, so Einstein believed that both space and time are modes of perspective—nomistic devices of the mind for locating ourselves vis-a-vis the world of our experience. We repeat: Man is limited by his sensory equipment. Lincoln Barnett observes that "the human eye is sensitive only to a narrow band of radiation" which lies between red and violet light, whereas it is insensitive to cosmic rays, gamma rays, x-rays, ultraviolet light, infra-red light, heat waves, radar, radio waves, etc.[25] Alan Watts illustrates the contingency of our perception by the example of a rainbow. The "existence" of a rainbow is dependent upon the exact angular coalescence of sun, atmospheric moisture, and an observer. The absence of any one of these negates the rainbow. In fact, Watts points out, all of our perceptions, including such seemingly substantial items as mountains, operate through such an interplay of factors.[26] In other words, both rainbows and mountains are contingent upon the particular context of the observer in space-time. To understand Watts' point, we must recognize that both rainbow and mountain are "events," which, when viewed in proper perspective, reveal the insubstantiality of all reality in our experience. For example, if we could imagine viewing the mountain through "time-lapse photography" over many millions of years, we would observe a wave or ripple on the constantly-flowing surface of our evolving planet. Indeed, the universe itself envisioned by this method would prove to be like a sparkler in the hand of God.

A further example may be drawn from Bertrand Russell's discussion of Galileo's discovery of the existence of Jupiter's satellites.[27] Both men of science and men of religion refused to believe Galileo. Aristotelians refused to look through the telescope and insisted that the moons were an illusion. In a footnote Russell quotes Father Clavius, who asserted that "to see the satellites of Jupiter, men had to make an instrument which would create them."[28] Although Russell does not elaborate, we would assume that Father Clavius' statement means something like "we know that those satellites cannot be real since our presuppositions (such as limiting the number of heavenly bodies to seven—the number of perfection) do not allow for their reality. Therefore those satellites must be an illusion created by that so-called telescope." However, Father Clavius' statement transposed into the context of modern physics assumes a meaning consonant therewith. To "see" the satellites of Jupiter *through the telescope* requires 1) an observer, 2) an instrument, 3) proper viewing conditions, and 4) the satellites themselves. In a real sense the satellites can be regarded as illusions created by the coalescence of the above factors in relative relationship. For in fact, due to the constant flux of reality from the sub-atomic level to the astro-physical, those *particular* satellites will recur again at *no other time* nor in any other *space*.* That is why they are not to be regarded as substantive entities. Heraclitus was right: you cannot step into the same river twice. This is not to deny the existence of Jupiter's satellites, but to assert that in our experience they constitute not an absolute, but a relative (albeit "consistent") phenomenon. Our description and calculations (such as mathematical equations) are abstractions and generalities— statistical approximations—which may or may not be quite confirmed by subsequent experience. Assuming that we could weigh and measure these satellites and photograph their molecular structure, we would quickly discover that their material configuration *was not static.* Even physical laws— springing from observational data as interpreted by hypotheses, and embodied in mathematical formulae and statistical approximation—are in fact extrapolations and generalizations from our experience. Although useful and necessary for calculation and orientation, these laws may no longer be invested with the status of absolute or irrevocable truths existing apart from our experience, or considered as ultimate propositions about the nature of reality. At the same time, since the organic order seems to evince a certain consistency, we may assume the general applicability of our laws when weighed against the contingency of our experience. As Don K. Price asserts concerning the study of man:

> Man in society is hard to study scientifically less because he is a complicated object of observation than because he is the instrument of observation, and a refractory one indeed. If modern psychology has taught man anything, it is just how irrational and perverse and unreliable an instrument he is for scientific purposes . . .[29]

Although Price's comment concerning man as an "irrational and perverse and unreliable" instrument may be extreme, one thing is certain: man himself *is* the primary instrument of all human knowledge, and however "objective," consistent, and reliable the "laws of nature" may seem to be, they are always

---

*Moreover our vision of the satellites is not simultaneous to their present. Since light takes *time* to traverse space, we are actually seeing their "past."

known only within our limited (or mathematically- and technologically-extrapolated) experience. Even if they could be confirmed by some intelligent beings dwelling on another planet within our galaxy, it would only prove that these laws operate consistently within similar space-time frames; but there could be other space-time frames outside of our functional experience where other laws might be operative.

With these observations in mind, we may return to the work of Einstein. Levi writes that the main consequence of Einstein's work is

> that it vindicates the objectivity of the laws of nature, and demonstrates that the laws of electrodynamics and optics are independent of the standpoint of the observer.[30]

The wording of Levi's statement might be misleading, for the objectivity of the laws of nature may be substantiated only by postulating uniformly moving systems or by relating systems to each other by the equations of the Lorentz transformations. Thus however objective the laws of nature may be, the relative space-time orientation of man must be considered. Newtonian dynamics had assumed that the laws of motion are the same with respect to all inertial frames of reference ("inertial" meaning that they are in uniform relative motion). Newton regarded "space as a physical reality, stationary and immovable."[31] According to Newtonian concepts, space, time, and matter are separable "things," largely independent of one another. (The word "real" derives from the Latin *res*, "thing.") Thus the Newtonian System assumes that space and time are veritable entities with substantial existence (as opposed to descriptions of event-relationships). Einstein, though positing the objectivity of certain laws of nature, such as the constancy of the speed of light and the equation of matter and energy, at the same time destroyed the objectivity and absoluteness of Newton's laws. Absolute Space, Time, and Motion illustrate what Whitehead has called "the fallacy of misplaced concreteness" in that they are the *projection* of relative human experience into the cosmos. Einstein, on the other hand, recognizes space-time as a continuum of modes of relationship—a frame of reference which constitutes the human understanding of self-location and the location of the dynamic components of the material universe.

Perhaps our understanding of Einstein's contributions will be enhanced by pursuing several examples. First we may imagine ourselves from a stationary point observing an ascending escalator. Picture the escalator conveniently cross-sectioned so that we can observe the movement of its passengers. Although a passenger is standing still, we will observe him moving at the same rate as the escalator. On the other hand, a passenger who is walking up the escalator could be seen passing the stationary passenger, and from our vantage point the second, walking passenger is clearly moving faster than the escalator itself. If the escalator is moving at a rate of five kilometers per hour, and the passenger walking up the escalator is moving at an

identical rate, we would clock this second passenger at ten kilometers per hour (whereas, if measuring solely the propulsion of his legs the passenger would clock himself moving at five kilometers per hour). Furthermore, if a passenger were to walk *down* the same ascending escalator at a rate of five kilometers per hour, he would appear to us to be stationary (or from the cross-sectioned view, merely walking "in place"):

If we were to ask whose measurements were correct—ours or the passenger's, the answer obviously is that both are correct. For we are operating in different frames of reference.

We switch our analogy to a moving train, focusing on a particular car. A person standing in the middle of a moving car will discover that, upon speaking, the sound waves from his voice will reach both ends of the car simultaneously, traveling in each direction at 340 meters* per second. On the other hand, if we were stationary observers outside of the train, watching it pass by, and could "see" the sound waves of the passenger's voice, we would discover that the sound waves were accelerated in the direction of the train's motion by a factor of 340 + X, or retarded in the opposite directon by a factor of 340 - X (where X equals the number of meters per second traveled by the train). However, when we conduct a similar experiment with light, we find a curious anomaly. If the aforesaid passenger flashes a beam of light

---
*1,100 feet.

simultaneously visible in both directions, it, like the sound of his voice, would reach both ends of the car simultaneously. But for us on the outside, the light, like the sound, would reach the approaching wall of the car faster than the receding wall, and would thus appear to travel at variant speeds. But in this case we would be incorrect. The velocity of the light would be the same in both directions. Why the discrepancy? Sound waves traverse space via the medium of air molecules, but light traverses *empty space* according to its electromagnetic properties *apart from any medium.* Barnett notes that:

> This curious fact has also been confirmed by studies of double stars which revolve around a common center of gravity. Careful analysis of these moving systems has shown that the light from the approaching star in each pair reaches earth at precisely the same velocity as the light from the receding star.[32]

Considering the foregoing observations, we may now cite two conclusions of Einstein's theory of special relativity, summarized in his paper of 1905:

> 1. The laws according to which the states of a physical system change do not depend on which of the two coordinate systems, in uniform relative motion, these laws refer to.
>
> 2. Every light ray moves in a "rest" coordinate system with a definite speed, c, whether emitted from a stationary or a moving source.[33]

The first statement is a restatement of the Galileo relativity principle, that "all laws of nature are the same in two systems in uniform relative motion."[34] Since the old mechanical system had also accepted this principle, how does Einstein's theory differ? The mechanical system postulated a correlate principle, namely the rule of adding velocities. We illustrated this rule with the passengers on the moving staircase and the sound waves of a passenger's voice in a train car. But we concluded that the rule broke down when we attempted an experiment with a beam of light. The speed of light, not traveling through a specified medium, was unaffected by the relative space-time locations of the passenger or an outside observer. This constitutes the second statement within Einstein's special relativity theory, namely that the speed of light is a universal constant (approximately 186,000 miles per second, or 3×10^8 m/sec) regardless of our frame of reference.

Leopold Infeld clearly summarizes the implications of Einstein's theory as over against classical physics. First he enumerates three principles:

> One: Relativity principle
> Two: Constancy of the velocity of light
> Three: Addition of velocities[35]

It is impossible to accept all three principles in an absolute way. If we accept *one* and *three,* we must reject *two* (the position of classical physics). However, if we accept *one* and *two,* we discover that *three* has only limited validity; this is the solution of Einstein. Thus Einstein introduces

> a new relativistic physics to which the old Newtonian physics becomes only

> an approximation, useful and valid for bodies moving with speeds small compared to that of light, but invalid if the velocities of moving bodies approach that of light.[36]

Thus, concludes Infeld, when we are measuring the speeds of cars or airplanes or even the planets of our solar system, classical mechanics provides a workable and accurate model. However, when we move into the realm of atomic physics where speeds may approach the speed of light, classical mechanics is no longer accurate.

A further consequence of the theory of special relativity is the breakdown of an old constant of classical physics—the ether theory—postulated to avoid the seemingly ridiculous idea of empty space. Ether was hypothesized to be a universal invisible medium in space through which all things traveled, roughly analogous to the ocean through which a ship travels. In 1881 Michelson and Morley designed an experiment to confirm the existence of this sea of ether, through which the earth was assumed to move, just as our ship through the sea. Since the sea of ether was pictured as being motionless, the situation resembles a ship moving through absolutely calm waters. Newton had suggested that it would be impossible to detect the movement of a ship in calm waters by any mechanical means *aboard* ship, thus it would be necessary (as sailors often did), to throw a log *overboard* and watch "the unreeling of the knots of the log line."[37] Michelson and Morley hypothesized that, since the earth moves through the ether in a comparable fashion, a beam of light projected in the direction of the earth's movement should be slightly retarded by the ether, whereas one sent with the ether stream should be conversely accelerated.[38] For their experiment, Michelson and Morley devised an instrument called an *interferometer* by which a light beam could be split in two and flashed in opposite directions simultaneously. When the experiment had been completed, it was discovered that the velocity of the speed of light was the same in both directions; there was no evidence whatever for the supposed sea of ether. Although resisted by classical mechanists for some years, this and subsequent experiments completely relegated the phantom ether to the fantasy world from which it had emerged.

Einstein's pondering of the significance of the Michelson and Morley experiment resulted in the special theory of relativity which, extrapolating from the constancy of the speed of light, asserted that "the laws of nature are the same for all uniformly moving systems."[39] At the same time special relativity asserts that there is no absolute, stationary frame of reference (such as universal ether or Newton's Absolute Space, Time, and Motion) in the universe. Special relativity moves us one step away from projecting relative human perceptions (such as space, time, and substance) upon the cosmos as absolutes. At the same time the cosmos is removed a step further away from our experience. "Space" is now simply a descriptive mode of relationship—

not an external absolute. Furthermore, there is no universal flow of time, abstracted from a concrete frame of reference. For time, too, is a mode of location, of reference, of relationship. According to classical mechanics, by the principle known as the Galileo transformation, the time coordinate of an event is the same in all systems moving uniformly relative to one another; if clocks are coordinated, an event which is simultaneous in one system should be measured as simultaneous in another. Although this principle is valid when we are dealing with relatively low cosmic velocities, under relativity theory a new principle—valid for systems moving uniformly relative to each other *at any velocity*—the Lorentz transformation, is introduced. The Lorentz transformation, assuming the relativity of both space *and* time, connects the coordinates of *both* from an event in one system to the same event in another.[40] Thus Einstein concluded that space and time must be envisaged together, as a space-time *continuum,* a four-dimensional field of action and reference. Reichenbach insists:

> The theory of relativity shows that space and time are neither ideal objects nor forms of order necessary for the human mind. They constitute a *rational system* expressing certain general features of physical objects and thus are *descriptive of the physical world.*[41]

Relativity particularly shifts the ground of conceptualizing the material world in a critical fashion: the world is not a mechanical system of various "things" bumping into each other in space and moving through time; it is rather a complex series of *events* evincing varying modes of interaction which we call space-time. The philosophical movement here is away from a universe of static "being" and "substance" towards a cosmos of dynamic "becoming" and "fields of energy." Moreover, our sense of past, present, and future as absolute points in a linear frame or time line is false. To the passenger standing in the middle of a moving train car, a beam of light will strike either end simultaneously. To the observer outside, the light reaches the rear of the car slightly before the front (and yet its velocity is the same in either direction). The simultaneous *present* event of the passenger on board becomes two events for the outside observer, one *past* and one *future.* Yet deductions of the outside observer to the effect that the speed of light therefore varies would be false. The variation is *not* in the speed of light, but in the relative space-time frames of the passenger and the external observer. The situation is similar to the relative time frames of our earth with regard to a distant star:

> Arcturus is 38 light years away. A light year is the distance light travels in one year, or roughly six trillion miles. If we should try to communicate with Arcturus by radio "right now" it would take 38 years for our message to reach its destination and another 38 years for us to receive a reply.[42]

Thus the cosmos into which we gaze on a brilliant starlit night is, with regard to time, a phantom of the past. The Arcturus of 1982 lies in our future in our year 2020; whereas the Arcturus which we survey in our present—say 1982—

is the Arcturus of our 1944. "Whether or not Arcturus even exists "now" nature forbids us to know . . ."[43]

Furthermore, special relativity illustrates that measuring instruments themselves are affected by the relative motion of varying frames of reference. Moving clocks are retarded and moving rods contract as the velocity of the frame of reference increases. Such an effect is infinitesimal with regard to reasonably low velocities. But on a theoretical rocket ship approaching the speed of light, time appears to pass more slowly (since time is a measure of the relative motion of events in the space-time frame of "spaceship earth"). George Gamow offers the following illustration:

> Suppose you decided to visit one of the satellites of Sirius, which is at a distance of nine light-years from the solar system, and use for your trip a rocket ship that can move practically with the speed of light. It would be natural for you to think that the round trip to Sirius and back would take you at least eighteen years, and you would be inclined to take a very large food supply . . . In fact if you move, for example, at 99.99999999 percent of the speed of light, your wrist watch, your heart, your lungs, your digestion, and your mental processes will be slowed down by a factor of 70,000 and the 18 years (from the point of view of people left on the Earth) . . . would seem to you as only a few hours. In fact, starting from Earth right after breakfast, you will feel ready for lunch when your ship lands on one of the Sirius planets. If you . . . start home right after lunch, you will, in all probability, be back on Earth in time for dinner. But . . . you will find on arriving home that your friends and relatives have given you up as lost in the interstellar spaces and have eaten 6570 dinners without you! . . . 18 terrestrial years have appeared to you as just one day.[44]

In addition to time change, mass itself is relative to motion, increasing by significant proportions only at speeds approaching the speed of light. An electron travelling at 99 percent of the speed of light increases its mass by seven times.[45]

A further consequence of the Theory of Special Relativity is embodied in Einstein's famous formula $E = mc^2$, the basis of atomic physics. This formula is a logical derivation from earlier observations. Heat had been envisioned in two ways, both thermal and mechanical. According to the thermal model, heat seemed to be a uniform "substance" which could flow from a warmer to a colder object. According to the mechanical principle, heat could be produced by two cold objects engaged in friction (as in making sparks by rubbing two pieces of flint together). The thermal heat seemed invariable in amount, but what about the frictional heat? Physicists established that the amount of frictional heat was equal to the energy expended. Both thermal and frictional heat were incorporated in a conservation principle where heat and energy are equivalent.[46] But the conservation principle was soon extended to include chemical and electromagnetic processes. It appeared that whatever material changes occurred, the total amount of energy remained the same. To this principle of the conservation of energy was added the principle of the conservation of mass. Mass is defined as "the resistance that a body opposes to its acceleration (inert mass)" or "the weight of the body (heavy mass)."[47] Physicists had assumed that the total mass remained unchanged regardless of physical and chemical changes. However, special relativity (as we have seen) challenged this conclusion. Although as a single principle the conservation of mass failed, it was incorporated by Einstein into the theory of the conservation of energy. Einstein found that mass and energy are interchangeable, and that although mass may be converted into energy and vice versa, no mass/energy is ever lost from the cosmos. This principle is embodied in the formula $E = mc^2$ where c represents the velocity of light, E the energy of a stationary body, and m, its mass.[48] Because of the enormity of the speed of light (3×10^8 m/sec or 186,000 mi/sec), its square represents an immense figure of energy release for even the smallest mass unit. This is the principle behind the great destructiveness of the atomic bomb. Moreover, $E = mc^2$ constitutes another fundamental law of nature (as we know it).

Einstein submitted his first statement of special relativity in 1905, and his second statement, general relativity, followed in 1915. Special relativity was designed to explain the relationship of natural laws vis-a-vis the shifting space-time frames of observers moving uniformly with respect to each other. General relativity was Einstein's attempt to posit an absolute law independent of any frame of reference in equations which could transpose the laws of nature to any space-time frame in any kind of relative motion. Einstein's new principle redefined gravitation. Gravitation is no longer a mysterious force associated with matter, but a complex curvature of space-time near every material object, "the distortion being greatest near large masses."[49] Gravitation thus describes primarily the *structure of space* around material objects.

> Just as Maxwell and Faraday assumed that a magnet creates certain properties in surrounding space, so Einstein concluded that stars, moons, and other celestial objects individually determine the properties of the space around them. And just as the movement of a piece of iron in a magnetic field is guided by the structure of the field, so the path of any body in a gravitational field is determined by the geometry of that field.[50]

Newton's "force theory"—based on the attraction of masses—is still adequate for dealing with most phenomena, but Einstein's theory predicts slightly different results in very strong gravitational fields.

> Three predictions from the theory for strong fields—slight irregularities in the orbit of Mercury, the deflection of starlight passing close to the sun, and displacements of lines in the spectra of very dense stars—have been verified by observation, suggesting that the theory does actually give a truer description than Newton's for gravitational effects near large masses.[51]

Einstein discovered that such events follow the laws not of Euclidean geometry (which is adequate for describing a broad range of simple phenomena in our experience), but the principles of Riemann's geometry of curved surfaces. Actually, Einstein considered both special and general relativity not so much "discoveries" as new perspectives—more useful and accurate *models* of reality as we know it. Concerning the new geometry of the universe assumed by relativity theory, Barnett writes:

> the universe is not a rigid and immutable edifice where independent matter is housed in independent space and time; it is on the contrary an amorphous continuum, without any fixed architecture, plastic and variable, constantly subject to change and distortion. Wherever there is matter and motion, the continuum is disturbed. Just as a fish swimming in the sea agitates the water around it, so a star, a comet, or a galaxy distorts the geometry of the space-time through which it moves.[52]

The second great revolution in the physical theory of the cosmos is the quantum theory. Quantum physics calls into question basic notions of *physical description* and *causality*. On the one hand, the quantum theory has exposed a dualistic tension in the theory of light, arising from seemingly contradictory pictures of its behavior; and on the other hand it has challenged the status of deterministic causality. Deterministic causality is expressed in the following classical passage from La Place:

> We must envisage the present state of the universe as the effect of its previous state, and as the cause of that which will follow. An intelligence that could know, at a given instant, all the forces governing the natural world, and the respective positions of the entities which compose it, if in addition it was great enough to analyze all this information, would be able to embrace in a single formula the movements of the largest bodies in the universe and those of the lightest atom: nothing would be uncertain for it, and the future, like the past, would be directly present to its observation.[53]

As F. S. C. Northrop points out, the quantum theory has penetrated the comfortable predictability of the state of mechanical systems.

> With respect to [the state of mechanical systems], the concept of probability and the attendant uncertainty enter theoretically and in principle; they do not refer merely to the operational and epistemological uncertainties and errors, arising from the finiteness of, and inaccuracies in, human behavior, that are common to any scientific theory and any experimentation whatsoever.[54]

To understand the shift in perspective regarding the dualistic conception of light, we must review the triumph of the classical "wave theory of light." When Thomas Young (1773-1829) attempted to revive the wave theory of light, the proponents of the old corpuscular theory (expounded by Newton) greeted his efforts with derision. Young's definitive experiment was quite simple. Aiming a beam of light through a small hole in a card towards a second card containing two small holes, Young found that light passed through the second card to a third in patterns which were partially overlapping. In the region of their overlapping, bright and dark stripes called "fringes" were formed. Since the twin sources of light emanating from the second card alternately vibrate together or in opposition (creating bright and dark areas) according to the relative distance from the two holes, the behavior of the light manifests wave characteristics.[55] A further development of the wave theory was the contribution of the Scottish physicist James Clerk Maxwell (1831-1879), who first proposed the idea that "radiation consists of electromagnetic waves caused by oscillations of electrons within the atom."[56] The spectrum of electromagnetic radiations is now depicted as ranging from very long radio waves through infrared, visible, ultraviolet, and x-rays, to the waves of highest energy—the gamma rays. These radiations overlap with no discrete boundaries, and range in their vibrational patterns over 67 octaves. (The human eye, by contrast, has a visible range of only one octave.)

In 1901 the German physicist Max Planck (1858-1947), having encountered discrepancies in the wave theory when analyzing the sharp spectral lines on a spectrogram and the mysterious behavior of incandescent solids, found that the accompanying phenomena of radiation were not continuous, and thus proposed that atoms absorb and emit energy in units which he called *quanta*. But these *quanta* really betray a two-fold character of radiation, "for the energy of a quantum was equal to a constant (called "Planck's constant") multiplied by the frequency; and frequency depends on the wave length, which we measure only in terms of wave theory."[57] Thus light appears to behave both as "corpuscles" and as "waves." In 1913 Niels Bohr (1885-1962) introduced the quantum theory of the atom—the well-known model in which electrons revolve about the nucleus in various "shells." In 1925, Heisenberg, contrary to Bohr's model, proposed a new theory of quantum mechanics based upon the measurable radiation absorbed and emitted by the atom. In the following year Erwin Schroedinger confirmed Heisenberg's mathematical results with a system of wave mechanics in which elementary particles behave like wave systems.[58] In Levi's words, Heisenberg demonstrated that the "measurement of the position of an electron by some device like a high frequency microscope will involve an exchange of momentum between the electron and the agency of measurement" which means "that our knowledge of the state of an atomic system will always involve a peculiar *indeterminacy*."[59]

In 1936 Niels Bohr introduced his *complementarity principle*, which postulates that "the description of a system in terms of position is complementary to the description of a system in terms of momentum."[60] Bohr's principle underscores the significance of both the particle and wave models as equally fundamental to an understanding of micronature. Norwood Hanson writes that with quantum theory

> it becomes a reasonable metaphysical possibility that nature is fundamentally indeterministic; that elementary particles are, ontologically, always in partially defined states; that they do not in any sense that is scientifically respectable and philosophically intelligible have both a precise position and an exact energy. This position lacks the aura of

familiarity and intellectual comfort that Newtonian determinism had come to possess by the nineteenth century, but it has what determinism in micromechanics completely lacks—an extensive observational support structured by an inferentially well-made theory.[61]

Between relativity theory and quantum mechanics, which have not yet been welded into a satisfactory unified "field theory," fundamental philosophical problems have been raised. The chief of these are summarized by Levi:

> The first is the metaphysical issue of whether our direct representation of physical reality in space and time shall ultimately use a model of continuity or discontinuity. The second is the epistemological issue of whether physics can grasp reality as what actually goes on in nature independent of the act of observation (and thus employ strict causality), or whether it must confine itself to making statistical predictions based upon the results of all measurements which can be carried out upon a physical system. In each case Einstein himself (somewhat quixotically according to his colleagues) favors the first alternative.[62]

Einstein has been frequently cited for his famous statement, "God does not play dice." Accordingly, since he was imbued with the ideals of classical mechanism, Einstein was resistant (in particular) to assertions of *indeterminacy* within nature itself. The fuller implications of the new physical theory are summarized below, paraphrasing Levi:[63]

1. Time does not exist independently, but only in relation to an observer whose empirical status is relative to the speed of light.

2. Hypothetical geometries do not describe "reality" as such, and are relevant only when applied by experimental method to specific space-time frames.

3. Scientific objectivity is mainly the province of formal mathematics. The space-time of every observer is subjective.

4. Quantitative measurement at the atomic level is always approximate, and describes only mean values.

5. The speed of light, which is finite, determines our perceptions. Thus we perceive cause followed by effect, or before followed by after. We do not perceive simultaneous events.

6. Space, time and causality do not exist *a priori*. Euclidean geometry does not describe quantum or astrophysical dimensions.

7. Classical materialistic and atomistic concepts are inadequate for describing quantum events.

8. Relativity theory necessitates conceiving physical reality as lines of force comprising a "field." Material objects are not ultimate constituents of reality, but dynamic moments of such a field.

The new cosmology and its accompanying physical theory have radically altered our picture of the world, and have left us with fundamental and unresolved questions of basic philosophical import, such as "what is matter?" Moreover, just as the conception of religious dogmas as *a priori* truths deriving from eternal absolutes, apart from temporal referents, has broken down in the light of historical and scientific study of religious origins, so too, the

Newtonian cosmos of absolute laws has broken down before contextualized and historicized nature. Levi concludes that it is ironic "that at the very moment when Spengler and Toynbee have been converting History into Nature, Einstein and Planck have been converting Nature into History."[64] Furthermore, the world of objects, mechanically and atomistically heterogeneous and discrete, has given way to a world in which "what we call an enduring object is merely a repetition of pattern sustained by a plurality of successive events."[65] We shall examine further consequences of the new cosmology in the section that follows.

THE NEW COSMOLOGY AND THE STATUS OF MAN

The pressing question which emerges from the perusal of the contours and laws of the cosmos as it is known to us today is, "what is the status of man in this new world?" Actually, we shall be approaching this question from somewhat different vantage points in the ensuing chapters. However, in the present context, we shall set forth a series of propositions which we will rather loosely call "losses" and "gains"—since some would construe what we shall call "losses" as "gains" and vice versa. In any case, these propositions will attempt to capture the main dimensions of the altered world picture in which man now "lives and moves and has his being."

"Losses"

1. *The new cosmology shatters the foundations of anthropocentrism, geocentrism, and heliocentrism, and depicts the center of the cosmos as far removed from our own galaxy.*

The Mount Palomar telescope has enabled us to penetrate 3000 million light years (20,000 million million million miles) into the cosmos. Once the cosmos, though very big, was clearly bounded by the "fixed stars," and the planets ran their course across the heavens. The ultimate dissolution of the Ptolemaic cosmos came with the revolutionary Copernican heliocentric hypothesis. But even though man's earth was removed far from the center of the universe, the *sun* remained; and man still was considered to occupy an exalted position. Yet with the decentralization of the sun, with the recognition that our solar system does not lie in the center of the galaxy, and with the realization that our galaxy itself is only one of a myriad of "island universes," the insignificance of man's cosmic status seems demonstrably underscored.*

Harlow Shapley describes the awe of his first discovery, early in his career, that the center of the universe was not to be found even in our own galaxy. At first the universe appeared to be eccentric, out of focus. But gradually, Shapley recalls, a new orientation emerged with the realization that

---

*For a graphic artistic depiction of the status of our solar system vis-a-vis the cosmos, the reader should refer to the May, 1974 *National Geographic,* pages 596 and 597.

the trivial observer is far from the magnificent, star-filled center! He is the peripheral, the ephemeral one. He is the incidental by-product of water, soil, air, and sunlight. He is off in a cosmic corner, invisible from the central nucleus around which billions of stars revolve and to which, we, like they, pay gravitational homage.[66]

Later, Shapley offers his opinion concerning man's lack of comprehension of new cosmological perspectives:

My simple, perhaps too simple, diagnosis of our failure to comprehend the universe is that we have been and still are bedeviled by a natural and persisting anthropocentricism.[67]

Doubtless Shapley is correct, and one might ask, does man wish to surrender this anthropocentricism? Indeed is it psychologically possible? For, as we have seen, man must ever filter the cosmos through the limited scope of the lenses of his own sensory equipment and its technological extensions. Yet the *awareness,* the *consciousness* that accompanies human being, must gradually change in the light of our new cosmic location. Freud once identified three separate blows to human narcissism.[68] The Copernican revolution exiled man from his central cosmic position. The Darwinian revolution established man's integral relationship to the animal kingdom (but we might add, established a model for progress). The psychoanalytic revolution revealed forces of control seemingly not under the dominion of human "narcissistic consciousness."[69] The cosmological revolution must surely be added as a fourth. But are we to diagnose these blows to the ego as fatal? We shall return to this question.

2. *The new cosmology disavows the objectivity of the material world and challenges the perspectives of simplistic realism.*

One of the most threatening aspects of the new cosmology for man's world security is the loss of the objectivity and solidity of the material world. Heisenberg discusses the reluctance of scientists to abandon their materialistic predispositions, and their attendant desire to return to the more simple and predictable world of classical physics.[70] It is no wonder that physicists, not to mention the average person, would prefer a world which may be regarded as apparently and objectively solid. Heisenberg recalls that the word "real" derives from the Latin word *res* which means "thing."[71] It is part and parcel of our desire for security (and perhaps, as Korzybski suggests, part of the structure of our language), to *reify* the world for its easy manipulation and categorization.

The loss of objective materialism is not only disconcerting to the common man, but a challenge to ideologies whose foundations require materialistic presuppositions, including in particular Marxism and capitalism. Heisenberg observes that Soviet scientists have challenged his work on dogmatic grounds; for certainly the introduction of *probability* and *uncertainty* into the material world brings no comfort to dialectical materialism!*

---

*The author is not informed as to the consensus of opinion regarding Heisenberg's theories among Soviet physicists at the present time.

Heisenberg asserts:

> The ontology of materialism rested upon the illusion that the kind of existence, the direct 'actuality' of the world around us, can be extrapolated into the atomic range. This extrapolation is impossible, however.[72]

Don K. Price cites a similar resistance to the emergence of modern physics:

> Physicists began to lose that kind of confidence [intellectual faith] in the nineteenth century as they went beyond the solid and predictable matter that seemed to correspond to the ordinary man's notion of what was real. The electromagnetic theory of Faraday and Maxwell, for example, made Kelvin uncomfortable because he could not devise a mechanical model of it. And as the physicist got inside the atom, he entered a universe to which some of the older generation never became reconciled; to them it seemed to contain phenomena that were for the first time, even in principle, unknowable and unmeasurable; and individual bits of inanimate matter seemed to behave without obeying the classical laws of cause and effect.[73]

The vast ideological and cosmic superstructures of mechanism, materialism and determinism have slowly eroded away during the last century. Price remarks that the idea of determinism now carries validity "only within a controlled experiment of reasonable size," and that discussion of cosmic determinism is all but meaningless.[74] Moreover, Heisenberg adds that

> It has been the thesis of several philosophical systems of the past that substance or matter cannot be destroyed. In modern physics, however, many experiments have shown that elementary particles, e.g., positrons and electrons, can be annihilated and transmuted into radiation.[75]

Although Heisenberg does not argue that these philosophies are thereby necessarily "wrong," he does propose that their models of reality are no longer adequate vehicles for our present understanding of the world.

For some, this disintegration of the material world is taken as an affirmation of the ultimacy of the "spiritual" or "psychic" realm. Says physicist Raynor Johnson:

> We must leave behind the ingrained common-sense view that physical objects are clear-cut insulated entities different in kind from our thoughts and memories. We must think rather of one psychic continuum . . .[76]

Johnson's suggestion is evocative within the framework of traditional philosophical debate; the question of a monistic philosophy of mind is one which now merits fresh consideration. From Johnson's perspective Whitehead's sophisticated ruminations about "actual entities" may betray an unconscious desire (British to the core) to retain common sense at all costs.

3. The new cosmology entails the loss of a static world order.

The new cosmological world of novae and supernovae presents the universe as a dynamic—indeed an explosive—panorama, contrasting widely with the stable mechanical cosmos of Enlightenment heritage. As Holton observes

> from the beginning to the present day, science has been shaped and made meaningful . . . by its thematic content. The reigning themata until about

the mid-nineteenth century have been expressed most characteristically by the mandala of a static, homocentric, hierarchically ordered, harmoniously arranged cosmos . . .[77]

Modern cosmological theory has "demythologized" man's stable home, casting him adrift in an unbounded sea both vast and restless. Holton suggests that, for the modern intellectual,

The ground is trembling under his feet; the simple interpretations of solidity, permanence, and reality have been washed away, and he is plunged into the nightmarish ocean of four-dimensional continua . . .[78]

Holton further acknowledges that one by one the great syntheses which have sustained Western thought have been uprooted. Consequently, modern man himself is uprooted and threatened to the core by the anomie of his cultural and cosmic situation.

At the present time no one authoritative model of the cosmic process commands uniform recognition among cosmologists. There are certain constants. Most astronomers agree that the primal state of the universe was "congested," and erupted in a magnificent explosion (commonly called the "Big Bang") which eventually resulted in the current systems of celestial bodies. Furthermore, it seems certain that the universe is presently expanding rapidly,[79] with the most distant galaxies apparently hurtling out into the vast reaches of the unknown at phenomenal speeds (as suggested by the "Doppler Effect"). If such an expansion continues indefinitely, at some remote point in the future, the universe will become virtually an empty "place." Others surmise that the universe may follow a cyclical pattern of expansion and contraction over vast eons, so that a final convergence of all matter results in an explosion comparable to the initial big bang, precipitating a new expansion in an endless repetitive drama.

Finally, Fred Hoyle (who has since retracted the theory) and his associates proposed the "Steady State Hypothesis." This hypothesis asserts that, although the universe does indeed expand, it does so only with the correlate of "continuous creation." Although at the farthest reaches of the universe galaxies may be disappearing at velocities approaching the speed of light, new matter in the form of hydrogen atoms is continuously appearing, and eventually collects into new stars and galaxies, maintaining a "constant density" in the universe. Although Hoyle's theory may appear bizarre, we must remember that the "Big Bang" theory of Canon Le Maitre also asserts a kind of "creatio ex nihilo" at a mythical cosmic beginning.[80] The fact of the matter is that we are living in a dynamic universe whose origins and goals remain to us looming mysteries, like the remote receding bounds of the cosmos itself, fading just beyond our perception at the horizons of our knowledge.

4. *The new cosmology implies a loss of absolute reference points.*

Classical physics hoped to establish for man an absolute frame of reference, external to himself and to the shifting shadows of history. Relativity theory, which indeed seeks to establish the independence of the laws of nature from man's mobile frame of reference, has nevertheless underscored both in theory and in fact the necessity of considering that frame in all cosmic calculations. Though relativity has succeeded in establishing the overt intent of classical physics, it has emptied that system of its absolute contents (and perhaps its secret intent, which was to posit man as a privileged observer who held the key to nature's absolutes). Relativity is a continuous reminder to man of his historical and cultural conditioning and location (not to mention his organic limitations). Even "pure" mathematics is a humanly-contrived system. Relativity replaces the substantial nature of space, time, and matter in Newtonian physics with a four-dimensional spatio-temporal continuum whose single constant is the speed of light. Thus, as Heisenberg acknowledges, what we call "future and past are separated by a finite time interval, the length of which depends on the distance from the observer. Any action can only be propagated by a velocity smaller than or equal to the velocity of light."[81]

5. *The new cosmology betokens the loss of immediate sensory experience as verification of physical law.*

Before the telescope, even the shape and structure of the cosmos could be determined through immediate sensory reference. Likewise,

> The old physics assumed that we observed directly real things. Relativity theory says that we observe "relations," and that these relations must be relations between physical concepts which are subjective.[82]

The world of modern cosmology is *not* directly apprehensible to man. Sophisticated and hermetic instruments and esoteric mathematical formulae have robbed the world of its *immediacy*. Heisenberg suggests that

> The philosophic thesis that all knowledge is ultimately founded in experience has in the end led to a postulate concerning the logical clarification of any statement about nature. Such a postulate may have seemed justified in the period of classical physics, but since quantum theory we have learned that it cannot be fulfilled.[83]

The quantum theory and Heisenberg's *uncertainty principle* both signify to us that empirical knowledge—at least in its more original sense as rooted in man's sensory equipment (and perhaps its technological extensions)—and its positivisitic claims are ultimately unfounded as regards any exhaustive and comprehensive understanding of nature. Both relativity and its location of man cosmically in space-time, and uncertainty, and its location of man organically in his perceptual field, have strong cultural implications (though many scientists balk at such "extrapolations"). At least we can assert that any human claim to absolute knowledge, infallible revelation, etc., cannot be substantiated by, or grounded in, nature. For nature's absolutes are *not* translucent to our gaze.

6. *The new cosmology entails the loss of any ultimate deterministic prognostication of events.*

As we have seen, concomitant with man's empirical limitations is the inability to make dogmatic future projections or prognostications (at least with regard to predictions rooted in mathematical formulae or natural law). Heisenberg asserts that

> . . . we can never know beforehand which limitations will be put on the applicability of certain concepts by the extension of our knowledge into the remote parts of nature, into which we can only penetrate with the most elaborate tools.[84]

This limitation is reinforced as we recall the loss of objective status of material reality. These two points (the inability to make dogmatic predictions and the loss of the objective status of material reality) are interlinked by Heisenberg as follows:

> . . . atoms are not *things;* the electrons which form an atom's shells are no longer things in the sense of classical physics, things which could be unambiguously described by concepts like location, velocity, energy, size. When we get down to the atomic level, the objective world in space and time no longer exists, and the mathematical symbols of theoretical physics refer merely to *possibilities, not to facts.*[85]

Thus in the invisible realm of subatomic particles physicists can cite only statistical probabilities; exact locations and measurements seem, at this point, impossible. Science here is robbed of its control. The oft-feared Frankenstein monster seems to have retreated at the sight of his own shadow.

Because of our finite location in one space-time system, final mechanical laws and their correlative absolute predictions are not within the bounds of present (or perhaps future) possibility. Heisenberg writes that:

> Consequently, only if the whole universe is included in the object of scientific knowledge can the qualifying condition "for an isolated system" be satisfied for even the weaker form of mechanical causation.[86]

7. *The new cosmology must be described as agnostic as opposed to gnostic.*

The previous propositions may be summarized by asserting that the new cosmology is necessarily agnostic. We have written of the secret triumph of Mithraism in the absorption of militancy by Christianity. In the context of the history of ideas, we could also speak of another secret victor—gnosticism. Christianity defeated gnosticism (which claimed to have direct knowledge of the inner-workings of the cosmos) only at the expense of absorbing its opponent's stance, i.e., by laying claim to a sure and absolute knowledge of the nature of things. In this way Christianity both prepared for and hindered the advance of science. The secret victory of gnosticism is the belief that finite man can know the hidden structure of the divine scheme. This naive pretense to a knowledge of absolutes is apparent from Augustine to Newton and beyond (and has imbued secular science with a faith that has yielded a great store of knowledge). Nonetheless Christianity hindered the advance of science (by serving as a medium of gnostic consciousness), insofar as the emergence of a genuine empiricism and historicism was a slow, painstaking, against-the-grain process. But one of the fruits of this process now seems to be a new sense of mystery and humility before the universe.

As we have seen, the new cosmology is agnostic in its conception of the empirical method. As Northrup writes:

> We know the object of scientific knowledge only by the speculative means of axiomatic theoretic construction or postulation; Newton's suggestion that the physicist can deduce our theoretical concepts from the experimental data being false . . .[87]

An additional exemplar of the agnosticism of contemporary cosmology (and its hypothetical nature) is the dual wave-particle depiction of the subatomic world. As Heisenberg explains, these two pictures are mutually exclusive, since a certain thing cannot be a particle (a substance confined to a very small volume) and a wave (a field spread out over a large space) at the same time.[88] Furthermore we ask

> What is an elementary particle? We say, for instance, simply "a neutron" but we can give no well-defined picture and what we mean by the word. We can use several pictures and describe it once as a particle, once as a wave or as a wave packet. But we know that none of these descriptions is accurate. Certainly the neutron has no color, no smell, no taste . . . If one wants to give an accurate description of the elementary particle—and here the emphasis is on the word "accurate"—the only thing which can be written down as description is a probability function . . .[89]

Thus, we are unable to attribute even the "quality of being" (in any traditional sense) to the subatomic world according to Heisenberg. With a cosmic eye (recalling our time-lapse photography model) we could see a mountain as a wave and the universe itself as a sparkler. It is doubtlessly the peculiarities of the sub-atomic space-time frame that create for our imagination a dualistic picture. It is conceivable that if we learn the proper coefficients *of* this space-time frame, the mystery will be unraveled. Even a new field theory and a new gnosticism will be fundamentally different from the old, since by necessity we presuppose the *relativity* of our space-time frame and the inevitability of contextual transposition for even an analogous understanding of another dimension. Heisenberg's uncertainty principle reminds us that nature in its fulness is furtive before our anthropomorphic glance, for there is

> a subjective element in the description of atomic events, since the measuring device has been constructed by the observer, and we have to remember that what we observe is not nature in itself but nature exposed to our method of questioning . . . In this way quantum theory reminds us, as Bohr has put it, of the old wisdom that when searching for harmony in life one must never forget that in the drama of existence we are ourselves both players and spectators.[90]

Moreover, although in the past man has rooted his hopes in great cosmic myths with their cosmogonic and eschatological credos and programmatic schema of world order and harmony, the new cosmology, which is not without its myths of beginnings and ends, acknowledges all such visions as hypothetical. In actuality, questions of cosmological import such as the beginning and end of the universe, and its outer limits and inner nature, remain largely speculative and unknown. As Heisenberg has shown us, even the fundamental law of motion for matter is unknown at this time, and thus it is presently impossible to derive the simple properties of elementary particles from that law.[91] It is likely that we must agree with Heisenberg's conclusion—as mystics have taught for centuries—

> Any concepts or words which have been formed in the past through the interplay between the world and ourselves are not really sharply defined with respect to their meaning; that is to say, we do not know exactly how far they will help us in finding our way in the world . . . we practically never know precisely the limits of their applicability. This is true even of the simplest and most general concepts like "existence" and "space and time." Therefore, it will never be possible by pure reason to arrive at some absolute truth.[92]

Thus, it is a fairly safe assumption that our world picture is always peculiarly agnostic and anthropocentric, dependent as it is upon our own observation and mythological constructs. Jean Charon observes that man "projects himself in the image that he believes he can see objectively in the world in which he lives."[93]

"Gains"

With the secularization of the sacred comes the sacralization of the profane.[94] The loss of a clearly definable, reasonably limited, cognitively apprehensible, and spiritually anthropocentric universe is not without certain compensations, which we will now explore.

1. The new cosmos, for what it has lost in localization and simplicity, has gained far more in majesty and its capacity to inspire awe.

The magnificence of the vast and illimitable cosmos, whose dimensions we have sketched, seems to render it far more worthy of our imagination and excitement than the locally devised and comfortable—if perhaps somewhat boring—world pictures of former ages.

2. Concomitantly, the cosmos can no longer be construed as "lifeless matter." The panorama of the known universe spans our vision as a dynamic, expanding, organic continuum—a vast, living macrocosm.

Materialism raped the world of its sacred mystery; and as Sam Keen has pointed out, man lost his capacity for wonder. But the burgeoning popularity of science fiction (still considered by purists to be a peripheral literary form) should suggest to us the evocative power, the new mythopoeic capacity of the new cosmology. Once more the universe becomes a frontier of adventure and wonder—a virtually infinite panorama in which a veritably endless repertoire of cosmic dramas may unfold.

3. *Man is perhaps not alone in the cosmos. Solipsistic models of the isolate self, propagated especially through Western individualistic and existentialist myths, may have cultural validity but lack cosmic verification.*

One interesting and remote, but conceivable "remedy" for our myopia as human beings, might be the establishment of contact with other intelligent life in the universe. Although this is the "stuff" of science fiction, it is not merely that. The famed Harvard astronomer Harlow Shapley estimates that twenty percent of the hundred thousand million billion stars within our calculations "are essentially identical with our sun in size, luminosity, and chemistry."[95] He concludes that habitable planets (according to human standards) are abundant, and that many of these have experienced evolutionary processes comparable to those which have led to the present state of earth life.[96] Ervin Laszlo argues in a similar vein:

> That we do not consider ourselves cosmic accidents, limited for some inscrutable reason to a small planet of a smallish solar system toward the edge of a galaxy, is not due to rampant mythologizing but to our belief that what has occurred in one place is bound to manifest itself somehow in another, provided the conditions are similar.[97]

Shapley arrives at his staggering estimate of a possible ten billion planets suitable for organic life similar to earth life by the following calculations:

> . . . let us say that only one star in a hundred is a single star, and of them only one in a hundred has a system of planets, and of them only one in a hundred earth-like planets is in that interval of distance from the star that we call the liquid-water belt (neither too cold nor too hot), and of them only one in a hundred has a chemistry of air, water and land something like ours— suppose all those five chances were approximately true; then only one star in ten billion would have a planet suitable for biological experimentation. But there are so many stars! We would still have, after all that elimination, *ten billion* planets suitable for organic life something like that on earth.[98]

At the same time such calculations seem to rob man of his uniqueness, they also paint a vast new horizon before which human consciousness inevitably must be expanded. The vision itself is mind-boggling.

Although actual contact with other intelligences is problematic, it is not inconceivable. The problems of such contact are three-fold. First of all, the great cosmic distances between stars seem to forbid rapid communication. A message sent in 1985 to a planet some thirty light years away would be received in 2015, and if a reply were immediately sent, would reach earth only in the year 2045. We have of course *already* been sending signals for over sixty years since the first radio broadcasts left our planet hurtling into space at the speed of light. The second problem of extraterrestrial communication is that we have no real clues as to where to beam our messages. Furthermore, there is the problem of recognition and decipherment of a message even if it is received: can we or they "break the code?" Aside from such speculations, the very possibility of such communication casts the human phenomenon in a new light, a divergent frame of reference. Although Harlow Shapley takes a "dim view" of the *human* organism existing elsewhere,[99] Jean Charon asserts:

> The most important steps in the evolution of the cosmos were the changing of radiation into matter, matter into life, and life into man. It follows that the human phenomenon is spread over the universe in the same way as the phenomena of life, matter and radiation.[100]

On the other hand, Carl Sagan, the Cornell University exobiologist who designed the famous communication plaque placed aboard Pioneer 10 (1972), although believing that communication with extraterrestrials is possible, labels chauvinistic the views that other intelligences must conform to humanoid expectations and that other planets must have earth-like conditions to cultivate life.[101] As a humorous—though telling—aside, illustrative of variegated world views informing contemporary reactions to the new cosmology, Sagan quotes two letters from the Los Angeles *Times* commenting on his plaque* designed for Pioneer 10:

> I must say I was shocked by the blatant display of both male and female sex organs on the front page of the *Times*. Surely this type of sexual exploitation is below the standards our community has come to expect from the *Times*.
>
> Isn't it enough that we must tolerate the bombardment of pornography through the media of film and smut magazines? Isn't it bad enough that our own space agency officials have found it necessary to spread this filth even beyond our own solar system?[102]

A second letter read:

> I certainly agree with those people who are protesting our sending those dirty pictures of naked people out into space. I think the way it should have been done would have been to visually bleep out the reproductive organs of the drawings of the man and the woman. Next to them should have been a picture of a stork carrying a little bundle from heaven.
>
> Then if we really want our celestial neighbors to know how far we have progressed intellectually, we should have included pictures of Santa Claus, the Easter Bunny, and the Tooth Fairy.[103]

The new cosmology has intensified and dramatized the continuing struggle between open and closed world views.

4. The universe, though not to be contained by man's limited models and formulations, seems on the whole to be homogeneous and isotropic.

According to Heisenberg, there are limited systems which "have already attained their final form."[104] Newtonian mechanics is adequate for the description "of all mechanical systems, of the motion of fluids and the elastic vibration of bodies," including acoustics, statics, and aerodynamics.[105] The theory of heat, seemingly unrelated to space-time variables, seems to have been formulated adequately. Thirdly, the phenomena of electricity and magnetism, including electrodynamics, special relativity, optics and

---

*Sagan's plaque included stylized depictions of the male and female forms.

magnetism, seem to be understood. Finally, Heisenberg feels that the quantum theory has achieved similar utility.[106] Some would challenge Heisenberg. For as Holton suggests, "the existing scientific concepts cover always only a very limited part of reality, and the other part that has not yet been understood is infinite."[107] We can also add Einstein's constant of the speed of light as a datum which seems to have universal validity. However, dogmatism about absolutes, however fruitful experimentally, is a dangerous business and does not stand up well in the light of history.

5. *The new cosmology, unlike old world pictures, cannot serve to legitimate particularistic ideologies.*

Throughout this work we have cited various instances of ideological analogues constructed according to the supposed pattern of cosmology. The best example remains the Neoplatonism of the medieval hierarchy, but there are innumerable others, including the fascist appeal to a quasi-religious cosmos. At the same time, institutional structures may mirror (a) tacit and hidden cosmic pattern(s), such as the strange coalition in modern techno-bureaucracy between a secularized hierarchy and the mechanical cosmos. But the new cosmology betrays no such system designed expressly for the legitimation of anthropomorphic institutions.

In the final chapter we will propose that the new cosmos and the organic world itself—of which we are a part—provide ample, conspicuous, and significant clues to the meaning of a healthily functioning organic order. But our appeal reverses former appeals; rather than *projecting* a presupposed order on the cosmos, we stand before the cosmos as alert and respectful apprentices waiting to learn our trade—waiting to hear the *cosmic logos*, not simply the echoes of our own prejudices. Admittedly as we have reiterated, the world which we perceive will inevitably bear our stamp—the shape which we as humans must perceive (albeit simply the shape of our limited sensory range). Nevertheless, within the limited freedom of an open empiricism we may learn from the cosmos certain pristine lessons which might help renew our institutions and enliven our ideas. We shall return to this point, but for now a single example will suffice. The magnificent pictures of earthrise taken from the moon exhibit the beauty, unity, and isolation of our local world. From this perspective alone we must recognize that all human beings are indeed fellow adventurers on our global spaceship. We are hurtling through space together and our destinies are inextricably interlinked. This simple and incontestable fact is a presupposition for all future global planning.

6. *The new cosmology, though rendering us agnostic before a vast and mysterious world, at the same time reveals to us that* res natura, *novelty and evolution are part and parcel of the cosmos.*

Former world pictures in the West have generally depicted the cosmos—and derivative cultural forms and *ethos*—as fixed, static and permanent. Although providing a sense of security, such sessile schemes have saturated Western culture with a sense of inevitability: *moira, ananke,* divine predestination, atomistic determinism, etc. Concomitantly, fatalism and pessimism have been persistently recurrent, if not dominant, in the West. The understanding that not only is history "natural," but that nature is historical, and the correlate principle of *indeterminacy* in nature, should teach us that the future is an *open*—and *not* a closed—book. James W. Dye, speaking of Berdyaev's debt to Jacob Boehme's *Ungrund,* writes:

> meonic freedom (from Greek *me,* "not"; and *on* "being"), [is] intended to designate ultimate reality as dynamic, nonobjective, indeterminate. The essence of every existent is process; and meonic freedom is nothing but the creative energy underlying the forms and directions of all processes. The *Ungrund* does not exist, but precedes being in the sense that it is the possibility of being, the negative ground essential for the realization of the novel, creative aspects of existence.[108]

Whether or not it is expedient to use metaphysical jargon, the fact is that evolutionary freedom *is* part of the world order, and to succumb to a sense of deterministic despair is cosmically, if not culturally, illegitimate—and certainly self-defeating. Such a perspective is *not* a rosy-eyed idealism, but in fact a thorough-going realism. If we may coin a term, what we are suggesting is *optimum realism,* which means maximizing the realistic potentials of our situation vis-a-vis the cosmos. A supportive truism is, "what has been can be." History and nature do not appear before us solely as the tragic residue of absurdity. Beauty, vitality, health, creativity, and fulfillment are equally a part of what is. To a great extent our destiny is still a matter of choice.

7. *One legacy of the new cosmology may be stated as follows: With the loss of anthropocentrism cosmic anonymity ensues.*

At first glance the loss of security of being center-stage in the cosmic drama seems to rob man of his uniqueness and his identity. But such a loss, however traumatic, is not necessarily deleterious. Just like a first-born or only child, mankind has considered itself worthy of special favors, marked by perfectionistic demands, and burdened with intense guilt and anxiety of failing to measure up before the all-seeing scrutiny. Ancient Israel carried within itself the self-conscious pride and fear of being Yahweh's first-born and chosen child. With the sense of election, she vascillated between feelings of smug superiority and exclusiveness in good times to empty despair and feelings of desertion—of being orphaned—during the tougher years. By analogy, we humans (in particular Western man, imbued with the Judeo-Christian sense of election) have considered ourselves the chosen ones of the cosmos, commanding legions of angels and devils doing battle for our souls.* Like an only child who all of his life has had preordained self-images and expectations, man has always operated within the rigid confines of clearly defined roles.

---

*Since the completion of this manuscript in 1975 the author has discovered Fritjof Capra's *The Tao of Physics*—a stimulating description of the encounter of contemporary physics with *Eastern* philosophy. Capra's volume is heartily recommended.

But now man has discovered his cosmic anonymity. Suddenly the spotlight has shifted from (what was once taken to be) center stage and focused vast eons away in some other cosmic quarters. Bereft of cosmic blessings, yet unhaunted by divine threats of damnation, for the first time we are faced with real decision. For the first time we are challenged to develop our *own* integrity. Not under the aegis of placating promises, nor under the dim shadow of some impending cosmic axe, we must now find ourselves.

If we are faced with the urgency of very real and pressing global social concerns, we are likewise reminded by the cosmos of the leisure of a single cosmic year within which the entire sweep of human history has come and gone. If we can calm down a bit and begin to create there is no one to number our days but ourselves.

FOOTNOTES

[1] Donald H. Menzel, *Astronomy* (New York: Random House, 1970), p. 50.

[2] Ibid., p. 51.

[3] Ibid., p. 52.

[4] Ibid., p. 55.

[5] Sir Isaac Newton, *Principia* in *Newton's Philosophy of Nature: Selections from His Writings*, ed. H. S. Thayer (New York: Hafner Publishing Co., 1953), pp. 42-44.

[6] Sir Isaac Newton, *Mathematical Principles of Natural Philosophy* in *Great Books of the Western World*, ed. R. M. Hutchins (Chicago: Encyclopedia Britannica, 1953), p. 8.

[7] Jean Charon, *Cosmology* (New York: World University Library/McGraw-Hill, 1970), p. 157.

[8] Ben Bova, *The New Astronomers* (New York: New American Library, Mentor, 1972) p. 22.

[9] *The Encyclopedia of Philosophy*, s.v. "John Herschel," by W. F. Cannon.

[10] Charon, P. 167.

[11] Ibid., pp. 167, 171.

[12] Ibid.

[13] Ibid.

[14] Ibid., p. 175.

[15] Ibid.

[16] Menzel, p. 59.

[17] Ibid., p. 61.

[18] Ibid., pp. 63-67.

[19] Harlow Shapley, *The View from a Distant Star* (New York: Dell/Laurel, 1967), p. 38.

[20] Ibid., p. 62.

[21] Albert William Levi, *Philosophy and the Modern World* (Bloomington: Indiana University Press, 1970), p. 245.

[22] Ibid.

[23] Ibid.

[24] Ibid., p. 246.

[25] Lincoln Barnett, *The Universe and Dr. Einstein* (New York: Bantam Books, 1973), pp. 20-21.

[26] Alan Watts, *Beyond Theology* (New York: Vintage Books, 1973), pp. 218-19.

[27] Bertrand Russell, *Religion and Science* (London: Oxford University Press, 1970), pp. 35-36.

[28] Ibid.

282

[29] Don K. Price, "The Established Dissenters," in *The Scientific Estate* (Cambridge: Belknap Press, 1965), rpt. in *Science and Culture,* ed. Gerald Hoton (Boston: Beacon Press, 1967), p. 132.

[30] Levi, p. 249.

[31] Barnett, p. 40.

[32] Ibid., p. 50.

[33] Leopold Infeld, *Albert Einstein* (New York: Scribner's, 1950), pp. 23-24.

[34] Ibid., p. 24.

[35] Ibid., p. 25.

[36] Ibid., p. 26.

[37] Barnett, p. 42.

[38] Ibid., pp. 42-43.

[39] Ibid., p. 45.

[40] Infeld, p. 34.

[41] Levi, p. 252.

[42] Barnett, p. 48.

[43] Ibid.

[44] George Gamow, *One, two, three . . . infinity* (New York: Viking, 1970), pp. 101-02.

[45] Konrad Krauskopf and Arthur Beiser, *Fundamentals of Physical Science* (New York: McGraw-Hill, 1966), p. 255.

[46] Albert Einstein, *Out of My Later Years* (New York: Philosophical Library, 1950), p. 50.

[47] Ibid., p. 51.

[48] Ibid.

[49] Krauskopf and Beiser, p. 229.

[50] Barnett, p. 84.

[51] Krauskopf and Beiser, pp. 229-30.

[52] Barnett, p. 85.

[53] Jeremy Bernstein, *Einstein* (New York: The Viking Press, 1973), p. 30.

[54] Werner Heisenberg, *Physics and Philosophy* (New York: Harper Torchbooks, 1962), p. 8.

[55] Menzel, p. 75.

[56] Ibid., p. 76.

[57] Ibid., p. 77.

[58] Levi, p. 257.

[59] Ibid., pp. 257-58.

[60] Ibid., p. 259.

[61] *The Encyclopedia of Philosophy,* s.v. "Philosophical Implications of Quantum Mechanics," by Norwood Hanson.

[62] Levi, pp. 264-65.

[63] Ibid., pp. 268-69.

[64] Ibid., p. 271.

[65] Ibid.

[66] Shapley, p. 12.

[67] Ibid., p. 36.

[68] David Bakan, *The Duality of Human Existence* (Boston: Beacon Press, 1966), p. 37.

[69] Ibid.

[70] Heisenberg, pp. 128-29.

[71] Ibid., p. 130.

[72] Ibid., p. 145.

[73] Price, p. 127.

[74] Ibid., p. 129.

[75] Heisenberg, p. 119.

[76] Raynor C. Johnson, *Nurslings of Immortality* (New York: Harper Colophon, 1957), p. 127.

[77] Gerald Holton, *Thematic Origins of Scientific Thought* (Cambridge: Harvard University Press, 1973), pp. 35-36.

[78] Gerald Holton, "Modern Science and the Intellectual Tradition," *Science* 131 (April 22, 1960): 1187-1193, rpt. in *The New Scientist: Essays on the Methods and Values of Modern Science*, ed. Paul C. Obler and Herman A. Estrin (New York: Anchor, 1962), pp. 33-34.

[79] Charon, p. 199.

[80] Menzel, pp. 270-72.

[81] Heisenberg, p. 115.

[82] W. C. Dampier, *A History of Science and Its Relation to Philosophy and Religion* (Cambridge: Cambridge University Press, 1966), p. 491.

[83] Heisenberg, p. 85.

[84] Ibid.

[85] Arthur Koestler, *The Roots of Coincidence* (New York: Vintage Books, 1973), p. 51.

[86] Heisenberg, pp. 24-25.

[87] F. S. C. Northrup, "Introduction," in Heisenberg, p. 9.

[88] Heisenberg, p. 49.

[89] Ibid., p. 70.

[90] Ibid., p. 58.

[91] Ibid., p. 72.

[92] Ibid., p. 92.

[93] Charon, p. 10.

[94] The secularization/sacralization process is evident in a continuing series of encounters since the Middle Ages. In his superb essay, "Man, God, and the Church in the Age of the Renaissance," Roland H. Bainton illustrates how the Hellenizing secularizing components of the Renaissance entailed an extension of the sacral domain (and a modification of its meaning) into arenas formerly relegated to the profane. (Erasmus is a good example.) Concomitantly, in the Reformation "return" to Hebraic-biblical legitimations, the broader vision of an Erasmus was challenged. See Roland H. Bainton, "Man, God, and the Church in the Age of the Renaissance," in *The Renaissance: Six Essays* (New York: Harper Torchbooks, 1962), pp. 77-96. Another example is Sir Isaac Newton, whose new mechanical system was both a secularization and a sacralization process. J. Bronowski, *The Common Sense of Science* (New York: Vintage Books, n.d.), writes of Newton's order, "From the moment that it was seen that this lightning flash of clarity was sufficient — 'God said "Let Newton be" and there was light'—from this moment it was felt that here plainly was the order of God. And plainly therefore the mathematical method was the method of nature, a model for all scientific orders" (p. 47). Finally Albert Einstein, *Out of My Later Years*, in a discussion of modern tensions between science and religion, illustrates this principle. Einstein argues that to give up the anthropomorphic belief in a personal deity (secularization) does not necessitate abandoning the real intent of religion: "If it is one of the goals of religion to liberate mankind as far as possible from the bondage of egocentric cravings, desires, and fears, scientific reasoning can aid religion in yet another sense . . . It [science] also seeks to reduce the connections discovered to the smallest possible number of mutually independent conceptual elements. It is in this striving after the rational unification of the manifold that it encounters its greatest successes, even though it is precisely this attempt which causes it to run the greatest risk of falling prey to illusions. But whoever has undergone the intense experience of successful advances made in this domain, is

284

moved by *profound reverence* for the rationality made manifest in existence. By way of the understanding he achieves a far-reaching emancipation from the shackles of personal hopes and desires, and thereby attains that humble attitude of mind towards the grandeur of reason incarnate in existence . . . This attitude, however, appears to me to be *religious,* in the highest sense of the word. And so it seems to me that science not only purifies the religious impulse of the dross of its anthropomorphism but also contributes to a *religious spiritualization of our understanding of life*" (p. 29).

⁹⁵Shapley, p. 43.

⁹⁶Ibid., p. 63.

⁹⁷Ervin Laszlo, *The Systems View of the World* (New York: George Braziller, 1972) p. 59.

⁹⁸Shapley, p. 62.

⁹⁹Ibid., p. 58.

¹⁰⁰Charon, p. 231.

¹⁰¹Carl Sagan, *The Cosmic Connection: An Extra-terrestrial Perspective* (New York: Dell, 1973), p. 41 ff.

¹⁰²Ibid., p. 25.

¹⁰³Ibid.

¹⁰⁴Heisenberg, p. 98.

¹⁰⁵Ibid.

¹⁰⁶Ibid., pp. 99-100.

¹⁰⁷Holton, p. 201.

¹⁰⁸*The Encyclopedia of Philosophy,* s.v., "Nicolas Berdyaev," by James W. Dye.

CHAPTER ELEVEN

COSMOLOGY AS ESCHATOLOGY

OUR WORLD pictures are the *programs* we have for the future—the "maps," the "working" or "effective" myths which establish cultural latitudes, longitudes, and contours. But we must distinguish between tacit beliefs and overt creeds, between apparent desires and hidden intentions. How we imagine ("image"-ine) the future—the shape we give it—shapes us also as the future impinges upon each present moment. But many of our most basic beliefs and our most potent imaginings, just because of their subtlety and pervasiveness, elude our grasp. Thus our ostensible conscious wishes, if in conflict with our hidden assumptions, may seem impotent indeed. For each of us is located upon the maps of culture and history, and many of its tacit shapes have become our own. Moreover, as we bear the particular stamp of our own social and biographical location, it is only with persistent, vigorous effort that we may establish consciously and clearly the *general* structures and implications of our own consciousness. In addition, it is only with greater persistence and effort that we are able to extrapolate ourselves to the extent that our actions reflect a modicum of freedom and initiative. For an effective role in shaping even our local vicinity we require a *perspective* which, through exposing underlying structures of consciousness, illumines the interplay of our psyches and culture.

"Cosmology as eschatology" implies that the frame of reference which is our Alpha (our root beliefs, whether recognized or unrecognized) predisposes the hidden content of our Omegas. We project our root assumptions through the dialectical[1] process of society. In a legitimate sense the future is as tangible as our present presuppositions. We are the (albeit unwitting) agents of our own *eschaton*. The hues of future horizons are mixed on the palettes of present consciousness. If our legacy is to be a conscious, intentional "will" for the future, the understanding of cosmological assumptions implicit in eschatological pictures is mandatory.

We have indirectly approached the theme of cosmology as eschatology where we have attempted to illustrate how present institutions and ideologies reflect historical structures of consciousness. The task of this chapter is to examine contemporary cosmology in the light of its prominent structures of consciousness which are suggestive of pictures of the future. The extensiveness of the topic again demands critical limitations of scope. Two fruitful sources for probing future projections of cosmology (and its technological expressions)—science fiction and futurology—must be regrettably ignored. The reader is advised that these sources abound in (often traditional) eschatological imagery. In the present context we will seek structures of consciousness and accompanying attitudes which underly eschatological expectations of the new cosmology. We will suggest tentatively how a new eschatology might be appropriate to the new cosmology.

HISTORICAL ORIGINS OF ESCHATOLOGICAL SCHEMES

In chapter five we examined two early Christian eschatologies which define the status of the "unbelieving world." The apocalyptic tradition, mediated via Post-Exilic Judaism, established a clear dichotomy between this present age controlled by demonic powers and the messianic age to come (present spiritually to "believers"). This historical-cosmic scheme assumes that all mankind is divided into two camps—the unbelieving world, constituting the larger bulk of mankind under the sway of cosmic forces of darkness, and the believing Christian world, a stalwart "remnant" representing the cosmic forces of light. Apocalypticism has imbued the West with a strong suspicion of history and a tacit "faith" that the present earth and heavens are doomed to ultimate violent conflagration—the physical manifestation of the final spiritual conflict between divine and demonic forces.

The second cosmological picture derived from the Hellenistic *oikoumene* (which influenced both Pharisaism and Stoicism, each of which developed some sense of world brotherhood). The extension of the evangel to Gentile "Godfearers" (as well as to Hellenistic Jews) by Paul and other early Christian missionaries is an obvious instance of this more universal perspective. In both Ephesians and Colossians, and probably Romans 9-11, Paul (or in the case of Ephesians and Colossians, probably disciples of Paul), seem(s) to entertain hopes for the eventual salvation both of all mankind and the cosmos itself:[2]

> ... a hardening has come upon part of Israel, until the full number of the Gentiles come in, and so all Israel will be saved ... For God has consigned all men to disobedience that he may have mercy upon all.
> (Romans 11:25,26,32)
> For he has made known to us ... the mystery of his will ... a plan for the fulness of time, to unite all things in him, things in heaven and things on earth ... For he is our peace, who has made us both one, and has broken down the dividing wall of hostility ... To me ... this grace was given ... to make *all* men see what is the plan of the mystery hidden for ages ...
> (Ephesians 1:9,10; 2:14,15; 3:8,9)
> And through him [God intends] to reconcile to himself all things, whether on earth or in heaven, making peace by the blood of his cross ... Him we proclaim, warning every man ... that we may present every man mature *(telos)* in Christ.
> (Colossians 1:20,28)

In Colossians 3:11, "Here there cannot be Greek and Jew, circumcised and uncircumcised, barbarian, Scythian, slave, free man, but Christ is all, and in all," the universal *logos* (interpreted as Christ) is shared by all men. In spite of this more utopian and optimistic outlook in the New Testament, it is not too surprising that apocalypticism has dominated the West. Christianity remained for some years a repressed minority, and the graphic imagery and vindictive spirit of apocalyptic literature seemed to strike a more responsive chord, appealing in times of persecution to the sense of helplessness, impotency, and despair of this world.[3] The ecumenical vision, appearing from time to time among sensitive souls such as St. Francis, gained fresh impetus with the triumph of evolution in the nineteenth century, but has retreated before the tumultuous twentieth century.

A final and malignant element added to apocalypticism's triumph: the ontological dualism of Pythagorean-Platonic-gnostic heritage. The world became not only the temporal stage upon which spiritual warfare raged, but also the impure realm antipathetical to the spiritual realm of pure being. As the last and lowest emanation of the cosmos, the material order (including and in particular the body) was regarded as the most virulent medium of demonic power.

In considering eschatological projections attached to the new cosmology, our age seems faced with a set of options—the apocalyptic and the ecumenical—similar to those entertained by early Christianity.

IMAGES OF THE END: EMPIRICISM AND THE ESCHATON

Gerald Holton observes that this age has witnessed the dissolution of great syntheses which have provided an "intellectual and moral home" for Western man: notably the world views "of the Book of Genesis, of Homer, of Dante, of Milton, of Goethe";[4] and, we might add, the cosmologies of Ptolemy, of Augustine, of Pseudo-Dionysus, of Copernicus and of Newton.

The latest model of the cosmos to enter its demise is the deterministic, mechanistic universe of modern science. This model, when coupled with the Western sense of autonomous ego, bore paradoxically the promise of freedom and the terror of helplessness, a sense of predictability and control and the threat of determinism. On the one hand, like a machine the cosmos could be understood and, within reasonable limits, tinkered with (an attitude prominent in modern technology, as Berger, Berger and Kellner have pointed out in *The Homeless Mind*). On the other hand, the cosmos appeared to be quite stubborn in its inexorable course—insensitive to the plight of man or of the world. The empirical method, which in early modernity may have been understood mainly as a means of penetrating the inner workings of the cosmic machine, became a virtual ethos in itself; it emerged as a kind of world view quite disparate from the comfortable gnosticism (which Newton himself seemed alternately to propagate and to disavow) of Newtonian rationalism. We recall Cassirer's useful distinction between seventeenth and eighteenth century conceptions of reason:

> The whole eighteenth century understands reason . . . not as a sound body of knowledge, principles, and truths, but as a kind of energy, a force which is fully comprehensible only in its agency and effects.[5]

Cassirer identifies two particular functions of this "force": the power to bind and the power to dissolve.

> It dissolves everything merely factual, all simple data of experience and everything believed on the evidence of revelation, tradition and authority; and it does not rest content until it has analyzed all these things into their simplest component parts . . .[6]

Following this dissolution is the work of binding or building, the assemblage of the scattered parts into a new structure; man by reason has now gained "complete knowledge of the structure of its product."[7] Paradoxically this twin-pronged function of empirical reason proved the undoing of the world machine. Einstein himself, in the interest of salvaging a total cosmos in which cosmic premises could be established independently of man's limited space-time frame, signaled the death knell of Newton's absolutes and the mechanical system built upon them. Though the status of cosmic absolutes (in any case apprehensible only relative to man) continues to be debated, the quantum theory and Heisenberg's uncertainty principle have left the second task of Cassirer's two-fold function, i.e., binding, on very uncertain grounds. In general, "pure" empiricism has left us to ponder the wave-particle duality, quasars, pulsars, and a host of other odd phenomena (such as the less certain, but ominous black holes).

In addition, knowledge of what appears to be the most basic law of the cosmos, $E = mc^2$, should bring us a sense of gnostic security; ironically this knowledge constitutes the most effective ideological weapon of terror since eternal damnation. As we are all too aware, hidden behind the deceptive simplicity of this mathematical cipher is the greatest force of destruction* heretofore known. Here apocalypticism has come into its own. Yet if this demonic threat teaches us to resolve world conflicts by non-violent means we will have won a very great victory.

Thus scientific empiricism seems an anomalous paradox indeed. It has dissolved the certain grounds of old cosmologies. It must surely appear to many to be a chief apocalyptic tool of the devil. Coupled with classical mechanism, empiricism has created a vast technology (the ethos of which is a strange admixture of ancient and modern). Others see the exponential expansion of technology as the over-arching demonic specter of our age. Yet the empirical method has opened the door to an unprecedented knowledge of both history and the universe, and likewise to an unprecedented awareness

---

*and of course, *construction,* if we acquire the wisdom to so use it.

of our own ignorance and limitations. Perhaps by a kind of *via negativa,* empiricism has revealed to us routes which a new world view must travel.

TECHNOLOGY, COSMOLOGY AND APOCALYPTICISM

The fundamental apocalyptic truism is that man's greatest enemy is himself. Harlow Shapley, concluding a discussion of possible threats to man's future, suggests that we should *not* look for disaster from the stars, instellar dust, the sun's radiation or its diminution, from the deviation of the earth from its orbit, or from chemical or other natural agents in the earth's land, air and water. He agrees that "the real danger . . . is man himself;" for it is man who "goes on fighting thoughtless, futile wars" and behaves "in a fashion more beastly than angelic."[8] Likewise, it is man who has polluted the waters and the atmosphere, who has endangered various species of animal life, and who threatens the supply of foodstuffs and energy resources of the world. Impelled by very real socio-economic interests and ideological concerns which cannot be ignored, it is nevertheless man who retains the destructive polarity of "we" versus "them"—the hostilities of mutually exclusive nationalistic, territorial, or provincial concerns. Man himself remains the chief apocalyptic agent.

A popular myth of the technological age is the story of *Frankenstein.* The myth has two forms, each of which is pertinent to apocalyptic visions attached to technology. The story originally developed by Mary Shelley in her novel *Frankenstein* recounts the work of a brilliant young Dr. Frankenstein who "discovers the secret of life through the study of electricity, galvinism and chemistry,"[9] and creates a mechanical monster. In Ms. Shelley's novel, the monster becomes the superior, not only in strength, but also in intelligence. A more contemporary example of the theme of the mechanical creation becoming master occurs in Arthur Clarke's *2001,* where "Hal"—the Computer which controls all systems on a space flight bound for Jupiter—usurps authority over the hapless astronauts. In each case man creates an intelligent mechanical monster which rebels against its creator. Such a spectacle seems to reflect a technological and secularized version of the archetypal Judeo-Christian myth of the Fall, where it is feared that man will become "like gods, knowing good and evil." (Genesis 3:5)

But these images are blatant and dramatic, whereas the real threat of the machine's rule over man is far more subtle. Not only is the subjugation of man to technology somewhat anti-dramatic, it is frankly just plain boring. The scenario is man's reduction to a mindless functionary whose inner self and creativity are arrested by the systematic routinization of all facets of life, now governed by machines or machine-like processes. This image of technologized (or similarly, "organization") man has been thoroughly exploited by contemporary literature. But it is this more mundane image of man and technology to which the second form of the Frankenstein myth, the popular cinematic version, seems more relevant. Here the monster is not an intelligent, but an unreasoning, dumb monster who, maltreated by Frankenstein's assistant, wreaks vengeance and havoc upon the innocent peasant townsfolk. This cinematic version approaches the truth that machines are *not*—even at their most sophisticated—creative beings who have expressed themselves in art, music, philosophy, religion, literature, and science. Moreover, it is the *dumb* monster of the machine, however apt in learning its task, that triumphs over man by eliminating human creativity in the service of mechanized competence. Man, the creator of the technological monster, is threatened with violence to his creative autonomy and culture. Just as Marx envisaged man becoming slave to the products of his own labor, man's technological creation also threatens to enslave him. As Harry Levin says, "man himself becomes less and less a culture-bearer, more and more a codifier of programs, and manipulator of electronics."[10] Oscar Handlin observes that "the machine, the factory, and the city became identified (in the rise of technology) as a single entity oppressive to man."[11] Man as a cultural being—a "species being"—is redefined as an electronic coefficient or integer; he has become reified to himself.

A second mythical figure can be enlisted as a more ominous symbol of technological apocalypse—the Faustian *Mephistopheles*. When Mephistopheles defines himself to Faust, he says, "I am the spirit of negation." The ultimate act of Mephistophelian technology is the atomic bomb—the rending of matter into pure energy in an apocalyptic blast. Mephistopheles, the Spirit of Negation, sounding a secret Siren's call, beckons us (as Freud has suggested) to return to the *womb*—the womb (as it seems) of pure nothingness.*

From the more immediate and present threats, we move to visions of a remote cosmic end. Contemporary cosmological theory posits two contradictory visions or myths of the end. Each assumes that the universe is a finite system. There are some few dissidents who believe that the universe is infinite, and thus approach the question of cosmic directions in an entirely different manner.

The first of these visions recalls the mythical replication of prototype in antitype, or alpha in omega. Jean Charon writes that "if theory and observation are to be trusted, the universe began in an apocalyptic state not unlike that of an atomic explosion—apart from the fact that there was no matter."[12] This legendary "Big Bang," first proposed by Canon LeMaitre (1894-1966), assumes that approximately ten to twenty billion years ago a primeval "atom" or some unknown phenomenally-dense condition erupted in a violent explosion; the ostensible effects are still measurable (e.g., in terms

---

*We might also recall here the ancient Orphic equation of womb and tomb (*soma = sema*). To what extent is this nuclear self-destructiveness the very quintessence of the ascetic tradition (of ontological dualism)?

of an appropriate black body radiation temperature of 3° absolute throughout the universe) and still visible (in the rapidly expanding fringes of the known universe). A final explosion in the estimation of some will rival the scenario of the "Big Bang." Informed by relativity theory and assuming a finite radius of the universe, this interpretation envisions the expansion of the cosmos reaching a terminal point when it will then begin to contract. The galaxies will enventually converge in a monumental cataclysm. At this point the temperature will have risen to thousands of millions of degrees and all life will have vanished. Matter will be converted into radiation, and everything will return to a primal state of light, with a volume of approximately nil.[13] Some cosmologists see this entire process as recurrent; the universe becomes a pulsating affair and its history is essentially cyclical. When depicted as a one-time unique process the history of the cosmos simulates the Judeo-Christian historical model. Represented as cyclical it recalls the Greco-Roman cosmic scheme.

There are several objections to the apocalyptic-cataclysmic end. The 3° temperature may suggest, following Einstein's intuitions, that the universe is like an expanding balloon—finite and spherical.[14] But this is only one interpretation of the data. Furthermore, Charon cites the "non-reversibility of time,"[15] which he believes evident empirically from two sources: the history of a star and the history of a living cell:

> The mechanisms of living matter remain totally inexplicable in the light of simple physical and chemical laws if we assume that time is reversible— that is, if we do not agree that the universe is evolving; it began 10,000 million years ago and will end up in a different state in the future.[16]

Thus contrary to the linear and cyclical myths equating primal and terminal explosions, Charon proposes an evolutionary model. The chief feature of this cosmic model is the irreversibility of evolutionary processes and the inevitability—albeit unpredictability—of future metamorphoses.

But there is a second myth of the end often linked to the so-called "Big Bang." The universe is expanding. If it continues to do so beyond an imagined terminal radius where some say it should begin to shrink, the individual stars and galaxies will grow farther and farther apart; the universe will become "less and less dense," and will "finally develop into an essentially empty, dead world."[17] This myth portrays an eventual isolation of all matter by sheer trajectory into infinity. Such a termination seems strangely parallel to another Western myth—the "existential predicament"—the solitary ego contemplating its solipsistic futility.

For both the pulsating universe and the infinitely expanding universe the Second Law of Thermodynamics is of critical significance. This law, formulated by Rudolph Clausius and William Thomson (Lord Kelvin), states that "the entropy of an isolated system never diminishes."[18] Entropy (derived from the Greek *he trope*, "a transformation," or *entrope* "turning") refers to an irreversible process of a thermodynamic system in which the distribution of energy reaches a point where energy is no longer available for "work." Therefore, the Second Law suggests that every physical system is losing heat energy from transformations within that system. Because of the random nature of molecular activity in the state which we call "heat," heat energy is inevitably wasted, escaping into cooler external environs around a physical system (such as heat escaping from a room in cold weather). In the case of an infinitely expanding universe, the implications of entropy may be stated as follows:

> The law implies that the universe in the past had more energy in forms capable of doing work than it has at present. It seems to imply also that the distant future will bring a time when there is no energy but heat energy, heat energy evenly distributed so that no part of the universe is warmer than another, the so-called "heat death" of the universe.[19]

However, the continuous increase in entropy can apply only as long as the universe is conceived as a uniform or expanding system. If the pulsating model of the cosmos is correct, when the universe is contracting entropy is minimized, and the exact opposite conditions of the predictions of the Second Law would occur.

If the universe continues to expand until it is virtually "empty," and the attendant "heat death" of maximum entropy occurs, T. S. Eliot's suggestion that the universe may end "not with a bang, but with a whimper," may be most appropriate. Such a cosmic fate is contravened by the model of a pulsating cosmos. There is no conclusive evidence for either model at this time. E. A. Milne in 1931 challenged the entropy theory on the grounds that the universe cannot be conceived as an isolated system: on the one hand the rest of the universe is always present (whereas the Second Law logically requires that it be fragmented into two or more systems); and on the other, there is nothing physical outside of the universe (so far as we know) to constitute a physical system to which it is related.[20]

Furthermore, G. T. Whitrow writes that, with regard to the whole universe, "there is no evidence that the law of entropy increase applies on this scale," and therefore

> The various doubts that have arisen concerning the concept of world entropy have serious repercussions on any attempt to derive the irreversibility of time from the Second Law of Thermodynamics.[21]

This statement, of course, applies to the "heat death" of the universe, but not to Charon's "irreversibility of time" which is derived by analogy from evolutionary processes, and portrays the universe as destined towards an undetermined end.

Moreover, those who follow an evolutionary model seem to favor some purposeful (but not predetermined) end, characterized by order as opposed to disorder. Teilhard de Chardin (who is informed by religious presuppositions) is a case in point. A similar, but secular point of view is proposed by Lancelot

Law Whyte. Whyte, like Milne, argues that there is no evidence for cosmic entropy. But, Whyte suggests, there is abundant evidence for a cosmic *morphic* process ("morphic" meaning "generating order, form, or symmetry in ordinary 3D space").[22] He asserts:

> The entropic tendency merely disturbs, while the morphic builds up structures, replicates them, develops them from egg to adult, and reproduces them. So the morphic tendency has a remarkable privilege over the entropic: it leaves cumulative records, while the entropic has nothing to show for itself, being merely a randomizer or disturbing agent. One might almost say, misusing language slightly: the morphic tendency leaves a memory; the entropic doesn't.[23]

The French cosmologist, Jean Charon, shares Whyte's faith in a cosmic ordering tendency, and concludes his work on this mystical note:

> The universe is language; it is thought; it is, finally, the Word. All through the progress of cosmological thought, we have been able to make a better appreciation of the profound significance of the intuition 'In the beginning was the Word.'[24]

Further relevant data should be considered in the question of cosmic ends. In 1960, strange "quasi-stellar objects" (quasars) with strong radio emission were discovered. These objects seem to be neither stars nor ordinary galaxies. Their blue color indicates that their heat is intense, and their large red shifts seem to indicate that they are at the remote edges of the known universe, racing away at speeds of (apparently) up to 90% of the speed of light.[25] Another possible cause for the red shift, posited by Einstein,[26] is that light emitted in an intense gravitational field exhibits the red shift. Thus we could be viewing "the gravitational field of an extremely massive object."[27] Therefore, though some would suggest that quasars seem to be the most distant objects yet observed, others consider them to be more local. Hoyle has postulated that quasars are "superstars" or "star clusters" whose red shifts are indicative of intense gravitational fields as these objects are collapsing in upon themselves.[28] Still others envisage quasars as "a sort of 'shrapnel' fired out of exploding galaxies."[29] In any case, the most baffling question regarding the quasars is the source of their remarkable energy. One hypothesis suggests that gravitational collapse from the collision and explosion of "billions of stars in the galaxy's core as they are squeezed together"[30] creates this phenomenally potent display.

Theoretical explanations of galactic explosions are numerous. One of the more stunning and provocative theories is the theory of anti-matter, first suggested by P. A. M. Dirac in 1931.[31] In 1932 the anti-electron, called *positron* for its positive charge, was discovered. Since that time anti-particles have been found corresponding to all kinds of atomic particles, including protons, neutrons, mesons and neutrinos.[32] The encounter of a particle of matter and a particle of anti-matter results in an explosion in which both are annihilated and pure energy is produced. Although anti-matter has been witnessed only for "fleeting fractions of a second" in the laboratory, "matter/anti-matter annihilation may be an energy source for the quasars and exploding galaxies."[33] The status of anti-matter is uncertain; theoretically the model seems to parallel the dual symmetry of much of the known physical universe.

Among other apocalyptic portents in the universe are two theoretical bodies of great interest: the neutron star and the black hole. The neutron star is ostensibly a collapsed massive star resulting from a supernova explosion. The fantastic nature of the neutron star is its remarkably small size and incredible density. After all matter has been converted to neutrons in the process of the violent collapse, the star is squeezed into a diameter of 10 to 100 kilometers, with a density of 15 billion tons per cubic centimeter—a measurement which defies the imagination.[34] "A teaspoon of a neutron star material would weigh a billion tons"—the equivalent of some 200 million elephants.[35] Furthermore, the crust of the tiny star would be made of crystalline material 10^{15} times tougher than steel.[36] Neutron stars are believed to exist in the universe in the form of rapidly rotating objects called "pulsars" because of their emission of radio signals at precisely-timed blinking intervals.

The neutron star, already bizarre beyond any practical comprehension, is surpassed only by the black hole. The black hole, with a density exceeding 150 billion tons per cubic centimeter, surpasses even the neutron star in its gravitational collapse.[37] Under these unimaginable conditions, nothing can escape from its gravitational field, not even light. Obviously such an invisible phenomenon cannot be known directly—but only by its *effects*. It is postulated that some black holes may be collapsed mates of binary stars, and thus be detectable by the influence which they exert on their companion, i.e., powerful X-ray activity which may be caused by exploding gases drawn from the visible star just before the gases are sucked into the blackness. Evidence for one black hole exists in the form of

> a powerful but invisible X-ray object called Cygnus X-1, about 8,000 light-years away. It is estimated to be much greater than three times the mass of the sun, too massive for a neutron star. And it revolves with a super-giant star known as HDE 226868, from which gas clouds seem to be swirling around and disappearing into the invisible partner . . .[38]

The actual inner physics of the black hole are, of course, unknown and widely debated. It has been suggested that the black hole is like a tunnel leading from one space-time frame to another—a kind of warp in the fabric of the universe. "Some cosmologists . . . suggest that the quasars themselves might be the reemergence of collapsed galaxies, explosively bursting back into our universe after digging a tunnel through space-time."[39] That is, a quasar could be an inverted black hole.

The relevance of this data is ultimately unknown, since we are dealing with the medium of variant, and often contradictory, theories or mythic structures. Thus it seems somewhat precipitous to marshal full-scale philosophical arguments and prognostications based on data which are still highly theoretical and in need of far more substantiation, analysis, and interpretation. It is not surprising, though somewhat disheartening, that such phenomena as black holes are already being fully exploited (as for example, in *Black Holes: The End of the Universe,* an incautious blend of science fact and science fiction by the University of London professor John Taylor).[40]* However, as we examine the menagerie of new cosmic beasts postulated by astro-physicists, we are struck by a recurrent apocalyptic theme: the inherent violence and explosiveness of the universe. In addition, many accounts suggest the eventual dissolution of all matter. The one dissident theory, the Steady State Universe proposed by Bondi, Gold, and Hoyle, although enjoying initial prestige and heated debate, has fallen somewhat (though not entirely) into disrepute since the discovery of quasars. The Steady State hypothesis avoids secularized Judeo-Christian imagery and depicts the universe, expanding at a steady rate, as infinite in both space and time.[41] Stars and galaxies arise and disappear, but the continuous creation of matter maintains a constant density throughout the universe. The origin of matter *ex nihilo* is, as might be guessed, the chief weakness of the idea of "continuous creation."

What relevance do theories speculating about events exceedingly remote in time and in space have for human culture? At first glance this query may appear to be a convincing objection. Yet as we have suggested repeatedly there is a dialogical and dialectical interplay between cosmology and culture: cosmology shapes culture, just as initially culture shapes cosmology. The preponderant cosmological myths of the end generally share violent, cataclysmic apocalyptic imagery. It is a legitimate question to ask how much such theories divulge archetypal apocalyptic predispositions peculiar to Western (or Near Eastern) traditions. H. P. Owen writes that it is doubtful whether eschatology in a cosmic or social sense

> is to be found anywhere outside of Zoroastrianism and Judaism—together with the religious and philosophical systems that have drawn inspiration from them: Mithraism from the first, Christianity and Islam, and Western thought in general, from the second.[42]

Owen's claim is profoundly significant insofar as eschatology may not be a universal or necessary human phenomenon. It is significant that apocalypticism is a widespread phenomenon of consciousness in the modern West,†e.g., fundamentalist pronouncements of Billy Graham or the Jehovah's Witnesses, social prophets of doom, the Marxist historical vision, cosmological theories, etc. It is imperative that we recognize that to a great extent our beliefs create our reality (just as they derive from it). We must assume responsibility for our

---

*And since the first writing of this manuscript, the Walt Disney film "The Black Hole" has appeared!

†As it is in resurgent Islam which reflects Zoroastrian roots.

beliefs, just as we must assume responsibility for our acts. What is the impact of apocalypticism upon popular culture? Upon the self-consciousness of persons considering their own futures? Can we assume that the eschatological hypotheses of modern cosmology are "pure scientific hypotheses"—or are they, like all human thought-constructions, variant forms of anthropomorphic and historical myth?

Human reflection is expressed in human language. Although we have doubtlessly added immensely to our knowledge, *we still interpret the data in terms of anthropomorphic symbols, myths, and schema.* This universal constant does not negate the relative truthfulness of our knowledge. However, if we remain unaware of this constant, a danger appears which becomes *proportionately greater* as we intrude further into dimensions of the unknown: whether the distant past or the distant future, the outer reaches of the cosmos or its innermost nature (or prognostications of human historical destiny). Consider two commonplace structures of Western consciousness. On what grounds do we assume that cultural concepts of "good" and "evil" are relevant on a cosmic scale? It is noteworthy that popular space-fantasy often depicts the universe as populated by an array of beings usually more evil than ourselves in what seems all too typical of our anthropocentric arrogance and fears! Moreover, why should we assume that our human temporal concepts of beginning and end are cosmological constants? Einstein has warned us of the peculiarity of our own space-time frame. Such considerations should deter us from extrapolating ready analogies from human culture into the unknown.

In terms of the *known,* both psychology and the history of culture teach another historical constant—"self-fulfilling prophecy." This socio-psychological pattern has beneficial as well as destructive implications. The beliefs which we assume and their ramifications *are* the fate of future culture.

Empirical Consciousness and the Shape of Culture

Rene Dubos asserts that "either by choice or from necessity, the cultural evolution of man will be molded in the future by scientific concepts and technological forces."[43] If our world picture is an approximate blueprint of the future, and if Dubos' assessment of the role of science and technology is correct, it is of vital importance to understand the structures of consciousness at the root of the general scientific world view. Our discussions of technology and the new cosmology, though fragmentary and incomplete, have been addressed to that end. A few summary observations follow.

Technology, at least as it is propagated institutionally, commonly mirrors a world picture that is quite traditional. The great threat of technology to the future of man is *not* technology, per se, but rather the way in which technology has become institutionalized and politicized. For example, the sophisticated technological innovations of implements of death, whether

Hitler's gas chambers, the atomic bomb or the proliferation of modern missiles, must not be blamed abstractly on technology or science, but rather upon men and institutions who, operating out of quite primitive structures of consciousness, have seduced science and technology for their own ends. We may argue that such a seduction is suggestive of moral weakness, indifference, or schizophrenic separation of personal beliefs from professional duties.

John Wren-Lewis shares a pertinent anecdote. When speaking from his concentration camp cell of a "world come of age," Dietrich Bonhoeffer is not an addlewitted anachronist, for he correctly perceived that what "was killing him was not the modern world, but a deliberate attempt to go back on the most distinctive characteristic of the modern world" (which Wren-Lewis identifies as scientific-democratic consciousness).[44] The definition of "modern" is of course problematic. Certainly Hitler employed "modern" organizational methods successfully,[45] and created a myth which effectively defined the destinies of millions of persons living in the modern era. Yet at the same time, Hitler's use of power to control his subjects seems quite comparable to ancient Oriental "divine" despots, whose word could determine the life and death of "worshipers"/subjects. (The most potent of these despots is Yahweh himself, whose arbitrary will, imbedded in the *ethos* of the Western mind, Hitler seems to have grasped intuitively.)[46] Hitler's authority was indeed hierarchical, but in a sense more primitive than the carefully-ordered hierarchy of the Middle Ages.[47]

As Lewis Mumford observes, the regimentation and mechanization of persons is not the result of modern science so much as the age-old enslavement of the masses in the *megamachine* for the vested interests of a few. Regimentation and mechanization are not peculiarly modern dangers,[48] though unquestionably there are considerations* of the use of technology in our particular era that require a unique awareness.

In addition, if the most characteristic feature of modern science is its empirical, *a posteriori* approach to the world, we should avoid the Inquisitor's Temptation of blaming the evils of modern society on science. It is the voice of tradition that speaks with the staccato of *a priori* absolutes, and which *uses* science and technology as tools to secure ancient ends: power, mystification, manipulation, genocide, etc. When allowed free intercourse with the world, the empirical disposition of science does not easily or readily submit to authoritarian ideological interests. (There is a limited kind of empiricism which is adaptable to a cultural schizophrenia separating means and ends.) Wren-Lewis asserts that "the dangers we face are not products of science and technology at all, but rather aspects of traditional culture which people fail to see because they have been encouraged to look at culture through rose-coloured spectacles."[49] Science and Technology have become means to highly

---

*(such as global ramifications)

dangerous ends. But Wren-Lewis' point might be illustrated by the alliance of interests manifest in the so-called "military-industrial complex" which reveals an age-old penchant for the union of ideology and militant action in behalf of economic gain.* A prime example is the Crusades.[50] Certainly technological sophistication has enhanced the efficiency of the military in modern times. But the legitimation of military action by ideological referents with the intent of economic profit is a recurrent historical phenomenon which, in itself, is hardly the *product* of science or technology. Science and technology do not necessarily create the habits of thought responsible for their use.

At the same time, neither science nor technology is value-free. Technology bears the marks of its creator's intents. In this respect Wren-Lewis' judgment must be modified, since (for example) neither a heart machine nor a bomb are neutral instruments. Each—however it is used—is a value-laden artifact of culture (and a product of science and technology). In addition, science is not simply an idealistic discipline practiced in rarefied laboratories untouched by ideological or practical issues. For science itself implies certain views of the world for scientists who, as social beings, must by necessity encounter questions of cultural ethos. The scientist's cultural role obviously has become far more dramatic in the Nuclear Age, since many decisions (pertaining to military, ecological, or energy matters, for example) bear eschatological weight for world history. Heisenberg declares:

> The invention of nuclear weapons has also raised entirely new problems for science and scientists. The political influence of science has become very much stronger than it was before World War II, and this fact has burdened the scientist, especially the atomic physicist, with a double responsibility. He can either take an active part in the administration of the country in connection with the importance of science for the community; then he will eventually have to face the responsibility for decisions of enormous weight which go far beyond the small circle of research and university work to which he was wont. Or he may voluntarily withdraw from any participation in political decisions; then he will still be responsible for wrong decisions which he could possibly have prevented had he not preferred the quiet life of the scientist.[51]

Scientists face enormous responsibilities—the magnitude of which demands as much as possible a critically-informed and supportive public. Furthermore, science—for its own sake and for our own—cannot be invested with quasi-divine status. How can such a dilemma be resolved?

No ready or simple resolution to determine the proper role of science in future culture is available. Complex socio-economic, political, and ideological concerns, which often define the course of science, defy neat solutions. However, to lessen the burden which the scientific community must bear, it seems that a wider appreciation of a scientific world view by a

---

*It should be added that such alliances are equally prominent in Soviet Russia.

much greater portion of the educated public might create a broader base for decision-making.[52] Of course, scientific empiricism has already affected many facets of education besides the physical sciences (e.g., history and the social sciences). If it is to be one functional integer of viable world views of the future, empiricism merits closer analysis.

First we must distinguish between two kinds of empiricism, one limited and immediate in scope, and exclusive in focus; the other (which may include the former as a limiting case for utilitarian purposes such as data gathering, experimentation, and analysis) is ultimately unlimited and general in scope. The first case might be called "factical empiricism," and the second, "holistic empiricism."

Factical empiricism focuses upon immediate sensory experience (or extended experience through technical instruments) for the purpose of analysis, quantitative understanding, and categorization. Factical empiricism operates as if it is "doing business" with reality in an immediate—and not mediate—sense. Observations and instruments tell us what reality is. As such, factical empiricism mirrors presuppositions which are compatible with classical physics, namely that we can know the real world *as it is,* and that we can immediately relate to physical absolutes (such as Newtonian space and time). Factical empiricism is *gnostic,* because it presumes that the data with which it deals is knowledge of *the* real world. It is *literalistic,* because it assumes that the data literally describe what is. It is *substantialistic,* because it assumes that the data gathered are about a solid material world, and that as part of such a world the objects analyzed are objects *as they are.* According to Whitehead, this limited and literalistic empirical mentality errs according to "the fallacy of misplaced concreteness," which means we have mistaken our abstractions from and about the real world *as* the concrete real world itself.

The attitude of factical empiricism has enabled a schizophrenic science to prosper in the Western world, from the Renaissance to Newton (who played the dual role of physicist-theologian), and into our own era. Factical empiricism operationally assumes a secret (or often overt) dualism. This dualism may appear in various guises, but it essentially fosters the fallacy that there are two kinds of reality—the world of things and the world of culture, religion, ideology, art, etc. Though discrete spheres of operation and commitment, these two worlds may be quite parallel in terms of their basic functioning structures of consciousness. The world of real things may be conceived as orderly, obeying absolute laws parallel to the social or religious absolutes of the human or ethical world: "the starry skies above and the moral law within." Such dualism always implies a kind of gnostic certainty in both worlds of knowing.

It is the attitude of factical empiricism which accounts for that strange, paradoxical being—the hybrid scientist, who wears two hats: the orthodox Christian scientist, the Marxist scientist, the scientist allied with the tacit ideology of technobureaucracy, etc. In each case the empirical method is conceived as appropriate only to the physical world as a means of understanding its composition and laws. The world of culture is envisaged as operating by its own separate set of laws. The real "material world"—the concrete world of things—is susceptible to empirical *a posteriori* analysis in the probing of its rational structure. But the real "ideological world"—the realm of cultural commitments—operates on the basis of its own *a priori* structural presuppositions, such as Christian revelation (with its dogmas of guilt and grace, good and evil, etc.), Marxist socialism (with its dogmas of class warfare, the historical dialectic, etc.), or technobureaucracy (with its hidden dogmas of social necessity, deterministic hierarchies, etc.). This cosmological schizophrenia divulges deeply-embedded structures of consciousness, the foremost of which in this case is the Greco-Christian dualism of matter/mind, body/spirit, or nature/grace, etc.

As long as we envision science as operating out of this first kind of empiricism—"factical empiricism"—we can be sure that scientific discovery will be subjugated to particularistic ideological interests.

Given the cultural preconditioning of consciousness and belief structures, it is far more difficult to carry empiricism to its logical conclusion—namely as an attitude or stance towards the world *as a whole*. Holistic empiricism is first of all based upon the recognition of the *limitations* of all human knowing. This premise may seem contradictory—holism/limitations—but in fact it is quite consistent. The consistency of holistic empiricism rests upon the epistemological certainty that the limitations of our human equipment precondition *all* our encounters with the world, and therefore precondition the *whole world* of our experience. As we have suggested, holistic empiricism does not exclude the validity of factical empiricism for particular experimental cases or methods. It does, however, carry the empirical approach much further than factical empiricism, beyond the surface physical world to the inner workings of the atom and the remote frontiers of the known cosmos, and to the inner depths of the human psyche and the extensive sweep of all human culture.

Holistic empiricism acknowledges that we are never "doing business" immediately with the real world, but ever and always only *mediately*. As Karl Popper suggests:

> We must give up the view that we are passive observers, waiting for nature to impress its regularity upon us. Instead we must adopt the view that in digesting our sense-data we actively impress the order and the laws of our intellect upon them. Our cosmos bears the imprint of our minds.[53]

Both relativity and the uncertainty principle seem to imply Popper's judgment, and we may recall also Noam Chomsky's hypothesized innate mental structures. Holistic empiricism recognizes our physical sensory limitations and the bias of our technical instruments (as products of our particular space-time frame). It recognizes that (as Holton paraphrases Einstein) the physical "picture of the world (*Weltbild*) is one among all possible pictures."[54] Ideally, holistic empiricism is able to embrace the "paradox of the world" in its own bosom. The "paradox of the world" means that the world upon which we imprint the order of our minds is thus always *within us*: yet at the same time there is a vast, unknown world always at the fringes of our knowing, on the boundaries of our perception, and beyond the horizon of our experience. Thus holistic empiricism may be *im*mediately gnostic and nomistic, but ultimately agnostic and open-ended; (and the *im*mediate world is progressively modified by its expansion into the unknown). Einstein, in a 1918 address summarized by Holton, suggested that the scientific world view

> demands vigorous precision in the description of relationships. Therefore the physicist must content himself from the point of view of subject matter with "portraying the simplest occurrences which can be made accessible to our experience"; all more complex occurrences cannot be reconstructed with the necessary degree of subtle accuracy and logical perfection. "Supreme purity, clarity, and certainty, at the cost of completeness."[55]

Here is another historical constant—the recurrent danger of empirical nomism: "supreme purity, clarity, and certainty" *is* "at the cost of completeness"; such "knowledge" must therefore remain open to further clarification, modification, and correction.

Holistic empiricism as penultimate and not ultimate, and recognizing that we are dealing with *appearances of reality* as we encounter the world, acknowledges then that "reality itself" as some mythical, static thing will always elude our grasp.

But holistic empiricism is also *holistic*. The ramifications of this term are two-fold. First of all, *holism* implies that an empirical approach of systematic (but not atomistic) analysis—which understands parts in terms of wholes, and vice versa—is applicable to the *whole world of our experience*. Dismissing, or at least as much as possible holding in suspension ("bracketing") all *a priori* assumptions (including materialistic), holistic empiricism accepts and affirms the validity of *all experience* (physical, social, ethical, religious, mythical, etc.) as true expressions of the human condition, and therefore as worthy of understanding. By suspending apriority in the interest of analysis, holistic empiricism does *not* imply reductionism to bare data. For it identifies at the outset one *a priori*: the human condition, which itself is a limiting case of a greater reality always beyond the frontiers of our knowing. The continuous reminder is that "the whole is greater than the sum of its parts." Holistic empiricism assumes that there is only one kind of *known* reality—the reality of our human experience, qualitatively wealthy, rich in its variegation. By inference we can assume that the real world *beyond* the horizon of our present knowledge can be no less remarkable; thus as it gradually impinges upon our known world it will only add further richness and brilliant diversity to our cosmos.

The second implication of the term *holism* is its appositeness to all persons as knowers and shapers of the world. Here the burden of the future cannot be carried by science alone. All persons participate in world construction. To that extent it would seem appropriate and useful to disseminate an holistic conception of empiricism to as much of the modern public as possible. Holistic empiricism suggests a universal bank of human experience, since all men bear the limitations of human knowing, share some form of social life, strive for similar basic goals (survival, security, health, fulfilment, etc.), and live on a common planet.

It is at this point that the eschatological dimensions of holistic empiricism emerge. We have asserted that all human enterprise is informed by cosmological presuppositions, whether covert or overt. The cosmological presuppositions of holistic empiricism include the whole world of experience and all persons as knowers; the unique diversity and validity of human experience; the limitations of the human condition, the tentativeness and mediate character of all knowledge, and thus an ultimate agnosticism (implying not that we cannot know, but that *what* we know is always incomplete). The eschatological implications of these presuppositions should be obvious.

First of all, closed ideological systems—whether religious, political, or scientific—which lay claim to ultimate knowledge, defy empirical validation and ultimate usefulness. Absolutism, exclusivism, and claims to gnostic certainty find no substantiation in the empirical reality of the human condition. An holistic empirical model, though appreciating both the real socio-historical conditions which have given rise to such systems, and the needs to which they are addressed, seeks to create a broader frame of reference which will expose the limitations of such systems, and mitigate the concomitant hostile encounters between them.*

If holistic empiricism implies an open universalism, it is *not* to be inferred that the world must become a chaotic mass of discrete experiences unordered by norms and qualitative distinctions. On the contrary, norms and qualitative distinctions are a valid part of the whole scope of experience, in fact recurring universally (though not in a single fixed and changeless pattern). We *do* suggest that norms and distinctions will be most effective if 1) they are informed by the widest possible sampling of human wants and needs; 2) they fit the appropriate context(s); 3) they remain subject to periodic reassessment and healthy modification.

Secondly, this universalism does *not* imply that pluralistic experience and values could or should be eliminated. Part of the qualitative richness of the whole is the colorful variegation and unique distinctions of its parts. But holistic empiricism does affirm the value of implementing the creative

---

*See Appendix II for a further discussion of this point.

homeostasis and growth of the whole, so that local and particularistic expressions interrelate to each other felicitously, eliciting mutual appreciation and affirmative, if critical perspective.

We have sketched in very broad terms the character of holistic empiricism as an appropriate world stance for the future. In the final chapter possible implications of such a stance for human consciousness will be examined. The following represent the kind of premises which holistic empiricism (H.E.) might affirm:

1. H.E. acknowledges the limitations, tentativeness, and mediate character of all human knowing, and suggests that an agnostic openness is an appropriate ongoing attitude;

2. H.E. affirms the validity of the whole world of human experience as appropriate for analysis and understanding, without implying reductionism;

3. H.E. recognizes all persons as knowers and world-builders, and advocates ordering the world in such a way that there is always room for a wide variety of expressions of human experience considered to be appropriate and healthy, without establishing or encouraging any single dogmatic and absolute system of truth or social structure to which all must conform;

4. H.E. seeks to appreciate and to integrate truths from all quarters of human experience in a way in which various encounters will facilitate understanding, mitigate destructive exclusive claims, and encourage dynamic and continued interchange, growth and expansion of experience and consciousness.

5. These goals should be appropriate not only within the scientific and academic worlds, but in political and social deliberations, inter-religious and secular-religious dialogues, personal relationships, etc.;

6. H.E. implies a faith that in expanding the frontiers of experience and consciousness the quality of life will not be diminished, but greatly enhanced.

7. Finally, H.E. suggests that persons, institutions and societies, all automatically interrelated, must consider the ramifications of their beliefs and deeds for the whole of which they are a part, at the same time affirming a plurality of expressions which through their eccentric character immeasurably enrich the cosmos as a whole.

304

FOOTNOTES

[1]See Peter L. Berger and Thomas Luckmann, *The Social Construction of Reality* (Doubleday, 1966; Anchor Books, 1967), pp. 61; 128 ff.; etc.

[2]See Richard L. Rubenstein, *My Brother Paul* (New York: Harper and Row, 1972), pp. 129 ff. for a discussion of Paul's development of this theme from Jewish Messianism.

[3]And as Richard Rubenstein notes, apocalyptic reflects an awareness of the tenuousness and fragility of all human constructions. As such, it is recurrently relevant in history. See Richard L. Rubenstein, *After Auschwitz, Radical Theology and Contemporary Judaism* (New York: Bobbs-Merrill, 1966), esp. pp. 133; 182-84; 198.

[4]Gerald Holton, "Modern Science and the Intellectual Tradition," in *Science*, Vol. 131 (Apr. 22, 1960), 1187-1193, rpt. in Paul C. Obler and Herman A. Estrin, eds., *The New Scientist: Essays on the Methods and Values of Modern Science* (Garden City, N. Y.: Anchor, 1962), p. 34.

[5]Ernst Cassirer, *The Philosophy of the Enlightenment* (Princeton: Princeton University Press, 1951), p. 13.

[6]Ibid.

[7]Ibid., p. 14.

[8]Harlow Shapley, *The View from a Distant Star* (New York: Dell, 1967), pp. 75 and 77.

[9]Oscar Handlin, "Science and Technology in Popular Culture," in Gerald Holton, ed., *Science and Culture* (Boston: Beacon Press, 1967), p. 191.

[10]Harry Levin, "Semantics of Culture," in *Science and Culture*, p. 13.

[11]Handlin, p. 196.

[12]Jean Charon, *Cosmology* (New York: McGraw-Hill/World University Library, 1970), p. 233.

[13]Ibid., pp. 235-37.

[14]Ibid., p. 234.

[15]Ibid., p. 238.

[16]Ibid., p. 239.

[17]Donald H. Menzel, *Astronomy* (New York: Random House, 1970), p. 270.

[18]*Encyclopedia of Philosophy*, s.v., "Entropy," by G. T. Withrow.

[19]Konrad Krauskopf and Arthur Beiser, *Fundamentals of Physical Science* (New York: McGraw-Hill, 1966), p. 136.

[20]*Encyclopedia of Philosophy*, s.v., "Entropy," by G. T. Withrow.

[21]Ibid.

[22]Lancelot Law Whyte, *The Universe of Experience* (New York: Harper Torchbooks, 1974), p. 43.

[23]Ibid., p. 81.

[24]Charon, p. 243.

[25]Ben Bova, *The New Astronomies* (New York: Mentor/New American Library, 1972), p.180.

[26]Menzel, p. 273.

[27]Ibid.

[28]Bova, p. 182.

[29]Ibid., p. 183.

[30]Ibid., p. 184.

[31]Ibid., p. 187.

[32]Ibid.

[33]Ibid.

[34]Ibid., p. 192.

[35]Kenneth F. Weaver, "The Incredible Universe," *National Geographic* 145 (May, 1974) p. 618.

[36] Ibid.

[37] Bova, p. 195.

[38] Weaver, p. 620.

[39] Bova, p. 199.

[40] John Taylor, *Black Holes: The End of the Universe?* (New York: Random House, 1973).

[41] Menzel, p. 271.

[42] *The Encyclopedia of Philosophy*, s.v. "Eschatology," by H. P. Owen.

[43] Rene Dubos, "Science and Man's Nature" in *Science and Culture*, p. 252.

[44] John Wren-Lewis, "Faith in the Technological Future," in Alvin Toffler, ed., *The Futurists* (New York: Random House, 1972), p. 293.

[45] Hannah Arendt. *The Origins of Totalitarianism*, notes that the novel features of totalitarian organization, especially as exemplified by Hitler or Stalin, revolve around its central character as a propaganda machine. The creation of front organizations, surrounding "the movements' membership with a protective wall which separates them from the outside, normal world" is a case in point (pp. 364 ff).

[46] Paul Tillich makes this connection in *The Courage to Be* (New Haven: Yale University Press, 1952): "God as a subject makes me into an object which is nothing more than an object. He deprives me of my subjectivity because he is all-powerful and all-knowing. I revolt and try to make *him* into an object, but the revolt fails and becomes desperate. God appears as the invincible tyrant, the being in contrast with whom all other beings are without freedom and subjectivity. He is equated with the recent tyrants who with the help of terror try to transform everything into a mere object, a thing among things, a cog in the machine they control" (p. 185). See also Richard L. Rubenstein, *Power Struggle* (New York: Charles Scribner's Sons, 1974), p. 162.

[47] Hannah Arendt points out that modern totalitarianism is not hierarchical in the sense of traditional stratified orders. "If the functionaries appointed from above possessed real authority and responsibility, we would have to do with a hierarchical structure in which authority and power are delegated and governed by laws . . . A hierarchically organized chain of command means that the commander's power is dependent on the whole hierarchic system in which he operates . . . In the language of the Nazis, the never-resting dynamic "will of the Fuehrer"—and not his orders, . . . becomes the "supreme law" in a totalitarian state . . .(pp. 364-65). Thus with Hitler we are dealing with a "fluctuating hierarchy, with its constant addition of new layers and shifts in authority . . . where new controls are always needed to control the controllers" (p. 369). Yet as Lewis Mumford observes, authoritarian technics date at least to the fourth millennium, B.C. His description reminds us of the primitive—as well as the modern—facets of Hitler's style (and his mythical appeal). "Under the new institution of kingship, activities that had been scattered, diversified, but to the human measure, were united on a monumental scale into an entirely new kind of theological-technological mass organization. In the person of an absolute ruler, whose word was law, cosmic powers came down to earth, mobilizing and unifying the efforts of thousands of men . . . for purposes that lay beyond the village horizon." See Lewis Mumford, "Authoritarian and Democratic Technics," in *Technology and Culture*, ed. Melvin Kranzberg and William H. Davenport (New York: Meridian/New American Library, 1975), p. 53.

[48] Peter Drucker illustrates that many of the same results of the first great technological revolution, seven thousand years ago, are visible today. In the creations of the "irrigation city" in Mesopotamia, Egypt, the Indus Valley, and China, the following social results ensued: 1) "It established an impersonal government with a clear hierarchical structure in which very soon there arose a bureaucracy . . ." (and attendent concepts of citizen, super-tribal deity, codified law, and standing army); 2) "it was in the irrigation city that social classes first developed," (including farmers, soldiers, government officials and priests); 3) "The irrigation city first had knowledge, organized it, and institutionalized it," (including engineering, economic data, astronomy, and education); 4) "the irrigation city created the individual" (apart from the tribal identity). Drucker continues, "If an educated man of those days of the first technological revolution—an educated Sumerian perhaps or an educated ancient Chinese—looked at us today, he would certainly be totally stumped by our technology. But he would, I am sure, find our existing social and political institutions reasonably familiar—they are after all, by and large, not fundamentally different from the institutions he and his contemporaries first fashioned." See Peter Drucker, "The First Technological Revolution and Its Lessons," in *Technology and Culture*, pp. 41-44; 49.

[49]Wren-Lewis, p. 295.

[50]C. Warren Hollister, *Medieval Europe: A Short History* (New York: John Wiley & Sons, Inc., 1968), writes "The Crusades represented a fusion of three characteristic impulses of medieval man: sanctity, pugnacity, and greed. All three were essential. Without Christian idealism the Crusades would be inconceivable, yet the pious dream of liberating Jerusalem and the Holy Land from the infidel was reinforced mightily by the lure of new lands and unimaginable wealth. The Crusades provided a superb opportunity for the Christian warrior-aristocracy to perform their knightly skills in the service of the Lord—and to make their fortunes in the bargain" (p. 154.) Hollister continues, "During the Crusading age European merchants established permanent bases in Syria and vastly enlarged their role in international commerce. As a surprising side effect of the Crusading movement, a considerable portion of the Byzantine empire passed for a time into Western Christian hands" (p. 157). "Sanctity, pugnacity, and greed"—or ideological legitimation, military investment and action, and economic gain—seemed to command equal motivating power in the Viet Nam War, for example.

[51]Werner Heisenberg, *Physics and Philosophy* (New York: Harper Torchbooks, 1962), p. 192.

[52]A recent series of articles in *The New Yorker* by Barry Commoner underscores both of these points. Commoner discusses some of the highly complex ramifications of the energy problem facing the United States. At the same time, Commoner laments the fact that significant decision-making offices—the President's Office of Science and Technology, for example—have neglected the relevance of a significant scientific datum, the Second Law of Thermodynamics. See Barry Commoner, "A Reporter at Large: Energy III" in *The New Yorker,* Feb. 16, 1976, pp. 64-103.

[53]Karl Popper, *Conjectures and Refutations: The Growth of Scientific Knowledge* (New York: Harper Torchbooks, 1968), pp. 80-81.

[54]Gerald Holton, *Thematic Origins of Scientific Thought: Kepler to Einstein* (Cambridge, Mass.: Harvard University Press, 1973), p. 377.

[55]Ibid.

CHAPTER TWELVE

TOWARDS A RENEWED HOLISM

IN THE previous chapter we introduced the term "holistic empiricism" as descriptive of a world orientation (incorporating the perspective of, but not limited to, the scientific enterprise) appropriate and useful to culture in the quest for new world views. The observations that follow are not propositions of a new world view, *per se*, but perspectives differing from cultural assumptions now commonly held. The author hopes that the following perspectives will serve as signposts pointing towards a new holism.

NATURE AND CULTURE

Culture is a special case of nature. A sharp dichotomy between nature and culture is misleading, since man is a natural being and his tools and artifacts are all extrapolations from nature and her elements. When the sociologist Peter Berger asserts that society, as a human product, has no being apart from its "human" being, he is only partially correct; for man and his culture cannot be isolated from their nurturing environs, out of which they spring and to which they are always inextricably interconnected. Furthermore, Berger's suggestion that culture's "patterns, always relative in time and space, are not given in nature, nor can they be deduced in any specific manner from the 'nature of man'"[1] is an overstatement.[2] Indeed, there is mounting evidence to suggest that human social structures, albeit historically and culturally multiform, are not only irrevocably part of a global ecosystem, but also exhibit recurrent basic patterns which are widespread in nature itself. Throughout this work we have affirmed that unique, humanly conceived world pictures—which emerge from, are embedded in, and continue to shape culture—are universal, though widely variegated and dynamic constants. Understanding such cultural structures as distinctive human creations is a critical assumption in their appraisal. However, an equally critical assumption dialectically related to this sociological perspective is the participant identity of man and nature, including their total interdependence, common physiochemical constituency, and intertwined destinies. Particularly in our own time, when the world is a malaise of mutually clashing cultural systems, each of which is the jealous guardian of vital self-interests, a firm reminder of the shared *natural* roots of all humanity is crucial.

Nature has much to teach us about ourselves. Social structures are not unique to man, and hierarchical and symmetrical organizations appear throughout the plant and animal kingdoms. There is a structural similarity between human, and all levels of natural, events. George T. Lock Land observes that all living beings exhibit organizational similarities of such detail that the sciences of cybernetics, general systems, biochemistry, biophysics, and molecular genetics now assume that all life forms evidence analagous behavioral processes.[3] The new scientist, according to Ervin Laszlo, concerned with structures "on all levels of magnitude and complexity," "discerns relationships and situations, not atomistic facts and events."[4] For

> . . . we can discern systems of organized complexity wherever we look. Man is one such system, and so are his societies and his environment. Nature itself, as it manifests itself on this earth, is a giant system maintaining itself . . . we can see that the solar system and the galaxy of which it is a part are also systems, and so is the astronomical universe of which our galaxy is a component.[5]

Now it is true, as we have seen before, that in one sense nature is also a special case of culture. As human beings we perceive the natural order through our peculiar sensory apparati—equipment already culturally preconditioned. Furthermore we may ask, why should some new alliance between culture and cosmology prove to be any more useful than previous such alliances, for example as in mythopoeic and mechanistic systems? Actually it is just the new recognition of the critical limitations of our human/cultural space-time frame that is suggestive of man's acute need, insofar as possible, to assess his anthropocentric chauvinisms and cultural particularisms in the light of holistic perspective. Holistic-empirical consciousness, unlike the great syntheses and *a priori* systems which have heretofore defined the course of Western (if not world) civilization, proceeds by *a posteriori* analysis and must remain open-ended and flexible. The new holism turns our native focus inside out: instead of looking at nature on the outside from the inside of culture, we attempt to look at culture from the vantage point of the encompassing and supportive natural order. We adjust the focus of the human/cultural world according to a tri-powered set of lenses: the global-ecological mesocosm, the trans-galactic macrocosm, and the atomic-molecular microcosm.

Naturally, there are inevitable objections to the apparent "belittling" of culture by juxtaposing it to nature. First, it seems, man is robbed of his unique status. In reality, such is not the case. An holistic-empirical point of view, informed by culture as well as cosmology, recognizes the uniqueness of humanity within the (known) natural order. On the other hand, human arrogation to superiority *is* seen as a cultural bias—an emotive expression—which can be supported only by the circular process of cultural presuppositions. There is nothing in nature (*per se*) to suggest that man is a superior being. But there is no reason to suspect that a realistic appraisal of the *uniqueness* of the human phenomenon should denigrate lofty ethical expressions. Such expressions should gain further anchorage to the extent that they are *not* isolated anomalies, but are rather rooted in and inclusive of the organic environs.

A second argument against an organic appraisal of culture finds typical expression in the words of John Wren-Lewis:

> The attempt to conform human life to the supposedly greater plan of organic nature, as all the great traditional religious cultures did in their various ways, inevitably condones and encourages cruelty and inhumanity, for biological nature is full of cruelty and has no place at all for human values such as respect for individual feelings.[6]

In response to Wren-Lewis, it seems unclear how "the great traditional religious cultures" attempted to conform human life to nature *per se*. If Wren-Lewis means Buddhism, Christianity, or Greek Olympian religion, for example, in each case nature is conceived from a mythopoeic or philosophic *a priori* upon which culture is also patterned (as for example the medieval Neoplatonic scheme), and not from an holistic-empirical perspective.[7] Secondly, it is not at all clear that "cruelty and inhumanity" are "natural," but not "human" traits. Wren-Lewis' judgment smacks of the old dualism which pits man's rational-ethical nature against his "animal"-physical nature. But historically there is no way to establish "rationality" in and of itself as necessarily *ethical*. On the contrary, it can be argued the other way around: that ethics are organically rooted, and that the peculiar versions of "cruelty and inhumanity" eccentric to man seem to spring from the isolation of reason (and here we must include "empirico-logical" or mythopoeic thought, as well) *from* its organic roots. By *reason* we mean not solely the logical canons of thought esteemed in deductive systems, but the recurrent rationalistic penchant of man in the enterprise of legitimating various cultural structures of belief and behavioral patterns. As a function of particularistic *a priori* cultural ideologies, "reason" has played a consistent apologetic role historically in attempts to vindicate a wide variety of cruel and violent acts among men. In our century alone the barbarities of warfare have been enacted from and legitimated by diverse ideological bases, including "democracy," "fascism," and "communism."

A recent report of highly "exclusive" and expensive black market pornographic films—"distinguished" by the "actual murder and dismemberment of actresses on screen"[8]—is a repugnant reminder of a peculiarly *human* form of depravity which can hardly be blamed on man's "animal" nature. The article continues:

> Viewers at private screenings reportedly pay up to $200 to witness the filmed killings, Detective Joseph Horman of the police department's organized crime control bureau said. "The thing that is really astonishing," Horman said, "is that there is such a market. That's almost as astonishing as the fact that somebody would actually commit a murder for the purpose of

> making a film. Based on the price, I would imagine the people who
> purchase these things are from affluent backgrounds," he said.[9]

Such behavior suggests that certain facets of "civilization" have rendered
man less sensitive to organic canons of commonality than the animal
kingdom. Although admittedly predatory behavior is commonplace in the
animal kingdom, its occurrences seem to follow fairly strict, predictable
patterns attuned to the larger homeostasis and survival mechanisms of the
ecosystem. On the contrary, man's alienation from his organic roots seems at
least partially responsible for his cavalier disregard for planetary health and
balance. Moreover, *altruism* (which, like "good," and "evil," is a human
cultural concept) seems to have *behavioral analogues* in the animal kingdom.

The thesis of "altruism" among animals is the subject of recent studies of
sociobiology, a budding discipline designed to explore the biological roots of
social behavior in the organic (both animal and human) world. Edward O.
Wilson, professor of zoology at Harvard, who asserts that "human social
evolution is obviously more cultural than genetic," and that "we cannot
afford an ignorance of history,"[10] nevertheless believes that we stand much to
gain by considering the data of sociobiology. Wilson notes that "minor
altruism does occur frequently" in the animal kingdom.[11] Various small birds,
at the risk of betraying their hiding places in the presence of predators (such as
hawks) emit audible whistles to warn their companions. Dolphins sometimes
come to the aid of a harpooned fellow, hoisting it up to the water's surface so
that it can continue to breathe. Wild dogs and chimpanzees both share their
food with members of their own species, and the chimps practice adoption.
The phenomenon of "altruistic suicide" is widespread among social insects.
Wilson reports that the theory of natural selection has now been broadened to
include a process termed "kin selection," which is the propensity of
organisms for altruism and self-sacrifice, designed for the maximum survival
potential of kin species.[12] An example is the sacrifice of the soldier termite to
insure the fertility of its brothers and sisters.

Wilson suggests that such data seem to require reinterpretations of some
of our cherished prejudices. For example, animal aggression, which has been
studied extensively since the early work of Lorenz, "occurs in a myriad of
forms and is subject to rapid evolution."[13] Thus Wilson objects to substantialistic interpretations of aggression, such as Erich Fromm's ("death
instinct") and even Lorenz's own generalities. Aggressive tendencies differ
markedly even among closely related species; and "most kinds of aggressive
behavior are perceived by biologists" not so much as continuous intrinsic
patterns, as "particular responses to crowding of the environment."[14]
Although Wilson feels that behavior does indeed have a genetic as well as a
social index, he believes that

> What the genes prescribe is not necessarily a particular behavior, but the
> capacity to develop certain behaviors and, more than that, the tendency to
> develop them in various specified environments.[15]

Thus Wilson presents convincing cases both for the organic roots of behavior and also the flexibility and indeterminacy of nature. He concludes that we must be in "constant vigilance" of "the naturalistic fallacy;" for "when any genetic bias is demonstrated, it cannot be used to justify a continuing practice in present and future societies."[16] Though destructive cultural expressions such as warfare between competing groups "might be in our genes," it is "bad biology" as well as bad culture to think that we are predetermined to global suicide. In other words, as both Julian Huxley and Teilhard de Chardin suggest, man does play a volitional role in the evolutionary process. An holistic empiricism may include an optimum realism, as man is not predestined to any one given cultural form or historical end.

WORLD ORDER: NOMOLOGY OR COSMOLOGY?

Nature—on all levels of its appearances—evinces orderly arrangements and processes. How does this *natural* order modify or clarify our understanding of cultural order? Perhaps we can compare the "kinds" of order represented by culture and nature as follows:

	NOMOLOGY (from *nomos*, "law")	COSMOLOGY (from *cosmos*, "world order")
roots	cultural	natural
structures	"artificial"	organic
norms	atomistic, isolated	holistic, contextual
system	"closed," dogmatic	"open," flexible
motivation/ actuation	authoritarian, *a priori*	heuristic, *a posteriori*
model	mechanistic, literalistic	analogical, aesthetic
scope	"universal," deterministic	universal, indeterministic
end	entropic	morphic

The chart simplifies and the typology is intended to be heuristic: cultural nomology represents rigid competing systems of belief and behavior which often reflect old models of the cosmos. The cosmic/organic analogy suggests that *all* orders must be conceived both more integrally (in terms of their effects, for instance, upon all human culture and the ecosystem itself) and more freely (allowing variant expressions of culture to function according to context and need without mutual exclusiveness and hostile encounters). A cosmic perspective of order rejects both a purely rigid sessility or a purely ephemeral motility in favor of a dynamic homeostatic holism. If we take the natural ecosystem as a model, the implications for social structures seem evident: neither the unyielding stance of traditionalism nor the indiscriminate myopia of revolution yield viable orders. A healthy order is a dynamic affair—exhibiting continuous natural rhythms of birth, growth, and death according to organic needs.

312

One of the most cogent expressions of the critical implications of cosmic order for cultural orders is to be found in recent suggestions of "General Systems Theory," developed by the Austrian biologist Ludwig von Bertalanffy. Ervin Laszlo's *The Systems View of the World*[17] and George T. Lock Land's *Grow or Die: The Unifying Principle of Transformation*[18] are recent representative works. (In certain respects these "systems" analyses resemble the works of Alfred North Whitehead and Lancelot Law Whyte, as well as the writings of Teilhard de Chardin and Julian Huxley.)

Just as Noam Chomsky hypothesizes that within the human brain there are innate structures of "grammar," so systems theory asserts that the entire natural cosmos exhibits a consistent and discernible order. A fundamental principle of the systems view of nature, according to Laszlo, is that "the characteristics of complex wholes remain irreducible to the characteristics of the parts."[19]   Systems theory opposes atomistic or mechanistic reductionism. Nature is envisioned as a complex whole built up in an expanding pyramid from atomic structure through human social organization to the world order itself. The following picture is an extrapolation from Laszlo's description:

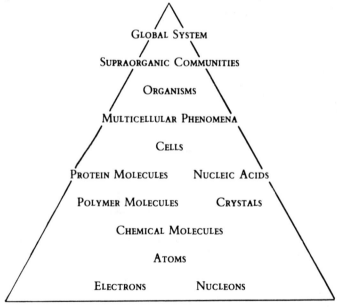

Systems theory proceeds on the assumption that the classical mechanical cosmos is no longer viable as a model for world order. Relativity and quantum theory have shattered the *absolute* (though not functional) value of the classical mechanistic view. Although mechanical and atomistic theories have proved to be highly useful models (for example) in molecular biology, they appear inadequate for explaining the ultimate vital interactions of living organisms. The comparative cosmological directions of the pre-scientific, the classical scientific, and the systems view of the world might be represented as follows (in highly general terms):

	PRE-SCIENTIFIC	CLASSICAL SCIENTIFIC	SYSTEMS
world order:	divine system	mechanical system	organic system
whole/parts:	macrocosm/ microcosm	atomistic	complex organic pyramid
derivation:	*a priori* revelation	*a priori* reason	*a posteriori* observation
matter/energy:	vital, substantialist	inert, substantialist	vital; matter = energy
organic/inorganic:	continuum	separate	continuum

As we have noted, systems theory asserts that "natural systems are wholes with irreducible parts."[20] The behavior and structural functioning of molecules, cells, animals, persons, etc., cannot be known by observation of an isolated example, but only through the examination of the system ("social" structure) of which they are a part. There are three levels of natural systems, according to Laszlo, the suborganic (the domain of the physical sciences), the organic (the domain of the life sciences), and the supraorganic (the domain of the social sciences).[21] On the suborganic level, quantum theory suggests that matter is not isolable into final discrete solid units; even though atoms have certain discernible characteristics, they are also processes and composites of interactions. On the organic level, as George T. Lock Land suggests, "the diversity of all life depends on the quantity and sequences of only two pairs of four nucleic acids in the hereditary information of DNA in chromosomes."[22] And yet the virtually infinite complexity of organic systems, from single-celled animals through the remarkable variety of systems within the human body, demonstrates the irreducible quality of organic wholes. Finally, on the supraorganic level, academic, political, and religious institutions, clubs, corporations, clans, states, ethnic groups, etc., involve complex structures of communication and organization which cannot be understood by the analysis of a single, isolated constituent member.*

Laszlo's second thesis is that "natural systems maintain themselves in a changing environment."[23] The natural world from microcosm to macrocosm is in a state of process, flux, or evolution. This second, universally apparent thesis, largely elucidates the failure of a mechanical model to do justice to the intricacies and the dynamics of the world order.

The direction of the process, flux, and evolution of world systems seems to be the increase in *entropy*—a postulate of the Second Law of Thermo-

*The cosmos as a whole must be conceived as an organic system.

dynamics which depicts every physical system as ultimately "running down," approaching a state of maximum disorganization. Although *entropy* has received ample experimental confirmation, there is a kind of circular argument to which it must appeal. Experiment demands isolating a physical system for observation. Entropy itself applies only to an *isolated, closed system.* Therefore entropy seems to be always confirmed by experiment. The question is not whether entropy is a true law of physical systems, but whether it is an ultimate or exclusive principle. Conceivably, entropy as a universal principle may be a last holdover of a mechanical cosmos, which *depicts* the physical world *as* a closed system.

Systems theory, which does not deny the *local* validity of entropy for isolated systems, also asserts that there is a comparable principle of ordering, which Lock Land calls "syntropy" (after Paul Kammerer)—a process analogous to L. L. Whyte's "morphic" process.[24]

This ordering principle, the converse of entropy, assumes that a natural system cannot ultimately be conceived *as* a closed, isolated system:

> The technical definition of a natural system is "open system in a steady state." *Openness* refers to the import-export activities of the system, which it needs to "stay in the same place," that is, to maintain its own dynamic steady-state. Man is an open natural system; so are the cells that compose his body, and the ecologies and societies which he constitutes jointly with his fellow human beings and organisms.[25]

If entropy can be aligned with classical causality, then "syntropy" is homologous to gravity. Syntropy as a force of attraction and ordering is complementary to entropy. Lock Land writes:

> Because no organization of information can reach an absolute state, entropy aids our reorganization by helping break down old materials. It is the catabolic function of the physical universe just as syntropy is anabolic. Life cannot exist without death, for life would have nothing to resynthesize into higher organizations if it were in static equilibrium.[26]

The entropy/syntropy duality seems analogous to the ancient yin/yang scheme.

But Lock Land challenges the "entropy bias" arising from experimental isolation. Experimental isolation only tells us what to expect in a "deprived subsystem" which, when subjected *to* such isolation, reverts to lower forms of growth.[27] As exemplary of a more holistic approach counter to classical experimentation Lock Land cites the classical "origin of life" experiment of Stanley Miller. In simulating the presumed primeval earth conditions of methane, ammonia, hydrogen and water, Miller found that when this environment was subjected to an electric spark, it yielded several amino acids and formaldehyde—the building blocks of life. By creating an entire environment, Miller was able to provide striking confirmation of the viability of a classical hypothesis of the origin of life. Many replications of Miller's experiment have followed. Lock Land finds this "holistic" experiment evocative, and suggestive of the emergence of order in nature. In the "origin of life" experiment, the simple primitive components themselves already exhibit certain orders which, when subjected to the appropriate electrical stimulus, yield even more exquisite and complex orders—the building blocks of life. Contrary to Lock Land,[28] the "origin of life" experiment does not necessarily suggest any strong rebuttal of the expectations of entropy law, since entropy can decrease locally as long as it increases in the system as a whole. However, as evidence for an "intelligent" direction manifest *in* the mounting hierarchies of nature, the "origin of life" experiment may be supportive of an hypothesized ordering principle standing in polar relation *to* entropy. Lock Land feels that such a principle suggests "an intelligence dedicated to providing even higher levels of organized, mutualized interrelationships."[29] Furthermore, Lock Land cites other studies which seem to indicate "that high levels of activity actually *increase* the working potential of organisms"[30]—a result again concordant with a principle of syntropy. Lock Land concludes that "Energy begets energy."[31] Of course at this time, there is no substantial evidence of the ultimacy of either entropy, syntropy, or—as in the case of the pulsating universe model—some rhythm of both principles. However, Ervin Laszlo agrees that the organic world strongly evidences a pervasive principle or order, and observes that organisms, unlike machines, make their own repairs, attain their own fuel, and maintain homeostasis, ("the precise regulative mechanisms of warm blooded creatures").[32] Indeed, Laszlo continues, "the whole of nature . . . is something like a vast, self-regulating and recycling system, drawing energy from the sun and running itself without surpluses and wastes."[33]

The third premise of systems theory proposed by Laszlo is that "natural systems create themselves in response to the challenge of the environment."[34] Indeed, "self-creativity is a precondition of evolution."[35] In a similar vein, Lock Land identifies the unifying principle of all organic systems as *growth*. From cells to galaxies, comparable processes of birth, maturity, and death occur. Laszlo defines two forms of change recurrent in nature. "Preprogrammed" change is the careful implementation of structural patterns, such as the emergence of characteristics from the precoded information in the genes. This kind of change is most characteristic of *ontogenesis* ("the growth and maturation of the young of self-reproducing species").[36] The second form of change, following Whitehead's terminology is the "creative advance of nature into novelty"—the "trailblazing self-transformation of entire species and populations of organisms."[37] This process occurs at the level of *phylogenesis* ("the evolution of the species . . . from one generation to the next").[38]

While Laszlo focuses more on general forms of evolutionary change as processes of ordering and novel transformations, Lock Land identifies three forms of growth: accretive, replicative, and mutual. Accretive growth is visible even in the simple process of atomic nucleation into crystals.[39] On other organic levels, this process of self-extension is visible in the reproduction processes of bacteria and algae, the maturation of complex organisms, and the exclusive legacy of primitive cultural tradition. Psychologically, accretion means self-seeking and autistic behavior.[40]

Replicative growth finds its simplest expression in the reproduction of viruses.[41] Replicative growth entails the reduplicating of an initial form, but does not exclude new information and mutations. Socially, replicative growth is visible in "missionary activity, imperial conquest, nationalism, and a host of other techniques" where "others become like us."[42] Psychologically, replication involves the duplication of forms of the external environment — "both modifications of the outside world to copy the internal, and the reverse, changing of the inside world to mimic the external."[43] (We are reminded here of the dialectic of the Sociology of Knowledge: internalization, externalization, and objectification.)

The third process, mutual growth, begins with the giant molecules which are distinguished by "the diversity of the elements (monomers) that they can incorporate into their carbon-based molecules."[44] Approximately one billion years ago meiosis emerged among more highly evolved organisms. This process allowed for "sexual fusion and *mutual* gene recombination."[45] This process assumes an ever more significant role in genetics. Mutual growth occurs in symbiotic mutualistic relationships "where each organism contributes directly, and often equally, to the growth of the others."[46] Success on this level involves "flexibility to evolve increasingly mutual relationships."[47] On a social level, mutuality is first preceded by the rejection of replication: anti-colonialism, wars of independence, nationalism, etc. But particularly within the contemporary milieu where *information* is disseminated rapidly via print and the electronic media, cross-cultural exchange and cultural hybridization are virtually inevitable processes. Psychologically, mutual growth means "self-extension through sharing."[48]

We have only traced a skeletal frame of the basic directions of systems theory. Both Laszlo and Lock Land elaborate the cultural implications of their positions in terms relevant to, but beyond the scope of, our present discussion. Here we accentuate the vital input of systems theory (and related perspectives) in the quest for a new global or cosmic consciousness.

The central contribution of systems theory is not merely its identification of the thoroughgoing orderliness of all nature (including culture), but also and in particular, its exposition of the characteristics of that order. Laszlo's final thesis of the systems view is, "natural systems are coordinating interfaces in nature's hierarchy."[49] As our pyramidal diagram is designed to illustrate, systems theory envisions nature as an hierarchical scheme of integrated systems. But the critical factor here is that, unlike authoritarian cultural hierarchies, *nature's* hierarchies (though homogeneously based) are heterogeneously integrated in a dynamic balance where particular structural integrity subsists in open-ended flexibility. By contrast, consider the cultural process of objectification defined by Peter Berger:

> This transformation of man's products into a world that not only derives from man, but that comes to confront him as a facticity outside himself, is intended in the concept of objectivation. The humanly produced world becomes something "out there." It consists of objects, both material and non-material, that are capable of resisting the desires of their producer . . . It stands outside the subjectivity of the individual as, indeed, a world. In other words, the humanly produced world attains the character of objective reality.[50]

When man forgets that culture is his own objectivation—that it is comprised of a network of artifacts devised by himself—then culture becomes *reified*.[51] Reification entails the attribution of substantial, cosmic, or quasi-divine status to cultural structures. As long as we remember the *flexibility* demonstrable throughout the ecosystem, a truly cosmic/organic analogue from nature to culture circumvents the tendency to reification.* "There is a high degree of internal plasticity within any natural system" writes Laszlo.[52] The simple phenomenon of H_2O is beautifully illustrative of this fact. According to context, H_2O appears as steam, clouds, water vapor, dew drops, total liquid environments (such as rivers, streams and oceans), ice, and an astounding, infinite array of symmetrical snowflakes. Any contemplation of the variety of life forms—in environs ranging from deserts to oceans and from mountains to river beds, (not to mention the proliferation of diverse human cultures)—must evoke a profound respect for the imaginative flexibility and adaptability of nature.

Moreover, nature, with her vast integrity and creative harmony, does indeed purvey her own values. Laszlo reminds us that "there is nothing in all the realms of natural systems which would be value-free when looked at from the vantage point of the systems themselves."[53] As we become increasingly aware of the exquisite balance of life systems on this planet, we recognize that nature is not merely "raw materials" for our exploitation, nor even a magnificent garden of "wonders" to excite our imagination. Nature is our nurturing environment out of which we are formed and to which we are responsible. As earth's most reflective children we are given the mandate of its fullest well-being; and we bear the responsibility not solely for ourselves, but for all our fellow species. Now that we have unleashed the energy of the atom, which has given us beyond our fellow species the sole and awesome power to annihilate earthly life, our responsibility is immeasurably greater.

At the same time, we possess the power to extend the world's energy resources, to create "artificial" environments, or to discover or create new

---

*It might be recalled that Italian fascism employed organic metaphors. But the fascist concept of organism was already attached to a highly limiting set of cultural presuppositions drawn by specious analogy to prior historical periods (e.g., the medieval and Roman worlds).

sources of food supply. Lock Land portrays the options which face us in lucid, poignant language:

> Yet evolution carries with it the message of extinction . . . if we do not find a balance of trade with our environment, we face a future known in all its frightening dimensions. We, as a culture, as a species even, will join with the other unfit systems of our world. The message is abundantly clear: Grow or die, evolution or extinction. It is in our hands, not just as governments or even cultures, but as humans.[54]

Finally, we must recognize that the greatest challenge which history poses to contemporary man is the evolution of human consciousness—an evolution of mind, of self-image, and of cognitive structures, which will not only precipitate a new and cosmic purview, but which will pave the way for new social and physical structures geared to a balanced and healthy ecosystem for the planet as a whole. The point cannot be overstressed: a new consciousness is not merely a luxury to add to the harmony of our days, it is a *necessity* of the most fundamental, life-and-death consequence for our continued life on earth.

PURPOSE

The classical mechanical world view, as we have discovered, is no longer an adequate *world* view in terms of the description of all processes. Modern physics has by no means abandoned mechanical descriptions. Yet both relativity and quantum theory, which underscore the particular space-time context of human observers, suggest that caution must be exercised in extrapolating mechanical explanations of local efficacy to universal significance. Minimally, we can assert that the new cosmology calls into question the utility of mechanistic hypotheses for addressing any of the more ultimate questions, such as the meaning of life and death, and the questions of world value and purpose.

Philosophically, the most important question that can be addressed to a mechanistic model of the world is "So what?" Freely accepting the tenet that all things may be described in terms of mechanical processes (which is at least questionable), we are still perplexed by the question, "So what?" Ultimately the mechanistic model does not answer satisfactorily the most basic question, which is of course, "what is the meaning of life? (or my life?)" Mechanism exhibits the "how," and the immediate "why," but never the intimate or the ultimate "why." Questions of meaning, value, or decision ("why this, and not something else?") are also not amenable to mechanical explanations.

On the other hand, an organic model proves acclimatable to questions of quality, meaning, and value, since phenomena of the world appear not as discrete "things," but rather as local expressions or extensions of a complex of interrelationships in a larger "field." "Organism" means the envisioning of phenomena in terms of their holistic setting or social nexus. Thus the explication of the organic world implies not simply the abstraction of physical cause-and-effect relations, but the exploration of implications of value inherent in an integral order or process. Homeostasis, growth, flowering, decay and death are susceptible to quantitative analysis on the level of physiochemical changes. But their *significance* to an organism or an environment requires an holistic qualitative perspective.

The contrast between the mechanical and organic models is nowhere more evident or more vital than in the question of purpose or teleology. Both, of course, are humanly devised *models* of reality constructed for the purpose of yielding the most extensive and intensive understanding for all ranges of phenomena. The real issue, then, between mechanism and organism is: which model most adequately incorporates the data of the other in a more comprehensive explanation? We must also remember that, as in the case of the wave/particle duality, *both* models may be necessary for the understanding of *all* processes. Or, yet a third model may arise which will supplant both of these. "Holistic empiricism" and also systems theory indicate directions toward a third option. An organismic model seems more capable of incorporating mechanism than vice versa.

Systems theory, which posits the emergence of order from the atom through the global ecosystem to the final superintegrated states of matter (white dwarfs, neutron stars, black holes) envisioned by astrophysicists, requires a minimum teleology. Although Laszlo balks at the idea of a plan "preestablished and realized by purposive manipulation,"[55] he does assert:

> But if by plan one means a recognizable pattern of development, then the answer is definitely *yes* . . . Among these forseeable characteristics of development are increasing coordination of formerly relatively isolated entities, the emergence of more general patterns of order, the consolidation of individuals in superordinate organizations, and the progressive replacement of certain types of functions and responses. There is a progression from multiplicity and chaos to oneness and order.[56]

Laszlo further proposes that "nature is 'permissive'" or "there is a plan, but it is not a preestablished one," or "There is purpose without slavery, and freedom without anarchy."[57] But such a plan is not amenable to mechanistic explanation:

> Suborganic nature turns out to be rather different from the mechanistic universe of Newtonian physics. It is a dynamic realm of interacting forces, resulting in the emergence of systems of increasingly organized complexity.[58]

In his article "Life and Quantum Physics," V. A. Firsoff defines the mechanistic approach to purpose as follows:

> The mechanist's point of view is essentially a prioristic and metaphysical, and he seeks to escape from this situation by substituting teleonomy for purposefulness and behavior for consciousness . . . Teleonomy may be defined as unconscious purposefulness, arising from the evolutionary adaptation of an organism, both internally in structure and externally in

behavior, through the blind forces of "chance and necessity," expressing themselves in random mutation and natural selection, which weeds out the unfittest . . . Thus what strikes us as purposeful in living organisms and the way they act would be only the outcome of ages of adjustment to the environment.[59]

In other words, purposeful behavior has emerged by *chance* and out of *purposelessness.*[60] Such a thesis is not only lacking in aesthetic or philosophical efficacy, it also reminds us of the circumscribed boundaries of the mechanical model, which itself is *a priori*-reductionistic. Mechanical causes can only be given for mechanical effects. But beyond this, we must *import* a mechanically irrelevant datum: in the case of Newton, God, and in the case of later mechanism, "chance" or "necessity" (equally as abstract as "God"). Firsoff raises the hotly debated question of intelligent behavior in cybernetic devices. For example, a robot tortoise has been constructed "to simulate intelligent behaviour in exploring a room, avoiding obstacles, seeking out and plugging itself into an electric contact when its batteries run low."[61] The analogy drawn by mechanists would be that a real tortoise has been comparably preprogrammed by evolution, only on a quantitatively far more sophisticated level. But "the evolutionary process" by this explanation is ultimately as mysterious as God; we are still left with the unsatisfactory appearance of purpose out of purposelessness.

Of course, in terms of consciousness, the greatest objection to the mechanical view arises from empirical data which defy simple mechanistic explanations: intuition, insight, emotions, and the whole realm of value—whether specifically human, or according to holistic perspective, also among other life forms. More sophisticated mechanical apparatuses may detect the "how" of these occurrences, but the question of their "why"—and their basic goal-directed character—remains outside of the scope of a mechanistic purview.

Presently there are many phenomena which seem recalcitrant to mechanistic reductionism (and hence to purposelessly-induced purpose).

Apart from manifold facets of human personality and creativity which seem to be explained inadequately by mechanism, various natural phenomena also appear to require some broader explanation. One example mentioned by Firsoff is an experiment conducted by V. A. Droscher, in which plants exposed daily to a cold draught exactly at 11:20 A.M. responded each day with drooping leaves (which recovered by the next day). After the cold draught was discontinued, the plants continued to respond for a few days with drooping leaves precisely at 11:20, apart from any exposure. Firsoff concludes that "plants can be taught a behavior and have a kind of memory."[62] Homing pigeons, and occasionally cats and dogs, seem to find their way home instinctively in circumstances of no prior exposure to, or learning of, the proper route. There are numerous similar examples which, though perhaps involving physical mechanism, nevertheless seem irreducible to pure atomistic mechanical causation.

Hypnotic effects also seem to evince a more complex model of behavior than simple mechanism. In an experiment at the University of Aberdeen, warts were willed away from one hand of a patient via hypnotic suggestion, while the other hand, as a control, retained its warts.[63] Firsoff also records a striking incident recounted by J. A. Hadfield, a London psychiatrist, Hadfield reports that a hypnotized seaman, a victim of combat hysteria, winced violently when told that a finger touching him was a red-hot poker. Moreover, a blister appeared at the spot touched, and filled with fluid.[64] Conversely, when the seaman was given an opposite suggestion while still under hypnosis, "he felt no pain on being touched with a red-hot iron rod . . . and the blisters which formed were very small and healed rapidly."[65] Similar examples could be multiplied from studies of hypnosis. Again mechanical explanations cannot be ruled out, but a reductionist mechanical model seems singularly unfit to account for the mental/organic facets of such experience.

Finally, Firsoff recounts an experiment conducted by Richard Sidman and G. R. Delong at Harvard in which they gently disarranged cells in developing brain tissue of a mouse embryo. Placed in test tube cultures, the cells spontaneously rearranged themselves in the original order.[66] Firsoff concludes (from this and other experiments and observations regarding the brain) that minimally we must assume some sort of "morphogenetic field" of mental organization—i.e., that there is not a one :: one relationship between the exact physical structure of the brain and its functioning. Furthermore, Firsoff suggests that more credence may be due the Lamarckian view of willed and purposeful mutations. Citing Lamarck's idea that giraffes acquired their long necks through a process of willing to reach the leaves of palm trees, Firsoff observes that the Darwinian view of random mutation and natural selection cannot explain why the gnu, sharing the same environs as the giraffe, should have a short neck. Firsoff feels that something like "will" must be considered as a factor.[67] Firsoff asserts that "the Lamarckian and the Darwinian interpretations are not mutually exclusive," and suggests that thought—which can "produce blisters and cure crocodile skin"—cannot be excluded necessarily from affecting even "the nucleotides in the DNA."[68]

It seems as though purposeful, intelligent, or goal-directed behavior demands purposeful, intelligent, and goal-directed causes and ends. The old deistic model of a clockmaker and his clock will not suffice, because the organic world itself exhibits *internal* direction, choice, flexibility, and at least functional "intelligence." Firsoff notes that

> an organism is an organization of statistical improbabilities, and if such an organization arose by mere chance it would seem to follow the arrow of time to that enzymatic chaos envisaged by Monod . . . in the absence of

> some controlling agency . . . An organism, however, is no machine, not even one operated by a ghost; it is an event propagated by continuous change in the four dimensions of spacetime. Its "structure" is like that of a river, which is never the same and cannot be stepped into twice . . . The real essence lies in the processes. The structure is only the product of the processes, seen in time cross-section, like a snapshot.[69]

Firsoff himself concludes that "the nature, origin and organization of life necessitate an intervention of mental forces. We cannot do without a 'ghost.'"[70] The most satisfactory explanation of purpose seems to be that the world itself is a purposeful, organic whole, directed by hierarchies of consciousness, and moving toward meaningful, but not preordained, ends. Such a view does not require a single personal intelligence, such as a theistic God, and in fact seems to lend itself more readily to a pantheistic or probably panentheistic model. Moreover, what we do know about the emergence of complexities of consciousness certainly does not rule out, but on a cosmic scale probably suggests, the existence of intelligences far more sophisticated and advanced than ourselves.

EXPANDING THE FRONTIERS OF CONSCIOUSNESS

In the preceding discussion we have introduced perspectives which seem to be probable components or directions of a new* consciousness—and suggestive of a new world view.

Reviewing the contours only of the new cosmology, we find that the universe at every point and in each known dimension challenges even the most grandiose world pictures by which human culture has lived for so many centuries. Relativity has emphasized the contextuality of human existence in a single space-time frame—a particular planet traveling at a particular speed around a particular sun, itself mobile within a particular galaxy—within a vast cosmos of innumerable stars and many known galaxies. Observational astronomy, especially enhanced by a sophisticated assortment of electronic equipment, has greatly expanded the horizons of the known universe. On another level entirely, quantum physics has revealed to us the complexity, uncertainty, and yet intricate orderliness of the atomic and subatomic worlds. Extrapolated from careful calculations, the patterns of electron waves resemble the symmetry and beauty of snowflakes.

> Ultimately all the regularities of form and structure that we see in nature, ranging from the hexagonal shape of a snowflake to the intricate symmetries of living forms in flowers and animals, are based upon the symmetries of these atomic patterns.[71]

Reality as a whole appears to be a vast dancing spectrum of electronic space-

---

*The term "new" must be used somewhat cautiously, since historical precedent certainly may be found (e.g., in the holistic conception of life of Native American cultures, etc.).

time configurations, the processes of which appear too complex for the simple geometries and mechanics of a static world order. Sir James Jeans writes:

> Today there is a wide measure of agreement, which on the physical side of science approaches almost unanimity, that the stream of knowledge is heading towards a non-mechanical reality; the universe begins to look more like a great thought than like a great machine.[72]

If the physical frontiers now exhibit an esoteric panorama of phenomena quite alien to the conceptions of reality by which we live from day to day, there is yet another frontier—every bit as remarkable and perhaps more immediately relevant to man—the frontier of the mind. We have alluded to the significance of the varying functions of the two lobes of the human brain, and we may marvel at the biophysical duality of apprehensional modes which seems implanted in man's head. Certainly holistic consciousness must be informed by a balanced perspective of this dual functioning, and consider relevant implications for the shape of culture.

Perhaps even more germane and mystifying is the age-old question of mind and body. Contemporary psychology seems to indicate firmly the integral unity of mind and body. In addition to hypnotic effects, psychosomatic medicine (an expanding field of exploration) is a dramatic exemplar of the holistic perspective, and promises to continue providing data evocative of cultural analyses. For example, David Bakan develops a convincing case (drawing upon Freud's conception of the "death instinct") for psychic inducement of cancer due to internalized aggression from sexual maladjustments or similar problems.[73] Confirming the influence of mental /emotional states upon cancer is a report from Drs. Carl O. and Stephanie Simonton at the first National Congress of Integrative Health. The Simontons produced statistically convincing evidence that cancer patients can strongly influence the course of their illness according to their mental attitudes. Dr. Simonton reports that "The cancer patient is a person who bottles things up. They don't have adequate outlets for their emotions."[74] At the other end of the spectrum of such mind/body interaction, Dolores Krieger of New York University has experimented since 1971 on the relationship between "therapeutic touch," (physical contact with healing intent, known in religious circles as the "laying on of hands") and the hemoglobin values in patients' blood.

> Krieger said she worked from a basic assumption that human beings are open systems, "perhaps a nexus for all fields . . . exquisitely sensitive to wave phenomena, i.e., energy." She saw the act of healing as the channeling of vital energy from an individual with an overabundance to the ill person. "On the physical level I felt that this occurs by electron transfer resonance. The resonance would . . . reestablish the vitality of the flow in this open system." The patient heals himself—as a resonant effect of the field.[75]

Controlling her experiments for age, sex, drugs, vitamins, nutritional intake, biological rhythms, smoking, and other factors, Krieger discovered shifts in hemoglobin values at the highly improbable statistical rate of one chance in a thousand.

In another report presented before the National Congress of Integrative Health, Dr. C. Norman Shealey, a University of Wisconsin surgeon, recounted that in an eighteen month study, a group of psychics had made accurate diagnoses of patients three times out of four—equivalent to the accuracy of more traditional procedures.

> Shealy said his study involved more than 200 patients and used the talents of clairvoyants, palmists, numerologists and astrologers, most of whom never even saw the patients they were diagnosing. "We did most of this by mail. We sent the clairvoyants photographs and provided birth dates for the numerologists and astrologers and palm prints for the palmists." The psychics were also given a body sketch. They would mark the portion of the body where the problem was and then fill out a form. In each case Shealy said the diagnosis was already known.[76]

Shealy's experiment included some unexpected events. One psychic diagnosed a patient as having "a malignant degeneration of the lymph system." Dr. Shealy counted this as a miss. Nine months later the patient died of lymphoma cancer of the lymph system. Such cases appear bizarre and offensive to our rational intellects, but the instances related here are only an incidental sampling of a burgeoning body of evidence, amassing over the past fifty or more years, of mental phenomena which defy mechanistic reductionism and known physical laws.[77]

Before rashly dismissing such phenomena, the skeptic would do well to remember Carl Jung's refusal "to commit the fashionable stupidity of regarding everything I cannot explain as a fraud."[78] Or as V. A. Firsoff asserts:

> Science is surely concerned with reality, quite objectively, which means that whatever observation and experiment reveal cannot be brushed under the carpet because it does not fit in with some preestablished set of propositions . . .[79]

An impressive body of strictly controlled experimentation, unknown generally to academia, and of a qualitatively different genre from popular tabloid sensationalism, presents formidable empirical evidence for the operation of "paranormal faculties" (as of yet poorly understood) in many human beings.*

Parapsychological research is in a position somewhat comparable to the quest for a unified field theory in physics—as of yet the experimental data have not been incorporated into a consistent theoretical frame. But we would venture to suggest that the eventual understanding of such phenomena will alter our concept of reality, including certain presumed physical laws, in a

---

*See Appendix III.

revolution which may prove as radical as Einsteinian relativity and quantum mechanics.

An holistic empirical approach must remain open to the relevance of such phenomena in the quest for understanding the world and human being. Considering the breakdown of the mechanistic world picture, we might add that an organic or holistic view renders the seeming anomalies of parapsychology far more integral, since holism envisions physical phenomena (including ourselves) not as isolated, atomistic entities, but as configurations of energy patterns, rather like "ripples in a cosmic field." We ourselves are peculiarly-conscious space-time warps. There is continuity, not just between "mind" and "body," but also between "self" and "world," suggesting that in particular the Western predisposition for a self-conceptualization of atomistic egotism is largely a cultural illusion.

Furthermore, the phenomena of life (from single-celled organisms to the complex "machinery" of the human body; from the mysterious world of subatomic particles to astrophysical bodies) overwhelm us with miraculous and once-unimagined processes which an earlier science might have dismissed as sheer fantasies. Indeed, if the mind can to a marked extent influence the health of the body, then perhaps a skeptical and pessimistic predisposition will, through its own effects on a particular organic field, precipitate appropriate evidence to substantiate its prejudices. The real issue, from the standpoint of an holistic empirical approach, is our *openness* to the whole world of experience. Only through such an openness can we hope to achieve a higher level of consciousness.

Toward a New Optimum Realism

In a real sense our exploration into culture and cosmology has revolved around a central problem—the problem of man, his condition and conditioning, his world perspectives and structures of belief. But as we are increasingly discovering, the problem of humanity is the problem of life itself. We must continuously oscillate between spheres of human relations, institutions, ideas and history, and the realm of nature and the universe, man's larger context. Here we begin to probe the organic interdependence of man with all other facets of nature. Here we search for interconnecting links which shed light upon the world of human artifacts and ideas. Here we move from nomology, where we address the cosmos with our static monologue, to cosmology, where we are continuously being addressed by the cosmos in a dynamic dialogue. Finally, in the midst of and beyond both man and history, nature and the universe, lies an ever greater realm of mystery. The whole is greater than the sum of its parts. Mystery unfolds before us at the most extreme frontiers of micro- and macrocosmic being, and the most profound depths of human reflection and analysis. The greatest mystery is ever life itself—the primal superfluity of experience (which engages us moment by moment).

The note of mystery resounds from a cosmos which appears vast and impenetrable. Vast it is, immense, infinite, and extraordinarily awesome, beyond the realms of our most extensive or intensive imagination. Impenetrable, however, it is not. Contemporary cosmology has not only expanded the perimeters of the known, it has exposed many of its hidden processes. The penetrability of both man and the cosmos is indicative of the possibility and reality of expanding awareness.

Penetrating realms formerly relegated to mystery not only solves certain problems, but uncovers afresh basic questions of human existence. Although the scientific elucidation of subatomic particles, the sociological and historical analysis of religion or culture, and the psychological probings of the unconscious have demystified large arenas of our experience, the age-old questions of the nature of reality, the nature of man, and the possibility of purpose only assume still more challenging roles. Yet because of the penetrability of things, it is not *realistic* to succumb to despair in the face of such questions, just as it is unrealistic to continue to propagate old myths— old wineskins unfit for new wine.

If we ponder the possibility of addressing the basic questions afresh there is one further *reality* which warrants consideration: the turbulent socio-political atmosphere of our world, which obviously affects the viability of future research. Following the traumatic incursion of the Atomic Age at the end of World War II, we entered an era in which pivotal powers—the U.S., Russia, and Europe—were speaking of "peaceful coexistence," while the Chinese and the emerging nations of the Third World seemed most concerned with establishing their nationalistic identities. "Peaceful coexistence"— however euphemistic in tone or outstanding in motivation—is too passive a term to define what is needed most urgently. The global crisis, not only in its socio-political, but in its *ecological,* and crucially, its *psychological* dimensions, demands not a passive "live and let live" attitude, but dynamic integral cooperation and interaction. All available resources—intellectual, physical and spiritual—are needed for engaging common problems (ecology, energy, population, food supplies, etc.) of human existence. Such an effort itself evinces the value of mutualism.

Finally, we must ask if the pursuit of fundamental questions of the meaning of existence, human nature, life and death, etc., is worthy of our time in the face of pressing practical crises? Are we afforded the luxury of thoughtful inquiry concerning world view, belief structures, and the subsequent shape of culture? The continuous commerce between world view and culture is as persistent as the daily news in which that interchange is so evident. Our beliefs do shape our reality (just as they are shaped by it). As a rejoinder to Feuerbach, we could say *Mann ist was Mann glaubt.** Not only can

---

*Man is what he believes.

we afford such inquiry, we cannot, by all means now, afford *not* to so inquire. Certainly, as many have insisted since Hegel, abstract theorizing must only and always be plugged into the real institutional and relational world of culture; intellectual endeavors must in fact spring out of that world of vital context. However, it may be argued with equal force that the very real world of culture will fare so much the better if informed by more universal structures of belief and orientation, whether supernovae, mind/body interactions, or starving persons in Cambodia.

For the cosmological precepts of culture, from hidden primeval archetypes to the overt projections of contemporary astrophysicists, indicate the range of mythical structures which *do inform* our self-concepts, world location, and ethos. Myths are the creative frameworks in which we live and out of which we operate. They are deliberate, albeit half-conscious, literal creations or projections of our psychic sensibilities into the cosmos. Only by realizing their vast psychic and spiritual potency, and our agency in their creation, can we begin to choose—to frame deliberately—new mythic structures attuned to the broader needs of mankind. Only by allowing for a healthy plurality of mythical constructs and cultural models can we mitigate destructive claims to ultimacy by any particular cultural system.

If we acknowledge that it is worth our efforts to strive for a new planetary consciousness, built not upon universal absolutes, but upon mutual understanding, respect, and tolerance, the task ahead is immense and long-range. From the first such a task calls for a dogged and courageous counterpoise to all forces—whether fleshly, technological or ideological—which seek to dehumanize or to denigrate life on this planet. As an optimum realism, such a task demands both disciplined understanding of socio-cultural forces we have created and an understanding of the transformative capacities of consciousness. Optimum realistic faith is hardly disembodied emotive melancholy, since it is based upon tangible experience of nature and history. However sporadic or particular their appearances—beauty, dignity, life-affirmation, progress, cosmos, novelty, and human caring—are recurrent historical phenomena. In this sense, optimum realistic faith is simple and verifiable: *what has been can be.* The historical recurrence of human creativity, of life-affirming myths and discoveries (e.g., medical advances or therapeutic breakthroughs in the meaning of human relationships) indicates realities as historically and empirically demonstrable as poverty, disease, death, famine, injustice, and warfare. One man or woman who has overcome poverty or injustice, or has risen to full stature, such as a Martin Luther King, provides us with a very real incarnate microcosm of human—and indeed global—potential, however long-range. We do not envision a glib, easy, short-term process. Such a commitment requires decade upon decade, generation upon generation, of cooperative and courageous endeavor. We must remember that we are but infants in the evolutionary time scale. An holistic human enterprise will necessarily encounter obstacles and setbacks. But as Laszlo writes, the evolution of culture "has now quickened, now slackened. But it has never reversed more than locally, and never for long."[80] Even if the quest for new consciousness points far beyond our day to some remote future, why should we not live in the superlative shadow of its promise, enriching the present with a cosmic quality which can transform our own identity and loyalties?

Behind the myths, masks, and models by which men live is the phenomenon of life itself, ever vital, ever rejuvenating. Attesting to this fact is one of the central archetypes of Western consciousness. Jesus, according to suggestions in John's Gospel, may never have intended to become a cult idol, leading persons away from the source of their own integrity.[81] Rather, probing beneath his generations's quest for belief, Jesus recognized a yearning for the inner Spirit, a Power which alone "will lead you into all truth." The point is that the *Spirit*, versus the letter of the law, versus ritual, cult, or dogma, is the most universal and the most particular referent of truth. The Spirit is most universal as the source of *all* life. Beneath the accretions of myth and tradition is the dynamic spirit of life, vivifying the evolutionary process in the unfolding novelty of the world. Like Jesus, the early Christian apostle Paul may have caught a glimpse of such a truth:

> Now the Lord is the Spirit, and where the Spirit of the Lord is, there is freedom. And we all, with unveiled face, beholding the glory of the Lord, are being changed (*metamorphoumetha*) into his likeness from one degree of glory into another; for this comes from the Lord who is the Spirit.
>
> (II Corinthians 3:17,18)

Although Paul may not have grasped the radical implications of his own words, the *metamorphosis* of which he speaks (according to the Greek tense a continuing, dynamic process) ever entails the shedding of old cloaks of tradition and old forms of life in the emergence of new life.

The precept may be extrapolated from Christian terminology. George T. Lock Land puts it simply: grow or die. There are cultural and psychic forms which bring men death, static structures which, unyielding to transformation, turn inward like a cancer, or outward like a scourge, striking down all who differ or do not conform. Such structures feed upon emotional insecurity, ignorance, intellectual timorousness, and spiritual lethargy. Their weakness is masked by a pretense of strength; their spiritual vacuity, by claims of absolute truth. This consciousness has brought down men and nations, and gloats at the death of the enemy. Though its way is narrow, it leads to destruction. But there is another way, and although a broader path, it knows no enemy except violence to the human spirit. This way calls as its witness the spirit of life, and celebrates the variegation of life forms—the plurality of beauty, springing from a single source. Such is the way of universal consciousness. But Life favors the living. We humans, who bear the curse or the blessing of decision, may yet choose to live.

FOOTNOTES

[1]Peter L. Berger, *The Sacred Canopy* (Garden City, N. Y.: Anchor Books, 1969), p. 7.

[2]A somewhat more moderate—and clearer position—is presented by Berger in his earlier work with Thomas Luckmann, *The Social Construction of Reality* (Garden City, N. Y.: Doubleday, 1966; Anchor Books, 1967). Here Berger and Luckmann assert that "man's relationship to the surrounding environment is everywhere very imperfectly structured by his own biological constitution . . . His species-specific sensory and motor equipment imposes obvious limitations on his range of possibilities" (pp. 47–48). In this context, Berger and Luckmann stress the "immense plasticity" of the human organism's response to its environment. "In other words, there is *no human nature* in the sense of *a biologically fixed substratum* determining the variability of socio-cultural formations . . . While it is possible to say that man has a nature, it is more significant to say that man constructs his own nature, or more simply, that man produces himself" (p. 49). Although this passage admits certain general natural and biological delimitations of human nature and culture, there is little suggestion that *psychological* and *cultural* patterns might be *structurally* predisposed by biological patterns—such as the brain's two hemispheres. Although we strongly endorse the protestations to the "immense flexibility" of the human organism, we would also suggest that an understanding of possible broad structural patterns recurring in both the psyche and in culture should in fact *enhance* man's realistic capacities to *reshape* his world (or to "produce himself").

[3]George T. Lock Land, *Grow or Die: The Unifying Principle of Transformation* (New York: Random House, 1973), p. 6.

[4]Ervin Laszlo, *The Systems View of the World* (New York: George Braziller, 1972), p. 13.

[5]Ibid., p. 12.

[6]John Wren-Lewis, "Faith in the Technological Future," in Alvin Toffler, ed., *The Futurists* (New York: Random House, 1972), p. 293.

[7]In the same way, the Nazis tried to legitimate their atrocities by reference to nature. Richard Rubenstein, *The Cunning of History: Mass Death and the American Future* (New York: Harper and Row, 1975), p. 90, writes, "When the Nazis sought to justify to themselves the extermination project, they often used arguments from nature. They argued that in nature it is the fate of the weak to perish. The Nazi argument rested upon the accurate perception that no political order upheld the rights of their victims or defined the relations between warring nations. In nature men have the same rights as flies, mosquitoes or beasts of prey. The Nazis emphasized this by using language that indicated that their victims had been expelled from the human world of politics and condemned at best to the status of beasts of burden."

[8]*The Palm Beach Post*, 3 October 1975, sec. A. p. 5.

[9]Ibid.

[10]"*The New York Times* 'Weekly Review,'" *The Gainesville Sun*, 13 October 1975, sec. D. p. 7.

[11]Ibid.

[12]Ibid.

[13]Ibid.

[14]Ibid.

[15]Ibid.

[16]Ibid.

[17]Laszlo.

[18]Lock Land.

[19]Laszlo, p. 8.

[20]Ibid., p. 27.

[21]Ibid., pp. 30–32.

[22]Lock Land, p. 6.

[23]Laszlo, p. 34.

[24]Lancelot Law Whyte, *The Universe of Experience* (New York: Harper Torchbooks, 1974), p. 43.

[25]Laszlo, pp. 37–38.

330

[26] Lock Land, p. 179.

[27] Ibid., p. 180

[28] Ibid., p. 181.

[29] Ibid.

[30] Ibid.

[31] Ibid.

[32] Laszlo, p. 41.

[33] Ibid., p. 43.

[34] Ibid., p. 46.

[35] Ibid.

[36] Ibid., p. 49

[37] Ibid.

[38] Ibid.

[39] Lock Land, pp. 42, 114.

[40] Ibid., p. 19.

[41] Ibid.

[42] Ibid., p. 43.

[43] Ibid., p. 114.

[44] Ibid., p. 19.

[45] Ibid., pp. 24-25.

[46] Ibid., p. 28.

[47] Ibid.

[48] Ibid., pp. 44, 45; 114.

[49] Laszlo, p. 67.

[50] Berger, pp. 8-9.

[51] Peter L. Berger and Thomas Luckmann, *The Social Construction of Reality* (New York: Anchor Books, 1967), pp. 88-89.

[52] Laszlo, p. 113.

[53] Ibid., p. 105.

[54] Lock Land, p. 187.

[55] Laszlo, p. 51.

[56] Ibid.

[57] Ibid., p. 52.

[58] Ibid., p. 58.

[59] V. A. Firsoff, "Life and Quantum Physics," *Parapsychology Review* 5 (November-December 1974): 11.

[60] This position is argued by Jacques Monod, *Chance and Necessity* (London: Collins, 1972), a work with which Firsoff takes issue.

[61] Firsoff, p. 11.

[62] Ibid., p. 12.

[63] Ibid., p. 13.

[64] Ibid.

[65] Ibid.

[66] Ibid.

[67] Ibid., p. 14.

[68] Ibid.

[69] Ibid.

[70] Ibid., p. 15.

[71] Victor F. Weisskopf, *Knowledge and Wonder* (New York: Anchor Books, 1966), p. 126.

[72] Arthur Koestler, *The Roots of Coincidence* (New York: Vintage Books, 1973), p. 58.

[73] David Bakan, *The Duality of Human Existence* (Boston: Beacon Press, 1969), pp. 154-96.

[74] Associated Press Release, date unknown.

[75] *Brain/Mind Bulletin* 1 (December 1, 1975): 1,3.

[76] *Palm Beach Times,* Monday, November 24, 1975.

[77] John L. Randall, *Parapsychology and the Nature of Life* (New York: Harper and Row, 1975), 256 pp., provides an excellent review of past and recent research. See Appendix III. For example, for an account of research in the year 1974 sponsored by a single foundation, the Parapsychology Foundation—only one of a number of such institutions pursuing research—see *Parapsychology Review*, 6 (January-February, 1975), "Annual Report for the Year 1974," pp. 5-9. This same issue includes a "Directory of Parapsychological Associations," pp. 22-28 (which is expressly qualified as non-exhaustive, omitting, for example, Soviet research), listing 186 organizations worldwide which are engaged in parapsychological research.

[78] Koestler, p. 91.

[79] Firsoff, p. 14.

[80] Laszlo, p. 100.

[81] John 3:8; 4:23,24; 13:5; 14:26; 16:12 suggest the possibility that the historical Jesus wished to point beyond himself, by stressing both the universality of servanthood and the final authority of God's Spirit. However, John's evangelistic and apologetic purposes (20:31) may or may not be responsible for a variety of statements to the contrary, such as John 3:31-36; 5:19-47; 8:39ff.; 10:7ff; 12:32; 14:6, etc.

APPENDIX I

TOWARDS A NEW WORLD VIEW

IN THE introductory comments to this writing we observed that what we commonly perceive as "reality" is only a "special case" of the larger cosmos, arising chiefly from the narrow band of frequencies available to our neurological equipment. For example, dogs hear certain high-pitched sounds that are inaudible to the human ear; and perhaps more poignantly, the human eye perceives radiation only in the narrow range of $4 \times 10^{-5} - 7 \times 10^{-5}$ cm., whereas the greater (though not exhaustive) range of radiation from γ-rays to VLF is 10^{12} to 10^7 cm.[1] Analogously, we must be wary of too quickly universalizing even the laws of nature, which are known only within the context of our experience (even if that experience is vastly enhanced through technological extensions of our physiological equipment or extrapolation by hypothesis and experiment). In light of our inherent structural bias, how can we speak of a *world* view, since only a very limited cosmos is available to our knowledge?

A second limiting factor, overlapping our physiological preconditioning, is the uniqueness of the particular space-time frame in which we operate. Einsteinian relativity establishes the necessity of considering that frame in our calculations and reconnoitering. From this frame alone, we conceptualize nature and establish our laws of nature. Einstein hoped by his relativity principles to insure the validity and universality of cosmic law; but even the redoubtable speed of light, which now appears to be a universal constant, is nevertheless an extrapolation from knowledge available to us in our own particular space-time frame.

Again the question emerges, how can we speak of a *world* view? We make two assumptions that seem to legitimate a world view: first, that reality is in some basic sense homogeneous and isotropic; and second, that it is therefore valid to make extrapolations from our partial experience to the whole of things. We peer at the macrocosmic trans-galactic domains and the microcosmic subatomic world from our ostensible median mesocosmic position. We might add that such a situation seems inevitable; and it would appear that we should learn to live with it.

However, a strange contradiction emerges as we examine classical conceptualizations of the world. We seem to have assumed consistently that our symbolic apprehensions of the world are literal descriptions of reality. We have attributed, either overtly or tacitly, absolute status to those assumptions. We may gaze back at our ancestors' mythopoeism with some

333

sense of appreciative tolerance, noting that their animated world brought life and power even to words and symbols. But as we begin to examine the great cognitive systems upon which our own "modern" civilization is founded—language, mathematics, and rational ideologies—we should be astounded by our form of subtle mythopoeism. As we observed in our analysis of language and world view, Indo-European languages, if not structurally and innately substantialistic, are at least by grammatical and common usage largely substantialistic in format, starting with the use of the verb *to be*. Secondly, the great rational systems of thought from Neoplatonism to scholasticism (with the exception of some surprisingly astute scholastic thought), to the Cartesian and Newtonian syntheses, all are imbued with abstracted absolute theorems to which the world of space-time is assumed to conform. Thirdly, mathematics abstracts and generalizes from the beginning. On an elementary level we speak of adding three apples (which vary in size, weight, color, volume, etc.) by a simple formula of 1 +1 +1 = 3, as if that were all there were to it.

Particularly in the *latter* case we may argue the necessity of such abstractions as foundational to rational thought, and also to social intercourse, technology, and commerce. Such arguments are quite valid. However, the real issue is not the validity of such generalizations, but their accuracy and universality. Just as Einstein recognized the genius and extensive fruitfulness of Newtonian concepts, yet continued to probe for more basic and universal foundations, perhaps we must examine afresh basic foundations—just as we applaud their inherent utility. For example, in addition to the system of classical mathematics—which will continue to exhibit its immense merit—we might be able to develop a parallel system which could prove to be fruitful both philosophically and descriptively for complex phenomena.

In analyzing anew our cosmological foundations, at least three *universals* seem apparent in nature that should serve as clues to reconstruction. These three universals are quite simple—and should be evident upon thoughtful reflection. We shall identify them, and then seek to explicate their relevance in the quest for new foundations. First of all, as Heraclitus taught us long ago, all of nature is a dynamic *process*. Even the most rigid artifacts of nature, such as rock crystals, are merely temporal expressions of physiochemical processes. Secondly, nature is neither perfectly symmetric nor asymmetric, but *eksymmetric*. We coin the term eksymmetric (with the prefix *ek* from the Greek "out of," to indicate something like "deriving from" symmetric principles) to observe that, although nature is fond of symmetry, it is never apparently a "perfect" symmetry (perhaps for the simple reason that nothing in nature is finally static). Most (if not all) natural forms derive from symmetrically-designed processes; but the actual processual expressions of natural forms are never completely, or at least *finally*, symmetric. "Perfect symmetry" would apparently entail a complete atomic rigidity (which would seem to be equivalent to a state of ultimate entropy increase where no further movement could occur). The fabled snowflake, beautifully expressive of symmetrical principles, when reduced to its molecular or atomic constituents is seen to be a temporary and general order.

Thirdly, and harmoniously allied with the first two "universals," all natural systems seem to occur as *functions* of a larger *field* or *organic whole,* as well as in temporary "bodies" or as separate "things." The significance of this latter observation is that all behavior affects a larger field; for all things are atomically—if not organically—interconnected.

These universals underscore a thesis to which we now return. Atomistic and mechanistic premises of the world, however fruitful and utilitarian pragmatically, analytically, or technologically, are not adequate explanations for the ultimate state of nature. For nature is ultimately an holistic process, manifesting itself in an infinite array of more or less temporary, more or less symmetrical expressions. How could it be otherwise, since permanence or perfect symmetry suggest a staticism which does not accord with our experience of reality.

On a more practical level, do these three premises alter the scope (for example) of mathematics? By great genius mathematics has been extended to symbolize all kinds of processes, and states of matter and energy. However, the present body of mathematical symbolism, which is of immense importance, still tends to represent the world as concatenations of discrete units or fragments. The world is atomized and mechanized. As such, we never engage the real world directly, but only the probable state of the real world as idealized in static space-time frames and symbolized in abstract formulae. For example, apples are still generalized as 1, 2, and 3 or, "assuming the average diameter of an apple to be 7 cm., how many apples would a container whose volume is 500 cm. accommodate, if 110 cm. of this space must be reserved as empty space for stacking?" Such calculations are quite valuable, but do not tell us much about the relative uniqueness of the individual apples, their ripeness, etc. Furthermore, rotten apples tend to collapse.

On a much more significant level, Raymond Sheline has demonstrated that as we examine the spectroscopies of atomic and molecular systems, of nuclei, and finally of the "bare" nucleon, we are struck by the following phenomenon:

> An intriguing aspect of the different realms of spectroscopy is, as the energy range of the system increases, the size of the mechanical systems which describe the spectra decreases. Historically, each time we find what for a short time appears to be an ultimate building block of matter, we also find that there seems to be a fine structure aspect in the spectroscopy, or an asymmetry in one of the fundamental properties of the ultimate building block. This is soon explained as a substructure and a separate spectroscopy in a considerably higher energy range. In some sense, the models we make

seem to be leading us by a series of successive approximations. We are forced to ask, having seen three spectroscopies and structures, should we not anticipate a fourth, fifth, and sixth . . . higher orders of spectroscopies and structure?[1]

In other words, as we descend the ladder in the size of physical systems (and concomitantly ascend the latter of energy coefficients), we are always dealing with series of successive approximations which exhibit imperfect symmetries in response to mathematical predictions. Sheline continues:

If we wish for a moment to be extremely speculative, we might ask, if our spectroscopies and structures are leading us to an ultimate understanding of the structure of matter by a series of successive approximations, is there not some way to understand that ultimate structure of matter directly—some more fundamental description which would bypass the series of successive approximations?[2]

Sheline cites as examples of the dilemma faced by physicists using our present mathematical systems the magnetic moment of a neutron, whose predicted value is 0, but actually measures -1.913 nuclear magnetons, and likewise the proton, with a predicted value of +2, yet actual measurement of 2.793 nuclear magnetons. Sheline's suggestion concerning "successive approximations" is provocative. Are we indeed consigned to a circular quandary, moving from abstraction to abstraction, and yet further away from the real world which we are describing? In other words, must we always deal with the world in terms of approximations or probable statements about reality, however satisfactory such statements may be for a wide variety of purposes? Is there no means or alternate model for bypassing such approximations? Or to put the question somewhat differently, is there no way we can incorporate the processual, eksymmetric, and field properties of the real world into our symbolic analyses of the world?

Before addressing these questions directly, let us consider a paradigmatic depiction of our dilemma which we call event x—an unknown atomic event which we will represent as an high energy spiral:

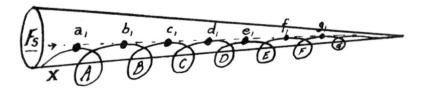

Now, let us assume that our technological sensors can only detect a certain range of frequency, represented as Fs (our "focus") which includes only the top peaks of the spiralling event, a1 b1 . . . g1, whereas the larger sweep of motion and frequencies of event x include the entire spiral pattern ascribed by moments A, B, C . . . G. If event x occurs "fast" enough, our perception of that event might be represented as a rapid and continuous sequence of linear points a1 b1 . . . g1, a depiction of event x which would be partial, and thus inadequate as an expression of the true course of the whole. The fuller course of A, B, C . . . G would remain unknown to us. Our space-time frame is too "narrow" to appreciate the full event. What could we do to remedy our myopia?

First of all, all descriptions of physical phenomena must remain tentative and open-ended as we remain alert to any further developments, either technological or theoretical, which will expand our range of perception or sharpen the accuracy of our descriptions. However, secondly, it seems that we *can* search for means of enhancing the utility of our symbolism. The suggestions that follow—uninformed by technical and mathematical expertise—must be considered quite tentatively and paradigmatically, and stand in need of more lucid expression.

However, we will attempt to sketch at least the *dimensions* of the problem, if not a proper solution. Our mathematical symbolism might be of considerably more value for depicting fundamental processes of nature if it could carry within its basic premises (and not just as advanced algebraic functions) expressions of nature's processes, eksymmetry, and field relationships. A processual mathematics would carry within its most basic principles, exponents or terms representing the uniqueness of each moment of reality, as well as expressions of continuous process and modification. The following premises would seem to be endemic also to a processual mathematics: 1) every moment of reality envisioned as a "thing" in space-time must also be regarded as a process undergoing internal changes and affecting (on whatever slight or significant level) external environs; 2) every moment of reality envisioned as a "thing" in space-time must also be regarded as an expression of a larger field; 3) every moment of reality envisioned as a "thing" in space-time must retain its character of uniqueness and the integrity of its own "societal" constituency.

We would represent these premises in the following illustrative form, which is offered merely as a suggestive paradigm of what may need to be done. (See page 338.)

In other words, we suggest the possible development of a system parallel to traditional mathematics (which would continue to serve most purposes). This system would incorporate processual premises, eksymmetric expressions, and field relationships. The ostensible value of such a system would be to correct for probability functions not inherent in our current symbolism.

In addition to organic systems, psychological and social systems seem to exhibit processual, eksymmetric, and field properties. Ideas and beliefs,

Every $1 \; \beta$ (becomes) 1_0 indicating its process through space-time

Every $1 \vDash$ (consists of) 1_c where c is equivalent to component processes or configurations

Every $1 \ll$ (exists as a part of) S_1 where S is a larger "society" or organic whole

Every $1 \rightsquigarrow$ (effects and is effected by, reciprocally) fS_1 where f is the field of S and its effectual exchanges

Every $1_0 \vDash 1_c \rightsquigarrow 1_{0c}$ where ($\rightsquigarrow$ = "transformed into") and (1_{0c} = or $\neq$ to 1_c)

Every $1_0 \ll S_{10}$ where $S_1 \rightsquigarrow S_{10}$ (and where S has further constituent expressions)

Every $1_0 \rightsquigarrow fS_{10}$, etc.

On a simple operational level, a parallel to $1 + 1 = 2$ would be:

$1a_1 + 1a_2 = 2a_{(1+2)}$ where $1a_1$ and $1a_2$ retain their separate identity in the process;

$1a_1 + 1a_2 = 2a_{(1\&2)}$ where the process involves a commingling of $1a_1$ and $1a_2$;

$2a_{(1+2)} \neq 1a + 1a$

$2a_{(1+2)} \vDash 1a_{1c} + 1a_{2c}$

$2a_{(1+2)} \ll Sa_1 \; \& \; Sa_2$ where Sa_1 may = or $\neq Sa_2$

$2a_{(1+2)} \; \beta \; 1a_{10} + 1a_{20}$

$2a_{(1\&2)} \; \beta \; 2a_{(1\&2)\,0}$

"healthy" or "unhealthy" psychological profiles, institutional forms and norms, aesthetic and ethical ideals, and historical processes all may be understood more fully by reference to these three universals. "Holistic empiricism" recognizes field properties as holistic effects (of all individual and institutional occurrences) in the global ecosystem of which we are a part. The three "universals" should insure both a broader understanding of, and more balanced judgments concerning, culture.

FOOTNOTES

[1]Raymond Sheline, Lecture, April 10, 1970, Tallahassee, Florida.
[2]Ibid.

APPENDIX II

A POSTSCRIPT TO CHAPTER ELEVEN: IMPERIALISM, THIRD WORLD CONSCIOUSNESS AND THE CHALLENGE TO HOLISM

WITH THE appearance of bourgeois imperialism in the mid-Victorian era, the middle class triumph, which had heretofore been fundamentally economic, was extended into the political sphere. Hannah Arendt writes that

> The central inner-European event of the imperialist period was the political emancipation of the bourgeoisie, which up to then had been the first class in history to achieve economic preeminence without aspiring to political rule.[1]

The situation in England is probably most typical. Perhaps the greatest symbol of this new politicizing of bourgeois interests occurred on November 1, 1858 when in India a royal proclamation announced that Queen Victoria (who ruled from 1837 to 1901) "had assumed the government of India"[2] (which had heretofore been held in trust by the East India Company). The proclamation announced (among others) these ostensible policies:

> We desire no extension of our present territorial possessions; and, while we will permit no aggression upon our dominions . . ., we shall sanction no encroachment on those of others. We shall respect the rights, dignity, and honour of native princes as our own; and we desire that they, as well as our own subjects, should enjoy that prosperity and that social advancement which can only be secured by internal peace and good government . . . Firmly relying ourselves on the truth of Christianity . . ., we disclaim alike the right and the desire to impose our convictions on any of our subjects . . . we do strictly charge and enjoin all those who may be in authority under us that they abstain from all interference with the religious belief or worship of any of our subjects . . . And it is our further will that, as far as may be, our subjects, of whatever race or creed, be freely and impartially admitted to offices in our service, the duties of which they may be qualified by their education, ability, and integrity, duly to discharge . . .[3]

The following day in London, the *Times* concluded an editorial with these words:

> Providence, so we are proud to say, has cast them upon our care. They are become our children. How shall we feed so many? How shall we double or treble the productiveness of the peninsula, which, between seas and impassible mountains, is hardly less an island than our own? How shall we save them from worse famine—the superstitions that enslave and degrade them? These are questions that will present themselves to-day, and which have long been clamorous for a reply.[4]

On January 1, 1877, amid great pomp and ceremony, Queen Victoria was proclaimed Empress of India. Prime Minister Benjamin Disraeli "prevailed upon the Queen . . . against much opposition in Britain, to assume the new 'un-English' title."[5]

Meanwhile on the home front, sentiments reflecting the same ethos were addressed to the proletariat by the most widely-read book of the nineteenth century, Samuel Smiles' *Self Help* (1859). "The aim of *Self Help* was to aid the working classes in improving themselves so as to reach the top. This path was marked by the improvement of the individual character of those who desired to be a success in life."[6] At the same time that this virtuous work ethic was being proclaimed to the working classes, their actual condition, as Karl Marx perhaps most poignantly realized, was too often a seething repository of poverty and injustice. Many significant voices joined in protest:

> callousness, poverty, ugliness, and degradation caused Carlyle, Ruskin, and others to protest against the very foundations of this civilization, alleging it to lie in selfishness and materialism . . . Shelley had burned with indignation at the factories of England . . . Certainly, until near the end of the century, the slums in London and other cities showed a subhuman degradation seldom if ever equalled in Europe, and until the 1880's very little concern about this was displayed by anyone; it was not society's business, but the individual's . . . Dickens in *Hard Times* (1854) flagellated a society that had just finished congratulating itself, upon the occasion of the great Crystal Palace Exhibition, for its infinite progressiveness. It is a world made up of Bounderbys; greedy capitalists unscrupulously pursuing success, and Gradgrinds, who, aided by utilitarianism and Political Economy, have reduced life to statistics and forgotten its beauty . . .[7]

But the *status quo* at home was perhaps too close, and not only lacked the mystique for arousing general missionary ardor (which seemed appropriate for faraway places such as India), but fit in far too well with the fundamental ambitions of bourgeois economics. Exploitation at home is too obvious to be veiled under the same official paternalistic euphemisms as expansion abroad (which is not to say that slogans have been absent from the home front). Hannah Arendt observes:

> Expansion as a permanent and supreme aim of politics is the central political idea of imperialism. Since it implies neither temporary looting nor the more lasting assimilation of conquest, it is an entirely new concept in the long history of political thought and action. The reason for this . . . is simply that this concept is not really political at all, but has its origin in the realm of business speculation, where expansion meant the permanent broadening of industrial production and economic transactions characteristic of the nineteenth century.[8]

In our own times the wave of bourgeois economic imperialism has only just begun to recede. In many places around the globe the bitter memories of this "capitalist imperialism" still linger, mixed with the ambivalent desires for national identity, "progress," and "modernization," (and the last two terms *are* largely bourgeois tenets). Berger, Berger and Kellner write:

> In recently colonial countries the vivid memory of discrimination against indigenous personnel in political and economic institutions still remains.

Even in countries where such memories are fading, resentment against the West is a powerful motivating force among the educated classes. This resentment may be increased by the often unadmitted recognition that while the West and all its works are violently rejected, the nation's goals of development and modernization cannot be achieved without accepting at least a measure of Westernization and Western-derived institutions . . .[9]

At the same time, even further tensions add to the cultural discrepancies between Western and emerging nations:

On the level of everyday experience, there are the massive realities of hunger, disease and early death. But the same facts . . . are also definitions of the situation and elements of consciousness . . . modernization entails an expansion of the individual's social horizon . . . Inevitably, he begins to compare his own situation with that world . . . What previously was perceived as being part of the human condition and its destiny now comes to be perceived as a very particular condition, an unjust one, and one that at least in principle might be changed. For this reason there is . . . increasing linkage between modernization and the rise of social dissatisfaction and revolutionary consciousness . . .[10]

The purpose of this brief review of bourgeois imperial beginnings and the response of emerging nations during the (ostensible) waning years of imperialism, is simply to raise the question of the efficacy or evocative force of the holistic model which has been proposed. Could such a model—seemingly itself the product of bourgeois society—command any respect from antagonistic peoples of socialist, Marxist, or a variety of indigenous nationalistic persuasions?

As we have stated in the introduction, this study does not claim to offer any facile solutions to such very real tensions. However, an holistic empirical model does seem capable of addressing itself to such issues. Both terms—"holistic" and "empirical"—are relevant to the question. "Empirical" means that the very concrete data of persons and their socio-economic, ideological, and political situations must be considered in any viable quest for new consciousness. "Holistic" implies, as we have suggested, that the indigenous integrities of all "parts"—that is of all peoples—must be affirmed. Thus holistic empiricism requires the recognition of the broad variety of human social expressions, of human sufferings and ambitions; it also implies that the health of the whole may be achieved only through the health of the constituent parts. Thus no artificial unity can be imposed upon the discrete peoples of the world.

On the other hand, holistic empiricism likewise implies the recognition that the world itself has "shrunk," as every schoolboy in New York City or Beirut knows. The problem of an *ecosystem* is not simply the leisure-time diversion of bourgeois intellectuals; if the world runs out of resources or blows itself up, there will not only be no emerging peoples but perhaps no peoples at all. Thus the *responsibility* for the *whole*—indeed for the health of the planet—can be escaped neither by the "rich" nor by the "poor." However uncomfortable we may be with it, we all live in a community of nations (if not an idealistic world community *a la* Ferdinand Tonnies, at least a world where our actions are inextricably interlinked). In this sense the whole is indeed greater than the sum of its parts, for without a world we are all lost.

Thus holistic empiricism as a model, though not intended as a panacea for struggling and suffering persons, does seek to create an awareness, a consciousness, which will underscore the mutual responsibility which all peoples share, whether by choice or by necessity, for the welfare *both* of the whole *and* of all constituent parts.

FOOTNOTES

[1]Hannah Arendt, *The Origins of Totalitarianism* (New York: Harvest Books, 1973), p. 123.

[2]Hans Kohn, ed., *The Modern World: 1848 to the Present* (New York: Macmillan, 1968), p. 121.

[3]Ibid., p. 123.

[4]Ibid., p. 127.

[5]Ibid., p. 121.

[6]George L. Mosse, *The Culture of Western Europe: The Nineteenth and Twentieth Centuries* (Chicago: Rand McNally, 19740, p.97.

[7]Roland N. Stromberg, *An Intellectual History of Modern Europe* (Englewood Cliffs: Prentice-Hall, 1975), pp. 288-89.

[8]Arendt, *The Origins of Totalitarianism,* p. 125.

[9]Peter L. Berger, Brigitte Berger, and Hansfried Kellner, *The Homeless Mind: Modernization and Consciousness* (New York: Random House, 1973; Vintage Books, 1974), p. 133.

[10]Ibid., pp. 134-35.

APPENDIX III

NOTES ON PARAPSYCHOLOGICAL RESEARCH

THE ORIGINS of contemporary psychical research date to the founding of the British Society for Psychical Research in 1882. The founders of this society were men of eminent stature in a variety of scholarly fields, including the philosopher Henry Sidgwick, the classical scholar F. W. H. Myers, and the physicist William Barrett. In America, formal research began with the establishment of the Duke University laboratory under the direction of Drs. J. B. and Louisa Rhine, who were encouraged and supported by the prominent psychologist Dr. William McDougall.

The Rhines' earliest studies elicited a variety of criticisms, mainly directed at alleged weaknesses in experimental methods or faulty use of statistics. J. B. Rhine responded by encouraging such criticisms, and devised his testing procedures with increasing rigor. In 1937 the American Institute of Statistical Mathematics officially commended the statistical methodology employed by the Duke researchers. Obviously, the greater the sampling in statistical studies, the more convincing the results. Jeffrey Mishlove reports that "By the end of 1941, a total of 651,216 experimental die throws had been conducted (by Rhine). The combined results of these experiments pointed to a phenomenon with 10^{155} to 1 odds against chance occurrence."[1]

Numerous similar tests have been conducted with increasing sophistication in experimental apparatus since the Rhines' early work. Such testing is now entirely automated. Today significant research is expanding in the investigation of "extrasensory perception" and a wide variety of related phenomena.[2] Some of the organizations in America sponsoring such research are the Academy of Parapsychology and Medicine, The Parapsychological Association (in December, 1969 granted affiliate status by the American Academy for the Advancement of Science), the American Society for Psychical Research, and the Foundation for Research on the Nature of Man. A sample of important research centers includes the Menninger Foundation of Topeka, Kansas; the Division of Parapsychology of the School of Medicine, the University of Virginia; the Maimonides Dream Laboratory in Brooklyn, New York; the University of California at Davis; and Stanford University. Serious research is now conducted worldwide, including universities in Great Britain, Europe, and the Soviet Union. There are also a number of scholarly journals devoted to parapsychological research.

An adequate summary of extensive recent parapsychological research would recount investigations of widely varied phenomena, including:

telepathy, clairvoyance, precognition, altered states of consciousness, "out-of-the-body" experiences, reincarnation, and bioenergetics.[3] Perhaps the issue of greatest consequence is that which motivated the founders of the British SPR: the investigation of the survival of human personality beyond physical death. Traditionally, this thesis has been highly suspect among educated persons because of its popular associations with superstition and the alleged hocus pocus of "madame mediums," depicted as preying upon the grief and gullibility of those recently bereaved.

Although significant "survival" research has been in progress for decades, the recent statements of the prominent psychiatrist Dr. Elizabeth Kubler-Ross (noted for her work with the dying) have precipitated wide discussion among intelligent inquirers. Dr. Kubler-Ross, whose *On Death and Dying*[4] has become a classic handbook for psychiatrists, counsellors and chaplains, began her research as a complete skeptic, operating on the popular materialistic assumption that death is the cessation of all life functions. After thousands of experiences with the dying, Dr. Kubler-Ross reports "I don't just believe that . . . I know, beyond the shadow of a doubt, that there is life after death."[5]

> The Swiss-born psychiatrist, who says she is not a religious person, bases her conviction on interviews with hundreds of men and women who were declared legally dead and then were revived. "We found some fabulous common denominators which you can't deny," she said.[6]

When Dr. Kubler-Ross and her associates questioned the patients who had been presumed dead,

> most of the patients said they were floating a few feet above their bodies, watching the resuscitation efforts. They could accurately describe the scene, the details of what was said, and the comings and goings of the rescuers and observers . . . "They have a fabulous feeling of peace and wholeness," Dr. Ross reported. "People who are blind can see, paraplegics have legs that they can move. They have no pain, no fear, no anxiety. In fact, it is such a beautiful experience that many of them resent being brought back to their physical body." Almost all of them reported that they were greeted by someone who had died before them.[7]

The research of one person (and her associates), however highly respected, certainly does not merit wholesale credulity. Dr. Kubler-Ross' observations call for further intensive study.[8] We must be wary of the siren-like "will to believe" which seems so persistent in human nature (and has fostered so many mass defections to groundless ideologies and superstitions). Perhaps we should be equally wary of the "will not to believe," which appears to be largely the legacy of a reductionist materialism. After all, the "will to believe" does not automatically negate the validity of all things believed. Science itself operates on a premise of faith in natural *laws* of the cosmos. The phenomena of parapsychology and related issues (such as the survival ques-tion—a matter upon which there is no agreement among parapsychologists)* merit further investigation, not merely because of their persistence, but because of their relevance to very ultimate human questions.

----

*A different approach to the survival question is that of Dr. Ian Stevenson, Carlson Professor of Psychiatry at the University of Virginia Medical School. Dr. Stevenson has subjected the reincarnational memories of (mostly) children to intense research, and has attained striking results which seem to support the reincarnation hypothesis. Of a series of his books published by the University of Virginia Press, *Twenty Cases Suggestive of Reincarnation* remains the most widely-read study.[9]

FOOTNOTES

[1] Jeffrey Mishlove, *The Roots of Consciousness* (New York/Berkeley: Random House/Bookworks, 1975), pp. 108, 111, 161.

[2] John L. Randall, *Parapsychology and the Nature of Life* (New York: Harper & Row, 1975), p. 175ff., for a history of recent research.

[3] Dr. Thelma Moss, *The Probability of the Impossible: Scientific Discoveries and Explorations in the Psychic World* (New York: Plume/New American Library, 1974), for a survey of phenomena under investigation.

[4] Elizabeth Kubler-Ross, *On Death and Dying* (New York: Macmillan, 1969).

[5] *Orlando Sentinel-Star,* 17 October 1975, sec. A, p. 14.

[6] Ibid.

[7] Ibid.

[8] Two recent volumes should be cited. On a somewhat popular level: Raymond A. Moody, *Life After Life* (New York: Bantam Books, 1976); a more exhaustive study: Karlis Osis and Erlendur Haraldsson, *At the Hour of Death* (New York: Avon Books, 1977).

[9] Ian Stevenson, *Twenty Cases Suggestive of Reincarnation* (Charlottesville: University Press of Virginia, 1974).

SELECTIVE BIBLIOGRAPHY

Aaronson, Henry S., "Behavior and the Place Names of Time," In *The Future of Time,* pp. 405-436. Edited by Henri Yaker, Humphry Osmond and Frances Cheek. Garden City, N.Y.: Doubleday, 1971; Anchor Books, 1972.

Albright, W. F., *From the Stone Age to Christianity.* Garden City, N.Y.: Doubleday Anchor Books, 1957.

"Annual Report for the Year 1974," *Parapsychology Review* 6 (January-February 1975): 5-9.

Anthes, Rudolf, "Mythology in Ancient Egypt," In *Mythologies of the Ancient World,* pp. 15-92. Edited by Samuel Noah Kramer. Garden City, N.Y.: Anchor Books, 1961.

Arendt, Hannah, *Between Past and Future: Eight Exercises in Political Thought.* New York: The Viking Press, 1968.

————, *The Human Condition.* Chicago: The University of Chicago Press, 1958.

————, *The Origins of Totalitarianism.* New York: Harcourt-Brace, Harvest, 1951-73.

Aristotle, *Politics.* Translated by Benjamin Jowett, In *Great Books of the Western World,* Vol. 9. Edited by R. M. Hutchins. Chicago: Encyclopaedia Britannica, Inc., 1952.

Augustine, *The City of God.* Translated by Marcus Dods.

Avineri, Shlomo, *Hegel's Theory of the Modern State.* Cambridge: Cambridge University Press, 1972.

Bainton, Roland H., "Man, God, and the Church in the Age of the Renaissance," In *The Renaissance: Six Essays.* New York: Harper Torchbooks, 1962.

Bakan, David, *The Duality of Human Existence.* Boston: Beacon Press, 1966.

————, *Sigmund Freud and the Jewish Mystical Tradition.* New York: Schocken Books, 1965.

Barbu, Zevedei, *Democracy and Dictatorship.* New York: Grove Press, 1956.

Barnett, Lincoln, *The Universe and Dr. Einstein.* New York: Bantam Books, 1948-73.

Barrett, C. K., ed., *The New Testament Background: Selected Documents.* New York: Harper Torchbooks, 1961.

Barth, Karl, "The Righteousness of God," Translated by Douglas Horton, In *Science, Faith and Man,* pp. 44-56. Edited by W. Warren Wagar. New York: Harper and Row, 1968.

————, *The Word of God and The Word of Man.* Translated by Douglas Horton. New York: Harper Torchbooks, 1957.

Bellah, Robert, "Religious Evolution." *American Sociological Review* XXIX, No. 3 (1964): 358-74.

Bem, Daryl J., *Beliefs, Attitudes and Human Affairs.* Belmont, California: Brooks-Cole, 1970.

Benedict, Ruth, "Child Rearing in Certain European Countries," In *Every Man His Way,* pp. 292-301. Edited by Alan Dundes. Englewood Cliffs, N.J.: Prentice-Hall, 1968.

————, "The Science of Custom," In *Every Man His Way,* pp. 180-88. Edited by Alan Dundes. Englewood Cliffs, N.J.: Prentice-Hall, 1968.

Bentham, Jeremy, "Principles of Legislation." In *Communism, Fascism, and Democracy: The Theoretical Foundations*. Edited by Carl Cohen. New York: Random House, 1972.

Berdyaev, Nicolas, *Truth and Revelation*. Translated by R. M. French. New York: Collier, 1962.

Berger, Peter L., *A Rumor of Angels*. Garden City, N.Y.: Doubleday, 1969; Anchor Books, 1970.

————, *The Sacred Canopy*. Garden City, N.Y.: Doubleday, 1967; Anchor Books, 1969.

Berger, Peter L.; Berger, Brigitte; and Kellner, Hansfried, *The Homeless Mind*. New York: Vintage Books, 1974.

Berger, Peter L., and Luckmann, Thomas, *The Social Construction of Reality*. Garden City, N.Y.: Doubleday, 1966; Anchor Books, 1967.

Bernstein, Jeremy, *Einstein*. New York: The Viking Press, 1973.

Bernstein, Richard, *Praxis and Action: Contemporary Philosophies of Human Action*. Philadelphia: University of Pennsylvania Press, 1971.

Black, Max, *Language and Philosophy*. Ithaca, N.Y.: Cornell University Press, 1949.

Bova, Ben, *The New Astronomies*. New York: Mentor, The New American Library, 1972.

Brain Mind Bulletin 1 (December 1, 1975): 1-3.

Bronowski, J., *The Common Sense of Science*. New York: Vintage Books, n.d.

Bronowski, J., and Mazlish, Bruce, *The Western Intellectual Tradition*. New York: Harper and Bros., 1960; Harper Torchbooks, 1962.

Brown, Norman O., *Love's Body*. New York: Vintage Books, 1966.

Burns, Edward McNall. *Western Civilizations: Their History and Culture*. 2 vols. New York: W. W. Norton, 1969.

Calder, Nigel, *The Mind of Man*. New York: The Viking Press, 1971; Viking Compass, 1973.

Caldwell, W. E., *The Ancient World*. New York: Holt, Rinehart and Winston, 1963.

Campbell, Alexander, *The Masks of the Gods: Occidental Mythology*. New York: The Viking Press, 1969.

Capra, Fritjof, *The Tao of Physics*. Berkeley: Shambhala Publications, 1975.

Cassirer, Ernst, *The Individual and the Cosmos in Renaissance Philosophy*. Translated by Mario Domand. New York: Harper and Row, 1963; Harper Torchbooks, 1964.

————, *Language and Myth*. Translated by Susanne K. Langer. New York: Harper and Bros., 1946; Dover Publications, 1953.

————, *The Philosophy of the Enlightenment*. Translated by Fritz C. A. Loellin and James P. Pettegrove. Princeton: Princeton University Press, 1951.

Cassirer, Ernst; Kristeller, Paul Oskar; and Randall, John Herman, *The Renaissance Philosophy of Man*. Chicago: The University of Chicago Press, 1948.

Charon, Jean, *Cosmology*. Translated by Patrick Moore. New York: World University Library, 1970.

Christian, James L., *Philosophy: An Introduction to the Art of Wondering*. San Francisco: Rinehart Press, 1973.

Clarkson, Jesse D., *A History of Russia*. New York: Random House, 1961.

Cochrane, Charles Norris, *Christianity and Classical Culture*. London: Oxford University Press, 1968.

Cohen, Carl, ed., *Communism, Fascism, and Democracy: The Theoretical Foundations*. New York: Random House, 1972.

Crombie, A. C., *Medieval and Early Modern Science*. 2 vols. Garden City: Anchor Books, 1959.

Cumont, Franz, *The Mysteries of Mithra*. Translated by Thomas J. McCormack. New York: Dover Books, 1956.

Dampier, W. C., *A History of Science and Its Relation to Philosophy and Religion*. Cambridge: Cambridge University Press, 1966.

Davies, W. D., *Paul and Rabbinic Judaism*. London, S.P.C.K., 1965.

Dewey, John, "The Future of Liberalism." *The Journal of Philosophy*, 32, April 25, 1935.

Dodds, E. R., *The Greeks and the Irrational*. Berkeley: The University of California Press, 1951.

Drell, Sidney D., "Electron-Positron Annihilation and the New Particles." *Scientific American*, June 1975, pp. 50-62.

Drucker, Peter. "The First Technological Revolution and Its Lessons," In *Technology and Culture: An Anthology*. Edited by Melvin Kranzberg and William H. Davenport. New York: Meridian, New American Library, 1975.

Dubos, Rene, "Science and Man's Nature," In *Science and Culture*, pp. 251-72. Edited by Gerald Holton. Boston: Beacon Press, 1967.

Dundes, Alan, Ed., *Every Man His Way*. Englewood Cliffs, N.J.: Prentice-Hall, 1968.

Einstein, Albert, *Out of My Later Years*. New York: Philosophical Library, 1950.

Embler, Weller, "Metaphor and Social Belief," In *Language, Meaning and Maturity*, pp. 125-38. Edited by S. I. Hayakawa. New York: Harper and Row, 1954.

Erikson, Erik H., *Childhood and Society*. New York: W. W. Norton, 1950-63.

Feine, Paul; Behm, Johannes; and (reedited by) Kuemmel, Werner G., *Introduction to the New Testament*. Translated by A. J. Mattill, Jr. Nashville: Abingdon Press, 1966.

Firsoff, V. A., "Life and Quantum Physics." *Parapsychology Review* 5 (November-December 1974): 10-15.

Fleming, William, *Arts and Ideas*. New York: Holt, Rinehart and Winston, Third Ed., n.d.

Fletcher, Amherst O.; Flatcher, Amos N.; Stanzo, Alonzo P.; and Lator, Fernando El, eds. *Field Studies Among Indigenous Archipelagoers*. Pointe-a-Pitre: Lesser Antilles Press, n.d.

Fourier, F. M. Charles, "The Mistakes of Industry," In *Selections from the Works of Fourier*. Translated by Julia Franklin. London: Swan Sonnenschein and Co., 1901.

Frankfort, H. and H. A., "Myth and Reality," In *Before Philosophy*, pp.11-36. Edited by H. and H. A. Frankfort, John A. Wilson and Thorkild Jacobsen. New York: Penguin Books, 1949-72.

Freud, Sigmund, *Civilization and Its Discontents*. Translated by James Strachey. New York: W. W. Norton, 1962.

————, *The Ego and the Id*. Translated by Joan Riviere and Revised and Newly Edited by James Strachey. New York: W. W. Norton, 1962.

————, *The Future of an Illusion*. Translated by W. D. Robson-Scott. New York: Anchor Books, 1964.

————, *New Introductory Lectures on Psychoanalysis.* Translated by James Strachey. New York: W. W. Norton, 1965.

Gamow, George, *One, two, three . . . infinity.* New York: Viking, 1970.

Gelven, Michael, *A Commentary on Heidegger's 'Being and Time.'* New York: Harper Torchbooks, 1970.

Goebbels, Joseph, *The Goebbels Diaries.* Edited, translated with an Introduction by Louis P. Lochner. Garden City, N.Y.: Doubleday, 1948.

Gordon, Cyrus H., *The Common Background of Greek and Hebrew Civilizations.* New York: Harper and Row, 1962; W. W. Norton, 1965.

Goering, Hermann, *Germany Reborn.* London: George Allen and Unwin, Ltd., 1934.

Green, T. H , "Liberal Legislation and Freedom of Contract," In *The Works of Thomas Hill Green,* Vol. 3. London: Longmans, Green and Co., 1888.

Greenleaf, W. H., "Hobbes: The Problem of Interpretation," In *Hobbes and Rousseau: A Collection of Critical Essays,* pp. 1-36. Edited by Maurice Cranston and Richard S. Peters. Garden City, N.Y.: Anchor Books, 1972.

Grube, G. M. A., *Plato's Thought.* Boston: Beacon Press, 1958.

Guthrie, W. K. C., *The Greeks and Their Gods.* Boston: Beacon Press, 1955.

Hall, Calvin, *A Primer of Freudian Psychology.* New York: Mentor Books, 1954.

Handlin, Oscar, "Science and Technology in Popular Culture," In *Science and Culture,* pp. 184-98. Edited by Gerald Holton. Boston: Beacon Press, 1967.

Hanson, Paul D., *The Dawn of Apocalyptic.* Philadelphia: Fortress Press, 1975.

Hardy, Alister; Harvie, Robert; and Koestler, Arthur, *The Challenge of Chance.* New York: Random House, 1974; Vintage Books, 1975.

Hayakawa, S. I., *Language in Thought and Action.* New York: Harcourt, Brace and World, 1964.

————, ed., *Language, Meaning and Maturity.* New York: Harper and Row, 1954.

Heidegger, Martin, *Being and Time.* Translated by John Macquarrie and Edward Robinson. New York: Harper and Row, 1962.

Heinemann, F. H., *Existentialism and the Modern Predicament.* New York: Harper and Row, 1953; Harper Torchbooks, 1958.

Heisenberg, Werner, *Physics and Philosophy.* Introduction by F. S. C. Northrup. New York: Harper and Row, 1958; Harper Torchbooks, 1962.

Hitler, Adolf, *Mein Kampf.* Translated by Ralph Manheim. Boston: Houghton Mifflin, Sentry Edition, 1971.

————, "Obedience uber Alles." In *Hitler's Words: the Speeches of Adolf Hitler from 1923 to 1943.* Edited by G. Prange. Washington: Public Affairs Press, n.d.

Hobhouse, Leonard T., *Liberalism.* New York: Henry Holt and Company, n.d.

Hofstadter, Richard, *Social Darwinism in American Thought.* Philadelphia: University of Pennsylvania Press, 1944; Boston: Beacon Press, 1955.

Hollister, C. Warren, *Medieval Europe: A Short History.* New York: John Wiley and Sons, Inc., 1968.

Holton, Gerald, "Modern Science and the Intellectual Tradition," In *The New Scientist: Essays on the Methods and Values of Modern Science,* pp. 19-38. Edited by Paul C. Obler and Herman A. Estrin. Garden City, N.Y.: Anchor Books, 1962.

————, *Thematic Origins of Scientific Thought.* Cambridge: Harvard University Press, 1973.

Homer, *The Iliad*. Translated by Richmond Lattimore. Chicago: Phoenix Books, 1967.

—————, *The Odyssey*. Translated by Richmond Lattimore. New York: Harper Torchbooks, 1967.

Hueber, Ernst R., "Constitutional Law of the Greater German Reich," In *National Socialism*. Washington: U.S. Government Printing Office, 1943.

Huxley, Julian, "Evolutionary Humanism," In *Science, Faith and Man*, pp. 87-98. Edited by W. Warren Wagar. New York: Harper and Row, 1968.

Hyppolite, Jean, *Studies on Marx and Hegel*. Translated by John O'Neill. New York: Basic Books, 1969.

Infeld, Leopold, *Albert Einstein*. New York: Charles Scribner's Sons, 1950.

Jaspers, Karl, "Nature and Ethics." Translated by Eugene I. Gadol. In *Science, Faith and Man*, pp. 125-39. Edited by W. Warren Wagar. New York: Harper and Row, 1968.

—————, *Philosophical Faith and Revelation*. Translated by E. B. Ashton. London: Collins, 1967.

Johnson, Raynor C., *Nurslings of Immortality*. New York: Harper and Row, 1957; Harper Colophon, 1972.

Johnson, William A., *The Search for Transcendence*. New York: Harper and Row, 1974.

Jung, C. G., *Psyche and Symbol*. Translated by Cary Baynes and F. C. R. Hull. Edited by Violet S. de Laszlo. Garden City, N.Y.: Anchor Books, 1958.

Kagan, Donald, rev., *Botsford and Robinson's Hellenic History*. New York: Macmillan, 1969.

Kaufman, Walter, ed., *Existentialism from Dostoevsky to Sartre*. New York: World, 1970.

Keen, Sam, *Apology for Wonder*. New York: Harper and Row, 1969.

Kierkegaard, Soren, *Concluding Unscientific Postscript*. Translated by David F. Swenson and Walter Lowrie. Princeton: Princeton University Press, 1968.

Kipling, Rudyard, "White Man's Burden," In *The Modern World: 1848 to the Present*. Edited by Hans Kohn. New York: Macmillan, 1968.

Kirk, Russell, *The Conservative Mind from Burke to Santayana*. Chicago, Henry Regnery Co., 1953.

Koch, Klaus, *The Rediscovery of Apocalyptic*. Translated by Margaret Koch. Naperville, Ill.: Alec R. Allenson, Inc., n.d., German edition, 1970.

Koestler, Arthur, *The Roots of Coincidence*. New York: Random House, 1972; Vintage Books, 1973.

Kohn, Hans, ed., *The Modern World: 1848 to the Present*. New York: Macmillan, 1968.

Konicek, Richard D., "Seeking Synergism for Man's Two-Hemisphere Brain." *Phi Delta Kappan* (September 1975): 37-39.

Krauskopf, Konrad and Beiser, Arthur, *Fundamentals of Physical Science*. New York: McGraw-Hill, 1966.

Kubler-Ross, Elizabeth, *On Death and Dying*. New York: Macmillan, 1969.

Laszlo, Ervin, *The Systems View of the World*. New York: George Braziller, 1972.

Le Fevre, Perry, *Understandings of Man*. Philadelphia: The Westminster Press, 1966.

Leff, Gordon, *Medieval Thought: St. Augustine to Ockham*. Baltimore: Penguin Books, 1958.

Levi, Albert William, *Philosophy and the Modern World*. Bloomington, Ind.: Indiana University Press, 1970.

Levi-Strauss, Claude, *The Savage Mind.* Chicago: The University of Chicago Press, 1966-1973.

Levin, Harry, "Semantics of Culture," In *Science and Culture,* pp. 1-13. Edited by Gerard Holton. Boston: Beacon Press, 1967.

Levy-Bruhl, Lucien, *Primitive Mentality.* Translated by Lilian A. Clare. Boston: Beacon Press, 1966.

Little, David, *Religion, Order, and Law: A Study in Pre-Revolutionary England.* New York: Harper Torchbooks, 1969.

Lock Land, George T., *Grow or Die: The Unifying Principle of Transformation.* New York: Random House, 1973.

Locke, John, "An Essay: Concerning the True Original Extent and End of Civil Government," In *Great Books of the Western World,* Vol. 35. Edited by Robero M. Hutchins. Chicago: Encyclopaedia Britannica, Inc., 1952.

Lovejoy, Arthur O., *The Great Chain of Being.* New York: Harper Torchbooks, 1960.

Lowith, Karl, *From Hegel to Nietzsche: The Revolution in Nineteenth Century Thought.* Translated by David E. Green. Garden City, N.Y.: Anchor Books, 1967.

Macpherson, C. B., *The Political Theory of Possessive Individualism.* New York: Oxford University Press, 1962.

Marcus Aurelius Antoninus, *The Meditations.* Translated by G. M. A. Grube. New York: The Bobbs-Merrill Co., 1963.

Marcuse, Herbert, *Reason and Revolution: Hegel and the Rise of Social Theory.* Boston: Beacon Press, 1960.

Marnell, William H., *Man-Made Morals: Four Philosophies That Shaped America.* Garden City, N.Y.: Doubleday, 1966; Anchor Books, 1968.

Marx, Karl, "Alienated Labor," In *Man Alone: Alienation in Modern Society,* pp. 93-105. Edited by Eric and Mary Josephson. New York: Dell Publishing Co., Laurel Books, 1962.

————, "Theses on Feuerbach," In *Writings of the Young Marx.* Translated and Edited by Loyd D. Easton and Kurt H. Guddat. Garden City, N.Y.: Anchor Books, 1967.

Marx, Karl and Engels, Friedrich, *The German Ideology: Parts I and III.* Edited with an Introduction by R. Pascal. New York: International Publishers, 1947.

————, Manifesto of the Communist Party, In *Great Books of the Western World,* Vol. 40. Edited by Robert M. Hutchins. Chicago: Encyclopaedia Britannica, Inc., 1952.

Maslow, A. H., *The Farther Reaches of Human Nature.* New York: The Viking Press, 1972.

Maximus of Tyre, "Oration VIII.10," In *Hellenistic Religions: The Age of Syncretism.* Edited and Introduced by Frederick C. Grant. New York: Bobbs-Merrill, The Library of Liberal Arts, 1953.

Mehta, J. L., *The Philosophy of Martin Heidegger.* New York: Harper Torchbooks, 1971.

Menzel, Donald H., *Astronomy.* New York: Random House, 1970.

Mill, John Stuart, *On Liberty.* New York: Bobbs-Merrill, The Library of Liberal Arts, 1956.

Mirandola, Giovanni Pico Della, "Oration of the Dignity of Man." Translated by Elizabeth Livermore Forbes, In *The Renaissance Philosophy of Man,* pp. 215-54.

Edited by Ernst Cassirer, Paul O. Kristeller and John H. Randall, Jr. Chicago: The University of Chicago Press, 1948; Phoenix Books, 1969.

Mishlove, Jeffrey, *The Roots of Consciousness*. New York/Berkeley: Random House /Bookworks, 1975.

Monod, Jacques, *Chance and Necessity*. London: Collins, 1972.

Moody, Raymond A., *Life After Life*. New York: Bantam Books, 1976.

Moss, Dr. Thelma, *The Probability of the Impossible: Scientific Discoveries and Explorations in the Psychic World*. New York: Plume/New American Library, 1974.

Mosse, George L., *The Culture of Western Europe: The Nineteenth and Twentieth Centuries*. Chicago: Rand McNally, 1974.

Mumford, Lewis, "Authoritarian and Democratic Technics," In *Technology and Culture: An Anthology*. Edited by Melvin Kranzberg and William H. Davenport. New York: Meridian, The New American Library, 1975.

————, "Technics and the Nature of Man," In *Technology and Culture: An Anthology*. Edited by Melvin Kranzberg and William H. Davenport. New York: Meridian, The New American Library, 1975.

Munsinger, Harry, *Fundamentals of Child Development*. New Yort: Holt, Rinehart and Winston, 1975.

Mussen, Paul Henry; Conger, John J.; and Kagan, Jerome, *Child Development and Personality*. New York: Harper and Row, 1969.

Mussolini, Benito, "The Doctrine of Fascism," In *The Social and Political Doctrines of Contemporary Europe*. Michael Oakeshott. New York: Cambridge University Press, 1950.

Musurillo, Herbert, "Bonaventure's 'The Soul's Journey to God'," *Thought: A Review of Culture and Idea* 46 (Spring 1971): 110-13.

Newton, Sir Isaac, "Mathematical Principles of Natural Philosophy," In *Great Books of the Western World*, Vol. 34. Edited by R. M. Hutchins. Chicago: Encyclopedia Britannica, Inc., 1952.

————, *Newton's Philosophy of Nature: Selections from His Writings*. Edited by H. S. Thayer. New York: Hafner Publishing Co., 1953.

Northrup, F. S. C., "Introduction," In *Physics and Philosophy* by Werner Heisenberg. New York: Harper and Row, 1958; Harper Torchbooks, 1962.

Osis, Karlis, and Haraldsson, Erlendur, *At the Hour of Death*. New York: Avon Books, 1977.

Owen, Robert, *The Book of the New Moral World*. Glasgow: H. Robinson and Company, 1837.

Palmieri, Mario, *The Philosophy of Fascism*. Chicago, 1936.

Papalia, Diane E., and Olds, Sally Wendkos, *A Child's World*. New York: McGraw-Hill, 1975.

Pelczynski, Z. A., *Hegel's Political Philosophy*. Cambridge: Cambridge University Press, 1971.

Piaget, Jean, *The Child and Reality*. Translated by Arnold Rosin. New York: The Viking Press, 1973; Viking Compass Edition, 1974.

————, *The Origins of Intelligence in Children*. Translated by Margaret Cook. New York: W. W. Norton, 1963.

Popper, Karl, *Conjectures and Refutations: The Growth of Scientific Knowledge*. New York: Basic Books, 1962; Harper Torchbooks, 1968.

Price, Don K., "The Established Dissenters," In *Science and Culture*, pp. 109-44. Edited by Gerald Holton. Boston: Beacon Press, 1967.

Randall, John L., *Parapsychology and the Nature of Life*. New York: Harper and Row, 1975.

Richardson, Herbert W., and Cutler, Donald R., ed., *Transcendence*. Boston: Beacon Press, 1969.

Ringgren, Helmer, *Israelite Religion*. Translated by David E. Green. Philadelphia: Fortress Press, 1966.

Robinson, John A. T., *The Body: A Study in Pauline Theology*. London, SCM Press, Ltd., 1952.

Robinson, John Mansley, *An Introduction to Early Greek Philosophy*. Boston: Houghton Mifflin Co., 1968.

Rolland, Romain, "Jean-Jacques Rousseau," In *French Thought in the Eighteenth Century*. Presented by Romain Rolland, Andre Maurois and Edouard Herriot. New York: David McKay Co., 1953.

Rosenberg, Alfred, "The Myth of the Twentieth Century," In *National Socialism*. Washington: U.S. Government Printing Office, 1943.

Rousseau, Jean-Jacques, *The Social Contract*. Translated and Introduced by Maurice Cranston. Baltimore: Penguin Books, 1968.

Rubenstein, Richard L., *After Auschwitz: Radical Theology and Contemporary Judaism*. New York: Bobbs-Merrill, 1966.

————, *The Cunning of History: Mass Death and the American Future*. New York: Harper and Row, 1975.

————, *My Brother Paul*. New York: Harper and Row, 1972.

————, *Power Struggle*. New York: Charles Scribner's Sons, 1974.

————, *The Religious Imagination: A Study in Psychoanalysis and Jewish Theology*. Boston: Beacon Press, 1971.

Russell, Bertrand, *Religion and Science*. London: Oxford University Press, 1970.

Sagan, Carl, *The Cosmic Connection: An Extraterrestrial Perspective*. New York: Doubleday, 1973; Dell Publishing Co., 1975.

Saint-Simon, Henri de, *Social Organization, The Science of Man and Other Writings*. Edited and Translated by Felix Markham. New York: Harper Torchbooks, 1964.

Sartre, Jean-Paul, *The Reprieve*. Translated by Eric Sutton. New York: Vintage Books, 1973.

————, *Search for a Method*. Translated by Hazel E. Barnes. New York: Alfred A. Knopf, 1963.

Schacht, Richard, *Hegel and After: Studies in Continental Philosophy Between Kant and Sartre*. Pittsburgh: University of Pittsburgh Press, 1975.

Schleiermacher, Friedrich, "Speeches on Religion to Its Cultured Despisers," In *Romanticism*, pp. 138-49. Edited by John B. Halsted. New York: Harper and Row, 1969.

Schneider, Herbert W., *The Puritan Mind*. Ann Arbor: The University of Michigan Press, Ann Arbor Paperback, 1958.

Scott, Sir Walter, "Dedicatory Epistle, *Ivanhoe*," In *Romanticism*, pp. 239-50. Edited by John B. Halsted. New York: Harper and Row, 1969.

Scroggs, Robin, *The Last Adam: A Study in Pauline Anthropology*. Philadelphia: Fortress Press, 1966.

Shapley, Harlow, *The View from a Distant Star.* New York: Basic Books, 1963; Dell Publishing Co., 1967.

Smith, Adam, "An Inquiry Into the Nature and Causes of the Wealth of Nations," In *Great Books of the Western World,* Vol. 30. Edited by R. M. Hutchins. Chicago: Encyclopaedia Britannica, Inc., 1952.

Smith, Morton, "Palestinian Judaism in the First Century," In *Israel: Its Role in Civilization,* pp. 67-81. Edited by Moshe Davis. New York: Harper and Row, 1956.

Stalin, Joseph, *Dialectical and Historical Materialism.* New York: International Publishers, 1940.

Stevenson, Ian, *Twenty Cases Suggestive of Reincarnation.* Charlottesville: University Press of Virginia, 1974.

Stromberg, Roland, *An Intellectual History of Modern Europe.* 2nd ed. Englewood Cliffs, N.J.: Prentice-Hall, 1975.

Taylor, John, *Black Holes: The End of the Universe?* New York: Random House, 1973.

Teilhard de Chardin, Pierre, *The Phenomenon of Man.* Translated by Bernard Wall. New York: Harper and Row, 1965.

Tillich, Paul, *The Courage to Be.* New Haven, Conn.: Yale University Press, 1952.

Tse-Tung, Mao, *Quotations from Chairman Mao Tse-Tung.* Peking: Foreign Language Press, 1967.

Vesper, Will, "Poem to Hitler." Translated by Carl Cohen. In *Communism, Fascism, and Democracy: The Theoretical Foundations.* Edited by Carl Cohen. New York: Random House, 1972.

von Treitschke, Heinrich, *Politics.* Translated by B. Dugdale and T. de Bille. London: Constable and Company, Ltd., 1916.

Wagner, Richard, "The Revolution," In *Romanticism,* pp. 232-38. Edited by John B. Halsted. New York: Harper and Row, 1969.

Walzer, Michael, *The Revolution of the Saints: A Study in the Origins of Radical Politics.* Cambridge: Harvard University Press, 1965.

Watts, Alan, *Beyond Theology.* New York: Vintage Books, 1973.

————, *The Book: On the Taboo Against Knowing Who You Are.* New York: Vintage Books, 1972.

Weaver, Kenneth F., "The Incredible Universe." *National Geographic* 145 (May 1974): 589/625.

Weber, Max, *The Protestant Ethic and the Spirit of Capitalism.* Translated by Talcott Parsons. New York: Charles Scribner's Sons, 1950.

Weisskopf, Victor F., *Knowledge and Wonder.* Garden City, N.Y.: Anchor Books, 1966.

Werkmeister, W. H., *A Philosophy of Science.* Lincoln, Neb.: University of Nebraska Press, 1940.

Wheelwright, Philip, ed., *The Presocratics.* New York: The Odyssey Press, 1966.

Whitehead, Alfred North, *Science and the Modern World.* New York: The Macmillan Co., 1925; The Free Press, 1967.

Whorf, Benjamin Lee, "Science and Linguistics," In *Every Man His Way,* pp. 318-29. Edited by Alan Dundes. Englewood Cliffs: Prentice-Hall, 1968. From *Language, Thought and Reality.* Cambridge, Mass.: M.I.T. Press, 1956.

————, "The Relation of Habitual Thought and Behavior to Language," In *Language, Meaning and Maturity,* pp. 225-51. Edited by S. I. Hayakawa. New York: Harper and Row, 1954.

Whyte, Lancelot Law, *The Universe of Experience*. New York: Harper and Row, Harper Torchbooks, 1974.

Wilson, John A., "Egypt," In *Before Philosophy*, pp. 39-113. Edited by H. and H. A. Frankfort, John A. Wilson and Thorkild Jacobsen. Baltimore: Penguin Books, 1949-72.

Windelband, W., *A History of Philosophy*. New York: Macmillan, 1935.

Wollenhauer, Hendrikus Theodoric, and Siraff, Edward Farragut, *Grain Constructs of Artificial Phenomena*. Hamburg: Geschwindigkeit International, 1950.

Wren-Lewis, John, "Faith in the Technological Future," In *The Futurists*, pp. 290-97. Edited by Alvin Toffler. New York: Random House, 1972.

Yankelovich, Daniel, and Barrett, William, *Ego and Instinct: The Psychoanalytic View of Human Nature—Revised*. New York: Random House, 1970.

About the Author . . .

Harry Coffin Stafford (B.A., Samford University; M.Div., Columbia Theological Seminary; Ph.D., The Florida State University) was born in 1944 in Birmingham, Alabama. He has taught at Columbia Theological Seminary, Presbyterian College, the Florida State University, the University of Montana, Queens College (Charlotte), and the University of North Carolina (Charlotte). He currently resides in Tallahassee, Florida where he teaches at the Florida State University.